# Utilizing Smart Technology and AI in Hybrid Tourism and Hospitality

Sanjeev Kumar
*Lovely Professional University, India*

Mohammad Badruddoza Talukder
*Daffodil Institute of IT, India*

Ana Pego
*Nova University of Lisbon, Portugal*

A volume in the Advances in Hospitality, Tourism, and the Services Industry (AHTSI) Book Series

IGI Global
PUBLISHER of TIMELY KNOWLEDGE

Published in the United States of America by
IGI Global
Business Science Reference (an imprint of IGI Global)
701 E. Chocolate Avenue
Hershey PA, USA 17033
Tel: 717-533-8845
Fax: 717-533-8661
E-mail: cust@igi-global.com
Web site: http://www.igi-global.com



Library of Congress Cataloging-in-Publication Data

CIP PENDING
2024 Business Science Reference

TITLE: Utilizing Smart Technology and AI in Hybrid Tourism and Hospitality
EDITORS: Sanjeev Kumar, Mohammad Badruddoza Talukder, and Ana Pego

ISBN: 9798369319789
eISBN: 9798369319796

This book is published in the IGI Global book series Advances in Hospitality, Tourism, and the Services Industry (AHTSI) (ISSN: 2475-6547; eISSN: 2475-6555)

British Cataloguing in Publication Data
A Cataloguing in Publication record for this book is available from the British Library.

# Advances in Hospitality, Tourism, and the Services Industry (AHTSI) Book Series

ISSN:2475-6547
EISSN:2475-6555

Editor-in-Chief: Maximiliano Korstanje, University of Palermo, Argentina

## MISSION

Globally, the hospitality, travel, tourism, and services industries generate a significant percentage of revenue and represent a large portion of the business world. Even in tough economic times, these industries thrive as individuals continue to spend on leisure and recreation activities as well as services.

**The Advances in Hospitality, Tourism, and the Services Industry (AHTSI)** book series offers diverse publications relating to the management, promotion, and profitability of the leisure, recreation, and services industries. Highlighting current research pertaining to various topics within the realm of hospitality, travel, tourism, and services management, the titles found within the AHTSI book series are pertinent to the research and professional needs of managers, business practitioners, researchers, and upper-level students studying in the field.

## COVERAGE

- Leisure & Business Travel
- International Tourism
- Health and Wellness Tourism
- Service Training
- Service Management
- Food and Beverage Management
- Cruise Marketing and Sales
- Hotel Management
- Tourism and the Environment
- Service Design

IGI Global is currently accepting manuscripts for publication within this series. To submit a proposal for a volume in this series, please contact our Acquisition Editors at Acquisitions@igi-global.com or visit: http://www.igi-global.com/publish/.

The Advances in Hospitality, Tourism, and the Services Industry (AHTSI) Book Series (ISSN 2475-6547) is published by IGI Global, 701 E. Chocolate Avenue, Hershey, PA 17033-1240, USA, www.igi-global.com. This series is composed of titles available for purchase individually; each title is edited to be contextually exclusive from any other title within the series. For pricing and ordering information please visit http://www.igi-global.com/book-series/advances-hospitality-tourism-services-industry/121014. Postmaster: Send all address changes to above address. 

## Titles in this Series

*For a list of additional titles in this series, please visit:*
*http://www.igi-global.com/book-series/advances-hospitality-tourism-services-industry/121014*

***Career Pathways and Professional Identities for Front-Line Workers in the Service ndustries***
Mark Peter Vitale (University of Phoenix, USA)
Business Science Reference • © 2024 • 370pp • H/C (ISBN: 9781668425282) • US $255.00

***Experiences, Advantages, and Economic Dimensions of Pilgrimage Routes***
Vítor João Pereira Domingues Martinho (Agricultural School, CERNAS-IPV Research Centre, Polytechnic Institute of Viseu, Portugal) João Augusto Guerra da Rocha Nunes (School of Education, Polytechnic Institute of Viseu, Portugal) Maria Lúcia de Jesus Pato (Agricultural School, CERNAS-IPV Research Centre, Polytechnic Institute of Viseu, Portugal) and Liliana Andrade de Matos Castilho (School of Education, Polytechnic Institute of Viseu, Portugal)
Business Science Reference • © 2023 • 367pp • H/C (ISBN: 9781668499238) • US $240.00

***Exploring Culture and Heritage Through Experience Tourism***
Yashwant Singh Rawal (Parul Institute of Hotel Management, Parul University, India) Rupa Sinha (Amity Institute of Travel and Tourism, Amity University, India) Sankar Kumar Mukherjee (Amity Institute of Travel and Tourism, Amity University, India) and Debasish Batabyal (Amity Institute of Travel and Tourism, Amity University, India)
Business Science Reference • © 2023 • 348pp • H/C (ISBN: 9781668499573) • US $240.00

***Sustainable Development Goal Advancement Through Digital Innovation in the Service Sector***
Vipin Nadda (University of Sunderland, UK) Pankaj Kumar Tyagi (Chandigarh University, India) Rubina Moniz Vieira (St. Mary's University, London, UK) and Priyanka Tyagi (Chandigarh University, India)
Business Science Reference • © 2023 • 272pp • H/C (ISBN: 9798369306505) • US $275.00

*For an entire list of titles in this series, please visit:*
*http://www.igi-global.com/book-series/advances-hospitality-tourism-services-industry/121014*

IGI Global
PUBLISHER of TIMELY KNOWLEDGE

701 East Chocolate Avenue, Hershey, PA 17033, USA
Tel: 717-533-8845 x100 • Fax: 717-533-8661
E-Mail: cust@igi-global.com • www.igi-global.com

# Table of Contents

# Detailed Table of Contents



The spa and wellness industry, focusing on holistic well-being, has witnessed remarkable growth in recent years, becoming a prominent niche in the broader tourism landscape. This transformation has been significantly influenced by the pervasive presence of social media, which has revolutionized communication and decision-making processes. This chapter synthesizes the relevant literature to elucidate the intricate relationship between social media reviews and consumer choices in the spa and wellness sector. The academic significance lies in the propositions, providing a solid foundation for future empirical research in consumer behavior within the spa and wellness context. Practically, this study offers actionable insights for spa and wellness businesses, emphasizing the need to actively encourage and promote high-quality, credible reviews and prioritize customer engagement strategies. Moreover, this study highlights the significant prospective contribution of this study towards the sustainable development goals (SDGs).

The advent of information and communication technologies (ICTs) has sparked a significant transformation within the tourism and hospitality sector. The prevalence of travel websites, which are known for their open sharing of information, has been established for a considerable duration. These platforms are now facilitating the adoption of increasingly advanced intelligent systems within the tourism and hospitality industry. Given the intricate nature of decision-making processes in the context of travel, intelligent systems and tourism are highly compatible. The advent of service automation, artificial intelligence, and robotics has presented tourism companies and organizations with a plethora of novel prospects. The utilization of artificial intelligence in different sectors of the tourism industry has been observed to a certain degree. However, there remains a limited amount of scholarly literature available on this topic. This chapter aims to further explore the emerging field of artificial intelligence applications in the tourism industry, as well as the key trends in this field.



Malaysia's smart tourism framework is a collaborative and visionary strategy designed to revolutionize the country's tourism industry. It focuses on key elements, including robust digital infrastructure, data-driven personalization, eco-friendly transportation, and cultural preservation. Through strategic partnerships and continuous monitoring using key performance indicators, the framework aims to create a sustainable, competitive, and inclusive smart tourism ecosystem. This approach promises increased revenue, job opportunities, and enriched visitor experiences while safeguarding Malaysia's natural and cultural heritage in the digital age.

The chapter delves into futuristic trends in hospitality, propelled by artificial intelligence (AI), the internet of things (IoT), and blockchain. AI drives personalized guest interactions, IoT enables smart hotels, and blockchain ensures security. Data analytics personalize experiences, VR/AR engage guests, while contactless services address pandemic concerns. Sustainability aligns with eco-consciousness, and cybersecurity safeguards guest data. Embracing innovation is imperative for thriving in the evolving hospitality landscape.



The advance in technology has influenced human beings and artificial intelligence (AI) is most discussed considering the similarity of human-like thinking process. AI has become inevitable in the hospitality industry both for the customers and the employees. Human resource management in hospitality has enormous challenges including high turnover rate, recruitment and retention, training, and development of the employees. A considerable gap is found between the expectations and the reality of artificial intelligence in human resource management. The study aims to find how human resource managers in hospitality effectively use artificial intelligence in their regular operations and in the well-being of the employees. The study takes a qualitative research approach to state how artificial intelligence is incorporated into regular functions of hospitality human resources and its impact on the organization. The findings of the study will state how AI will assist in redefining the role of hospitality human resources management in enhancing their efficiency and agility.

# Preface

Welcome to this exploration of the transformative intersection between Smart Technology, Artificial Intelligence (AI), and the dynamic realms of Tourism and Hospitality. In an era where technological innovation is reshaping industries, the fusion of virtual and physical experiences is becoming increasingly vital. This document delves into the multifaceted ways in which Smart Technology and AI are reshaping the landscape of hybrid tourism and redefining hospitality services.

Integrating Smart Technology and AI in the tourism and hospitality sector is not merely a futuristic vision but a present-day reality. The possibilities are vast, from personalized customer experiences to contactless services, predictive analytics, and immersive technologies. This edited book sets the stage for an in-depth exploration of the key trends, challenges, and opportunities that arise when smart technologies and AI converge with the diverse and dynamic world of tourism and hospitality.

The edited volume, " Utilizing Smart Technology and AI in Hybrid Tourism and Hospitality," spearheaded by Sanjeev Kumar, Mohammad Badruddoza Talukder, and Ana Pego, delves into the multifaceted landscape of AI in Hybrid Tourism and Hospitality. This compilation is a compass for navigating the diverse initiatives across the Tourism and Hospitality industries. It underscores the expansive opportunities of embracing Smart Technology in Hybrid Tourism and Hospitality.

The journey through the book will unravel the innovative strategies industry leaders employ to enhance customer satisfaction, operational efficiency, and sustainability. Whether it is the deployment of virtual assistants, the implementation of IoT in smart rooms, or the use of blockchain for data security, each facet contributes to a more prosperous and more adaptive industry.

As we navigate this exploration, let us acknowledge the rapid pace of change and the importance of staying attuned to travelers' evolving needs and expectations. The synergy between technological advancements and the human touch in hospitality is a delicate balance that requires thoughtful consideration.

We invite you to delve into the following chapters, each offering insights into the role of Smart Technology and AI in shaping the future of hybrid tourism and hospitality. May this document guide industry professionals, innovators, and enthusiasts alike as we embark on a journey into the exciting and transformative landscape of Smart Tourism and Hospitality.

Happy reading!

## SUMMARY OF THE BOOK

"Smart Tourism and Hospitality" explores the dynamic synergy between cutting-edge technologies and the evolving landscape of the tourism and hospitality industry. The book comprehensively overviews how Smart Technology and Artificial Intelligence reshape virtual and physical travel experiences.

The journey begins with a deep dive into personalized customer experiences, where AI algorithms analyze user preferences to offer tailored recommendations for destinations, accommodations, and activities. Integrating virtual assistants and AI-powered chatbots enhances customer support, helping travelers plan their trips and navigate a seamless booking process.

Contactless services take center stage, with mobile check-ins, digital room keys, and IoT-enabled bright rooms providing guests with a safe and convenient environment. The book explores the role of AI in predictive analytics, optimizing pricing through dynamic algorithms and managing inventory effectively to meet the demands of modern travelers.

Immersive technologies such as Augmented Reality and Virtual Reality open new frontiers, offering virtual tours of accommodations and enhancing wayfinding through AR applications. Biometric technology, including facial recognition and biometric payments, contributes to secure and efficient processes within the hospitality sector.

Integrating the IoT devices ensures smart energy management in hotels, aligning with sustainability goals. Blockchain technology emerges as a key player in securing guest data and ensuring transparency in handling information.

"Smart Tourism and Hospitality" serves as a guide for industry professionals, offering insights into innovative strategies that enhance customer satisfaction, streamline operations, and contribute to the overall transformation of the tourism and hospitality sector. As travelers seek a balance between technology and human touch, this book navigates the path toward a more connected and adaptive future in Smart Tourism and Hospitality.

## ORGANIZATION OF THE BOOK

In this edited reference book, we bring together diverse perspectives on the intersection of artificial intelligence (AI) and the hospitality, tourism, and entertainment industries.

The contributing authors, experts in their respective fields, explore the multifaceted applications of AI, offering insights into its impact on human resource management, marketing strategies, visitor patterns, guest expectations, safety measures, and various sectors within the broader tourism landscape. From the transformative effects of COVID-19 to futuristic trends in hospitality, each chapter contributes a unique perspective on how AI is shaping the present and future of these industries.

## Chapter 1: Social Media Reviews' Influence on Spa and Wellness Consumer Choices: Conceptual Framework, Prospective Significance, and Future Research Directions (Md. Tariqul Islam, Biswabhusan Pradhan, Jeetesh Kumar)

Focusing on the spa and wellness industry, this chapter synthesizes literature to elucidate the relationship between social media reviews and consumer choices. Providing propositions for future research, the study offers actionable insights for businesses in the spa and wellness sector, emphasizing the importance of high-quality reviews.

## Chapter 2: The Technology Impacts and AI Solutions for the Tourism Industry (Dina Darwish)

Examining the impact of Information and Communication Technologies (ICTs) on tourism, this chapter explores the compatibility of intelligent systems with decision-making processes in the context of travel. Highlighting the potential of AI, robotics, and automation, the chapter aims to bridge the gap in scholarly literature on this emerging field.

## Chapter 3: Malaysia's Smart Tourism Framework (Mooi Kwong, Anthony Tee)

This chapter introduces Malaysia's Smart Tourism Framework, a strategic initiative aiming to revolutionize the country's tourism industry. The framework focuses on digital infrastructure, data-driven personalization, eco-friendly transportation, and cultural preservation to create a sustainable and competitive smart tourism ecosystem.

## Chapter 4: Voyage Virtuoso: Artificial Intelligence in Transforming Tourism in the Travel (Geetha Manoharan, C V Rao, Sunitha Ashtikar, Sanjeev Kumar, M Nivedha)

This chapter delves into how AI, with its complex algorithms and processing power, is transforming tourism. From information processing to personalized experiences, the authors discuss the role of AI, machine learning, and deep learning in enhancing traveler experiences, managing destinations, and optimizing sector organizations' services.

## Chapter 5: A Review of the Pre-and Post-Covid-19 Effects on the Tourism and Entertainment Industries: Innovative Methods and Predicted Challenges (Saumendra Das, Rao N. V. J, Dwipanita Mishra, Rohit Bansal)

Focusing on the profound impact of the COVID-19 pandemic, this chapter examines the challenges faced by the tourism and entertainment industries. It provides intelligent solutions for sustainable recovery, making it an essential read for academicians, researchers, and policymakers seeking to navigate the post-pandemic landscape.

## Chapter 6: Managing Guest Expectations and Safety with AI and Smart Solutions (Dr. Ruby Jindal)

Exploring the transformative impact of AI and smart solutions on the hospitality sector, this chapter covers AI-driven personalization, communication tools, safety innovations, and data analysis. An essential guide for industry experts, scholars, and students navigating the evolving landscape of guest management and safety in the digital era.

## Chapter 7: Predictive Analytics for Heritage Site Visitor Patterns (Aditi Nag, Smriti Mishra)

This chapter explores the relationship between predictive analytics and heritage site management, emphasizing cultural sensitivity and the impact of diverse backgrounds on visitor behaviors. The research provides insights for sustainable heritage management, conservation efforts, and community engagement initiatives.

## Chapter 8: Exploring the Prospects of Artificial Intelligence in the Tourism Sector (Mandeep Kaur, Uma Pandey)

Focusing on AI's role in travel and tourism, this chapter explores key areas such as chatbots, predictive analytics, smart infrastructure, and personalized suggestions. Drawing from secondary sources, the authors provide an overview of AI's integration into the tourism sector, offering insights for stakeholders aiming to leverage AI's influence.

## Chapter 9: The Future Prospect of Online Travel Agencies in Hotel Bookings (Jagjit Singh, Shikha Sharma)

This chapter traces the evolution of online travel agencies (OTAs) and their transformative impact on travel reservations. Discussing the shift from traditional travel agencies to internet-based booking, the authors explore the changing consumer attitudes and behaviors that have shaped the online travel business.

## Chapter 10: AI-Powered Marketing Strategies in the Tourism and Hospitality Sector (Rina Daline, Joby Thomas)

This chapter explores the competitive environment in the tourism and hospitality industry and the role of AI in personalized services. From customer analysis to revenue improvement, the authors discuss how AI and Virtual Reality (VR) technologies are reshaping marketing strategies for enhanced customer experiences and effective operations.

## Chapter 11: Enhancing Competitive Advantages through Virtual Reality Technology in Hotels of India (Milan Sharma & Amrik Singh)

The chapter begins by highlighting the 360-degree virtual reality film, "Incredible India," produced in collaboration between the Indian Ministry of Tourism and Google India in 2018. This film serves as a prime example of the immersive experiences that VR technology can offer to showcase the diverse facets of India as a getaway destination. The chapter underscores the limited adoption of VR technology in Indian hotels and emphasizes the need for comprehensive research to understand its potential impact. The primary objective is to identify and explore the competitive benefits that VR technology can bring to the hotel industry in India. The methodology employed for this study involves interviews with industry professionals and a thorough review of existing literature, combining insights from both practical experiences and theoretical perspectives.

## Chapter 12: Embracing Technological Advancements A Futuristic Approach to Hospitality Management (Baljit Kaur, Sanjeev Kumar Saxena)

This chapter explores futuristic trends in hospitality driven by AI, the Internet of Things (IoT), and blockchain. From personalized guest interactions to smart hotels and enhanced security, the authors discuss how innovation is imperative for thriving in the evolving hospitality landscape.

## Chapter 13: Artificial Intelligence in Human Resource Management in Hotels: A Qualitative Approach (Partho Seal, Parul Gupta)

This chapter delves into the challenges faced by human resource managers in the hospitality industry and explores the integration of AI into regular HR functions. The qualitative research approach aims to uncover how AI enhances efficiency and agility in managing high turnover rates, recruitment, training, and development of employees.

## Chapter 14: Implication of Artificial Intelligence in Hospitality Marketing (Iva Das, Mohammad Talukder, Sanjeev Kumar)

Investigating the impact of AI on marketing strategies, this chapter discusses machine learning, natural language processing, and computer vision. Emphasizing AI's role in learning and adapting to customer behavior, the chapter explores practical applications, predictive analytics, and the marketing significance of augmented and virtual reality.

In this comprehensive collection, each chapter offers valuable insights, making this edited reference book an indispensable resource for scholars, industry professionals, and policymakers navigating the dynamic intersection of artificial intelligence and the hospitality, tourism, and entertainment industries.

*Sanjeev Kumar*
*Lovely Professional University, India*

*Mohammad Badruddoza Talukder*
*Daffodil Institute of IT, Bangladesh*

*Ana Pego*
*Nova University of Lisbon, Portugal*

# Chapter 1
# Social Media Reviews' Influence on Spa and Wellness Consumer Choices:
## Conceptual Framework, Prospective Significance, and Future Research Directions

**Md. Tariqul Islam**
https://orcid.org/0000-0002-7367-2989
*Taylor's University, Malaysia*

**Biswabhusan Pradhan**
*Central University of Jammu, India*

**Jeetesh Kumar**
https://orcid.org/0000-0001-9878-1228
*Taylor's University, Malaysia*

## ABSTRACT

*The spa and wellness industry, focusing on holistic well-being, has witnessed remarkable growth in recent years, becoming a prominent niche in the broader tourism landscape. This transformation has been significantly influenced by the pervasive presence of social media, which has revolutionized communication and decision-making processes. This chapter synthesizes the relevant literature to elucidate the intricate relationship between social media reviews and consumer choices in the spa and wellness sector. The academic significance lies in the propositions, providing a*

DOI: 10.4018/979-8-3693-1978-9.ch001

*solid foundation for future empirical research in consumer behavior within the spa and wellness context. Practically, this study offers actionable insights for spa and wellness businesses, emphasizing the need to actively encourage and promote high-quality, credible reviews and prioritize customer engagement strategies. Moreover, this study highlights the significant prospective contribution of this study towards the sustainable development goals (SDGs).*

## INTRODUCTION

A spa is a facility that offers a range of treatments and services to enhance physical, mental, and emotional well-being (Okech, 2014). Lehto et al. (2006) described a spa as a place where therapeutic services enhance an individual's physical, mental, and spiritual well-being. In contrast, wellness encompasses a holistic approach to health, encompassing physical, mental, and emotional well-being, it involves engaging in activities and adopting lifestyles that promote optimal health and vitality (Kumar et al., 2023). Global Wellness Institute (2019) defines wellness as the intentional endeavor to engage in activities, make choices, and adopt lifestyles that foster overall well-being and holistic health.

However, Spa and wellness tourism has emerged as a prominent niche sector within the tourism industry (Ahani et al., 2019; Trihas & Konstantarou, 2016). The demand for enhancing physical fitness, access to knowledge regarding healthy lifestyles, nutritional guidance, healing therapies, preventive healthcare, solutions for psychological challenges such as stress and depression, and the promotion of spiritual well-being is increasingly met through the diverse range of health and wellness programs currently offered; spas are now a top priority for many vacationers since they provide a health and relaxation element to the typical vacation or break(Didascalou & Lagos, 2009). According to Suttikun et al. (2018), the International Spa Association (ISPA) has released a study revealing that 184 million spa visits were made in 2016, generating $16.3 billion in revenue. Moreover, the expansion of the spa sector and customer visits reflects broader shifts in consumer attitudes toward integrating health and leisure activities, as well as beliefs that spa treatments may assist in achieving the optimal health outcomes for customers (Ahani et al., 2019; Chen et al., 2013).

In the contemporary digital age, social media has seamlessly integrated into our everyday existence, fundamentally transforming how we communicate, disseminate information, and make decisions (Dentzel, 2013; Garg & Kumar, 2021). With the rise of social networking platforms, consumers have gained unprecedented access to a vast array of information and opinions from fellow users. It has profoundly impacted various industries, including the spa and wellness sector (Kaur & Kumar, 2022). Choosing a spa or wellness center can be challenging for consumers as they seek a reliable and reputable establishment that aligns with their needs and preferences. In this context, social media reviews have emerged as a significant source of information for consumers, shaping their decision-making processes (Varkaris & Neuhofer, 2017). These reviews, shared by individuals who have experienced the services or facilities of a particular spa or wellness center, provide firsthand insights and evaluations that influence potential customers (Riswanto & Kim, 2023). Therefore, this study aims to explore the impact of social media reviews on consumers' choices in this context, focusing on the mediating role of review helpfulness, which will assist concerned stakeholders in formulating marketing strategy and product development to attract customers.

Various factors of online reviews influence customer purchase intention, as stated in previous literature, and the most influential factors of online reviews include review quality, source credibility, and perceived review helpfulness. Among these factors, review quality is a significant factor that significantly impacts review helpfulness and customer purchase intention. Because the higher the quality of reviews, the more likely it is to benefit consumers. The persuasiveness of reviews, reflected in an informational message, determines the quality of an online review. A critical factor in the success of an information system model is information quality, which is determined by how well-suited information features for information consumers (Jiang et al., 2021). Studies on online reviews have defined information quality as the specific attributes of content quality found within customer reviews (Park et al., 2021). Studies have shown that reliable reviews significantly impact how consumers evaluate products (Park & Lee, 2008). Several research studies have separated information quality into different aspects as a multi-dimensional variable in diverse circumstances. Information quality was evaluated by Salvatore et al. (2021) based on its usability, credibility, accessibility, and usefulness. Abu-Taieh et al. (2022) described information quality as combined with four distinct factors: intrinsic, accessible, contextual, and expressive, each comprising different aspects of information qualities. Filieri (2015) examined the depth, factuality, breadth, relevance, and trustworthiness of e-WOM in online review studies to assess the information quality by depth. However, the quality of online review influence positively both review helpfulness and customer purchase intention (Bigne et al., 2021; Brazil et al., 2022).

The utility of online reviews and customers' intent to make a purchase is significantly shaped by the credibility of the information source. Online platforms acquire more diverse information and need more social connections between users. This will make it challenging for a recipient to judge the credibility of online information sources. Source credibility refers to the good traits of communicators that can enhance the value of the information in a message and, as a result, affect how information is received (Rusdiana et al., 2020). Vafeiadis (2021) defines source credibility as a group of traits that identify a message source and may affect how the recipient assesses the information. In contrast, Muda and Hamzah (2021) described source credibility as the degree to which a piece of information and its source may be trusted. Research has shown that trustworthiness, competence, and knowledge, which distinguish reliable sources of online reviews, may be able to affect a consumer's assumptions and evaluations while making a purchase (Shin & Choi, 2021). The credibility of a review is contingent upon the customer's perception of its source. Higher credibility associated with the source of a review positively influences customers' purchase intentions.

Review helpfulness is a subjective assessment of the information's perceived value as contained in an online customer review. If the information is favorable, a helpful online review raises the perceived value of the information it contains, which raises the perceived value of the product or service being assessed and influences the consumer's purchase intention (Huang et al., 2015). Furthermore, Reviews are considered more valuable if they include credible sources and high-quality information that considerably impact consumers' buying intentions. However, the increasing popularity of social media has sparked renewed interest in various commercial sectors, including spa and wellness. Unfortunately, the different critical components of online reviews have received scant attention. This study will provide valuable insights for stakeholders in the spa and wellness industry and for social media platforms catering to tourists, enabling a deeper understanding of consumer preferences and behaviors. Moreover, the study will highlight its significance towards the Sustainable Development Goals (SDGs).

## LITERATURE REVIEW

### Role of Artificial Intelligence (AI) in the Spa and Wellness Industry

The hospitality sector including lodging facilities, restaurants, travel agencies, and hotels has unique difficulties in meeting the increasingly high standards of contemporary guests. Spa and wellness is a major sector of the hospitality and tourism industry. Guests' expectations of the spa and wellness industry have increased with the rise of social media, review websites, and online booking systems (Pandey et al., 2023). The role of AI is becoming more important in changing the spa and wellness business since today's guests need personalized experiences, seamless connections, and efficient services. The use of artificial intelligence (AI) in the spa and wellness industry has great potential to improve guest services, optimise operational efficiency, and strengthen safety and security measures. Through the incorporation of AI technologies, spa and wellness can provide guests with personalized recommendations tailored to their unique interests, use chatbots and virtual assistants to automate repetitive activities, and implement voice recognition systems for smooth control over in-room commodities. In addition, AI plays a role in revenue management by implementing dynamic pricing methods, facilitating predictive maintenance to minimize interruptions, and using data analytics for informed decision-making.

## Social Media Reviews' on Choosing Spa and Wellness Destination

As defined by Szromek and Polok (2022), Spa is dedicated to promoting overall well-being through professional services that rejuvenate the mind, body, and spirit. The primary objective of spa destinations is to assist visitors in adopting a healthier lifestyle. Traditionally requiring extended stays, this transition can now be achieved through comprehensive programs encompassing spa services, physical fitness activities, wellness education, healthy cuisine, and special interest programs. However, choosing products or services is a facet of consumer behavior that encompasses a consumer's deliberate decision to invest in a product (Lu et al., 2014). According to Beneke et al. (2016), purchase intention refers to the likelihood of a consumer purchasing a specific product based on the interplay between consumer demands, attitudes, and perceptions of the product or brand. Purchase intention is a predictive indicator closely linked to buying behavior, capturing the interest of marketing scholars. Authors such as Kim and Kim (2004) have measured the intention to purchase or consumers' propensity to act on products or services. Previous research has unveiled many factors that influence purchase intent, including product knowledge and involvement (Lin & Chen, 2006), internal and external motivation, and the attitudes and behaviors of customers.

Additionally, in various industries, including tourism, user-generated content (UGC) has gained significance due to the proliferation of Web 2.0 technologies. The reason for studying UGC in tourism is rooted in the fact that travelers assign substantial weight to social media content as reliable and credible sources of travel information, influencing their future travel decisions. Furthermore, Jalilvand and Heidari (2017) asserted that recommendations from previous visitors hold immense credibility for prospective travelers. However, in an environment where most social network users can readily generate electronic word-of-mouth (eWOM) while interacting with others, the quality and credibility of eWOM information become paramount (Erkan & Evans, 2016). Information quality and credibility are pivotal factors that aid consumers in assessing the usefulness of information when selecting products or services.

According to Li et al. (2022), information quality is how individuals perceive information to be timely, accurate, valuable, and of good quality. It encompasses a user's evaluation of the quality of product or service information presented on a website, facilitating the comparison of purchased products with those available on other online shopping platforms, covering aspects such as pricing and product quality. Low-quality information adversely affects the helpfulness of customer information and the decision-making process, also imposing additional costs, time, and effort due to the consumption of irrelevant messages (Nabella, 2021). Conversely, high-quality information benefits not only the service providers offering it but also the customers seeking insightful details about a particular product or service. By delivering high-quality information, service providers can enhance their reputation and public perception (Kim et al., 2021).In social media and other online platforms, information is presented in several ways, including sound, images, text, and video, and these properties of the information define its quality (Barbosa et al., 2023; Kumar et al., 2020; Tarute et al., 2017). To eliminate ambiguity and make the best purchasing decisions in online transactions, consumers heavily rely on the quality of the information available(Chen & Chang, 2018; Lee & Min, 2021). In contrast, Lee and Min (2021) identified information quality as one of the key factors promoting the online transaction process and stimulating customer purchase intention.

According to Vafeiadis (2021), positive attributes exhibited by online review providers, which impact how the recipient accepts and assesses information, are collectively known as source credibility. Additionally, Dou et al. (2012) asserted that messages from trustworthy sources hold greater persuasiveness than those from less reputable ones. Source credibility comprises two key dimensions: expertise, which pertains to the source's knowledge, skills, and experience on a subject, and trustworthiness, which signifies the level of confidence one places in the source's reliability (Vafeiadis, 2021). Furthermore, in the bustling online environment, source credibility wields even more influence because consumers employ it as a heuristic cue during information processing, ultimately shaping the persuasiveness of online reviews (Hu et al., 2008; Sundar, 2008).

## Review Quality and Choosing Spa and Wellness Destination

The term information quality encompasses the correctness, completeness, relevance, and timeliness of data and the clarity and timely delivery of information. Furthermore, information quality is closely tied to how information is presented to potential consumers, necessitating it to be well-organized, current, suitable, accurate, and easily comprehensible (Hartanti et al., 2021). According to Xie et al. (2022), information quality is the extent to which individuals perceive content as current, precise, effective, and valuable. A customer's perception of the quality of information about a product or service offered by a website is characterized as information quality. Online customer reviews have become an essential form of long-term word-of-mouth (WOM) in e-commerce. However, it is worth noting that low-quality reviews can frustrate readers (Park, 2018). This is because consumers who have made purchases write online product reviews to assist future customers in making informed decisions. As Mudambi and Schuf (2010) explain, reviews are peer-generated, open-ended comments about a product posted on a company's or third-party websites. However, customers may need help to read all reviews as they accumulate. Poorly written, low-quality reviews can add to this challenge. Therefore, it is crucial for businesses to identify and selectively share positive feedback with their customers. Chen and Tseng (2011) suggest that high-quality reviews are subjective and include in-depth remarks about various product attributes. Consumers rely heavily on information quality in online purchases to reduce uncertainty and make well-informed decisions (Chen & Chang, 2018). Consequently, Lee & Min (2021) identify information quality as a primary motivator stimulating customer purchase intentions. According to the information richness theory, electronic media provide information and encourage e-commerce, albeit to a lesser extent than more prosperous face-to-face encounters (Chesney et al., 2017). The availability of more information enhances reliability and, consequently, increases the likelihood of customers purchasing goods or services. Moreover, better information quality provided by sellers leads to higher customer satisfaction and a greater intention to purchase (Chen & Chang, 2018; Ramadanty & Kartikasari, 2021). Matute et al. (2016) established that high-quality information significantly influences consumers' decision-making. Similarly, Mathur et al. (2021) found that information quality positively affects customer attitudes toward user-generated content on YouTube, influencing purchasing decision-making. However, several studies have described information quality as multi-dimensional (Brazil et al., 2022; Gaberamos & Pasaribu, 2022; Kang & Namkung, 2019). Kang and Namkung (2019) noted that different researchers have categorized information quality dimensions (e.g., correctness, timeliness, adequacy, dependability, etc.) differently, and there currently needs to be standardized information quality features. In this context, Li et al. (2022) employed a four-dimensional approach to information quality, including intrinsic, contextual, symbolic, and accessible dimensions, comprehensively encompassing the majority of information quality characteristics systematically. Notably, various studies have revealed that review quality positively influences customer purchase intentions (Lee & Min, 2021; Li et al., 2022). Therefore, the first proposition is proposed as:

Proposition 1: Review quality is significantly related to choosing a spa destination.

## Reviewer Credibility and Choosing Spa and Destination

Reviewer credibility pertains to the perception of a message recipient regarding the trustworthiness of the source delivering the message. Similarly, as stated by Muda and Hamzah (2021), credibility involves assessing certain information and its source in terms of trustworthiness. Furthermore, according to Sharif (2016), source credibility is defined as how perceivers judge the communicator's credibility. Rusdiana et al. (2020) described, the source credibility theory posits that information from credible sources can influence the recipient's attitudes, opinions, and behavior. Review source credibility is a comprehensive construct comprising three sub-dimensions: trustworthiness, which pertains to the recipient's confidence in the communicator; expertise, which relates to the sender's knowledge regarding the message; and attractiveness, which concerns the communicator's ability to persuade the recipient to engage with products or services (Sudheer et al., 2019). According to Ismagilova et al. (2020), credibility can be defined as the readiness or intention to rely on another person. In the context of planned behavior and reasoned action theories, where positive feelings lead to intention, confidence in the source leads to purchase intention (Saleem & Ellahi, 2017). The reliability of content providers influences the purchase intention of fashion goods on social media websites. Source credibility positively influences behavioral intention. Another study conducted by Dou et al. (2012) revealed that source credibility had a favorable impact on purchase intent in the context of online video reviews. The two fundamental aspects of source credibility are trustworthiness and expertise. Trustworthiness is the degree of confidence in the communicator's intention to convey valid propositions. This concept pertains to message receivers' trust in the communicator's integrity and honesty, which the communicator's reputation can influence (Zhang et al., 2019).

On the other hand, expertise was described as "the degree to which a communicator is considered as a source of valid assertions (Walten & Wiedmann, 2022), indicating how the communicator's ability and competence to provide information are perceived (Zhang et al., 2019). Several studies have affirmed that source credibility positively influences customer purchase intention (Li & Peng, 2021; Liang et al., 2021). Therefore, the second proposition is proposed as follows:

Proposition 2: Reviewer credibility is significantly related to choosing a spa destination.

## The Mediating Role of Perceived Review Helpfulness

According to Mudambi and Schuff (2010), perceived review helpfulness refers to the extent to which customers consider a peer-generated product assessment to aid in their purchase decision-making process. Chevalier and Mayzlin (2006) discovered that individuals who peruse online reviews are interested in the content and statistical data, such as the total number of reviews or the average review rating. Consequently, readers' responses are contingent upon the quality of the review's content, determined by its helpfulness. Online sellers frequently employ review helpfulness as a vital metric for gauging how customers assess a review and highlighting the most helpful reviews on a product's information page. Customers often organize reviews based on their perceived helpfulness level (Ping et al., 2023). Many review websites have implemented peer-review systems, allowing users to vote on whether they found a review valuable in their decision-making process. These valuable votes not only signal the diagnosticity of a review but also serve as a means to differentiate valuable reviews from the rest and assist customers in effectively filtering through various reviews (Ghose & Ipeirotis, 2008). Filieri et al. (2018) argue that users are more inclined to avail a service if they believe that the information provided on the e-tailer website will help them become acquainted with the service and evaluate its quality and performance before making a purchase.

Similarly, Chen et al. (2021) suggested that reviews with the highest degree of helpfulness can assist buyers in assessing and enhancing the reliability of reviews, thus boosting customer trust in selecting products and services. Chen et al. (2021) also point out that an analysis of the helpfulness of online reviews can aid in understanding the impact of reviews on the decision-making process, with the depth of reviews having a significant relationship with perceived usefulness and purchase intention. Empirical studies in the electronic word-of-mouth (eWOM) literature have shown that information quality affects perceived information helpfulness, perceived information diagnosticity, information adoption, and purchase intention (Chen et al., 2021; Filieri, 2015). Moreover, various aspects of information quality, such as review length/depth, readability, timeliness, relevancy, and correctness, have been observed to impact review usefulness positively (Filieri et al., 2021; Yang et al., 2017). Customers who find information in online reviews helpful tend to have a higher purchase intention. The influence of reviewer expertise on the perceived usefulness of user-generated content further underscores the significance of consumer trust and source credibility in this context (Zhang et al., 2019). Therefore, one of the primary factors affecting how people perceive online reviews as applicable is their confidence in the reviewer's knowledge and reliability as a review source (Bigne et al., 2021).

Additionally, research in psychology literature has shown that individuals assess message content differently based on the credibility of the message source (Ozdemir et al., 2021). Credible sources have been found to impact the decision-making processes of information seekers significantly. Perceived review helpfulness is a subjective evaluation of the perceived value of information contained in online customer reviews (Sharma et al., 2023). When the information is favorable, a helpful online customer review enhances the perceived value of the information it conveys, consequently elevating the perceived value of the assessed product or service and influencing the consumer's purchase intention (Huang et al., 2015). As mentioned earlier, various attributes of online customer reviews can influence how the review's helpfulness is perceived. Therefore, it is vital to comprehend the impact of the perceived usefulness of online customer reviews on purchase intention at this juncture. According to Filieri et al. (2018), online customer reviews positively influence customers' purchase intentions, meaning that the greater the perceived helpfulness, the higher the purchase intention. Therefore, the third, fourth, and fifth propositions are proposed as follows:

Proposition 3: Review quality has a significant relationship with perceived review helpfulness.

Proposition 4: Reviewer credibility has a significant relationship with perceived review helpfulness.

Proposition 5: Perceived review helpfulness is significantly related to choosing a spa destination.

*Figure 1. Proposed conceptual research framework*

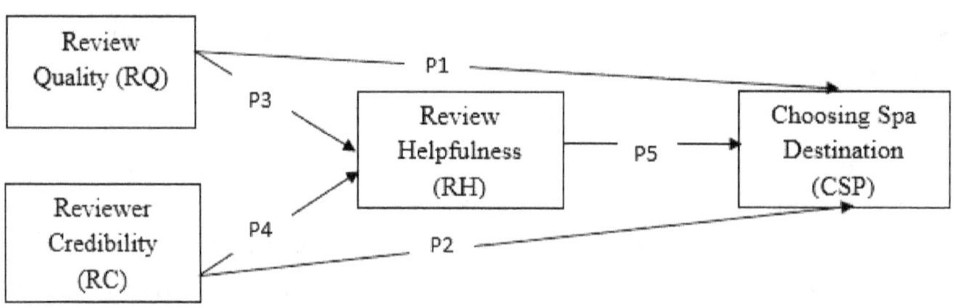


## DISCUSSION AND CONCLUSION

This article highlights the important role of social media reviews in influencing consumer choices within the spa and wellness industry. The review emphasizes the transformative impact of social media in modern communication and decision-making processes and the growing importance of spa and wellness as a niche sector in the broader tourism landscape. It underlines the significance of review quality and reviewer credibility as pivotal factors shaping consumer purchase intentions, with perceived review helpfulness mediating these relationships. Spa and wellness establishments can actively encourage high-quality, credible reviews and prioritize customer engagement strategies to enhance their online reputation and attract more customers. The proposed conceptual framework provides a solid foundation for future empirical research in consumer behavior within the spa and wellness context, offering valuable insights for businesses in the industry. This comprehensive exploration bridges theory and practice, making it a valuable resource for academia and the spa and wellness industry, ultimately empowering businesses to thrive in an increasingly competitive market.

## Prospective Academic Significance

The propositions presented in this literature review hold significant academic importance. They offer a foundation for future research endeavors in consumer behavior, specifically within the spa and wellness industry. Researchers can use the identified factors, such as review quality, reviewer credibility, and perceived review helpfulness, as variables in empirical studies, seeking to validate and expand upon the proposed relationships. Further investigation into the nuances of consumer decision-making in this context can contribute to developing more comprehensive theories and models in tourism and hospitality management. This review's multi-dimensional information quality and credibility approach allows in-depth exploration and measurement development. Thus, this literature review provides a stepping stone for scholars to advance their understanding of consumer behavior in the spa and wellness sector and to contribute novel insights to the broader marketing and tourism research field.

## Prospective Practical Significance

From a practical perspective, the insights from this literature review offer valuable implications for business operations in the spa and wellness industry. Spa and wellness centers can leverage the knowledge that review quality and reviewer credibility are pivotal in influencing consumer choices. By actively encouraging and promoting high-quality, credible reviews, these businesses can enhance their online reputation and attract more customers. They may also invest in customer engagement strategies on social media platforms to foster positive reviews and bolster their online presence. Furthermore, by recognizing the mediating role of perceived review helpfulness, spa and wellness businesses can prioritize efforts to ensure that customers find reviews valuable and informative, thus increasing the likelihood of converting potential customers into actual patrons. Overall, the practical significance lies in the ability of spa and wellness establishments to tailor their marketing and customer engagement strategies to better align with the dynamics of consumer decision-making in the digital age, ultimately leading to improved business outcomes.

## Prospective Significance of Sustainable Development Goals (SDGs)

The study on the impact of social media reviews on consumers' choices in the spa and wellness industry can be significant for the Sustainable Development Goals (SDGs) in several ways. The SDGs are a set of global goals adopted by the United Nations to address various global challenges, including health, well-being, and sustainable tourism. More broadly, this study contributes to SDG 3 (Good Health and Well-being), SDG 8 (Decent Work and Economic Growth), SDG 9 (Industry, Innovation, and Infrastructure), SDG 12 (Responsible Consumption and Production), SDG 13 (Climate Action), SDG 17 (Partnerships for the Goals).

The study focuses on the spa and wellness industry, which directly contributes to promoting physical, mental, and emotional well-being. Therefore, understanding the factors influencing consumers' choices in the spa and wellness sector can lead to the development of more effective health and wellness programs, contributing to improved health outcomes. Moreover, the study mentions the revenue generated by the spa industry, indicating its economic significance. By providing insights into consumer preferences and behaviors, the study can inform strategies for spa businesses, potentially leading to economic growth in this sector. In addition, the study explores the role of social media in influencing consumer decisions in the spa and wellness industry, highlighting the impact of technology and innovation on this sector.

Furthermore, understanding factors influencing consumer choices can lead to more informed and responsible consumption patterns. Hence, the study emphasizes the importance of reliable and reputable establishments, which aligns with promoting responsible consumption in the spa and wellness sector. Moreover, when managed sustainably, the spa and wellness industry can contribute to climate action by promoting eco-friendly practices. In contrast, Insights from the study can guide businesses in adopting sustainable practices, contributing to climate resilience. In addition, the study provides valuable information for stakeholders in the spa and wellness industry, encouraging collaboration and partnerships to improve the overall well-being of consumers. In summary, the study on the impact of social media reviews in the spa and wellness industry can contribute to various Sustainable Development Goals by promoting health and well-being, supporting economic growth, encouraging responsible consumption, and fostering partnerships for sustainable development.

## Applications of Artificial Intelligence in the Spa and Wellness Industry

Artificial intelligence systems evaluate information about guests, including previously taken services, preferences, and feedback, to customize their experience. This encompasses personalized services, suggestions for food and entertainment, and even exclusive presents upon arrival. In addition, artificial intelligence-driven chatbots and virtual assistants provide round-the-clock customer care, managing frequently asked questions, making reservations and payments, and checking different services. They enhance quickness of response and efficiency, hence improving overall guest satisfaction. In addition, dynamic pricing refers to pricing methods that are powered by AI that adjust product prices in real-time. These modifications are made depending on criteria like as demand, occupancy levels, competition rates, and other important factors. This assures the most effective handling of revenue and increases profitability. Moreover, AI utilizes data obtained from sensors and equipment to forecast the timing of necessary maintenance. This minimizes the amount of time that the system is not functioning, improves the security of the guests, and decreases the expenses related to operations.

Furthermore, voice recognition technology enables visitors to effortlessly operate various amenities like as lighting, temperature, and other features with voice-activated AI systems. Additionally, these systems can provide details on spa and wellness centres' amenities and nearby points of interest, consequently elevating visitor convenience. In addition, recommendation engines use AI algorithms to propose consumption choices, nearby attractions, and facilities based on visitor preferences and previous information. This encourages customers to further explore the many amenities and facilities offered by the spa and wellness centres as well as its neighboring areas. Artificial intelligence can analyze security camera footage to detect unusual activity and identify possible security risks. Additionally, it can identify unauthorized transactions and enhance the security of visitor data. Moreover, AI-driven translation services dismantle linguistic obstacles, facilitating efficient communication between staff and international visitors. AI examines guest evaluations and comments from many online platforms to detect patterns and highlight areas that need improvement. By swiftly addressing difficulties, spa and wellness centres can improve their reputation. Staff optimization involves the use of AI to analyze previous data and present demand patterns to aid with staff scheduling, work allocation, and training. This ensures that the appropriate staff members are assigned to the correct locations at the appropriate times. AI can manage and enhance energy consumption in spa and wellness centres by regulating heating, cooling, and lighting systems according to occupancy levels and environmental factors, resulting in decreased energy expenditures. AI can improve inventory management for spa and wellness by aligning supply levels with demand, minimizing waste and maximizing profitability. These AI solutions enhance guest satisfaction and result in cost savings, operational efficiency, and a competitive advantage in the constantly evolving spa and wellness business.

## Future Research Directions

Future studies can delve into the influence of user-generated visual content, the long-term impact of reviews on business sustainability, the potential of Artificial intelligence and natural language processing (NLP) in analyzing reviews, multi-channel consumer behavior, innovative user engagement strategies, the intersection of sustainability and wellness, customer journey mapping, and strategies for crisis management in the digital age. These avenues of inquiry can provide valuable insights into how social media reviews impact consumer choices and guide businesses in optimizing their marketing strategies in a competitive market. Moreover, Future research directions for the article could encompass a cross-cultural analysis to explore cultural influences, examine the role of review moderation and ethical considerations, investigate the impact of emerging social media platforms, and assess the effectiveness of influencer marketing in the spa and wellness industry.

## CONCLUSION

In conclusion, this literature review comprehensively explores the relationship between social media reviews and consumer choices in the spa and wellness industry. Defining the critical concepts of spa and wellness emphasizes the transformative role of social media in modern communication and decision-making. Highlighting the impact of social media reviews as significant sources of firsthand information, the review identifies critical factors influencing individual behavioral intention. This thorough examination sets the stage for further research by proposing valuable research propositions. It offers essential insights for businesses and stakeholders in the spa and wellness sector seeking to optimize their strategies in an increasingly competitive market.

## REFERENCES

Abu-Taieh, E., AlHadid, I., Masa'deh, R., Alkhawaldeh, R. S., Khwaldeh, S., & Alrowwad, A. (2022). Factors Influencing YouTube as a Learning Tool and Its Influence on Academic Achievement in a Bilingual Environment Using Extended Information Adoption Model (IAM) with ML Prediction—Jordan Case Study. *Applied Sciences (Basel, Switzerland)*, *12*(12), 5856. doi:10.3390/app12125856

Ahani, A., Nilashi, M., Ibrahim, O., Sanzogni, L., & Weaven, S. (2019). Market segmentation and travel choice prediction in Spa hotels through TripAdvisor's online reviews. *International Journal of Hospitality Management*, *80*, 52–77. doi:10.1016/j.ijhm.2019.01.003

Barbosa, B., Saura, J. R., Zekan, S. B., & Ribeiro-Soriano, D. (2023). Defining content marketing and its influence on online user behavior: A data-driven prescriptive analytics method. *Annals of Operations Research*, 1–26. doi:10.1007/s10479-023-05261-1

Beneke, J., de Sousa, S., Mbuyu, M., & Wickham, B. (2016). The effect of negative online customer reviews on brand equity and purchase intention of consumer electronics in South Africa. *International Review of Retail, Distribution and Consumer Research*, *26*(2), 171–201. doi:10.1080/09593969.2015.1068828

Bigne, E., Ruiz, C., Cuenca, A., Perez, C., & Garcia, A. (2021). What drives the helpfulness of online reviews? A deep learning study of sentiment analysis, pictorial content, and reviewer expertise for mature destinations. *Journal of Destination Marketing & Management*, *20*, 100570. doi:10.1016/j.jdmm.2021.100570

Brazil, C., Neri, S. B., Soriano, A. Y., Victorio, C. F., & Grimaldo, J. R. (2022). The Effect of Online Wet Markets Website Quality on the Purchase Intention of Consumers in Caloocan City. *Journal of Business and Management Studies*, *4*(2), 136–149. doi:10.32996/jbms.2022.4.2.11

Chen, C.-C., & Chang, Y.-C. (2018). What drives purchase intention on Airbnb? Perspectives of consumer reviews, information quality, and media richness. *Telematics and Informatics*, *35*(5), 1512–1523. doi:10.1016/j.tele.2018.03.019

Chen, C. C., & Tseng, Y.-D. (2011). Quality evaluation of product reviews using an information quality framework. *Decision Support Systems*, *50*(4), 755–768. doi:10.1016/j.dss.2010.08.023

Chen, K.-H., Liu, H.-H., & Chang, F.-H. (2013). Essential customer service factors and the segmentation of older visitors within wellness tourism based on hot springs hotels. *International Journal of Hospitality Management, 35*, 122–132. doi:10.1016/j.ijhm.2013.05.013

Chen, Y.-L., Chang, C.-L., & Sung, A.-Q. (2021). Predicting eWOM's Influence on Purchase Intention Based on Helpfulness, Credibility, Information Quality and Professionalism. *Sustainability (Basel), 13*(13), 7486. doi:10.3390/su13137486

Chesney, T., Chuah, S.-H., Dobele, A. R., & Hoffmann, R. (2017). Information richness and trust in v-commerce: Implications for services marketing. *Journal of Services Marketing, 31*(3), 295–307. doi:10.1108/JSM-02-2015-0099

Chevalier, J. A., & Mayzlin, D. (2006). The effect of word of mouth on sales: Online book reviews. *JMR, Journal of Marketing Research, 43*(3), 345–354. doi:10.1509/jmkr.43.3.345

Dentzel, Z. (2013). How the internet has changed everyday life. *Ch@ Nge, 19*, 235–252.

Didascalou, E., & Lagos, D. (2009). Wellness tourism: Evaluating destination attributes for tourism planning in a competitive segment market. *Tourismos, 4*(4), 113–126.

Dou, X., Walden, J. A., Lee, S., & Lee, J. Y. (2012). Does source matter? Examining source effects in online product reviews. *Computers in Human Behavior, 28*(5), 1555–1563. doi:10.1016/j.chb.2012.03.015

Erkan, I., & Evans, C. (2016). The influence of eWOM in social media on consumers' purchase intentions: An extended approach to information adoption. *Computers in Human Behavior, 61*, 47–55. doi:10.1016/j.chb.2016.03.003

Filieri, R. (2015). What makes online reviews helpful? A diagnosticity-adoption framework to explain informational and normative influences in e-WOM. *Journal of Business Research, 68*(6), 1261–1270. doi:10.1016/j.jbusres.2014.11.006

Filieri, R., Lin, Z., Pino, G., Alguezaui, S., & Inversini, A. (2021). The role of visual cues in eWOM on consumers' behavioral intention and decisions. *Journal of Business Research, 135*, 663–675. doi:10.1016/j.jbusres.2021.06.055

Filieri, R., McLeay, F., Tsui, B., & Lin, Z. (2018). Consumer perceptions of information helpfulness and determinants of purchase intention in online consumer reviews of services. *Information & Management, 55*(8), 956–970. doi:10.1016/j.im.2018.04.010

Gaberamos, O., & Pasaribu, L. H. (2022). The Effect Of Information Quality, Customer Experience, Price, And Service Quality On Purchase Intention By Using Customer Perceived Value As Mediation Variables (Study On Gofood Applications On The Millenial Generation). *Jurnal Mantik*, *5*(4), 2470–2480.

Garg, A., & Kumar, J. (2021). Social media marketing influence on Boutique Hotel customers' purchase intention in Malaysia. *Tourism & Management Studies*, *17*(3), 51–62. doi:10.18089/tms.2021.170304

Ghose, A., & Ipeirotis, P. G. (2008). *Estimating the socio-economic impact of product reviews: Mining text and reviewer characteristics.*

Global Wellness Institute. (n.d.). *Home.* Global Wellness Institute. https://globalwellnessinstitute.org/

Hartanti, F. T., Abawajy, J. H., Chowdhury, M., & Shalannanda, W. (2021). Citizens' Trust Measurement in Smart Government Services. *IEEE Access : Practical Innovations, Open Solutions*, *9*, 150663–150676. doi:10.1109/ACCESS.2021.3124206

Hu, N., Liu, L., & Zhang, J. J. (2008). Do online reviews affect product sales? The role of reviewer characteristics and temporal effects. *Information Technology and Management*, *9*(3), 201–214. doi:10.1007/s10799-008-0041-2

Huang, A. H., Chen, K., Yen, D. C., & Tran, T. P. (2015). A study of factors that contribute to online review helpfulness. *Computers in Human Behavior*, *48*, 17–27. doi:10.1016/j.chb.2015.01.010

Ismagilova, E., Slade, E., Rana, N. P., & Dwivedi, Y. K. (2020). The effect of characteristics of source credibility on consumer behavior: A meta-analysis. *Journal of Retailing and Consumer Services*, *53*, 101736. doi:10.1016/j.jretconser.2019.01.005

Jalilvand, M. R., & Heidari, A. (2017). Comparing face-to-face and electronic word-of-mouth in destination image formation: The case of Iran. *Information Technology & People*, *30*(4), 710–735. doi:10.1108/ITP-09-2016-0204

Jiang, G., Liu, F., Liu, W., Liu, S., Chen, Y., & Xu, D. (2021). Effects of information quality on information adoption on social media review platforms: Moderating role of perceived risk. *Data Science and Management*, *1*(1), 13–22. doi:10.1016/j.dsm.2021.02.004

Kang, J.-W., & Namkung, Y. (2019). The information quality and source credibility matter in customers' evaluation toward food O2O commerce. *International Journal of Hospitality Management*, *78*, 189–198. doi:10.1016/j.ijhm.2018.10.011

Kaur, K., & Kumar, P. (2022). Social media: A blessing or a curse? Voice of owners in the beauty and wellness industry. *The TQM Journal, 34*(5), 1039–1056. doi:10.1108/TQM-03-2021-0074

Kim, E. Y., & Kim, Y.-K. (2004). Predicting online purchase intentions for clothing products. *European Journal of Marketing*.

Kim, Y., Wang, Q., & Roh, T. (2021). Do information and service quality affect perceived privacy protection, satisfaction, and loyalty? Evidence from a Chinese O2O-based mobile shopping application. *Telematics and Informatics, 56*, 101483. doi:10.1016/j.tele.2020.101483

Kumar, J., Konar, R., & Balasubramanian, K. (2020). The impact of Social Media on Consumers' purchasing behaviour in Malaysian Restaurants. *Journal of Spatial and Organizational Dynamics, 8*(3), 197–216.

Kumar, J., Nazir, F., & Nisar, Q. (2023). Empowering wellness worldwide: A critical analysis of the Global Wellness Institute (GWI) journey 2014-2021. *Journal of Tourism & Development, 41*, 263–287. doi:10.34624/rtd.v41i0.29731

LEE, S. K., & MIN, S. R. (2021). Effects of Information Quality of Online Travel Agencies on Trust and Continuous Usage Intention: An Application of the SOR Model. The Journal of Asian Finance. *Economics and Business, 8*(4), 971–982.

Lehto, X. Y., Brown, S., Chen, Y., & Morrison, A. M. (2006). Yoga tourism as a niche within the wellness tourism market. *Tourism Recreation Research, 31*(1), 25–35. doi:10.1080/02508281.2006.11081244

Li, K., Zhou, C., Luo, X. R., Benitez, J., & Liao, Q. (2022). Impact of information timeliness and richness on public engagement on social media during COVID-19 pandemic: An empirical investigation based on NLP and machine learning. *Decision Support Systems, 162*, 113752. doi:10.1016/j.dss.2022.113752 PMID:35185227

Li, Y., & Peng, Y. (2021). Influencer marketing: Purchase intention and its antecedents. *Marketing Intelligence & Planning, 39*(7), 960–978. doi:10.1108/MIP-04-2021-0104

Liang, X., Hu, X., Islam, T., & Mubarik, M. S. (2021). Social support, source credibility, social influence, and solar photovoltaic panels purchase intention. *Environmental Science and Pollution Research International, 28*(41), 57842–57859. doi:10.1007/s11356-021-14750-4 PMID:34097220

Lin, L.-Y., & Chen, C.-S. (2006). The influence of the country-of-origin image, product knowledge and product involvement on consumer purchase decisions: An empirical study of insurance and catering services in Taiwan. *Journal of Consumer Marketing*, *23*(5), 248–265. doi:10.1108/07363760610681655

Lu, L.-C., Chang, W.-P., & Chang, H.-H. (2014). Consumer attitudes toward blogger's sponsored recommendations and purchase intention: The effect of sponsorship type, product type, and brand awareness. *Computers in Human Behavior*, *34*, 258–266. doi:10.1016/j.chb.2014.02.007

Mathur, S., Tewari, A., & Singh, A. (2021). Modeling the factors affecting online purchase intention: The mediating effect of consumer's attitude towards user-generated content. *Journal of Marketing Communications*, 1–20.

Matute, J., Polo-Redondo, Y., & Utrillas, A. (2016). The influence of EWOM characteristics on online repurchase intention: Mediating roles of trust and perceived usefulness. *Online Information Review*, *40*(7), 1090–1110. doi:10.1108/OIR-11-2015-0373

Muda, M., & Hamzah, M. I. (2021). Should I suggest this YouTube clip? The impact of UGC source credibility on eWOM and purchase intention. *Journal of Research in Interactive Marketing*, *15*(3), 441–459. doi:10.1108/JRIM-04-2020-0072

Mudambi, S. M., & Schuff, D. (2010). Research note: What makes a helpful online review? A study of customer reviews on Amazon. com. *MIS Quarterly*, 185–200.

Nabella, S. D. (2021). Improve Consumer Purchasing Decisions Through Quality of Service, Promotion And Quality of Information At PT. Ng Tech Supplies. International Journal of Science. *Technology & Management*, *2*(3), 880–889.

Okech, R. N. (2014). Promoting the spa tourism industry: Focus on coastal resorts in Kenya. *Athens Journal of Tourism*, *1*(1), 67–77. doi:10.30958/ajt.1-1-4

Ozdemir, D. Y., Singh, H., & Sarkar, S. (2021). *Credibility*. Novelty and Helpfulness in Online Reviews.

Pandey, U., Islam, M. T., & Hossain, M. I. (2023). Servicescape, E-WoM, and satisfaction on tourists' revisit intention to yoga tourist destination: Evidence from Patanjali Yogpeeth, India. *Revista Turismo & Desenvolvimento (Aveiro)*, *44*, 313–333.

Park, C. W., Sutherland, I., & Lee, S. K. (2021). Effects of online reviews, trust, and picture-superiority on intention to purchase restaurant services. *Journal of Hospitality and Tourism Management*, *47*, 228–236. doi:10.1016/j.jhtm.2021.03.007

Park, D.-H., & Lee, J. (2008). EWOM overload and its effect on consumer behavioral intention depending on consumer involvement. *Electronic Commerce Research and Applications*, *7*(4), 386–398. doi:10.1016/j.elerap.2007.11.004

Park, Y.-J. (2018). Predicting the helpfulness of online customer reviews across different product types. *Sustainability (Basel)*, *10*(6), 1735. doi:10.3390/su10061735

Ping, Y., Buoye, A., & Vakil, A. (2023). Enhanced review facilitation service for C2C support: Machine learning approaches. *Journal of Services Marketing*, *37*(5), 620–635. doi:10.1108/JSM-01-2022-0005

Ramadanty, M. L., & Kartikasari, D. (2021). *Purchase Intention of E-Payment: The Substitute or Complementary Role of Brand.* Sales Promotions, and Information Quality.

Riswanto, A. L., & Kim, H.-S. (2023). An Investigation of The Key Attributes of Korean Wellness Tourism Customers Based on Online Reviews. *Sustainability (Basel)*, *15*(8), 6702. doi:10.3390/su15086702

Rusdiana, A., Suroso, A., & Suwandari, L. (2020). The Effect of e-WOM Source Credibility on Purchase Intentions with Consumer Involvement as a Moderating Variable. *ICORE, 5*(1).

Saleem, A., & Ellahi, A. (2017). Influence of electronic word of mouth on purchase intention of fashion products in social networking websites. [PJCSS]. *Pakistan Journal of Commerce and Social Sciences*, *11*(2), 597–622.

Salvatore, C., Biffignandi, S., & Bianchi, A. (2021). Social media and Twitter data quality for new social indicators. *Social Indicators Research*, *156*(2), 601–630. doi:10.1007/s11205-020-02296-w

Sharif, M. A. (2016). Electronic word of mouth: Investigating the influence of electronic message source credibility, message appeal and brand equity on consumer purchase intention. *City University Research Journal, 6*(1).

Sharma, S. P., Singh, L., & Tiwari, R. (2023). Prediction of Customer Review's Helpfulness Based on Feature Engineering Driven Deep Learning Model. [IJSI]. *International Journal of Software Innovation*, *11*(1), 1–16.

Shin, H.-R., & Choi, J.-G. (2021). The Moderating Effect of 'Generation'on the Relations between Source Credibility of Social Media Contents, Hotel Brand Image, and Purchase Intention. *Sustainability (Basel)*, *13*(16), 9471. doi:10.3390/su13169471

Sudheer, S., Reddy, M. S. K., & Manideep, A. S. (2019). The Influence of Source Credibility, Endorser Credibility and Message Appeal on Consumers' Purchase Intention: An Empirical Analysis. *International Journal of Recent Technology and Engineering*, *8*(1), 2845–2850.

Sundar, S. S. (2008). *The MAIN model: A heuristic approach to understanding technology effects on credibility*. MacArthur Foundation Digital Media and Learning Initiative Cambridge.

Suttikun, C., Chang, H. J., & Bicksler, H. (2018). A qualitative exploration of day spa therapists' work motivations and job satisfaction. *Journal of Hospitality and Tourism Management*, *34*, 1–10. doi:10.1016/j.jhtm.2017.10.013

Szromek, A. R., & Polok, G. (2022). A Business Model for Spa Tourism Enterprises: Transformation in a Period of Sustainable Change and Humanitarian Crisis. *Journal of Open Innovation*, *8*(2), 72. doi:10.3390/joitmc8020072

Tarute, A., Nikou, S., & Gatautis, R. (2017). Mobile application driven consumer engagement. *Telematics and Informatics*, *34*(4), 145–156. doi:10.1016/j.tele.2017.01.006

Trihas, N., & Konstantarou, A. (2016). Spa-goers' characteristics, motivations, preferences and perceptions: Evidence from Elounda, Crete. Almatourism-Journal of Tourism. *Culture and Territorial Development*, *7*(14), 106–127.

Vafeiadis, M. (2021). Message interactivity and source credibility in online dental practice reviews: Responding to reviews triggers positive consumer reactions regardless of review valence. *Health Communication*, 1–11. PMID:34080513

Varkaris, E., & Neuhofer, B. (2017). The influence of social media on the consumers' hotel decision journey. *Journal of Hospitality and Tourism Technology*, *8*(1), 101–118. doi:10.1108/JHTT-09-2016-0058

Walten, L., & Wiedmann, K.-P. (2022). How product information and source credibility affect consumer attitudes and intentions towards innovative food products. *Journal of Marketing Communications*, 1–17.

Xie, D., Xiao, F., & Pedrycz, W. (2022). Information quality for intuitionistic fuzzy values with its application in decision making. *Engineering Applications of Artificial Intelligence*, *109*, 104568. doi:10.1016/j.engappai.2021.104568

Yang, S.-B., Hlee, S., Lee, J., & Koo, C. (2017). An empirical examination of online restaurant reviews on Yelp. com: A dual coding theory perspective. *International Journal of Contemporary Hospitality Management*, *29*(2), 817–839. doi:10.1108/IJCHM-11-2015-0643

Zeithaml, V. A. (1988). Consumer perceptions of price, quality, and value: A means-end model and synthesis of evidence. *Journal of Marketing*, *52*(3), 2–22. doi:10.1177/002224298805200302

Zhang, B., Ritchie, B., Mair, J., & Driml, S. (2019). Is the airline trustworthy? The impact of source credibility on voluntary carbon offsetting. *Journal of Travel Research*, *58*(5), 715–731. doi:10.1177/0047287518775781

# Chapter 2
# The Technology Impacts and AI Solutions for the Tourism Industry

**Dina Darwish**
*Ahram Canadian University, Egypt*

## ABSTRACT

*The advent of information and communication technologies (ICTs) has sparked a significant transformation within the tourism and hospitality sector. The prevalence of travel websites, which are known for their open sharing of information, has been established for a considerable duration. These platforms are now facilitating the adoption of increasingly advanced intelligent systems within the tourism and hospitality industry. Given the intricate nature of decision-making processes in the context of travel, intelligent systems and tourism are highly compatible. The advent of service automation, artificial intelligence, and robotics has presented tourism companies and organizations with a plethora of novel prospects. The utilization of artificial intelligence in different sectors of the tourism industry has been observed to a certain degree. However, there remains a limited amount of scholarly literature available on this topic. This chapter aims to further explore the emerging field of artificial intelligence applications in the tourism industry, as well as the key trends in this field.*

## INTRODUCTION

The term "travel technology" encompasses a wide range of technological advancements, including AI, information technology (IT), e-commerce, and other

DOI: 10.4018/979-8-3693-1978-9.ch002

related solutions. These advancements are specifically applied within the domains of tourism, travel, and hospitality. Hotel and tourism technology is designed to provide support to businesses and their staff, enhance the travel experience for customers, or fulfil both objectives simultaneously.

The underlying objectives or rationales for the implementation of travel technology encompass the automation of travel and associated procedures, the optimization of time utilization, the mitigation of expenses, and the facilitation of a more streamlined travel encounter for individuals. The utilization of technology can be employed to augment the customer experience prior to, during, and subsequent to the journey.

The utilization of travel technology has the potential to enhance operational efficiency for businesses by streamlining processes and automating tasks that have traditionally relied on human intervention. Implementing this strategy can potentially assist a business in minimizing their staffing needs, reducing expenses, and augmenting their revenue generation, thereby resulting in enhanced financial outcomes.

Furthermore, the integration of technology can provide substantial benefits to businesses by enhancing precision and efficiency, thereby mitigating the occurrence of human errors. Nevertheless, it is imperative to consistently stay abreast of the most recent advancements in tourism technology in order to employ optimal solutions and prevent other enterprises from gaining a competitive advantage.

It is imperative for businesses to consistently stay abreast of the most recent advancements in travel technology, as this practice is also adopted by their primary competitors. Allowing individuals to adopt new technology poses the potential risk of granting them a substantial advantage. Simultaneously, one may become complacent, particularly when the technology is intended to provide advantages to customers.

As emerging trends and established technologies continue to shape the market landscape, customers increasingly demand a specific level of experiential quality and seek the associated convenience. Customers are likely to experience a sense of disappointment in the event that your business does not meet the aforementioned expectations. Consequently, this may subsequently result in adverse evaluations and harm to one's professional standing.

Simultaneously, staying abreast of advancements in travel and tourism technology can also prove beneficial for employees and potentially facilitate the recruitment process, as prospective candidates are likely to be attracted to opportunities involving cutting-edge tools, particularly if they contribute to stress reduction.

A trend can be characterized as a broad advancement within a specific domain or as a broad alteration in conduct. In the field of hospitality, various factors contribute to alterations in consumer behavior, consequently driving the emergence of significant travel technology trends.

The adoption of smart speakers in hotels, virtual reality tours offered by travel companies, and streamlined check-in processes that eliminate the need for queuing and interacting with reception staff are examples of how emerging technologies, such as AI-based applications, voice search, virtual and augmented reality, facial recognition technology, and the Internet of Things, have influenced various industries.

In contemporary society, individuals have become more reliant on contactless payment methods, voice-activated search functionalities, and mobile applications in their daily lives. Consequently, it is logical to observe a similar trajectory in the adoption of technological advancements within the tourism industry. The COVID-19 pandemic has also expedited certain behaviors, thereby intensifying the demand for solutions such as cleaning robots. The main topics to be covered in this chapter includes the following;

- The Scope of Artificial Intelligence in the Tourism Industry
- The Application of Artificial Intelligence in the Tourism Industry: Prominent Use Cases
- The key technology trends in the tourism and travel industry
- The tourism industry presents various challenges for the implementation of AI technologies
- The future implications of artificial intelligence in the tourism industry

Also, this chapter is organized as follows; the first section includes the background, then, the second section contains the main focus of the chapter, including the main topics stated in the previous section, then finally, the conclusion section is provided.

## BACKGROUND

AI technology has emerged as a groundbreaking innovation that has significantly transformed numerous industries on a global scale in the era of technology-driven advancements. AI is commonly defined as the advancement of computer systems capable of executing tasks and activities that typically necessitate human intelligence (Russell and Norvig, 2016). The emergence of Artificial Intelligence can be traced back to the year 1956 when it was first introduced in John McCarthy's Dartmouth Summer Research Project. Throughout the years, numerous achievements in the field of AI have been observed, including advancements in heuristic searches, character recognition, facial recognition systems, natural language processing, and the development of mobile robotics. Significant advancements have been achieved in the technology-driven field by the 1980s, leading to substantial conceptual progress and a notable increase in its application (Issa et al., 2016). Throughout the

1990s, notable advancements were made in the realm of technology, with particular emphasis on the domain of Artificial Intelligence, facilitating the development of advanced technologies, enabling engineers to effectively utilize vast amounts of data and construct robots with enhanced efficiency.

Also, there is a focus on enhancing computational capabilities. Subsequently, the concept of artificial intelligence has undergone significant advancements, thereby revolutionizing the capabilities of technology. In the contemporary era, the field of Artificial Intelligence has attained a pinnacle of development, exhibiting the capacity to exert a substantial influence on individuals, organizations, and industries. Artificial Intelligence technology is being utilized across diverse industries, extending beyond the confines of the Information Technology sector, in the digitalized era (Nagaraj, 2019, 2020). For instance, individuals may encounter AI in the context of autonomous transportation, robotic healthcare assistants, navigational tools, conversational agents, human-computer competitions, and diverse domains (Russell & Norvig, 2016). Based on the forecast made by McCormick et al. (McCormick et al., 2016), the increasing adoption of Artificial Intelligence by various industries is expected to enable businesses to extract approximately $1.2 trillion in annual profits from their less knowledgeable competitors by the year 2020. Artificial Intelligence has significantly impacted various prominent sectors, including the manufacturing industry, automotive industry, banking and financial services, healthcare and life sciences, insurance, telecommunications, energy, travel tourism and hospitality, and media and entertainment.

The presence of AI is rapidly growing in various industries worldwide on a daily basis. The utilization and acceptance of AI technology are experiencing a notable surge within the industrial domain due to its capacity to enhance innovation and streamline human-dependent processes and activities. AI is being widely employed across multiple sectors, including sales and marketing, customer service, and finance, within organizations. The tourism industry has experienced significant expansion and success on a global scale in the 21st century. According to data from Statista (Statista, 2023), there has been a significant growth in international tourist arrivals, with numbers rising from 528 million in 2005 to 1.19 billion in 2015. In contemporary society, a significant number of individuals exhibit a willingness to allocate financial resources towards engaging in tourism and travel activities. The allocation of funds has resulted in an increase in demand and overall efficacy within the industry. The travel and tourism industry has experienced significant growth, positioning it as one of the largest sectors globally with the potential to influence a nation's economic well-being. According to a report from Statista (Statista, 2023), the integration of technology in the industrial sector has resulted in enhanced performance and improved quality of service provision. AI has permeated the tourism and hospitality industry, where its implementation is sought after as a means to attain a competitive edge within the ever-evolving market. The graph depicted below illustrates the utilization of diverse artificial intelligence strategies across various industries, encompassing the tourism and hospitality sector. The tourism industry has experienced a gradual integration of technology, resulting in a reduction of manual processes. The tourism industry, known for its propensity to embrace new technologies, has readily embraced AI. The concept of Artificial Intelligence has been introduced into the business context, offering marketers in the competitive industrial setting the opportunity to automate processes and optimize business activities. Originally, the utilization of AI technology aimed to streamline marketing procedures. However, in contemporary times, AI technology has made a significant impact on various facets of the tourism industry, including guest reception, service provision, and attentive customer care. AI along with emerging technologies is being utilized within the tourism sector for a multitude of objectives, including enhancing the degree of individualization, customizing customer recommendations, and ensuring prompt response times even in the absence of staff members. The utilization of artificial intelligence along with other emerging technologies has become increasingly indispensable in the industrial context, as it is employed to aid and facilitate customer interactions, thereby enhancing the level of engagement.

Studies conducted between 2015 and 2019 by Gajdošík (Gajdosik, 2018) indicate that emerging technologies are being utilized in the tourism and hospitality industry to enhance tourists' holiday and accommodation experiences. Additionally, it is being employed to offer innovative tourist services that enhance overall trip satisfaction (Jasrotia & Gangotia, 2018). In addition, the use of emerging technologies with AI enhances the competitiveness of these tourism firms by automating services and leveraging information communication technologies, so gaining a competitive edge over their rivals (Gretzel et al., 2015). Also, a smart tourist destination refers to a location that leverages information technology and innovations to provide tourists with high-quality services, enjoyable experiences, and exceptional travel opportunities (Jasrotia and Gangotia, 2018). Figure 1 shows impact of AI and emerging technologies on tourism industry. The purpose of this chapter is to examine the integration of Artificial Intelligence technology into the tourism sector and the transformative impact it has had on the industry. This perspective aims to provide a comprehensive understanding of the diverse artificial intelligence technologies being utilized, their implications, challenges, and future prospects within the Travel, Tourism, and Hospitality industry.

*Figure 1. Impact of AI and emerging technologies on tourism industry*

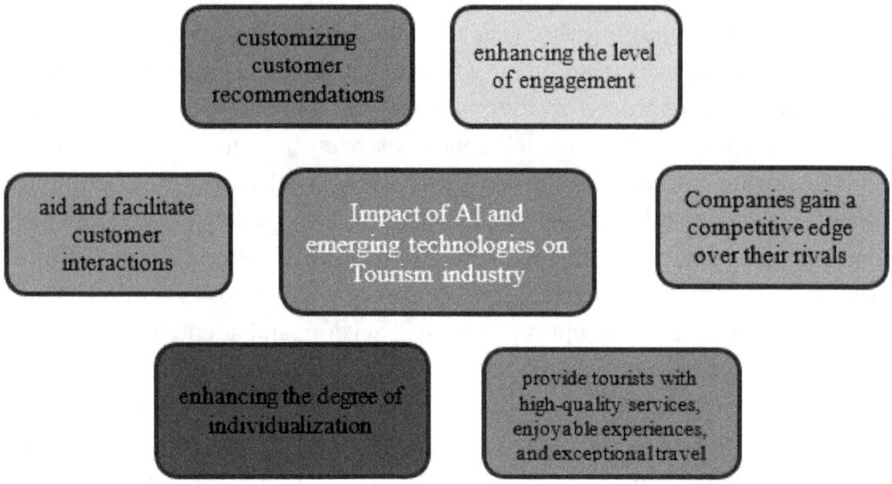


## MAIN FOCUS OF THE CHAPTER

Despite the ongoing discourse pertaining to AI, the practical implementation of AI within the travel, tourism, and hospitality industries remains constrained, with only a few noteworthy advancements observed thus far. Within the domain of the travel, tourism, and hospitality industry, there is a scarcity of recent research studies focused on the utilization of AI. According to research findings, the substantial increase in online travel sales, which are estimated to surpass $800 billion by the year 2020, could potentially account for the observed trend. According to a study conducted by Google Travel and Trip Advisor (Trip Advisor, 2023), a substantial majority of consumers rely on the internet as a primary tool for organizing their vacation plans. In addition, a significant segment of these consumers utilize smartphones in order to engage in vacation planning activities. The majority of customers exhibit a notable inclination towards utilizing self-service technologies as opposed to traditional service options.

Moreover, a significant percentage of these consumers utilize smartphones for the specific objective of planning their vacations. A substantial majority of customers indicate a preference for employing self-service technologies in lieu of conventional services. In a study conducted by thinkwithgoogle.com in 2016 (thinkwithgoogle, 2023), it was discovered that a substantial majority of customers, specifically 90%, possess the expectation of acquiring essential information relevant to their travel while in transit to their final destination. Upon analysis of the aforementioned aggregated data, it becomes apparent that consumers are displaying a growing propensity to utilize internet and technological resources that facilitate self-service functionalities. Based on the aforementioned findings, marketers may exhibit a propensity to incorporate AI into their organizations via interactive and self-service technology, with the objective of augmenting the overall consumer experience. The results of these surveys not only indicate that customers have a tendency to adopt technology, but they also suggest that the concept of "Timeliness" is of importance. A significant proportion of clients demonstrate a reluctance to avail themselves of services prior to their journey, instead expressing an anticipation of receiving said services throughout the course of their trip. A substantial majority of customers demonstrate a preference for self-service technologies over conventional service options.

The integration of artificial intelligence significantly improves the feasibility of creating self-service technology. In addition to the aforementioned elements, there are various additional factors that have an impact on the travel, tourism, and hospitality industry. The choice of Tourism, Travel & Hospitality services is impacted by various notable factors, such as the accessibility of natural resources, the standard of overall infrastructure facilities, and the preferences and requirements of tourists. The term "natural" pertains to phenomena or entities that are present or manifest in the physical world. The available resources encompass a diverse range of natural features, including aesthetically pleasing landscapes, extensive bodies of water, towering mountain ranges, and expansive desert regions. Furthermore, the geographical area exhibits a diverse array of botanical species, which can be identified by their unique and distinctive characteristics. The biodiversity of a given location is influenced by various factors, including its fauna and climatic conditions, encompassing temperature, precipitation, and humidity. Infrastructure facilities comprise various elements, including road networks and both public and private transportation systems. The establishment comprises a variety of amenities, including options for lodging and accommodation, dining establishments, bars, discotheques, clubs, and themed venues. Public parks, recreational and sporting facilities, aquatic parks, zoological gardens, gambling establishments, hiking trails, and other exhilarating outdoor activities are among the diverse range of options for individuals seeking leisure and entertainment. Additionally, various amenities, including retail malls, are also accessible to cater to the needs and preferences of visitors.

Destination tourism infrastructure refers to the diverse elements that play a role in the establishment and upkeep of a tourist destination. The availability and quality of human resources is a critical aspect of this infrastructure. The safety protocols that have been implemented at the specific location. The field of artificial intelligence shows great potential in offering comprehensive insights into various crucial sectors, including natural resources, general infrastructure, tourist infrastructure, destination tourism infrastructure, and more. The advantage of AI technology over human performance resides in its capacity to efficiently analyze and disseminate vast amounts of information related to critical components within a considerably compressed time frame. Considering the current circumstances, it is plausible to envision a scenario where artificial intelligence surpasses human capabilities in providing services. Artificial Intelligence efficiently caters to customer requirements by delivering timely information regarding essential elements such as Natural Resources, General Infrastructure facilities, Tourist Infrastructure facilities, Destination Tourism Infrastructure facilities, and other pertinent variables. The aforementioned information can be communicated through various methods including interactive messaging, self-service technologies, chatbots, audio tours, virtual tours, an interactive reservation process, facial recognition technologies, language translations, cross-selling and up-selling tactics, competitive pricing, user-friendly shopping interfaces, and other methodologies. In recent years, the field of artificial intelligence has enabled the development of several innovative technologies. These technologies have demonstrated their ability to provide a unique and beneficial experience to the customer base. This category encompasses a variety of advancements, including technologies such as facial recognition, virtual reality applications, chatbots, robots, artificial intelligence integrated into Google Maps, language translators, audio tours, and enhanced shopping experiences, among other examples.

Facial recognition, an AI technology, is gaining recognition for its substantial importance and extensive adoption across various industries due to a multitude of factors. The utilization of facial recognition technology has become increasingly prevalent within the travel and tourism industry on a significant scale. The present system employs facial recognition technology to accurately identify visitors and subsequently compares their facial characteristics with the data stored in their official identification cards, thereby streamlining the check-in procedure. By leveraging this sophisticated technology, travelers are afforded the convenience and comfort of seamlessly navigating airport check-in procedures and other pertinent stations. The check-in process can be carried out without the need for document verifications conducted by various authorities, including immigration, customs, and other relevant entities.

Virtual Reality (VR) technology commonly utilizes a VR headset to create a simulated environment. The simulated world provided offers to users for a highly immersive experience within the domain of virtual reality. The application of virtual reality (VR) technology enables consumers to engage in a three-dimensional (3D) setting, thereby augmenting their overall experiential encounter. The concept of the digital realm has been extensively examined in numerous scholarly investigations. In the present era, the adoption of this technology has become widespread within the travel and tourism sector. Hospitality companies exhibit tourist attractions and hotel destinations by means of their services.

A chatbot is a type of software application that engages in conversation through auditory or written communication channels. There are two main classifications of Chatbots, namely Text message-based chatbots and Voice-based chatbots. Text message-based chatbots provide messaging services to individuals. Customer inquiries are received in the form of text messages. Voice-based chatbots provide a method of communication utilizing spoken language. Chatbots are widely recognized as computer software programs that are specifically developed to replicate human conversation. The system has been developed utilizing pre-established algorithms that facilitate its ability to provide responses to fundamental inquiries presented by clients.

Additional technologies that can be utilized to improve the experience of tourists include wearable technology. This wearable technology refers to equipment that is worn on the body without the need for hands, and typically includes wireless connectivity (Terry, 2018). Android users have the option to incorporate a travel management itinerary application. This software enables people to easily get notifications on their smartwatch (Atemble, 2015). Travelers can access real-time flight warnings, gate changes, and other pertinent information on their smartwatches via an application called Trip case. This application is utilized in airports and travel agencies such as Sabre (Conyette, 2015).

Social media platforms are computer-mediated technologies that enable the creation and sharing of information, ideas, and various kinds of expression through virtual communities and networks. (Ensemble, 2020). Several agencies transitioned from in-person to online experiences in order to boost online booking revenues. (Gelter, 2017). Instagram has the potential to enhance the promotion and marketing of tourist destinations by facilitating the sharing of traveler's films, experiences, and images with a larger audience than ever before (Popesku & Zlatanov, 2019). Several hotels and resorts have implemented social efforts to safeguard their guests' credit (Strarkov, 2019).

Mobile technology refers to the use of mobile phones for various purposes such as web browsing, multimedia consumption, email communication, and accessing applications. Additionally, mobile phones can also be used for keyless entry and Vertical concierge. (Ivanov et al., 2017). The Smart app is a location-based application that provides targeted marketing services throughout the entire journey. It is particularly useful for searching and reserving accommodations, similar to popular platforms such as journey Advisor and Expedia (Gelter, 2017). Intelligent applications and platforms such as Expedia and Booking.com provide high-quality hotel room options and allow guests to provide feedback to assist in the decision-making process when selecting hotels and restaurants. (Popescu & Zlatanov, 2019).

The Internet of Things (IoT) refers to the extension of internet connectivity to various items, devices, and appliances within tourism or lodging establishments. (Geisler, 2018). Beacon technology, which utilizes GPS and Bluetooth, has expanded the potential for providing location-based information. This technology can be employed by travel agents and tour guides to transmit messages to tourists at the exact moment, thereby delivering current information about tourist services, nearby attractions, and other relevant details. The aim is to enhance the overall tourist experience. (Wisskirchen, 2017). The smart room is intended to be tailored to the specific interests of each guest, similar to the rooms seen in Hilton and Marriott hotels. These rooms utilize technology to synchronize the choices of loyalty members with their room experiences, including room temperature, lighting, bathing amenities, streaming options, media preferences, bedding, and more (Singer, 2016).

## The Scope of Artificial Intelligence in the Tourism Industry

The utilization of AI in the Travel, Tourism, and Hospitality Industry has garnered attention due to several intriguing discoveries, despite being a current topic. There have been limited research studies conducted in the recent years regarding the utilization of AI in the Travel, Tourism, and Hospitality Industry. Some notable companies, such as Tata Consultancy Services, Google Travel, and Trip Advisor, have contributed to these studies (Viglia et al., 2014). These studies have unveiled several significant findings that offer advantages to companies in the Travel & Tourism industry. According to a survey conducted by Tata Consultancy Services (TCS) (Tata consultancy services, 2023), it was found that a significant majority of 85 percent of travel and hospitality service providers incorporate AI into their business operations (Anurag, 2018). According to Chawla (Chawla, 2019), research indicates that this phenomenon can be attributed to the significant growth in digital travel sales, which are projected to surpass $800 billion by 2020. According to a study conducted by Google Travel and Trip Advisor, it was found that a significant majority of customers, specifically 74 percent, utilize the Internet to plan their tourism trips. Furthermore, it was observed that a substantial proportion, exceeding 45 percent, of customers rely on smartphones for their trip planning activities (Peranzo, 2019). According to additional surveys, it has been found that a significant majority of customers, specifically 85 percent, make decisions regarding their travel activities once they have arrived at their destination (Think with google, 2023). According to Peranzo (Peranzo, 2019), a study found that 36% of customers have a preference for the Interactive booking process, while a significant majority of 80% opt for self-service technologies over traditional services. According to a study conducted by thinkwithgoogle.com in 2016, a significant majority of customers, specifically

90 percent, have an expectation for receiving pertinent information regarding their trip as they journey towards their intended destination.

Collectively, these findings appear to indicate a proclivity among customers for utilizing internet and self-service technologies. These findings may incentivize marketers to integrate Artificial Intelligence through interactive and self-service technologies in order to provide an improved customer experience. The results of these surveys not only indicate the customers' inclination towards technology but also imply the importance of "Timeliness". The timeliness of the services received by customers is of great importance, as highlighted by Kim et al. (Kim et al., 2014). The majority of customers are unwilling to accept services prior to their travel; instead, they anticipate receiving these services at the time of their travel. The research findings also indicate that a significant proportion of customers exhibit a preference for self-service technologies as opposed to traditional service methods. The feasibility of these self-service technologies is primarily facilitated through the utilization of Artificial Intelligence (Ivanov and Webster, 2017; Ivanov et al., 2017). In addition to the aforementioned factors, there exist various other factors that exert influence on the travel, tourism, and hospitality industry. The selection of Tourism, Travel & Hospitality services is influenced by several significant factors, such as Natural Resources, General Infrastructure facilities, Tourist Infrastructure, and Destination tourism infrastructure (Beerli and Martin, 2004).

Natural resources encompass a diverse array of elements, such as aesthetically pleasing landscapes, bodies of water, elevated landforms, arid regions, as well as the distinctive and diverse plant and animal life. Additionally, weather conditions, including regional temperatures, precipitation levels, and humidity, also contribute to the overall composition of natural resources. The category of infrastructure facilities encompasses various elements such as roadways and both public and private transportation systems. The components of tourist infrastructure encompass a range of amenities and services, such as lodging establishments and accommodations, dining establishments, establishments offering alcoholic beverages, venues for dancing and live music, establishments for social gatherings and recreational activities, aquatic amusement parks, facilities for observing and interacting with animals, establishments for gambling, opportunities for hiking and other outdoor adventures, commercial centers for retail therapy, and more. The infrastructure for destination tourism encompasses various aspects, such as the availability of skilled personnel and the implementation of safety protocols (Beerli and Martin, 2004; Kaushik et al., 2010; Seyidov and Adomaitiene, 2016). Artificial Intelligence has the capability to offer comprehensive data pertaining to various crucial aspects, including but not limited to Natural Resources, General Infrastructure facilities, Tourist infrastructure facilities, and Destination tourism infrastructure facilities.

AI technology has the potential to outperform human capabilities by swiftly providing extensive information on various critical factors.

## The Application of Artificial Intelligence in the Tourism Industry: Prominent Use Cases

Companies operating in the travel industry employ AI tools in order to reduce expenses, expedite procedures, enhance services, and enhance the overall user experience. Let us explore several exemplary applications of artificial intelligence in the field of tourism.

### AI in the Context of Travel Agents

In the contemporary landscape, airlines and travel companies have begun to substitute human consultants with virtual agents in order to enhance the efficiency of their services. WestJet employs a virtual travel assistant named Juliet to assist customers in effectively managing their travel itineraries.

### AI for Enhancing Operations

AI has emerged as a valuable tool for enhancing operational efficiency and effectiveness. By leveraging advanced algorithms and machine learning techniques, AI can analyze vast amounts of data and identify patterns, and trends. The collaboration between The Boston Consulting Group (BCG) and KLM Royal Dutch Airlines (KLM) has resulted in the development of an artificial intelligence-based solution. This solution aims to assist airlines in achieving growth, fostering innovation, and optimizing operations in order to meet the prevailing benchmarks of quality and hospitality.

### AI Has Been Widely Utilized in the Field of Sentiment Analysis

The tool known as Brand24 serves as a notable illustration of artificial intelligence implementation within the tourism industry. However, there are emerging tools such as PureStrategy that employ the utilization of an Automated Neural Intelligence Engine (ANIE), which is a cognitive computing network, in order to monitor and analyze customer sentiment.

## The Utilization of AI in the Process of Customer Segmentation

An additional advantageous implementation of artificial intelligence within the travel industry pertains to the domain of customer segmentation. TravelPerk, a travel management platform with its headquarters in Barcelona, employs Twilio Flex and Twilio Segment to effectively segment the market and enhance the overall customer experience.

## AI for Personalization

Booking.com, Airbnb, and Tripadvisor exemplify the importance of AI in the tourism industry by offering personalized recommendations.

## AI in the Context of Customer Service

The integration of artificial intelligence and tourism has emerged as a promising alliance that holds potential for enhancing the tourism industry in the future. One illustrative instance involves the renowned hotel operator, Dorchester Collections, which employed an AI system to acquire crucial insights pertaining to the needs and preferences of their guests. The artificial intelligence system employed cognitive computing and machine learning techniques to analyze a dataset consisting of more than 7,000 guest reviews. Following this exercise, the hotel successfully implemented modifications to its menu in order to cater to a wider range of guests.

## The Application of AI in the Domain of Baggage Handling

The implementation of AI-powered baggage handling systems has the potential to optimize the efficiency of luggage transportation and monitoring. The aforementioned BagsID technology has undergone successful testing at Eindhoven Airport. Figure 2 shows Artificial Intelligence use cases in Tourism industry.

*Figure 2. Artificial intelligence use cases tourism industry*
*(author compilation)*

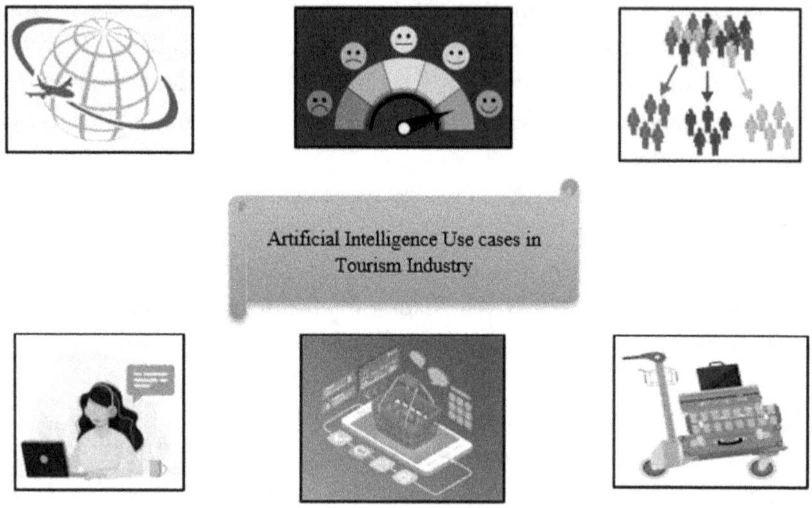


## The Key Technology Trends in the Tourism and Travel Industry

A comprehensive collection of the most recent and cutting-edge technological advancements in the fields of tourism and travel, encompassing the latest trends in technology projected for the year 2023 are mentioned below:

### 1. Artificial Intelligence

AI refers to the field of computer science that focuses on the development of intelligent machines capable of performing tasks that typically require human intelligence. In addition to its application in robotics, artificial intelligence is also being employed in various other domains. One of the most prominent applications in the travel and tourism sector is the utilization of chatbots for customer service functions. These chatbots are capable of providing prompt responses to issues or inquiries. Moreover, it possesses the capability to acquire knowledge through ongoing interactions with customers. Furthermore, establishments within the tourism sector, such as hotels and other relevant enterprises, have the potential to employ AI systems in order to effectively and consistently analyze and organize vast amounts of data. It possesses the capability to derive inferences regarding the performance of a business or the patterns linked to customer satisfaction, and furthermore, it can effectively oversee inventory management in an intelligent manner.

## 2. AI Chatbots

AI chatbots are computer programs designed to simulate human conversation and provide automated responses to users. The implementation of AI-powered chatbots in the travel industry can be considered a highly practical investment in technology. This is due to their ability to promptly address customer inquiries at any time, without being constrained by staff availability. Ensuring compliance with contemporary customer service standards is imperative in meeting the demands and expectations of customers. In general, chatbots demonstrate optimal performance when responding to frequently asked questions that possess standardized responses. However, the advancements in AI technology have resulted in a continuous enhancement of modern chatbots, as they accumulate a greater number of interactions. They are also proficient in addressing inquiries regarding policies and various measures or protocols.

## 3. Robotics

The field of robotics technology is regarded as a highly captivating domain within the realm of travel technology, exhibiting a perpetual state of advancement. Robots have been employed in concierge-like capacities within the hotel industry, wherein they assist in welcoming guests upon their arrival and dispensing relevant information. Certain hotels have extended their scope of services by incorporating additional responsibilities such as cleaning and luggage handling. Robotic entities possess the potential to assume responsibilities in both the preparation and service of food within the confines of dining establishments. Airports possess the capability to identify concealed weaponry, and certain manufacturers employ robotics to fabricate luggage cases that exhibit intelligent tracking abilities. In addition, travel agents employ automated systems to conduct pre-screening procedures, thereby enhancing the efficiency of waiting periods and increasing customer productivity. Similar to various other technological advancements in the travel sector, the utilization of robots has witnessed a notable surge in the wake of the COVID-19 pandemic. This is primarily attributed to their capacity to mitigate interpersonal interactions, thereby minimizing the risk of viral transmission.

## 4. Contactless Payments

Contactless payments refer to a method of conducting financial transactions without the need for physical contact between the payment device and the payment terminal. An additional significant aspect of travel technology pertains to the capability of facilitating contactless payment acceptance. This will enable travel companies to expedite payment processing, even in situations where customers lack access to physical currency or their credit or debit cards. Additionally, it has the potential to enhance the overall customer experience by saving time. The initial introduction of contactless payment options was primarily driven by the desire for convenience. However, in the aftermath of the global COVID-19 outbreak, it has evolved into a significant component of tourism marketing strategies. Due to concerns regarding the transmission of the virus, a significant number of travelers exhibit hesitancy in handling physical currency. Maximizing the utilization of contactless payment methods can additionally serve as a means of safeguarding the well-being of your personnel.

## 5. Virtual Reality

Virtual Reality (VR) refers to a computer-generated simulation of a three-dimensional environment that can be interacted with and experienced by an individual through the use of specialized electronic devices. Virtual reality (VR) has emerged as a prominent technology across various sectors, with its impact on the tourism industry being particularly noteworthy. Ultimately, virtual travel offers to individuals the opportunity to explore distant destinations without leaving the confines of their own residence. Moreover, it can significantly impact the decision-making process of potential travelers, potentially influencing their final choice to proceed with a booking. Through the utilization of virtual reality (VR) tours, individuals have the opportunity to engage in a wide range of immersive experiences, encompassing virtual tours of hotels, restaurants, renowned landmarks, national parks, and even specific activities. The utilization of interactivity and immersion in technology trends can confer a competitive advantage over competitors who have not yet embraced these advancements. Nowadays, the majority of virtual reality (VR) tours or 360 tours are compatible with widely used web browsers, thereby facilitating individuals who are hesitant to travel in perceiving the advantages more distinctly.

## 6. Augmented Reality

Augmented Reality (AR) refers to a technology that superimposes computer-generated elements, such as images, videos, or 3D models, onto the real world. Augmented reality (AR) bears resemblance to virtual reality (VR) in terms of its immersive nature, yet it diverges by focusing on enhancing an individual's existing physical environment rather than substituting it entirely. One notable advantage of this specific technological trend is its cost-effectiveness compared to virtual reality (VR), as users only need a smartphone or tablet device with internet connectivity. The utilization of graphical overlays in the tourism sector has the potential to significantly augment the overall customer experience by offering valuable information and even entertainment to customers. For example, some applications have the capability to enhance photographs by applying various filters and effects. Information regarding nearby destinations can be conveniently presented to customers by utilizing their smartphones. This approach ensures that the information is delivered precisely when it is most pertinent.

## 7. Voice Search

The utilization of voice search has become increasingly significant in the travel industry due to the emergence of smartphones, smart speakers, and AI assistants. An increasing number of travel consumers are utilizing voice search as a means to discover and reserve airline tickets, hotel accommodations, and travel activities. Therefore, it is imperative to strategically plan the design of your website with consideration for voice search, in order to effectively leverage this prevailing phenomenon. In addition, voice control is increasingly becoming a significant factor in real travel experiences as well. Voice-activated devices are employed within hotel accommodations to regulate room lighting and heating systems, as well as to access tourist-related information, thereby obviating the necessity of engaging with hotel personnel. It is probable that this trend will persist and extend its reach to additional sectors within the industry as well.

## 8. Internet of Things (IoT)

The Internet of Things (IoT) refers to the interconnected network of physical devices, vehicles, buildings, and other objects embedded with sensors, software, and network connectivity, enabling them to collect and exchange data. One of the most noteworthy emerging trends in the field of travel technology is the Internet of Things (IoT), which encompasses the utilization of internet-enabled connectivity among various commonplace devices, enabling them to exchange data in a bidirectional manner. There are already instances of its significance within the travel and tourism sector, and this trend is expected to further intensify. For example, the Internet of Things (IoT) technology can be implemented in hotel rooms to offer customers a unified device that facilitates connectivity with various amenities, including lighting systems, heating units, and air conditioning systems. This integration enables centralized control and management of these utilities from a single interface. In airport settings, luggage cases can be equipped with sensors that have the capability to notify passengers as they traverse the vicinity.

## 9. Recognition Technology

Recognition technology refers to the field of study and application that involves the identification and authentication of individuals or objects through various technological means. Recognition technology is particularly intriguing among the prominent technological trends, owing to its capacity to eliminate obstacles in the purchasing process and facilitate seamless interactions. The technology encompasses a range of biometric identifiers such as fingerprint recognition, facial recognition, retina scanning, and other similar methods. This technology is currently being implemented in certain hotels to facilitate room access through fingerprint recognition and enable partially contactless check-out processes. Nevertheless, it is anticipated that in subsequent times, this technological advancement may facilitate patrons to settle their bills for meals consumed at the hotel restaurant merely by traversing the exit.

## 10. Big Data

The concept of Big Data refers to the vast amount of information that is generated, collected, and analyzed in various domains. In contemporary tourism management, the utilization of big data has become an inherent aspect, with the majority of prosperous companies implementing their own methodologies for data collection. One of the primary applications of this data pertains to enhancing personalization, whereby travel companies leverage the gathered information to tailor their offerings in a targeted manner. Another significant application of data is the analysis of present business performance. Hotel owners can utilize big data for the purpose of revenue management, by leveraging historical occupancy rates and other previous trends to enhance their ability to predict levels of demand. When demand exhibits predictability, it becomes possible to optimize pricing and promotional strategies.

*Figure 3. Technology trends in tourism industry*

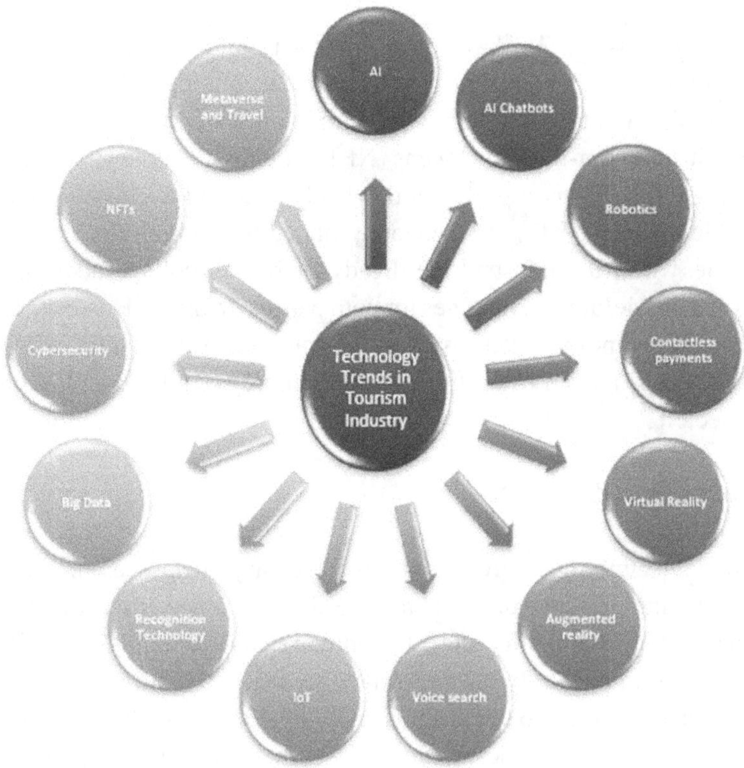


## 11. Cybersecurity Measures

Cybersecurity measures refer to the various strategies, protocols, and practices implemented to safeguard computer systems, networks, and data from unauthorized access. Cybersecurity holds significant importance for individuals in travel management positions, as companies within the industry face escalating threats from cyber-attacks and heightened susceptibility to various forms of data breaches. Travel companies are a significant focal point due to their substantial workforce and extensive access to customer data. Phishing attacks and ransomware attacks are among the prominent perils in this domain. Moreover, the contemporary dependence on data exposes organizations to potential vulnerabilities arising from inadvertent mistakes made by their own personnel. In order to ensure the security of your business, it is imperative to allocate resources towards cybersecurity training as well as the implementation of diverse hardware and software solutions. Staying abreast of current regulations and adhering to data protection laws is of paramount importance.

## 12. NFTs

Non-fungible tokens (NFTs) have made their way into the travel industry. Non-fungible tokens (NFTs) represent a noteworthy technological phenomenon that extends beyond general applications, warranting the attention of stakeholders within the travel industry. Non-fungible tokens (NFTs) are digital assets that are stored on a blockchain and serve as representations of distinct and exclusive digital items. Non-fungible tokens (NFTs) are frequently linked to the realm of digital art, and certain entities within the industry have already established collaborative partnerships with local artists, yielding advantages for both parties involved. However, it is worth noting that NFT technology also possesses the potential to facilitate customer loyalty programs. There is a need to examine NFT technology and its implementation in the travel sector.

## 13. Metaverse and Travel

One additional technological trend that travel industry businesses should take note of is the expanding presence of the metaverse. There is a need to further explore the advancements in virtual reality and augmented reality technologies, which enable the creation of immersive digital environments that facilitate social interactions. This feature enables users to engage in social interactions while navigating virtual simulations of various travel destinations. Also, there is a need to shed light on the current and potential effects of metaverse technology on the travel sector. Figure 3 shows technology trends in tourism industry.

# The Tourism Industry Presents Various Challenges for the Implementation of AI Technologies

Despite the rapid advancement of Artificial Intelligence, there remains a constraint on its utilization by individuals lacking literacy skills (Reddy, 2006). These limitations must and will be overcome as needed through the implementation of innovative solutions, integration of emerging technologies, and regular updates to policies. Regardless of the extent to which AI supplants human labor, the question of whether AI can replace human intelligence remains a topic of debate. However, there are still numerous unresolved questions in various sectors of the business world that AI must address and resolve. Although "Artificial Intelligence" has shown potential in generating financial gains through employee replacement and non-financial gains by offering customers a distinctive experience, it remains unable to surpass human intelligence due to its status as an emerging field (Laurent et al., 2015). One significant obstacle in the utilization of AI pertains to the safeguarding and protection of data, particularly in terms of safety and security.

The persistent challenge of implementing artificial intelligence in critical sectors such as finance and military is a matter of significant concern. One instance of employing Blockchain technologies in Facial Recognition software guarantees the preservation of data integrity and confidentiality. Despite the potential benefits, certain nations remain hesitant to adopt Facial recognition technology due to concerns surrounding privacy and data security (Bowyer, 2004). Hotels often retain the historical records of customers' previous purchases and travel experiences, thereby posing significant concerns regarding data privacy and security. Privacy and data security pose a significant challenge (Kannan and Bernoff, 2019). One significant concern associated with software-controlled services is the vulnerability to malware attacks, as even a minor incursion can result in the disruption of software programs and subsequent operational disturbances for service providers, thereby causing a state of disorder. While AI technology is considered advanced and forward-looking, smaller service providers may face financial constraints in adopting these technologies due to the substantial investment required (Murphy et al., 2017). While Chatbots and Robots have the potential to replace human workers, customers continue to rely on human workers for queries that involve complexity. Chatbots, such as machines, are restricted to responding solely to uncomplicated inquiries. These technologies utilize the keywords present in the questions in order to furnish the corresponding answers. In situations of emergency and intricate problems requiring resolution, customers continue to depend on the human workforce (Lommatzsch, 2018). Figure 4 illustrates challenges for adopting AI in tourism industry.

*Figure 4. Challenges for adopting AI in tourism industry*

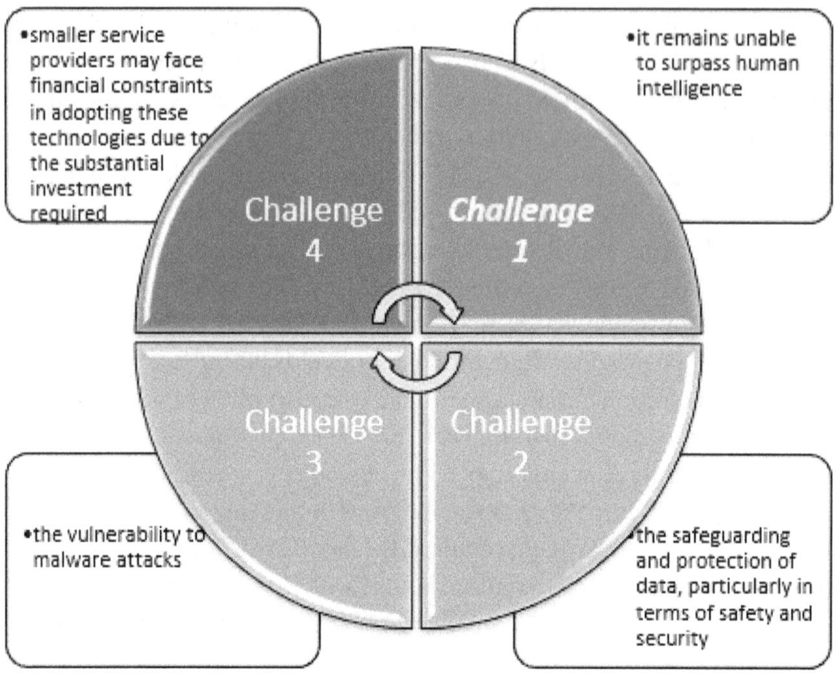


## The Future Implications of Artificial Intelligence in the Tourism Industry

Forecasting the future of AI in the tourism and travel sector proves to be a challenging task, given the rapid rate of technological advancements observed in the present era. However, some insights from experts were announced in order to make predictions about the future developments in this field. The task at hand involves the prediction of occupancy levels within a given space. Hotels and airlines are anticipated to allocate significant investments towards the integration of data science and deep learning algorithms, with the objective of enhancing their ability to accurately forecast and predict occupancy rates. This predictive ability will assist individuals in effectively allocating their resources to minimize expenditures and optimize financial gains. Furthermore, any travel management company has the ability to depend on this technology while strategizing and organizing travel packages.

Biometric identification refers to the process of using unique physical or behavioral characteristics of individuals to establish their identity. As reported by the New York Times (New York Times, 2023), airports are actively exploring the implementation of biometric verification techniques, such as facial recognition, as a means to enhance security and streamline passenger identification processes. According to findings by the National Institute of Standards and Technology, it has been determined that facial recognition technology exhibits a level of accuracy reaching 99.5%. In the near future, it is anticipated that airlines will mandate passengers to undergo biometric authentication prior to their embarkation onto aircrafts.

Natural Language Processing (NLP) and AI are two interconnected fields that have gained significant attention in recent years. NLP focuses on the interaction between computers. Technology companies will persist in collaborating with AI and natural language processing (NLP) technologies in order to advance the development of algorithms and neural networks that possess the ability to imitate and comprehend human emotions. Language model technologies such as GPT-4 have the potential to enhance translation and platform localization services for travel companies.

The concept of AIoT, which stands for Artificial Intelligence of Things, refers to the integration of artificial intelligence technologies with the Internet of Things (IoT) paradigm. The convergence of artificial intelligence and the internet of things is anticipated to result in a proliferation of devices that are optimized with AI capabilities. One of the most notable applications of AIoT is found in the field of autonomous vehicles.

In the near future, tourists will have the opportunity to utilize autonomous ride-hailing services as a means of transportation to reach their desired destinations. The concept of hyper-personalization refers to the practice of tailoring products, and services.

The concept of hyper-personalization is being explored by companies such as Amadeus in the tourism and travel industry, challenging the notion that these sectors cannot become more personalized. The predominant determinant in this context is consumer behavior, particularly among Generation Z and Millennials.

As a result of this AI-driven transformation along with emerging technologies incorporation, it can be anticipated that the emergence of personalized pricing, advertising, bundling, bidding, and subscriptions as viable forms of payment, can be realized. In addition, travel companies may offer exclusive insurance agreements to individuals embarking on their journeys. Through strategic collaborations such as the partnership between Amadeus and Setoo, travelers are afforded the opportunity to avail themselves of the most pertinent protection by means of an artificial intelligence-driven solution.

## CONCLUSION

In conclusion, it can be inferred that the tourism and travel industries are undergoing significant transformations due to the advent of artificial intelligence, particularly in the aftermath of the COVID-19 pandemic. Hotels, airlines, and providers of hospitality services currently depend on AI tools to enhance operational efficiency, increase financial gains, and enhance the overall user experience.

Furthermore, it is evident that AI undeniably enhances the provision of experiential services in the tourism industry. However, it is important to acknowledge that AI is unable to surpass the intrinsic value of human interaction, which serves as a crucial factor in determining the quality of experiential tourism. AI serves as a valuable supplementary component in shaping the future of the tourism industry. The advent of artificial intelligence in the field of travel has significantly streamlined the process of making travel arrangements. AI provides automated, personalized, and informative travel services. AI enables individuals who are travelling to gain insights into their behaviors, interests, and inclinations, thereby facilitating the provision of a customized and tailored experience. The era of seeking guidance from a travel agent, engaging in face-to-face interactions, and enduring a protracted series of cumbersome phone conversations to obtain information regarding travel plans has become a thing of the past.

The increasing presence of artificial intelligence along with emerging technologies in the tourism sector is a positive development in the current era of technological advancements. This is due to the fact that it signifies the industry's ability to effectively utilize cutting-edge technology in order to enhance operational efficiency and productivity. The clientele of the tourism sector will experience enhanced levels of satisfaction, resulting in various benefits. Simultaneously, tourism enterprises will gain enhanced operational oversight over their processes. The automation of business processes will be significantly increased, resulting in streamlined business operations.

## REFERENCES

Anurag. (2018). 4 Emerging trends of artificial intelligence in travel. *New Gen Apps*. www.newgenapps. com/blog/artificial-intelligence-in-travel-emerging-trends

Atembe, R. (2015, December). The Use of Smart Technology in Tourism: Evidence from Wearable Devices [Austria.]. *Journal of Tourism and Hospitality Management*, *3*(11-12), 224–234.

Beerli, A., & Martin, J. D. (2004). Factors influencing destination image. *Annals of Tourism Research, 31*(3), 657–681. doi:10.1016/j.annals.2004.01.010

Bowyer, K. W. (2004). Face recognition technology: Security versus privacy. *IEEE Technology and Society Magazine, 23*(1), 9–19. doi:10.1109/MTAS.2004.1273467

Chawla, S. (2019). 7 Successful applications of AI & machine learning in the travel industry. *Hacker Noon.* https://hackernoon.com/successful-implications-of-ai-machine-learning-in-travel-industry-3040f3e1d48c

Conyette, M. (2015). *21 Century Travel using Websites, Mobile and Wearable Technology Devices*. Research Gate. https://www.researchgate.net/publication/328712383_21_Century_Travel_using_We bsites_Mobile_and_Wearable_Technology_Devices.

Ensemble, Q. (2020). Ways Social Media Has Transformed Tourism Marketing. *Hospitality Tourism.* https://hospitalitytech.com/5-ways-social-media-has-transformed[REMOVED HYPERLINK FIELD]tourism-marketing

Gajdošík, T. (2018). Smart Tourism: Concepts and Insights from Central Europe. *Czech Journal of Tourism, 7*(1), 25–44. doi:10.1515/cjot-2018-0002

Geisler, R. (2018). *Artificial Intelligence in the Travel & Tourism industry Adoption and impact.* [Thesis, NOVA School of Business and Economics].

Gelter, H. (2017). Digital tourism -An analysis of digital trends in tourism and customer digital mobile behavior for the Visit Arctic Europe project. Report of Europe.

Gretzel, U., Siagala, M., Xiang Z., & Koo, C. (2015). *Smart Tourism: Foundations and Developments*. Springer. https://link.springer.com/article/10.1007/s12525-015-0196-8

Issa, H., Sun, T., & Vasarhelyi, M. A. (2016). Research ideas for artificial intelligence in auditing: The formalization of audit and workforce supplementation. *Journal of Emerging Technologies in Accounting, 13*(2), 1–20. doi:10.2308/jeta-10511

Ivanov, S., & Webster, C. (2017). Adoption of robots, artificial intelligence and service automation by travel, tourism and hospitality companies – a cost-benefit analysis. *International Scientific Conference Contemporary tourism – traditions and innovations.* Sofia University.

Ivanov, S., Webster, C., & Berezina, K. (2017). Adoption of Robots and Service Automation by Tourism and Hospitality Companies. *Revista Tur smo & Dese nv olvimento*, no. 27/28. https://ssrn. com/abstract=2964308.

Ivanov, S. H., Webster, C., & Berezina, K. (2017). Adoption of robots and service automation by tourism and hospitality companies. *Revista Turismo & Desenvolvimento (Aveiro)*, *27*(28), 1501–1517.

Jasrotia, A., & Gangotia, A. (2018). *Smart Cities to Smart Tourism Destinations: A Review Paper*. Research Gate. https://www.researchgate.net/publication/327536704_Smart_Cities_To_Smart_Touri sm_Destinations_A_Review_Paper_ISSN_2249-7307.

Kannan, P., & Bernoff, J. (2019). The future of customer service is AI-Human collaboration. *MIT Sloan Management Review*.

Kaushik, N., Kaushik, J., Sharma, P., & Rani, S. (2010). Factors influencing choice of tourist destinations: A study of North India. *IUP Journal of Brand Management*, *7*(1/2), 116–132.

Kim, T., Kim, M. C., Moon, G., & Chang, K. (2014). Technology-based self-service and its impact on customer productivity. *Services Marketing Quarterly*, *35*(3), 255–269. doi:10.1080/15332969.2014.916145

Laurent, P., Chollet, T., & Herzberg, E. (2015). *Intelligent automation entering the business world*. Deloitte. https://www2.deloitte.com/eg/en.html

Lommatzsch, A. (2018). A next generation Chatbot-Framework for the public administration. *International Conference on Innovations for Community Services*. Springer. 10.1007/978-3-319-93408-2_10

McCormick, J. Doty, C.A. Sridharan, S. Curran, R. Evelson, B. Hopkins, B. Little, C. Leganza, G. Purcell, B. & Miller, E. (2016). *Predictions 2017: artificial intelligence will drive the insights revolution*. FORRESTER research for customer insights professionals.

Murphy, J., Hofacker, C., & Gretzel, U. (2017). Dawning of the age of robots in hospitality and tourism: Challenges for teaching and research. *European Journal of Tourism Research*, *15*, 104–111. doi:10.54055/ejtr.v15i.265

Nagaraj, S. (2019). AI enabled marketing: What is it all about? *International Journal of Research in Commerce, Economics and Management*, *8*(6), 501–518.

Nagaraj, S. (2020). Marketing analytics for customer engagement: A viewpoint [IJISSC]. *International Journal of Information Systems and Social Change*, *11*(2), 41–55. doi:10.4018/IJISSC.2020040104

Peranzo, P. (2019). *AI assistant: the future of travel industry with the increase of artificial intelligence*. Imaginovation. www.imaginovation.net/blog/the-future-of-travel-with-the-increase-of-ai/

Popesku, J., & Zlatanov, S. (2019). Current Applications of Artificial Intelligence In Tourism And Hospitality. *International Scientific Conference on Information Technology and Data Related Research*. Research Gate. https://www.researchgate.net/publication/333242550_Current_Applications_of_Artificial_Intelligence_in_Tourism_and_Hospitality

Reddy, R. (2006). Robotics and intelligent systems in support of society. *IEEE Intelligent Systems*, *21*(3), 24–31. doi:10.1109/MIS.2006.57

Russell, S., & Norvig, P. (2016). *Artificial Intelligence: A Modern Approach*. Pearson.

Seyidov, J., & Adomaitiene, R. (2016). Factors influencing local tourists' decision-making on choosing a destination: A case of Azerbaijan. *Ekonomika (Nis)*, *95*(3), 112–127. doi:10.15388/Ekon.2016.3.10332

Singer, R. (2016). *Robots and Artificial Intelligence in The Hotel Industry*. ITB Berlin.

Starkov, M. (2019). Hospitality Digital Technology: Challenges, Priorities, and Buzzwords. *Next Guest.* https://www.nextguest.com/blog/hospitality-digitaltech/HARE

Terry, L. (2018). *Why Wearable Technology Is Hotel Management's Next Big Thing*. Samsung. https://insights.samsung.com/2018/10/19/why-wearable[REMOVED HYPERLINK FIELD]technology-is-hotel-managements-next-big-thing

Viglia, G., Furlan, R., & Ladron-de-Guevara, A. (2014). Please, talk about it! when hotel popularity boosts preferences. *International Journal of Hospitality Management*, *42*, 155–164. doi:10.1016/j.ijhm.2014.07.001

Wisskirchen, G., Biacabe, B., Bormann, U., Muntz, A., Niehaus, A., Soler, G., & Brauchitsch, B. (2017). *Artificial Intelligence and Robotics and Their Impact on the Workplace*. IBA Global Employment Institute.

## KEY TERMS AND DEFINITIONS

**Augmented Reality (AR):** An interactive experience that enhances the real world with computer-generated perceptual information.

**Automated Neural Intelligence Engine (ANIE):** This platform is the next evolution of AI driven analysis. ANIE is an artificial mind that not only listens to, but understands the voice of the customer and helps your business act on it. **Virtual Reality (VR):** is a simulated experience that employs pose tracking and 3D near-eye displays to give the user an immersive feel of a virtual world.

**Internet of Things (IoT):** Describes devices with sensors, processing ability, software and other technologies that connect and exchange data with other devices and systems over the Internet or other communications networks. **Non Fungible Tokens (NFTs):** are blockchain-based tokens that each represent a unique asset like a piece of art, digital content, or media.

**Natural Language Processing (NLP):** The application of computational techniques to the analysis and synthesis of natural language and speech.

**The Artificial Intelligence of Things (AIoT):** The combination of AI technologies with the Internet of things (IoT) infrastructure to achieve more efficient IoT operations, improve human-machine interactions and enhance data management and analytics.

# Chapter 3
# Malaysia's Smart Tourism Framework

**Mooi Kwong (Anthony) Tee**
https://orcid.org/0000-0001-5754-4015
*Universiti Tunku Abdul Rahman, Malaysia*

## ABSTRACT

*Malaysia's smart tourism framework is a collaborative and visionary strategy designed to revolutionize the country's tourism industry. It focuses on key elements, including robust digital infrastructure, data-driven personalization, eco-friendly transportation, and cultural preservation. Through strategic partnerships and continuous monitoring using key performance indicators, the framework aims to create a sustainable, competitive, and inclusive smart tourism ecosystem. This approach promises increased revenue, job opportunities, and enriched visitor experiences while safeguarding Malaysia's natural and cultural heritage in the digital age.*

## MALAYSIA'S SMART TOURISM FRAMEWORK

In our era of rapid technological advancement and global connectivity, smart tourism has emerged as a transformative force in the travel and hospitality sectors. It harnesses cutting-edge technologies and data-driven solutions to elevate travel experiences, optimize resource management, champion sustainability, and drive economic prosperity for destinations and stakeholders. Smart tourism leverages digital technologies, data analytics, and innovative methodologies to create intelligent and dynamic tourism ecosystems. It enhances various aspects of the traveller's journey, from pre-trip planning and booking to on-site activities and post-trip interactions. By integrating networked technology, artificial intelligence, big data analytics, and

DOI: 10.4018/979-8-3693-1978-9.ch003

the Internet of Things (IoT), smart tourism delivers personalized, efficient, and sustainable experiences for both tourists and host communities (Höjer & Wangel, 2015; Harrison et al., 2010; Gretzel et al., 2015; Hunter et al., 2015).

Smart tourism enhances the visitor's experience through key components, like digital connectivity, including high-speed internet and mobile apps; data analytics for informed decision-making; and smart mobility solutions for convenience and sustainability. Digitalized attractions employ AR, VR, and IoT, while AI-powered chatbots and location-based services offer personalized journeys. Sustainability is paramount, encouraging eco-friendly and responsible practices. Smart tourism boosts visitor satisfaction, promotes sustainable development, attracts tech-savvy travellers, and optimizes resource allocation, ultimately driving economic growth (Bakici et al., 2013; Buhalis & Amaranggana, 2014; Lee et al., 2014; Vanolo, 2013; Vasavada & Padhiyar, 2016).

Embracing smart tourism increases a destination's competitiveness, allowing it to carve out a niche by offering cutting-edge, technology-infused experiences. Malaysia is in the early stages of adopting smart tourism, with limited studies and a lack of a specific framework. The tourism industry is grappling with challenges such as global crises, which have negatively affected tourist arrivals and the environment. Additionally, insufficient digitalization has resulted in subpar tourist experiences and hindered overall tourism development in the country (Syakir et al. 2020).

Smart tourism faces significant obstacles as well. Due to technology inequalities, the digital divide impedes equitable access, potentially excluding segments. The collecting of visitor data raises privacy and cybersecurity issues. Adequate infrastructure, which includes connectivity and technology, is critical for successful deployment. Navigating cultural and ethical issues is critical for avoiding over-commercialization and ensuring technology advancement is consistent with cultural authenticity.

Smart tourism is a paradigm shift in how destinations connect with tourists, manage resources, and build their tourism economies in a sustainable manner. Destinations can offer seamless, personalised, and sustainable travel experiences that respond to the changing interests of modern tourists by leveraging the power of technology. Smart tourism's importance in the modern tourism scene is apparent, providing a route towards more efficient, engaging, and responsible tourism practises that benefit both visitors and host communities.

The objective of this chapter is to establish a comprehensive framework for smart tourism in Malaysia. It aims to create a roadmap for using technology to enhance the tourist experience, promote sustainability, and boost economic benefits in Malaysia's tourism sector. This involves exploring dimensions like digital infrastructure, data utilization, smart mobility, sustainability practices, and collaboration among stakeholders. This literature strives to provide a solid and practical foundation for smart tourism in Malaysia, equipping stakeholders with the knowledge to leverage technology for the industry's advancement while ensuring a sustainable and enriching experience for visitors and local communities.

## SMART TOURISM RESEARCH

Recent research in smart tourism within Malaysia has explored various dimensions. Ye's (2020) systematic review of 24 related articles highlights a predominant focus on technology's impact on tourists' perceptions and behaviours. Abumandil (2022) delves into mobile augmented reality and social media's role in Penang's smart tourism, emphasizing the benefits of interactive and informative ICT-based services. Topsakal et al. (2020) bibliometric analysis reveals a significant rise in smart tourism research interest since 2015, with collaboration among American, English, and South Korean institutions. The most cited journal is the Journal of Travel Research, and Buhalis and Gretzel are the most frequently cited authors. Key research topics include mobile guest behaviour and areas like destination websites, open data, smart systems, and visitor adaptation. Other studies discussed the development and challenges of implementing a smart tourism in Malaysia focuses on developing the Malaysia Smart Tourism Framework for Ecotourism (MSTF-Eco) based on the Malaysia Smart City Framework (Rahman & Dura, 2021). The study uses content analysis to identify the characteristics and sub-characteristics of MSTF-Eco. Amir et al. (2020) examines the challenges of implementing smart tourism in Malaysia, with a focus on eco-tourism destinations. The study identifies awareness, security and privacy, and implementation mechanisms as the main challenges. Azmi & Ahmad (2022) proposes the development of Malaysia's Smart Community-Based Tourism Model, aiming to explore the concept of smart community-based tourism (CBT) in Malaysia and investigate the readiness of CBT to adopt smart tourism.

Kim (2016) found that a higher intensity of green practices in hotels indirectly enhances customer satisfaction through perceived relative quality and suggest to conceptualize the generativity of the information systems content both in general and in the context of the smart tourism system. Sofian (2021) focuses specifically on smart tourism services and finds that smart tourism technology attributes are significantly associated with service satisfaction levels, which in turn positively affect the intention to use new technology. Abumandil (2020) highlights the lack of awareness and knowledge among employees in the tourism industry regarding the Islamic smart tourism concept, cultural sensitivity, and promotion of historical and interesting places. Sofian (2021) focuses on tourists' satisfaction with smart tourism services and identifies the relationship between smart tourism technology attributes, tourist service satisfaction levels, and the intention to use new technology. The study also examines the moderating effect of trust on this relationship. Hua (2017) explores the use of social media as a tool for selecting tourism destinations and emphasizes the influence of perceived usefulness, perceived ease of use, perceived risk, and electronic word-of-mouth on tourists' attitudes and intentions. The above papers collectively provide insights into the factors affecting the adoption of smart tourism apps and services among tourism stakeholders in Malaysia.

Azis (2020) found that smart tourism technologies and memorable tourism experiences play essential roles in enhancing tourist satisfaction and destination loyalty. Susanto (2020) revealed that attributes of smart tourism technology, such as smart information systems and e-commerce systems, influence visit intention and visits to tourist destinations. Zhang (2022) highlighted that the dimensions of smart technologies, including accessibility and interactivity, positively affect tourist experiences, satisfaction, and post-consumption behavioural intentions. Chen (2020) emphasized the importance of smart tourism products and services in improving destination competitiveness and enhancing tourist satisfaction. These papers collectively indicate that the adoption and implementation of smart tourism technologies positively influence tourist experiences, satisfaction, and loyalty to tourist destinations.

Obeidy (2018) presents the development of a smart glass-based augmented reality (AR) application called "TouristicAR" specifically designed for cultural heritage tourism in Malaysia. Fino (2013) introduces an AR tourist guide for exploring World Heritage cities, utilizing 3D animations of historic buildings along the route. Doğan (2019) examines the effects of interactive AR applications on visitors' experiences highlighting the practical usefulness and impact on visit intention. Fritz (2005) describes the development of an interactive visualization system based on AR technologies to enhance cultural tourism experiences. These papers demonstrate the potential of AR technology in providing context-aware and visually appealing tourism content, guiding visitors, and enriching their experiences at World Heritage sites.

Tung (2019) highlights the significant changes that smart mobility will bring to tourism management, particularly in terms of tourist travel patterns and decision-making. Additionally, Rahman (2020) identifies challenges in the application of smart tourism in Malaysia, including awareness, security and privacy, and the implementation mechanism. Overall, these papers emphasize the relevance and growing importance of smart mobility in the context of smart tourism in Malaysia. These papers collectively discuss the relevance of smart mobility in the context of smart tourism in Malaysia. Furthermore, according to Rahman & Dura (2021), a comprehensive smart tourism framework has yet to be introduced in Malaysia while Amir et al. (2020) said overall strategies, visions, and a comprehensive framework of smart tourism for Malaysia is unclear. These findings collectively reflect Malaysia's evolving landscape in smart tourism, touching on technology's influence, adoption, perception, behaviour and intention of tourists, augmented reality, and research trends.

## SMART TOURISM

The term "smart tourism," also known as "intelligent tourism" or "technology-enabled tourism," refers to a contemporary strategy for the travel and tourism sector that makes use of cutting-edge technologies and data-driven tactics to enhance destination management, improve the overall travel experience, and promote sustainable and ethical practises. It entails combining different digital tools, such as mobile apps, augmented reality, artificial intelligence, data analytics, and the Internet of Things (IoT), to offer individualised, effective, and innovative services to travellers while also assisting destinations in managing their resources more effectively and achieving sustainable growth (Buhalis & Amaranggana, 2015; Xiang et.al, 2017; Gretzel et al, 2015).

In Malaysia, the term "smart tourism" refers to the intentional blending of cutting-edge technology and data-driven strategies to enhance the overall travel experience, advance sustainability, and foster economic growth in the country's tourism sector. This framework makes use of digital platforms such as mobile apps, interactive displays, and real-time data analytics to deliver personalised recommendations, engaging experiences, and eco-friendly practises to tourists. Smart tourism in Malaysia aspires to improve visitor satisfaction, reduce environmental impact, and promote equitable accessibility, all while contributing to economic development through higher tourism revenue and investment in technology-related sectors. This strategy emphasises ongoing monitoring, data collecting, and revisions based on performance feedback to maintain the framework's efficacy and connection with tourism goals.

## MALAYSIA'S DIGITAL INFRASTRUCTURE

Malaysia has been making significant strides in developing its digital infrastructure and enhancing connectivity to keep pace with the demands of the modern digital age. The country's commitment to digital transformation is evident through various initiatives, policies, and investments that have contributed to shaping a robust and well-connected digital landscape. Malaysia boasts a commendable level of internet penetration, with a significant portion of its population having access to the internet. As of January 2023, there were 33.03 million internet uses and the internet penetration rate in Malaysia was 96.8%, indicating widespread digital access. While the internet connection speed is 36.34Mbps via cellular network and 91.50Mbps through fixed internet connection at beginning of 2023 (Kemp, 2023). The government has been actively working to extend high-speed internet connectivity to rural and remote areas through initiatives like the National Fiberisation and Connectivity Plan (NFCP) (MCMC, 2019). This plan aims to bridge the digital divide by providing equitable access to high-speed broadband services across the nation. Mobile connectivity has become a cornerstone of Malaysia's digital infrastructure.

The widespread adoption of smartphones has contributed to the growth of mobile internet usage. In line with global technological advancements, Malaysia has also embarked on the deployment of 5G networks, which promise even faster data speeds, low latency, and enhanced capabilities for IoT devices (MCMC, 2022). The Malaysian Communications and Multimedia Commission (MCMC) has been actively working on the 5G rollout to position Malaysia as a regional leader in connectivity. Malaysia has invested significantly in the development of broadband infrastructure, both in urban and rural areas. The implementation of the NFCP includes the expansion of broadband services to underserved regions, enabling digital inclusion, and supporting various smart initiatives. The Malaysian government has shown a strong commitment to fostering digitalization and smart city development. Initiatives like the Smart Cities Framework and Digital Government initiatives aim to leverage technology to enhance urban living, promote efficient governance, and elevate overall quality of life (Ministry of Housing and Local Government, 2018). Cities like Kuala Lumpur and Cyberjaya have been designated as testbeds for smart city solutions.

## HIGH-SPEED INTERNET AND 5G NETWORKS FOR SMART TOURISM

In the modern era, the tourism industry is undergoing a profound transformation fuelled by technological advancements. Among the most significant enablers of this transformation are high-speed internet and the emerging 5G networks. Malaysia launched 5G technology ahead of schedule at the end of 2021, making it one of the first countries in the region to establish a 5G ecosystem. The key advantages of 5G over 4G include significantly faster speeds (up to 1.5GB per second), extremely low latency (around 1ms), and the ability to connect a larger number of devices per square kilometre (1 million compared to 1,000 with 4G). The speed and low latency of 5G pave the way for improved communication, data transmission, research, and entertainment experiences on a global scale. This technology can download high-definition movies within seconds and reduce lag when connecting devices (The Star, 2022).

5G technology holds immense potential across diverse sectors, including Malaysia's digital economy goals and the "smart tourism" concept. Malaysia is integrating 5G through the National Digital Network (JENDELA) plan to stimulate economic growth, attract investments, and create high-value jobs. In smart tourism, 5G and high-speed internet empower travellers with real-time information on attractions, transport, events, and recommendations, enhancing their experiences. It ensures seamless communication, enabling contact with loved ones and local services. Location-based services and navigation apps are greatly improved, while augmented reality and virtual reality offer immersive, educational experiences. Personalization in tourism is driven by 5G, with businesses tailoring offerings based on data analysis. Moreover, 5G facilitates innovative solutions like smartphone check-ins, contactless payments, and data-driven marketing, enhancing business connectivity and competitiveness. Quick data transfers and low latency enable real-time data analysis, informing marketing campaigns and resource allocation. In summary, 5G and high-speed internet redefine tourism interactions, empowering destinations, and businesses to innovate, optimize operations, and offer personalized services. Strong connectivity is a linchpin for the evolving smart tourism landscape, shaping the future of the global tourism industry.

## ENHANCING DIGITAL CONNECTIVITY IN URBAN AND RURAL AREAS

Modern society's foundational element is digital connectivity, which supports communication, healthcare, education, and economic progress. The need of improving digital connectivity in both urban and rural communities cannot be overstated to close the digital divide and guarantee equal access to opportunities. The following provides an overview of a comprehensive strategy that makes use of cutting-edge technology and collaboration to improve digital infrastructure, in particular high-speed internet, in these various settings.

Making sure that everyone has affordable dependable access to high-speed internet is one of the key goals for improving digital connection in urban and rural areas. Encourage the use of digital inclusion as a tool for entrepreneurship, job creation, and economic growth. Enable digital literacy and promote creative solutions to empower local people and to make it easier to access online education, telemedicine, and government services.

To enhance digital connectivity, it is essential to collaborate with telecom companies, expanding high-speed broadband infrastructure across urban and rural areas. Public-private partnerships can drive investments in fibre-optic networks, 4G/5G towers, and satellite tech, with a focus on underserved regions. Encouraging policies and streamlining permitting processes for telecom investments are vital. Establishing Community Connectivity Centres in rural areas, backed by local authorities and NGOs, can provide digital literacy training and services. Mobile broadband units can offer temporary connectivity during events and emergencies, while satellite-based internet can reach remote areas. Implement digital literacy programs, raise public awareness about digital benefits, secure funding for infrastructure projects, and set up monitoring systems to track progress and inclusion metrics in both urban and rural areas.

Enhancing digital connectivity in urban and rural areas is not only a technological imperative but a social and economic one. By implementing this proposal, we can create a more inclusive and equitable digital society, unlocking opportunities for education, economic growth, healthcare, and community development. Collaboration among government entities, private sector stakeholders, and civil society will be instrumental in realizing this vision of a digitally connected and empowered nation.

## DATA COLLECTION AND ANALYSIS

The success of modern tourism increasingly relies on data-driven insights to enhance visitor experiences, optimize resource allocation, and promote sustainable practices. This exploration delves into the diverse data sources pertinent to the tourism industry, encompassing visitor data, environmental conditions, and cultural information. Visitor data, a cornerstone of informed tourism management, is sourced from multiple channels. Online booking platforms yield insights into travel inclinations and popular spots. Visitor surveys capture opinions and satisfaction levels, while foot traffic tracking via counters informs peak visitation periods.

In the realm of smart tourism, data from various sources are harnessed for holistic insights. Social media and tourism apps provide real-time sentiment and preferences. Environmental data includes weather, air quality, and disaster alerts. Cultural information stems from institutions, text analysis, archives, and community collaboration. Geospatial data aids attraction mapping, and economic data informs analysis. Technology data, such as Wi-Fi usage and beacon technology, enhances digital services. This wide array of data empowers the tourism industry to make informed decisions, tailor experiences, and ensure sustainability while preserving destinations.

## DATA COLLECTION METHODS AND TECHNOLOGIES FOR TOURISM INSIGHTS

Data collection methods and technologies are instrumental in gathering valuable insights to enhance the tourism industry's efficiency, customer experiences, and sustainability. Two prominent approaches in this realm are Internet of Things (IoT) devices and mobile apps. Examine their roles, benefits, and potential obstacles in data collection for tourism insights is necessary.

IoT devices, or networked things with sensors and communication capabilities, are essential for gathering data for the tourism industry. These gadgets provide the real-time data collection from numerous sources necessary for a thorough understanding of traveller behaviour and destination dynamics. Continuous and real-time monitoring of numerous factors, such as foot traffic at attractions, environmental conditions, and energy usage in hospitality places, is one of the features of IoT devices. IoT-enabled safety tools can help monitor and control visitor flows, ensuring secure interactions at busy tourist destinations or in emergency situations. Operational expenses and environmental impact are decreased because to resource management that is optimised thanks to data from IoT devices, such as electricity usage in hotels. By assessing visitor preferences and habits, IoT data also makes personalised experiences possible by providing customised recommendations and services. Destinations can identify trends and make wise decisions thanks to predictive analytics, which is made possible by the constant flow of data. Despite the obvious advantages of IoT, there are also drawbacks. IoT devices gather private information, which prompts worries about security flaws and data privacy. It might be challenging and technically demanding to integrate numerous IoT devices and manage the enormous volume of data they produce. Regular maintenance is necessary for reliable data gathering since it addresses technical issues or glitches and ensures the appropriate operation and dependability of IoT devices.

The use of mobile applications as a direct route for information gathering and communication with travellers has made them an essential component of the travel experience. These applications collect a plethora of data regarding user preferences, activities, and interactions. Mobile apps offer valuable benefits for tourism insights, including location-based understanding of attractions and preferences, direct user engagement for personalized recommendations and real-time feedback, diverse data collection spanning bookings, reviews, and social integration, and behaviour analysis to customize offerings. However, challenges encompass encouraging user adoption to ensure app utilization, addressing privacy concerns through robust policies, and ensuring app compatibility across devices and platforms for comprehensive data collection. Both IoT devices and mobile apps have transformative potential in data collection for tourism insights. While IoT devices offer real-time monitoring and predictive capabilities, mobile apps provide direct user engagement and diverse data acquisition. To harness their benefits effectively, stakeholders must address challenges related to data security, privacy, integration, and user adoption. Embracing these technologies can empower the tourism industry to make informed decisions, enhance visitor experiences, and drive sustainable growth.

## LEVERAGING DATA ANALYTICS AND AI FOR VISITOR INSIGHTS

Data analytics and artificial intelligence (AI) are transformative tools that hold immense potential for gaining deep insights into visitor preferences and behaviours within the tourism industry. By harnessing the power of data-driven analysis and AI-driven algorithms, destinations can create personalized experiences, optimize resource allocation, and enhance overall visitor satisfaction.

By gathering and combining various data sources, such as booking platforms and social media, data analytics and AI play a crucial role in modern tourism by giving an in-depth insight of each visitor's journey. AI-driven personalized recommendations enhance attractions, accommodations, and dining experiences, while behavioural analysis optimizes site layouts, event scheduling, and crowd management. Real-time insights from social media and mobile apps inform prompt responses to changing preferences, and demand forecasting ensures efficient resource allocation and staffing. Segmented marketing campaigns resonate with specific audience segments, and sentiment analysis gauges visitor satisfaction for proactive improvements. Data-driven insights facilitate continuous enhancements in offerings and operations, guided by AI's optimization strategies, while resource allocation optimization furthers sustainable practices without compromising visitor satisfaction. Finally, data analytics and AI are critical tools for gaining a better knowledge of visitor preferences and behaviours. Destinations can develop more enriched and individualised tourism experiences while supporting sustainability and innovation by analysing varied datasets, creating personalised experiences, forecasting trends, and optimising resource allocation.

## SMART MOBILITY

Malaysia's transportation systems are critical components of the country's economic and social development, connecting urban and rural areas, facilitating trade, and enabling tourism. However, these systems also face several limitations that impact efficiency, accessibility, and sustainability. Malaysia's transportation landscape encompasses an extensive road network, including highways and urban roads, which serves as the primary travel mode but contributes to congestion and pollution. The rail system comprises urban transit like MRT and LRT, along with intercity trains, enhancing connectivity but needing further expansion. Public transportation, crucial for urban mobility, faces challenges in reliability and accessibility, leading to reliance on private vehicles. The air transportation network, featuring international airports like KLIA, offers efficient long-distance travel but contends with congestion and capacity issues. Maritime transportation, vital for trade and tourism, encounters port congestion and infrastructure limitations. Addressing these aspects is vital for comprehensive and sustainable transportation solutions in Malaysia.

Malaysia's transportation landscape is marked by urban congestion, inadequate rural connectivity, and safety concerns, affecting both locals and tourists. Insufficient infrastructure investment hampers integrated travel experiences, while overreliance on personal vehicles worsens environmental issues. Addressing these challenges is vital for establishing an efficient, accessible, and sustainable transportation network that supports economic growth and enhances the quality of life for all.

The integration of smart mobility solutions, such as autonomous vehicles (AVs), electric transportation (EVs), and real-time navigation apps, can significantly enhance Malaysia's transportation landscape. AVs promise improved traffic flow and safety, especially for first-and-last-mile connectivity. Promoting EVs through infrastructure development and incentives can reduce the nation's carbon footprint, and real-time navigation apps optimize routes and encourage multimodal travel options. Smart city integration and infrastructure investments, like connected roads and smart traffic management, are key. Collaboration among the government, private sector, and technology providers, along with data-driven insights, plays a crucial role in this transformation.

Smart mobility solutions offer a wide array of advantages, including efficient traffic management, reduced environmental impact, enhanced safety, improved accessibility, seamless multimodal transportation, economic growth, data-driven urban planning, resource optimization, enriched user experiences, and informed decision-making. These benefits have the potential to transform transportation systems, rendering them more efficient, sustainable, and user-centric, with positive impacts extending to individuals, communities, the environment, and economies overall.

## DIGITALIZED ATTRACTIONS

IoT technology enhances tourist attractions by creating interactive and immersive experiences. For instance, at a historical site, IoT sensors embedded in artefacts or landmarks can provide real-time information to visitors' smartphones, offering historical context, stories, and multimedia content as they explore the site. By introducing more layers of involvement and information, this improves the visitor experience. IoT-powered navigation systems enhance the tourist experience at complex sites such as museums, botanical gardens, and theme parks. Indoor positioning systems and Bluetooth beacons offer tailored instructions through visitors' smartphones, optimizing their routes and providing detailed information about exhibits. IoT devices enable real-time data exchange between attractions and visitors, offering insights like weather conditions, trail availability, and wildlife sightings for informed exploration and improved safety. Augmented reality further enriches tourist attractions by overlaying digital information onto the physical environment. For example, visitors can use AR glasses or smartphones to witness historical reconstructions superimposed onto ancient ruins, creating immersive and educational experiences. Augmented Reality (AR) technology introduces gamified elements, language translation, interactive learning experiences, and virtual guides to tourist attractions, enhancing engagement and educational value. Visitors can use AR apps to find hidden elements, translate languages instantly, and interact with 3D models, while virtual guides provide personalized and entertaining tours. These technologies make tourist experiences more interactive, informative, and memorable, enriching their understanding and engagement at various attractions.

## Case Studies

**Case Study 1**: Louvre Museum, France - The Louvre Museum in Paris enriched visitor engagement by introducing an augmented reality (AR) app, providing historical context, artist biographies, and 3D models when pointed at artworks. The AR experience rejuvenated visitor interactions with art and boosted museum attendance.

**Case Study 2**: Singapore Zoo - IoT Safari Experience in the Singapore Zoo utilized the Internet of Things (IoT) and data analytics through a mobile app to enhance the safari experience. Real-time animal behaviour and habitat data improved visitor experiences, and data analytics optimized crowd control and exhibit layouts, benefiting both tourists and conservation efforts.

**Case Study 3**: Machu Picchu, Peru - 3D Scanning and Virtual Reality Machu Picchu in Peru employed 3D scanning and virtual reality to preserve its cultural heritage. A precise digital replica of the site allows remote visitors to explore its architecture, history, and significance, offering a unique opportunity to engage with Machu Picchu's cultural heritage.

**Case Study 4**: Tokyo Disneyland, Japan - Seamless Guest Experience Tokyo Disneyland streamlined visitor experiences by introducing a comprehensive smartphone app, providing maps, mobile food ordering, real-time attraction waits times, personalized recommendations, and virtual line reservations. This digitization initiative improved customer satisfaction, reduced wait times, and increased operational efficiency.

These case studies illustrate how digitalization initiatives in various locations have transformed visitor experiences, preserved cultural heritage, and enhanced operational procedures at tourist destinations globally.

## IMPLEMENTING DIGITALIZATION IN MALAYSIA'S KEY TOURIST DESTINATIONS

Key tourist destinations in Malaysia can greatly enhance visitor experiences through the strategic implementation of interactive displays, virtual reality (VR) experiences, and digital information boards. Interactive displays at historical sites and cultural destinations offer touch-screen interfaces for historical information and multimedia presentations, engaging visitors in the area's culture and significance. VR experiences transport tourists to different times or places, creating immersive encounters, such as virtual tower climbs or rainforest exploration. Digital information boards at key attractions provide real-time updates, maps, and essential information, ensuring visitors have access to vital details, whether they are exploring a cave or enjoying a beach. These technologies combine to create a more interactive, educational, and engaging tourism experience while highlighting Malaysia's rich cultural and natural heritage.

The implementation of interactive displays, virtual reality experiences, and digital information boards in Malaysia's prominent tourist destinations involves several key steps. First, an assessment of destinations with cultural, historical, or natural significance is conducted to identify suitable sites. Collaborating with technology providers, appropriate hardware and software are chosen to ensure compatibility and seamless interaction. Engaging and informative content is then created to align with each destination's narrative. The deployment of technology follows, including interactive displays, VR zones, and digital boards, integrated with existing infrastructure. Staff training ensures visitors have a smooth experience, while regular maintenance and updates keep the technology functional and content current. Effective promotion through various platforms raises awareness among tourists, enabling them to connect deeply with Malaysia's cultural and natural wonders through enhanced experiences.

## PERSONALIZED EXPERIENCE FOR TOURISTS

In modern tourism, personalized experiences are of paramount importance, aligning with the preferences and expectations of today's individualistic travellers. These tailored experiences offer numerous advantages, including increased visitor satisfaction, emotional connections to the destination, the creation of lasting memories, a competitive edge in the industry, higher rates of repeat visits, increased spending, data-driven decision-making, and contributions to tourism sustainability by reducing overcrowding and promoting responsible practices.

Personalized experiences are essential in modern tourism as they elevate visitor satisfaction, foster emotional connections, create memorable moments, and provide a competitive edge. By tailoring offerings to individual preferences, destinations can build strong relationships with travellers and offer unique, value-added experiences that contribute to a thriving and sustainable tourism industry. Advanced technologies, including AI-driven chatbots, mobile apps, and location-based services, are enhancing the overall tourism experience by providing personalized advice and support to travellers. These tools utilize sophisticated algorithms and data analysis to offer individualized guidance at various stages of a tourist's journey. AI chatbots, integrated into websites, apps, and messaging services, engage users in real-time conversations, responding to inquiries, offering recommendations, and creating customized itineraries based on user preferences and travel history. Travel-related mobile apps provide flexible resources for personalization, incorporating features like real-time navigation, interactive maps, and user-generated ratings to curate tailored recommendations by collecting user data such as location and interests. Location-based services utilize GPS technology to send location-specific notifications and suggestions as travellers move through an area, enhancing the relevance and timeliness of recommendations. Together, these technologies provide personalized connections, enhance convenience, and deliver insightful information to make each trip more memorable and enjoyable.

## POTENTIAL CHALLENGES AND ETHICAL CONSIDERATION

The implementation of personalized experiences using AI-driven systems presents significant challenges and ethical concerns. These include issues related to data privacy and security, potential algorithmic biases in recommendations, user discomfort with AI interactions and data sharing, the reliability of AI algorithms, and the risk of information overload. Addressing these challenges is crucial to responsibly and effectively integrating personalized experiences into the tourism industry. The integration of personalized experiences in tourism through AI systems has great potential, but ethical considerations are crucial. Transparency is essential, with clear communication about data use. Informed consent empowers users to control their data and preferences. Striking a balance between customization and user control is vital. Developers must work to reduce algorithmic biases for fair recommendations. Responsible data use means using data only to enhance user experiences. Safeguarding vulnerable groups, considering cultural sensitivities, and avoiding dehumanization are key to realizing the benefits of enhanced travel experiences while maintaining privacy and fairness.

## SUSTAINABLE PRACTICES

Malaysia has been making commendable efforts to promote sustainability in its tourism sector, recognizing the importance of balancing economic growth with environmental conservation and social responsibility. Malaysia has embraced eco-tourism through efforts to preserve its biodiversity, including national parks and marine parks, which promote conservation while benefiting local communities. Many hotels and resorts have adopted eco-friendly practices, and cultural heritage preservation initiatives provide authentic experiences for tourists. Wildlife conservation, such as orangutan sanctuaries, is a focus, along with community involvement in tourism activities. Certification programs and waste management efforts contribute to sustainability, while initiatives to reduce carbon emissions and promote responsible tourism practices are actively encouraged through educational campaigns. Malaysia demonstrates a commitment to preserving its natural and cultural treasures while promoting eco-friendly and sustainable tourism. These sustainability efforts reflect Malaysia's commitment to maintaining its natural and cultural treasures for both current and future generations. While progress has been made, ongoing collaboration between government agencies, tourism stakeholders, and local communities is vital to ensure the continued success of these initiatives.

## INTEGRATING SUSTAINABILITY CAMPAIGNS AND ECO-FRIENDLY PRACTICES INTO SMART TOURISM FRAMEWORK

Integrating sustainability campaigns and eco-friendly practices into a smart tourism framework in Malaysia can significantly enhance the positive impact of technology-driven tourism initiatives. Incorporating data-driven sustainability insights, smart destination messaging, green incentives, carbon footprint tracking, interactive eco-tours, smart transportation options, sustainability challenges and rewards, local community engagement, green accommodation choices, real-time environmental alerts, and education/cultural exchange into the smart tourism framework offers a holistic approach to promoting sustainable practices among tourists. Using cutting-edge technologies like mobile apps and augmented reality, Malaysia can enable visitors to make educated decisions, participate in environmentally beneficial activities, and support conservation initiatives. With the help of this comprehensive plan, responsible tourism practises may be fostered while also improving the overall visitor experience. Tourist conduct is matched with environmental and social aims. By intertwining sustainability campaigns and eco-friendly practices with the smart tourism framework, Malaysia can leverage technology's power to raise awareness, facilitate responsible choices, and foster a culture of sustainability among tourists, ultimately contributing to the preservation of the country's natural beauty and cultural richness.

## DIGITAL PLATFORM AS ENABLER OF SUSTAINABLE PRACTICES

Digital platforms serve as potent tools for raising awareness and advocating responsible tourism practices. Through social media, websites, and dedicated apps, destinations can disseminate educational content, highlight conservation efforts, and showcase sustainable initiatives. Engaging visuals, informative articles, and interactive campaigns can inform tourists about minimizing environmental impact, respecting local cultures, and supporting community development. These platforms facilitate real-time communication, enabling destinations to provide updates on eco-friendly activities, responsible travel guidelines, and ethical wildlife interactions. By fostering a sense of shared responsibility and providing accessible information, digital platforms play a pivotal role in inspiring travellers to make conscious choices that preserve the environment, support local communities, and contribute to a more sustainable and respectful tourism landscape.

## COLLABORATION AND STAKEHOLDER ENGAGEMENT

Collaboration between government agencies (Ministry of Tourism, Arts & Culture, Ministry of Communication & Digital, MCMC), private sector entities (Maxis, Digi Telecommunication, U Mobile, Celcom, Edotco, Time dotcom, BT, AT&T, Telekom Malaysia), local communities, and technology providers (Apple Inc, Alphabet Inc, Meta Platforms, Microsoft, Samsung) is paramount for the successful implementation of the smart tourism framework in Malaysia. This multi-stakeholder approach not only enhances the framework's effectiveness but also ensures its sustainability and alignment with the diverse needs of the tourism ecosystem. Collaboration is crucial to attain resource mobilization, capitalizing on diverse expertise, having balance decision-making, local empowerment, promote innovation and adaptability and generating economic growth.

Collaboration is a driving force behind effective smart tourism initiatives in Malaysia. It allows for the mobilization of resources from various stakeholders, including government agencies, private sector businesses, local communities, and technology providers. These diverse groups bring unique expertise to the table, facilitating well-rounded and effective initiatives. Collaborative decision-making ensures inclusivity and balanced solutions that reflect various stakeholders' interests. Engaging local communities fosters ownership and the preservation of cultural heritage, enhancing authenticity. This collaborative approach promotes innovation, stimulates economic growth, attracts tourists, and creates job opportunities.

Effective stakeholder engagement strategies are crucial for the success of smart tourism initiatives. These strategies include maintaining open and transparent communication channels through regular meetings, sharing a common vision, formalizing collaborations through agreements, offering incentives for participation, involving local communities, and being adaptable to changing circumstances. Collaboration among government agencies, businesses, communities, and technology providers is essential for building a sustainable and cutting-edge tourism ecosystem in Malaysia.

## Case Studies of Collaboration in Smart Tourism Destination

Barcelona, Spain, and Singapore serve as prime examples of successful collaborations in smart tourism. In Barcelona, a "Smart City" initiative involves cooperation between local administration, private businesses, and technology providers, resulting in a sophisticated system that enhances the visitor experience through real-time data and mobile apps, leading to improved waste management, reduced traffic congestion, and higher visitor satisfaction. Singapore's Gardens by the Bay is another case of effective teamwork, featuring government organizations, private sector businesses, and landscape architects who have created an environmentally sustainable attraction with a smartphone app offering real-time information and educational content for visitors. These case studies showcase how collaboration can create smart tourism destinations that are both appealing and eco-friendly.

## MARKETING AND PROMOTION

Digital marketing, social media, and influencer campaigns play a vital role in promoting smart tourism. Digital marketing leverages online channels to showcase the advantages of smart tourism, such as personalized experiences and cost-effective travel. Social media platforms provide interactive means for engaging with travellers, sharing information about smart destinations, and stimulating user-generated content. Collaborating with influential individuals with substantial online followings through influencer marketing allows for authentic experiences to be shared, building trust and inspiring potential visitors. These digital strategies collectively boost the visibility, credibility, and appeal of smart tourism offerings, enhancing awareness and fostering a positive perception of new travel experiences.

Data-driven marketing tactics are potent tools for precise and effective targeting of specific audiences. By utilizing comprehensive data and analytics, marketers can identify and comprehend their target audience's interests, behaviours, and needs. This insight facilitates the creation of tailored marketing strategies that resonate with distinct demographic or psychographic segments. Data segmentation based on factors like age, gender, location, interests, and past behaviour enables the delivery of highly relevant content, offers, and messages to each segment, thereby increasing engagement and conversion potential. Predictive analytics can also forecast future consumer behaviours and preferences, empowering marketers to proactively adjust their strategies. For instance, if data reveals a growing interest in eco-friendly travel within a particular segment, marketers can craft campaigns promoting smart tourism activities aligned with sustainability.

Data-driven personalized suggestions and retargeting strategies help re-engage individuals who have shown interest but have not completed desired actions, like booking a trip. By analysing prior interactions, marketers can send tailored offers or reminders that align with individual preferences, increasing the likelihood of conversion. Data-driven marketing also facilitates continuous evaluation and refinement. Marketers can monitor campaign effectiveness in real-time and make immediate adjustments based on insights. For example, if data analysis indicates that a campaign targeting millennials is underperforming, marketers can swiftly make the necessary refinements. Data-driven marketing strategies empower marketers to precisely target, engage, and convert specific demographics. Through data and analytics, marketing efforts can be fine-tuned to match the preferences and behaviours of the intended audience, ultimately driving more successful and impactful campaigns.

To effectively showcase Malaysia's smart tourism initiatives on digital platforms, a comprehensive approach is proposed. This includes a dedicated website section with engaging content, social media posts for visual storytelling, a comprehensive tourism app for real-time information, immersive VR content, video marketing, informative blogs, influencer collaborations, podcasts, webinars, targeted online ads, and email newsletters. This integrated strategy aims to present Malaysia's innovative approach to travel technology through a variety of engaging and informative digital channels.

## MONITORING AND EVALUATION

Measuring the success and impact of smart tourism initiatives is crucial for several reasons. It allows stakeholders to assess the effectiveness of their strategies, make evidence-based decisions, enhance accountability and transparency, identify strengths and areas for improvement, align policies with broader tourism goals, foster innovation, and ensure efficient resource utilization.

To assess the effectiveness of the smart tourism framework, it is crucial to track key performance indicators (KPIs) that provide insights into various aspects of the program. These KPIs include evaluating personalization success, measuring adoption rates of smart services, quantifying environmental impact reductions, analysing time spent at smart destinations, assessing digital engagement and campaign effectiveness, measuring return visitation rates, and evaluating environmental impact. By monitoring these KPIs collectively, it becomes possible to evaluate the framework's impact on enhancing visitor experiences and promoting sustainable practices within destinations. Establishing a robust system for continuous monitoring, data collection, and iterative adjustments is essential for ensuring the ongoing success and effectiveness of the smart tourism framework. This approach allows for continuous assessment, data-driven insights, and informed adjustments based on user feedback and analysis.

To ensure the ongoing success of our smart tourism framework, a robust system for continuous monitoring and data collection shall be established. This system will integrate real-time data from various sources, including mobile apps, interactive displays, social media, and visitor surveys, to create a comprehensive understanding of visitor engagement, preferences, behaviours, and trends. In line with the framework's objectives, a set of key performance indicators (KPIs) will be developed. These KPIs will encompass metrics related to visitor satisfaction, the utilization of smart services, the adoption of sustainability practices, digital engagement, and economic impact. These KPIs will be consistently monitored and assessed to gauge the framework's effectiveness. Furthermore, mechanisms for collecting visitor feedback will be implemented. Visitors will have the opportunity to provide qualitative input through surveys within mobile apps, interactive kiosks, and online platforms. This feedback will serve to clarify user expectations, identify areas for improvement, and gather suggestions for enhancing the overall smart tourism experience.

Advanced data analytics technologies will be used to glean valuable insights from the data gathered through continuous monitoring. These tools will examine the data and find patterns, correlations, and trends that might help with decision-making. These insights will be visually represented via interactive performance dashboards, allowing stakeholders including government organisations, business partners, and local communities to access and analyse the data cooperatively. In addition, tools for predictive analysis will be used to predict future trends and behaviours based on previous data, enabling proactive strategies to quickly take advantage of opportunities and handle obstacles.

With the participation of all stakeholders, monthly review meetings will create a continuous feedback loop. Discussions on performance insights, data-driven conclusions, and the framework's compatibility with its goals will be facilitated throughout these meetings. An iterative refinement strategy will be used to improve the smart tourism services using the data and insights gathered. According on user preferences, this process will involve modifying personalised recommendations, improving interactive displays, and adding new features. A flexible implementation technique will be used, allowing for quick and flexible adjustments. Government agencies, private sector companies, local communities, and technology suppliers will actively participate in decision-making to ensure collaboration, identifying areas for improvement and prioritising changes based on shared insights.

We have to make sure that the smart tourism framework is dynamic and in line with the changing demands and expectations of contemporary travellers by putting in place a thorough system for ongoing monitoring, data collection, and modifications. The proposal's strategy encourages a culture of data-driven decision-making, openness, and cooperation, which has a lasting impact on improving visitor experiences and encouraging ethical tourism practises.

## MALAYSIA'S SMART TOURISM FRAMEWORK

Malaysia's Smart Tourism Framework is a visionary strategy set to transform the nation's tourism landscape through collaboration between government agencies, private sectors, local communities, and technology providers. The framework's core components include digital infrastructure, data analysis, smart mobility, digital attractions, personalized experiences, sustainability, and stakeholder engagement. With a strong focus on robust digital infrastructure, including widespread high-speed internet and 5G networks, it aims to ensure seamless connectivity across urban and rural areas. Leveraging data analytics and artificial intelligence, the framework tailors' experiences, optimizes marketing, and enhances resource allocation. Sustainability practices are woven throughout, emphasizing eco-friendly transportation, responsible waste management, and the preservation of cultural heritage. Prioritizing inclusivity and cultural preservation, the framework bridges the digital divide while fostering cultural exchange. Investment in sustainable mobility and strategic public-private partnerships propels Malaysia toward a competitive, sustainable, and visitor-centric smart tourism industry. Continuous monitoring, guided by key performance indicators, facilitates iterative improvements to stay attuned to evolving trends and needs. This roadmap furnishes actionable insights to guide policy-making, investment allocation, and strategic planning for all stakeholders. Ultimately, Malaysia's Smart Tourism Framework positions the nation for socio-economic growth, bolstered by increased tourism revenue, job creation, enriched visitor experiences, and economic diversification, all while safeguarding its natural and cultural heritage in the digital era.

Digital infrastructure, data collecting and analysis, smart mobility, digitalized attractions, personalised experiences, sustainability practises, and stakeholder collaboration are all essential components of the framework. Every element plays a part in creating a well-rounded smart tourist environment.

In order to enable smart tourism, the framework emphasises the crucial role of digital infrastructure and improved connectivity, powered by high-speed internet and cutting-edge technologies like 5G. To learn more about visitor behaviour, it also explores data collection techniques and the use of IoT devices, mobile apps, data analytics, and AI. It is suggested that smart mobility solutions, such self-driving cars and real-time navigation software, will enhance travel. Personalised experiences, sustainable practises, stakeholder engagement, digital marketing, and effective monitoring and evaluation methods are all studied together with digitalized attractions through IoT and augmented reality. Together, these elements lay the groundwork for Malaysia's envisioned smart tourism framework, which provides practical advice and insights for a tourism sector that is both environmentally friendly and technologically advanced.

*Figure 1. Smart tourism framework*

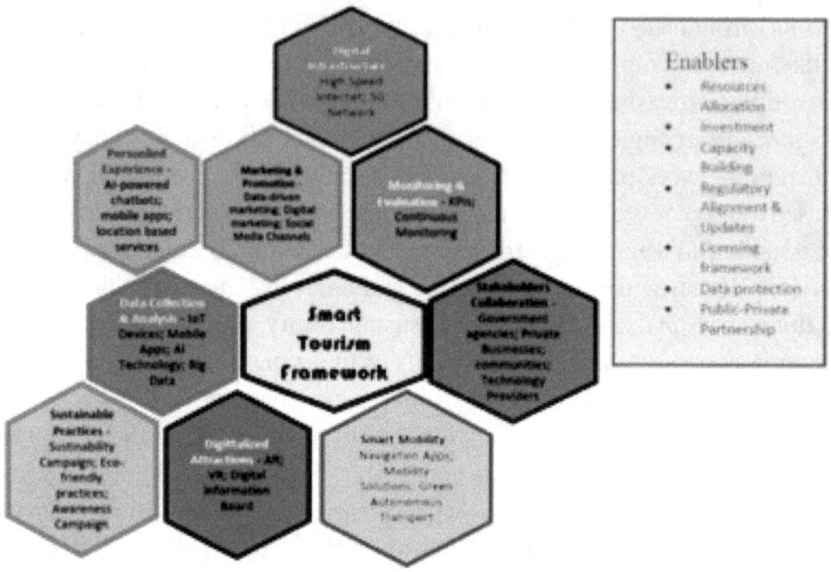


## IMPLEMENTATION OF SMART TOURISM FRAMEWORK IN MALAYSIA

The implementation of Malaysia's smart tourism framework is crucial for its success. To ensure a smooth transition, practical recommendations and strategies that take into consideration resource allocation, investment priorities, capacity building, and regulatory adjustments are required. A comprehensive approach to resource allocation, investment prioritisation, capacity building, and regulation adjustment is required to guarantee the successful implementation of Malaysia's smart tourism framework. This entails identifying a variety of financial sources, such as government budgets, public-private partnerships, and foreign grants, as well as creating a special fund for smart tourism activities. Prioritising projects based on alignment with framework objectives assures adequate financing for important components. The emphasis on resource efficiency and staggered deployment efficiently spreads expenses. Priorities for investment include modernising digital infrastructure, adopting data analytics and AI, improving smart transportation, and digitalizing significant attractions with IoT and augmented reality. Capacity building through training programmes and educational collaborations promotes a skilled workforce, while information exchange enables continuous learning and adaptation. Regulatory adaptation entails evaluating and updating rules, establishing licencing frameworks, and adopting stringent data protection safeguards, with public-private collaboration essential for innovation and responsible practises. This comprehensive strategy will promote long-term smart tourism growth, enhance visitor experiences, and protect cultural and natural heritage.

## BENEFITS OF ADOPTING THE SMART TOURISM FRAMEWORK

Adoption of Malaysia's smart tourism concept promises significant socioeconomic benefits. By improving visitor experiences and attracting a broader tourist base, it is possible to dramatically increase tourism revenue, encourage job development, and promote economic diversification, ultimately lowering dependency on conventional sectors. Furthermore, the framework's emphasis on sustainability coincides with worldwide trends and strengthens Malaysia's eco-friendly image. Investments in digital infrastructure benefit not only tourism but also other sectors, enhancing overall competitiveness. Furthermore, personalised encounters and cultural exchange opportunities boost tourism's appeal. However, issues such as the digital gap and data privacy must be addressed to achieve equitable and sustainable development.

## ACTIONABLE PLANS

Actionable insights derived from the smart tourism framework can guide policy decisions, investment priorities, and strategic planning for tourism stakeholders, government bodies, and businesses in Malaysia. Among the actions to be taken are collaboration, investment in digital infrastructure, develop data analytics and AI capabilities, integrating sustainable activities, invest in upskilling workforce, reviewing, and updating regulations. Embracing digital marketing, continuous monitoring, practice inclusivity, emphasize cultural preservation and fostering private-public partnership. These actionable insights collectively form an extensive guide for Malaysia's diverse tourism stakeholders, spanning government bodies, private enterprises, and local communities. At its core, collaboration emerges as a pivotal force, fostering knowledge sharing and innovative partnerships. The roadmap places a strong emphasis on the foundational role of digital infrastructure investments, specifically the expansion of high-speed internet and 5G networks, as the bedrock for smart tourism. Leveraging data analytics and AI to personalize experiences and allocate resources efficiently is highlighted, as is the integration of sustainability practices. Capacity building through workforce upskilling and a commitment to regular regulatory reviews ensures a responsible and ethical approach. Elevating visitor experiences through digital attractions and targeted digital marketing strategies caters to the expectations of tech-savvy tourists. Continuous monitoring, driven by key performance indicators, steers iterative improvements, while inclusivity and cultural preservation promote mutual understanding. Concurrently, investments in sustainable mobility and strategic public-private partnerships underpin Malaysia's journey towards a competitive, sustainable, and visitor-centric smart tourism industry, poised to make substantial contributions to the nation's socio-economic development.

## CONCLUSION

The proposed framework for smart tourism in Malaysia is designed to revolutionize the tourism experience by integrating cutting-edge technology, sustainability practices, and personalized services. Leveraging the power of data analytics, artificial intelligence, and digital platforms, the framework aims to offer tourists tailored and immersive experiences that align with their preferences and values. By incorporating interactive exhibits, virtual reality experiences, and real-time navigation apps, Malaysia's cultural, natural, and historical assets will become more accessible to visitors and their involvement will increase. The framework strongly emphasises sustainability, supporting environmentally beneficial behaviours, conscientious travel, and minimal environmental effect. To achieve the aims of the framework, cooperation between governmental organisations, commercial enterprises, local communities, and technology providers will be crucial. The smart tourism products will stay current, efficient, and in line with guest expectations thanks to ongoing monitoring, data collecting, and adjustments based on performance feedback. By putting this complete framework into practise, Malaysia will be better able to attract modern travellers with memorable, personalised, and sustainable travel experiences.

Adoption of the suggested smart tourism framework in Malaysia has the potential to bring about a wide range of advantages that will completely alter the tourism industry. The integration of personalised recommendations, interactive displays, and real-time navigation apps will produce unforgettable journeys catered to individual interests, cantering on improved visitor experiences. As a result, visitors will have more positive experiences, stronger emotional ties to their travel places, and lasting memories. In parallel, the framework's focus on sustainability will contribute to reduced environmental impact, fostering responsible tourism practices that conserve natural resources and promote eco-friendly behaviours. Moreover, the framework's technological advancements will attract tech-savvy travellers, boosting the country's image as an innovative and forward-thinking destination. This, in turn, has the potential to drive economic growth through increased tourism revenue, job creation, and investment in smart tourism-related industries. As Malaysia positions itself as a smart and sustainable tourism hub, the adoption of this framework will undoubtedly bring forth a new era of enriching, memorable, and environmentally conscious travel experiences that benefit both visitors and the nation.

The proposed smart tourism framework for Malaysia presents a transformative opportunity to revolutionize the tourism industry, enhance visitor experiences, and drive sustainable growth. However, its successful realization requires a concerted effort from all stakeholders. We call upon researchers, policymakers, technology providers, private sector businesses, local communities, and tourism professionals to collaboratively embark on further research, rigorous testing, and practical implementation of this framework. The fusion of expertise, insights, and resources is crucial to refining the framework's components, addressing challenges, and fine-tuning its mechanisms for optimal results. Let us collectively work towards making Malaysia a beacon of smart and sustainable tourism, setting new standards for visitor engagement, environmental responsibility, and economic prosperity. Together, we can shape the future of tourism in Malaysia and create lasting positive impacts for both travellers and the nation.

## REFERENCES

Abumandil, M. S., Ekmeil, F. A., Younus, A. M., & Alkhawaja, M. I. (2022). Mobile Augmented Reality Elements and Social Media Usage on Smart Tourism in Penang: Malaysian. *ECS Transactions*, *107*(1), 10935–10943. doi:10.1149/10701.10935ecst

Abumandil, M. S., Halim, M. S., & Alshuaibi, A. S. (2020). Ibrahim, & Siam, M.I. (2020). Factors Affecting the Adoption of Smart Tourism App Study Among Tourism Stakeholders In Malaysia. *Journal of Critical Reviews*, *7*(02).

Azis, N., Amin, M., Chan, S., & Aprilia, C. (2020). How smart tourism technologies affect tourist destination loyalty. *Journal of Hospitality and Tourism Technology*, *11*(4), 603–625. doi:10.1108/JHTT-01-2020-0005

Azmi, A., & Ahmad, J. A. (2022, August). Developing Malaysia's Smart Community-Based Tourism Model. *Jurnal Intelek*, *17*(2), 2022. doi:10.24191/ji.v17i2.18172

Bakici, T., Almirall, E., & Wareham, J. (2013). A smart city initiative: The case of Barcelona. *Journal of the Knowledge Economy*, *4*(2), 135–148. doi:10.1007/s13132-012-0084-9

Buhalis, D., & Amaranggana, A. (2014). Smart tourism destination, 553-564.

Buhalis, D., & Amaranggana, A. (2015). Smart tourism destinations enhancing tourism experience through personalization of services. In *Information and Communication Technologies in Tourism 2015* (pp. 377–389). Springer. doi:10.1007/978-3-319-14343-9_28

Chen, C. (2020). The Influence of Smart Tourism on Tourist Experience Toward Travel Intention and Satisfaction: Evidence from China. *International Journal of Marketing Studies, 12*(3), 65. doi:10.5539/ijms.v12n3p65

Doğan, M. (2019). The Effects of Interactive Applications On Visitors' Experience: A Case of Gobeklitepe, Turkey. *Social Science Studies Journal. Vol, 4*(27), 6125–6135. doi:10.26449/sssj.1084

Fino, E. R., Martín-Gutiérrez, J., López, D. C., Fernández, M. D., Hernández, V. M., & Penate, F. M. (2013). *An Augmented Tourist Guide of a World Heritage City*. Interacción. doi:10.1007/978-3-642-39476-8_58

Fritz, F., & Susperregui, A. (2005). *Enhancing Cultural Tourism experiences with Augmented Reality Technologies*.

Gajdošík, T., & Orelová, A. (2020). Smart Technologies for Smart Tourism Development. In R. Silhavy (Ed.), *Artificial Intelligence and Bioinspired Computational Methods. CSOC 2020. Advances in Intelligent Systems and Computing* (Vol. 1225). Springer. doi:10.1007/978-3-030-51971-1_27

Gretzel, U., Sigala, M., Xiang, Z., & Koo, C. (2015). Smart tourism: Foundations and developments. *Electronic Markets, 25*(3), 179–188. doi:10.1007/s12525-015-0196-8

Gretzel, U., Zhong, L., & Koo, C. (2016). Application of smart tourism to cities. *International Journal of Tourism Cities, 2*(2). doi:10.1108/IJTC-04-2016-0007

Harrison, C., Eckman, B., Hamilton, R., Hartswick, P., Kalagnanam, J., Paraszczak, J., & Williams, P. (2010). Foundations for smarter cities. *IBM Journal of Research and Development, 54*(4), 1–16. doi:10.1147/JRD.2010.2048257

Höjer, M., & Wangel, J. (2015). Smart Sustainable Cities: Definition and Challenges. In L. M. Hilty & B. Aebischer (Eds.), *ICT Innovations for Sustainability, Advances in Intelligent Systems and Computing* (pp. 333–349). Springer. doi:10.1007/978-3-319-09228-7_20

Hua, L. Y., Ramayah, T., Ping, T. A., & Cheah, J. (2017). Social Media as a Tool to Help Select Tourism Destinations: The Case of Malaysia. *Information Systems Management, 34*, 265–279. doi:10.1080/10580530.2017.1330004

Hunter, W. C., Chung, N., Gretzel, U., & Koo, C. (2015). Constructivist research in smart tourism. *APJIS*, *25*(1), 105–120. doi:10.14329/apjis.2015.25.1.105

Kemp, S. (2023). *Digital 2023: Malaysia.* Data Portal. https://datareportal.com/reports/digital-2023-malaysia#:~:text=Malaysia's%20internet%20penetration%20rate%20stood,percent)%20between%202022%20and%202023.

Kim, J., Hlee, S., & Joun, Y. (2016). Green practices of the hotel industry: Analysis through the windows of smart tourism system. *International Journal of Information Management*, *36*(6), 1340–1349. doi:10.1016/j.ijinfomgt.2016.05.001

Lee, J. H., Hancock, M. G., & Mei-Chih, H. (2014). Towards an effective framework for building smart cities: Lessons from Seoul and San Francisco. *Technological Forecasting and Social Change*, *89*, 80–99. doi:10.1016/j.techfore.2013.08.033

MCMC - Communications and Multimedia Malaysia. (2019). *National Fiberisation and Connectivity Plan (NFCP) 2019-2023.* MCMC.

MCMC - Communications and Multimedia Malaysia. (2022). *5G Drives Malaysia's Digitalisation.* MCMC. https://www.mcmc.gov.my/en/media/press-clippings/5g-drives-malaysia-s-digitalisation#:~:text=5G%20TECHNOLOGY%20was%20launched%20here,successor%20of%204G%20cellular%20networks

Ministry of Housing and Local Government. (2018). *Smart City Framework Malaysia*. MHLG.

Mohamed Sofian, I. N., Padlee, S. F., & Hussin, N. Z. (2021). Tourists Satisfaction Towards Smart Tourism Services in Malaysia. *Proceeding for Global Tourism Conference (GTC) 2021*. IEEE. 10.46754/gtc.2021.11.008

Obeidy, W. K., Arshad, H., & Huang, J. (2018). TouristicAR: A Smart Glass Augmented Reality Application for UNESCO World Heritage Sites in Malaysia. *Journal of Telecommunication, Electronic and Computer Engineering*, *10*, 101–108.

Rahman, S. A., Dura, N., Yusof, M. A., Nakamura, H., & Nong, R. A. (2020). Challenges of Smart Tourism in Malaysia Eco-Tourism Destinations. *Planning Malaysia Journal*, *18*(4), 442–451. doi:10.21837/pm.v18i14.844

Rula, A. (2022). How smart is e-tourism? A systematic review of smart tourism recommendation system applying data management. *Computer Science Review*, *39*, 2021.

Susanto, E. H., Novianti, S., Rafdinal, W., Prawira, M. F., & Septyandi, C. B. (2020). Visiting Tourism Destination: Is It Influenced by Smart Tourism Technology? *Journal of Indonesian Tourism and Development Studies*, *8*(3), 145–155. doi:10.21776/ub.jitode.2020.008.03.04

Syakir, A., Nur'hidayah, D., Asrah, Y. M., Hitoshi, N., & Abu, N. R. (2020). Challenges of Smart Tourism In Malaysia Ecotourism Destinations. *Journal of the Malaysian Institute of Planners VOLUME*, *18*(4), 442–451.

(2020). Syakir Amir1, Nur'Hidayah Dura, Muhamad Asrah Yusof, Hitoshi Nakamura & Rahmat Abu Nong. (2020). Challenges of Smart Tourism in Malaysia Ecotourism Destinations. *Journal of the Malaysian Institute of Planners.*, *18*(4), 442–451.

The Star. (2022). 5G Drives Malaysia's Digitalization. *The Star.* https://www.thestar.com.my/news/nation/2022/01/26/5g-drives-malaysias-digitalisation

Topsakal, Y., Bahar, M. & Yüzbaşioğlu, N. (2020). Review of Smart Tourism Literature by Bibliometric And Visualization Analysis. *Journal ofTourism Intelligence and Smartness*, *3*(1).

Tung, V. W., Cheong, T. M., & To, S. J. (2019). Tourism Management in The Era of Smart Mobility: A Perspective Article. *Tourism Review*, *75*(1), 283–285. doi:10.1108/TR-05-2019-0180

Vanolo, A. (2013). Smartmentality: The smart city as disciplinary strategy. *Urban Studies (Edinburgh, Scotland)*, *51*(5), 883–898. doi:10.1177/0042098013494427

Vasavada, M., & Padhiyar, Y. Y. (2016). "Smart Tourism"; Growth for Tomorrow. *Journal for Research*, *1*(12), 55–61.

Xiang, Z., & Fesenmaier, D. R. (2017). Big Data Analytics, Tourism Design and Smart Tourism. In Z. Xiang & D. Fesenmaier (Eds.), *Analytics in Smart Tourism Design. Tourism on the Verge*. Springer., doi:10.1007/978-3-319-44263-1_17

Ye, B. H., Ye, H., & Law, R. (2020). Systematic Review of Smart Tourism Research. *Sustainability (Basel)*, *12*(8), 3401. doi:10.3390/su12083401

Zhang, Y., Sotiriadis, M. D., & Shen, S. (2022). Investigating the Impact of Smart Tourism Technologies on Tourists' Experiences. *Sustainability (Basel)*, *2022*(14), 3048. doi:10.3390/su14053048

# Chapter 4
# Voyage Virtuoso:
## Artificial Intelligence in Transforming Tourism

**Geetha Manoharan**
https://orcid.org/0000-0002-8644-8871
*SR University, India*

**C. V. Guru Rao**
https://orcid.org/0000-0002-9210-6122
*SR University, India*

**Sunitha Purushottam Ashtikar**
*SR University, India*

**Sanjeev Kumar**
https://orcid.org/0000-0002-7375-7341
*Lovely Professional University, India*

**M. Nivedha**
*Robert Gordon University, UK*

## ABSTRACT

*AI employs complex algorithms and processing power to mimic human reasoning and perform tasks like recognition, interpretation, and decision-making. Artificial intelligence is helping more commercial and industrial sectors boost capacity, optimize operations, and provide better products and services to customers. Tourism has being transformed by AI. The travel industry has created adaptable and responsive environments using AI, machine learning, and deep learning to meet customer needs. The chapter discusses how artificial intelligence (AI) is being used in tourism to enable information processing, intelligent predictive applications, social media opinion deciphering, accommodation, personalized experiences, and destination management. AI's real-time data analysis has revolutionized how travelers plan and start their trips. AI will likely improve traveler experiences and sector organizations' management and services. AI-powered technology also assigns realistic responsibilities to employees, saving time, money, and effort, allowing firms to establish more competitive rates.*

DOI: 10.4018/979-8-3693-1978-9.ch004

## INTRODUCTION TO THE ROLE OF ARTIFICIAL INTELLIGENCE IN TOURISM/TRAVEL INDUSTRY

Advances in technology increase industry productivity. AI revolutionizes technology. Intelligence is quantified and defined. AI is far progressed and employed throughout fields. AI launched'sharing economy', 'IoT', and 'IoP'. AI impacts tourism and other businesses. Travel companies utilize chatbots and other smart tech. New personalized solutions may rearrange tourism's digital revolution. How can we adjust to AI's social disruption? Tech evolves continually. Tourism and hospitality face public health issues like COVID-19. Managers prioritize sustainability, customized services, and social alienation. This chapter discusses AI technology in service interactions and its consequences, advantages, and causes for consumers, personnel, and AI. AI can personalise services, streamline operations, and boost sustainability (Ramachandran K K., et al., 2022). AI chatbots and virtual assistants can swiftly and correctly answer client queries, enhancing customer satisfaction and response times. Machine learning algorithms may assess client behaviour to recommend hotels, activities, and holidays (Razak, A., Nayak, M. P., et al., 2023) Booking, occupancy, and pricing data help AI optimize operations. Inventory and supply chain logistics optimization and revenue management are provided. AI can analyze energy, waste, and environmental data to improve tourism and sustainability. Travel agencies employ AI for administrative and customer support. Cognitive process automation benefits tourism. AI integration may save time, money, remove errors, and speed up project completion at any moment (Hari Krishna S., et al., 2022). AI aids hotel and resort customer service. Artificial intelligence can customize, recommend, and reply fast without human interaction. Artificial intelligence helps and engages consumers, learning and improving future interactions. Hoteliers use AI for data processing, calculations, and complex difficulties.

### Transformation of AI in Travel/Tourism Sector

AI impacts tourism for several reasons. Vacationers must pick a destination, transportation, hotel, and activities. These decisions will considerably impact visitor satisfaction. Many locations, transportation, hotels, and activities need supervision. Tour operators struggle to personalize programs. Companies may get endless customers. Therefore, matching client demand with a product is a challenging AI task. Arriving travelers must traverse foreign customs, languages, cultures, cuisine, and more. AI can plan travel and help with language and culture. Companies may adapt visitor experiences using AI. Though tech-savvy, tourism has limited AI adoption. Most research is done in labs and development. Many industrial and data processing systems use AI. Prediction, robot, conversational, and speech recognition.

Travel and tourism will be dominated by AI. The chapter discusses AI's history and present impact on tourism. Our mission is to build, execute, integrate, and connect AI systems. We explore privacy, labor, and connection in the industry. Humans used to recognize, understand, and make intelligent judgments, but AI employs complicated algorithms and computers to do it. The travel industry has used AI, machine learning, and deep learning to build flexible and adaptable systems (Meenaakumari, M., Jayasuriya, P., et al., 2023). This helps the industry satisfy client requests swiftly. AI improves most travel processes. Integrate it with current platforms or do it separately. Customer chat, language translation, guidance, and personalization are provided by these machines. AI may change hotel room lights, temperature, and music without human intervention. Aviation security utilizes scanning or facial recognition, and travel guides use trend-analysis algorithms. A good reputation requires customer-centric management and great experiences by travel firms. Without human interaction, AI manages requests, customizes services, and satisfies needs. AI is improving tourist safety and comfort. Fast access to any information, regardless of language, improves mobility. Repetitive jobs suit AI. For repeatable, high-quality tasks, this is great. A robust online booking system like Rezdy helps streamline operations and reduce errors. AI can verify data, validate information, and create attractive graphs and charts. Let's examine six key AI travel and tourism applications.

1. Travel booking and planning

   Both tourists and travel specialists may find the process of making, confirming, and finishing travel arrangements tedious and stressful. Fortunately, AI can help. AI may create customized trip itineraries based on a client's prior travel experience or preferences. This lets you personalize services for all your customers with far less effort than before. It also simplifies trip planning since passengers may get customized advice and take virtual tours of places and landmarks before booking. Tour providers can help travelers plan every detail of their trip before leaving.
2. Revenue management

   AI does not immediately enhance tourism revenue. AI can speed up money management. AI is great at processing payments. It includes cash inflows and outflows, so you know your company's remaining capital. In addition, they excel at collecting money for each service, reducing the risk of overcharging customers. This drastically cuts administrative time. Furthermore, AI-driven accounting software for restaurants and tourism companies may help you see sales data in graphs and charts. These tools let you examine your finances and compare real income to projections.
3. Customer service

Every travel and tourism professional knows that customer happiness is crucial. The use of AI to improve customer service is beneficial. AI can do this using chatbots. While your employees are away, chatbots can help clients get the information they need. This protects them from having unanswered questions or difficulties. AI may also survey and poll customers after each interaction to determine satisfaction. This helps you learn how to improve customer service and discover areas of success.

4. Business finances and accounting

Running a business without good financial management and accounting is impossible, but AI helps. Employing self-service tax software helps improve your financial and accounting processes. This tool simplifies and reduces user stress during tax completion. AI-powered software helps companies comply with all rules and regulations, including 2022 ones announced by M. Lourens, R. Raman, P. Vanitha, R. Singh, G. Manoharan, and M. Tiwari. It's also ideal for evaluating and improving record-keeping methods, resulting in better-structured, easier-to-read data.

5. Self-service technology

Travel and tourism firms may not be able to afford specialists for all positions. Process optimization and efficiency are the benefits of self-service technology. AIs are well-suited to that technology. Since AIs are technical systems meant to be intelligent, the key point is obvious. Thus, unlike headphones, they can connect with people at a basic level. In self-service situations, people flourish because they can answer questions autonomously. They may help tourists book from start to finish. They can answer travel and insurance issues and recommend new solutions.

6. Marketing and advertising

Tourism relies on marketing (Manoharan, G., Durai, S., et al., 2024), and artificial intelligence may help. AI solutions like ChatGPT help businesses create excellent advertising campaigns. By helping experts discover and fix flaws in their ideas, they create a stronger final result. ChatGPT may also improve content brainstorming. In particular, ChatGPT simulates human conversations. This tool (Geetha M., et al., 2023) helps professionals finalize their content ideas to create blog posts that appeal to their target audiences and are relevant to their themes. You may use such tools to create SEO-focused content for your website and blog to boost your search engine ranking. Implementing this method will boost your company's popularity and enable you to provide engaging and useful content.

## Various Reviews of Literature That Support Artificial Intelligence in Travel/Tourism Sector

In their 2023 study, García-Madurga and Grilló-Méndez combined literature on artificial intelligence in tourism. Themes, strengths, and flaws will be identified and further studied in this synthesis. AI will also be discussed in tourism. Quickly growing AI technology is altering tourism and other sectors. A comprehensive 'overview of reviews' method was employed to discover, assess, and aggregate previous review articles. Web of Science allowed us to study 31 tourist AI scholarly reviews. AI technology in tourism is fully explained. AI solution professionals and academics may find this website useful. This academically significant study may influence tourism AI research, promote its efficient and sustainable use, and boost technology and sustainability research. Corporations enter a lot of consumer data into AI systems, yielding sensitive customer data, according to Mohd Shith Putera, N.S., Saripan, H., Mohd Bajury, M.S., and Ya'cob, S.N. However, privacy considerations arise. This portal helps AI researchers and professionals develop. Case studies and doctrinal techniques were used to organize AI-based tourist legal thinking. To prevent legal responsibility and maintain customer trust, tourist sector participants must ensure data privacy and security throughout life.

Dogru, T., Line, N.D., Mody, M., Hanks, L., Abbott, J., Acikgoz, F., Assaf, et al. (2023) state that generative artificial intelligence (GAI) offers hospitality and tourism (HT) opportunities in operations, design, marketing, destination management, human resources, revenue management, accounting and finance, strategic management, and more. In healthcare technology (HT), organizations must examine ethical, legal, social, and economic effects of General Artificial Intelligence (GAI). This study will explore how GAI applications affect HT stakeholders. This sector's academic research should integrate practical and intellectual understanding. Using the stakeholder theory of the corporation, researchers, professors, and businessmen assessed GAI's pros and cons. We also analyze how academics may address the problematic research aspects of this rapidly developing technological challenge.

The tourism industry uses AI and big data to engage and satisfy consumers. Report by Çeltek and İlhan, 2020. Tourism professionals improve customer service with big data insights. Due of its benefits, operations will utilize AI. Tourism, like other industries, uses AI to save expenses. AI-driven hotel marketing is common. Technology will enable tourism specialists to employ big data and AI to meet client expectations. Artificial intelligence will change tourism. Advantages and disadvantages of AI and big data are discussed here. This includes tourist examples. Theam, T.S., Veloo, P., Hussain, N.H., and Luu, Y.K. demonstrate in 2021 that AI can enhance tourism and hospitality operations and provide unique passenger experiences. Malaysia's tourism and hospitality operations leverage AI for e-Hailing, e-Wallet, e-Gate, and e-Visa. A study on tourist pleasure. These 200 self-administered questionnaires were from local and international over-18s with travel experience. E-Hailing, e-Gate, and e-Wallet boost passenger happiness dramatically. It seems that e-Visa does not affect passenger pleasure. Tourism and hospitality promotion in Malaysia is supported by this study. This may help Malaysian tourism and hospitality authorities use AI more.

Kong, Wang, Qiu, Cheung, and Bu, N.T. published research. AI research in hotels and tourism will be assessed in 2022. This study will cover AI research's substance, disciplines, terminology, and trends. After referrals, we chose 491 Web of Science core collection papers. Gephi and VOSviewer assess 1991–2021 documents. Publications and references in AI research have increased rapidly since 1991, especially after 2018. This increase indicates academic AI interest. AI research covers technology, adoption, consumer perception, and trends. Early AI technology was replaced by user views and AI openness. Results enhance comprehension, reveal research gaps, and guide further study. Travel destinations, governments, and hotels may learn from the findings. The results assist governments, tourist destinations, and hotels. An AI research project in tourism and hospitality is the first of its kind.

Solakis, Katsoni, A.B. Mahmoud, and N. Grigoriou carefully evaluated this. (2022) AI and automation recognize customer-related factors and technology that affect hospitality and tourism value co-creation. Tourist-related customer-based factors and technologies Theoretical literature analysis examines VCC. The authors provide a theoretical framework for VCC in AI-driven tourism by reviewing relevant research. Artificial intelligence is used to study VCC client traits. Credibility, trust, social influence, hedonic incentives, anthropomorphism, and prior experience of clients. Metaversal tourism, service robots, AI-enabled self-service kiosks, chatbots, and ML/NLP affect VCC. This paper lays the groundwork for future research on human and AI components to improve tourist VCC models. VCC customer engagement with automation and AI is understudied.

Studying Du, Sun, Jiao, Li, J., and Liu, L. Tourism confronts new "Internet + Ice and Snow Tourism." challenges in 2022. Internet integration has expanded tourism's market. This increasing market comprises internet users, purchasers, and buyers' means. In leisure and tourism, mobile ice and snow tourism is discussed. Analysis of this integration's projected expansion, notably in mobile Internet. absence of functional area definition, wide gap between industry innovation and demand, inadequate industrial informatization, and absence of market service credit were observed in the ice and snow tourist sector. Ice and snow tourism development via "one network, three places, and one platform" is our idea. The tourism network's "Three New Coverage Projects" and "Internet + Tourism." cross-business partnership mechanism are pushed. Internet and PR will boost tourism services' credibility and efficiency. The local economy should expand 51.28% with these strategies. With present conditions, "Internet + ice and snow tourism" is inevitable.

The authors of AI and interactive technology include Sobhani, Armaghan, Haghir, and Garmaroodi. Identifying users in 2022 will boost social connection and industrial customization. Interactive and smart technology influences visitor personalization and collective experience design. Promoting tourism online boosts reputation and efficiency. Researchers study human cognition and experience to better computer-human interaction. Sensation is non-linguistic, study shows. Happiness boosts mood and socializing. An intelligent building system and facial expressions evaluate users' emotions in this project. It innovates methods to connect customers' emotions to locations. This research measures how environmental changes affect users' social ties.

According to Goel, R., Singh, T., Baral, S.K., Sahdev, S.L., and Gupta, S. (2022), AI is helping the Indian tourism sector. It will explore safer and longer trips. Tech-friendly travel and tourism is the first thought. Technology powers booking and checkout. Report examines AI's impact on India's travel industry. Growing India may lead tourism. Only a few well-known innovations, such as multilingual translators, chatbots, and virtual reality, improve tourism and travel. We'll examine AI and robots in India's travel industry.

According to Fang W (2022), cultural tourism combines culture and tourism. Author suggests meeting spiritual, cultural, and recreational needs while promoting growth. Tourist attractions are spread, and each city often has the highest market value. Culture tourism market value affects growth and industry. Numerous cultural tourism business traits can be extracted and recognized. The Gabor wavelet and DT-CWT extract textural features. We use multiscale DT-CWT and Gabor-based algorithms to detect cultural tourism. Cultural tourism pictures are leveled by the Gaussian pyramid. Next, Gabor and DT-CWT extract multiscale image attributes. Fusions occur. Evaluation of SVM classifier feature extraction. This article's method appears to be common.

Research by Jabeen, Zaidi, and Dhaheri. Frameworks are needed to prioritize hospitality and tourism automation and AI in 2021. The analytic hierarchy prioritized automation and AI deployment. The study modeled 23 sub-criteria from earlier research into five criteria: human knowledge, services, robotics applications, internal environment, and institutional environment. A paired comparison questionnaire was inspired by this research's hierarchical structure. The importance of hierarchy factors was compared using a nine-point ordinal scale. Staff from 35 top UAE hotels and tourist firms tried it. Services, robots, and human skills drove automation and AI adoption. Sustainable automation and AI can be implemented by hotel and tourism professionals and academics. Paradigm may aid hotel and tourism AI research. This study has given policymakers a framework to address global hospitality and tourism automation and AI integration issues. Results inform sector research.

Travel is now a popular pastime as living standards rise. Global tourism is popular. The wealthy thrive on it. GT developers cater to this lifestyle. GT has promoted regional change, economic and social growth, and poverty reduction despite slow progress. M cited poor tourist marketing (Manoharan, G., & Narayanan, S., 2021), planning, management, and qualified staff as barriers to integrated tourism industry (TI) growth. Article authored by A., R., F. Effendy, G. Manoharan, M. John Paul, and M. Aarif in 2023. TI must build GT, resolve discrepancies, meet market demand, follow industrial progress, and sustain GT. An AI model and questionnaire assess GT TI development in this study. TI and local tourism will benefit from AI. Young and old use global technology as technology integration (TI) improves. More people don't know about TI integration, says the poll. In contrast to young and elderly people, middle-aged people understand this topic and support TI integration. Television and smartphones inform most respondents about GT. The authors are Wang, G., Dong, T., Chu, Y., Shi, D., Ding, J., and Chen, C. Practical, this method meets modern needs.

## NEED FOR THE CHAPTER

Its potential has made artificial intelligence in tourism important and popular. This chapter covers tourism's current situation and change using AI. AI was utilized to tailor consumer experiences, arrange travel and lodging, and investigate immediate customer care with chatbots, according to the literature. Traveler behavior and tastes were also analyzed using data analytics. Using predictive modeling helps estimate demand, allocate resources, and optimize resources. Smart destinations use artificial intelligence to optimize traffic management, infrastructure, and city planning. Information privacy and biases in tourist AI systems must be examined. The chapter studies how artificial intelligence revolutionizes the tourism sector and improves travel experiences for companies and visitors to solve and comprehend the possible difficulties from the aforementioned literature.

## AI Within the Tourism / TRAVEL INDUSTRY

### 1. Online Customer Service Chatbots

Tourism firms benefit from AI, particularly for online customer care. Chatbots on social networking and IM are popular. AI can provide valuable customer insights without human intervention. Online customers expect quicker response times, and AI helps companies perform faster.

## 2. Personal service

Despite being popular for online customer care, AI is increasingly employed in-person. According to A. Shameem et al., 2023, this technology minimizes information or reception desk wait times and boosts efficiency. Hilton's intelligent robot 'Connie' utilizes it. Tourists get travel advice from an AI-powered robot. Robots learn from every human interaction, improving future interactions.

## 3. Data Analysis/Processing

Travel & tourism AI extends beyond customer service. Its major and effective application is data collecting and analysis to figure out consumer, company, and price strategies (Kumar, S., Kumar, P., et al., 202). This domain's key advantage of artificial intelligence is its ability to quickly and accurately evaluate large amounts of data. Similar processes for people might take longer and may include more errors. AI examines survey, review, and online poll data at Dorchester Collection. Artificial intelligence helps the hotel analyze consumer sentiment in real time.

## 4. Speech-activated assistant

AI is being used in travel and tourism to provide voice-based digital assistance. Hotels may now have voice assistants that answer questions and make requests instantly. Controlling room functions and accessing tourist information 24/7 is possible using speech recognition technology. Voice-based digital help on robots allows customer care desks to function without humans, especially during off-peak hours (B. Nagarjuna, et al., 2022).

## 5. Flight Pattern Prediction

Travel flight projections are increasingly affected by AI. This field uses flight data. Big data analysis and pattern recognition benefit from artificial intelligence. Weather patterns, past flight durations, and aircraft speed trends may be used by AI-powered algorithms to accurately anticipate flight arrival timings and delay durations. Program users benefit from more reliable and exact estimates.

## 6. Social Media Channel Analysis

The tourist business may benefit from social media (S. Mekala, M. Bhuvana, et al., 2024; G. Manoharan A. VM, E., 2024). AI. AI can help social media companies comprehend content and users. Daily interactions on certain social media sites make manual monitoring and assessment difficult. AI can recognize trends, analyze sentiments, and improve audience understanding.

## 7. Flexibility Pricing

Tourist firms use dynamic pricing to modify rates depending on demand and supply. Tourism companies like hotels, airlines, and others may benefit from AI strategy optimization. AI can quickly organize and assess data, simplifying intelligent pricing adjustment and accuracy. Prices may be higher during high demand months than low demand months. Using new factors, artificial intelligence may make intelligent evaluations.

## 8. Intelligent Luggage Processing

Tourism uses AI for baggage security. AI can sort bags and reduce missing ones. AI can also categorize misplaced bags. Secure AI is possible. AI can detect questionable objects in baggage shots at airport security. Next, an alarm system may warn security of unusual activities.

## 9. AI Facial Recognition

Face recognition is automated by AI. Using face traits, this method compares real-time photographs to database images to identify people. Cutting-edge facial recognition technology can identify people in seconds. In tourism, AI-powered face recognition is used for security. This might be used at airports to identify interesting people. Facial recognition provides security by counting individuals.

## 10. Tailored Vacation

trip and tourism agencies employ AI to personalize trip experiences early on. Travel booking websites often experience this. The booking process may include smart recommendations. AI may utilize a user's search history and seen content to propose hotels and holidays (Abdulwahid, A. H., Pattnaik, M., et al., 2023) Amazon recommends items based on past purchases or browsing habits. The travel and tourism business customizes travel experiences early on using AI.

## 11. Managing Travel Delays

Forecasting in the tourism industry uses AI significantly. It may reduce travel interruptions and solve issues. Using historical data, AI can forecast flight delays.

Artificial intelligence may foresee problems and provide remedies using weather predictions and previous data.

## 12. Revenue Control Increased by AI

When the proper product, price, and technique are offered to the right customer, revenue management maximizes sales. Its data-driven approach helps the travel and tourism business maximize earnings. Cognitive computing helps categorize massive data sets. Reservations, available rooms or seats, forthcoming events, and past demand figures are included. J. K. S. Al-Safi, A. Bansal, M. Aarif, M. S. Z. Almahairah, G. Manoharan, and F. J. Alotoum wrote in 2023 that the AI may change pricing and distribution methods to optimize financial returns.

## 13. Airspace and airplane maintenance service reports

Airline investments in predictive analytics are rising because it may reduce financial costs from unexpected operational problems that stop planes. The best maintenance time and probable concerns may be determined via AI and predictive analytics. AI can help airlines and other travel and tourist companies adapt to circumstances with little inconvenience.

## 14. Employee scheduling software

AI may enhance workforce management and scheduling in hotels, airlines, and other tourist organizations. The various variables in big firms make scheduling difficult and time-consuming. Artificial intelligence (B. Bijeta Nayak G. Manoharan, et al., 2024) analyses data points like employees' working hours, the need for experienced staff during each shift, contractual obligations, approved holidays, and mandatory rest periods to generate feasible work schedules.

## 15. Demand and Price Forecasting

Modern customers want the best prices, yet several factors affect hotel, flight, and other business prices. Artificial intelligence-driven software may help travel and tourism clients comprehend pricing fluctuations. Customers may be notified when hotel room prices in a certain place will increase using the program. Meanwhile, the software helps customers understand abrupt demand changes to make the best travel or accommodation plans.

## 16. Enable consumer loyalty schemes

Incentivizing customers to return is vital to customer loyalty programs. Additionally, a customer loyalty program must give attractive benefits, which links the travel and tourist company to AI. Through online monitoring, transaction histories, and sign-up choices, AI can provide loyalty program participants with highly personalized benefits that enhance client retention.

## 17. Payment Fraud Detection and Intervention

Artificial intelligence can detect and minimize financial fraud in tourism organizations. Behavior analysis and pattern recognition aid with this. By analyzing historical fraud data, attempted payment fraud may be detected before it causes major damage. Human intervention may be prompted by alerts for potentially harmful conduct.

## 18. Travel Delay Communication

Flight delays, misplaced baggage, and lengthy security queues hinder travel. Customers require accurate information from travel companies, therefore they must communicate accurately. Travelers may get AI warnings. An AI system can anticipate delay time and send emails and texts in advance. AI-powered chatbots handle passenger inquiries for travel and tourist organizations.

# ISSUES RELATED TO TOURISTS' ADOPTION AND USE OF AI

Initial AI challenges include people's beliefs, attitudes, and impressions of the technology. As with other technology users, Rogers (2010) classifies tourists as innovators, early adopters, early majority, late majority, and laggards. Tussyadiah and Miller (2019) identified three sets of users based on the potential risks and benefits of AI: laggards (who see significant risks and minimal benefits), aficionados, and realists. Those who have not used AI technology likely to dislike it, according to Tussyadiah and Miller (2019). Users accept and employ robots based on their perceived usefulness and efficacy (Bowen and Morosan 2018). Gretzel (2011) advises researching actual use, use patterns, and nonuse rather than intentions of use. User benefits and risks of AI are many. AI helps visitors navigate unknown places, reducing their anxiety (Buhalis et al., 2019). It may also encourage new and meaningful interactions (Li et al. 2019). Visitors worry about being watched, artificial intelligence dividing them, and a tech-driven world. According to Gretzel (2011) and Tussyadiah and Miller (2019), AI systems may violate privacy. They can detect patterns in massive data sets. AI might create a separation as the digital divide did at the start of the century owing to restricted availability. Security concerns may limit AI use. In a tech-driven world, tourists may have to choose between highly automated, efficient, and cost-effective services or less automated, premium ones that emphasize human interaction. As said, hotels may connect.

## Challenges for AI in the Tourism Sector

Despite increasing AI growth, uneducated people use it little (Reddy, 2006). When required, fresh ideas, technology, and legislation will overcome obstacles. The topic of whether AI can replace human intellect is raised by its capacity to replace human efforts in various industries, yet many economic sectors are skeptical. Since "Artificial Intelligence" is still developing, it cannot yet outperform human intelligence (Laurent et al., 2015). However, it may replace workers and provide a unique customer experience. AI faces serious data security issues. Use of AI in finance and defense raises concerns. The blockchain secures Facial Recognition software data. Many governments are wary of facial recognition technology owing to privacy and data security concerns (Bowyer, 2004). Chatbots in hotels save prior purchases and trip experiences, posing data privacy and security issues. Data privacy and security are difficult (Kannan and Bernoff, 2019). Software-controlled services are vulnerable to tiny viral assaults, which may interrupt software programs and service providers' operations, causing chaos. Despite AI technology's sophisticated and forward-thinking character, small service companies cannot afford its high investment (Murphy et al., 2017). Although chatbots and robots may replace people, customers still need them for difficult tasks. Chatbots can only answer basic inquiries like machines. These tools answer inquiries using keywords. In emergency and complex issues, consumers rely on personnel (Lommatzsch, 2018).

# DISCUSSION AND CONCLUSION

Traveling smart helps cities become more connected. Use of new information technology has enhanced municipal services in cities. Innovating smart tourism demands several systems. Fast-track smart technology adoption and economic development model adaptation to boost tourist attractions and services (Manoharan, G., Durai, S., et al., 2023) Easy urban public services, social management, and other field informa-tion. Brainstorming to identify and solve problems promotes creativity and growth in cities. This will boost the city's importance and quality of life. New intelligent tourist service technology is developed by the intelligent customer service system for scenic locations employing unique information service approaches

(Ponduri, S. B., Ahmad, S. S., et al., 2024). Explore resources and extend gorgeous site information consulting services to enhance visitors' experiences. Intelligent scenic site customer service provides quick, secure, trustworthy, adaptive, and tailored information consultancy to international and domestic tourists. Instead, it highlights the information service process's advantages, ensuring sustained and positive tourism growth. Intelligent scenic areas will prioritize resources and environmental monitoring. IT, big data, and public services will integrate environmental protection information systems. Environmental consultancy can fully automate resources and settings. Sustainability is supported by tourism site selection.

In tourism, AI is quickly enhancing customer service, operational efficiency, travel experience customization, and sustainability. Despite an increase in research on this issue, a comprehensive and coordinated literature evaluation is required to establish the best AI applications and recommend topics for additional study. AI deployments in tourism have grown. The operational processes of major AI implementations are covered in this chapter (Thavamani, S., Mahesh, D., et al., 2022; Manoharan, K. G., Nehru, J. A., & Balasubramanian, S., AI can boost air and marine airline and company performance and satisfaction. As AI technology advances, new uses emerge. Overall, AI will benefit travel and tourism professionals. This technology is crucial for contemporary tourism firms. While examining humanity and human civilization, evaluate humanity's connection with other living creatures that manage human resources (Deviprasad, S., Madhumithaa, N., et al., 2023). Life is valued to preserve species diversity. A minimum renewable resource usage threshold and life system protection are needed. To thrive, historic tourism requires new values. New values will promote sustainable historical tourism (Satpathy, Samal, et al., 2023). Historical tourism sustainability stimulates expansion. It proposes a new path to responsible historical site tourist resource use. It connects humans and nature and instills environmental responsibility and morals in future generations. Sustainability expands heritage tourist development. It reinvents historical site responsible tourism resource development.

## REFERENCES

Abdulwahid, A. H., Pattnaik, M., Palav, M. R., Babu, S. T., Manoharan, G., & Selvi, G. P. (2023, April). Library Management System Using Artificial Intelligence. In *2023 Eighth International Conference on Science Technology Engineering and Mathematics (ICONSTEM)* (pp. 1-7). IEEE.

Al-Safi, J. K. S., Bansal, A., Aarif, M., Almahairah, M. S. Z., Manoharan, G., & Alotoum, F. J. (2023). Assessment Based On IoT For Efficient Information Surveillance Regarding Harmful Strikes Upon Financial Collection. *2023 International Conference on Computer Communication and Informatics (ICCCI)*, Coimbatore, India. 10.1109/ICCCI56745.2023.10128500

Bijeta, B., Sharma, V., Lourens, M., Kumar, A., & Hinge, P. (2024). Design and Empirical Analysis of a Artificial Intelligence-Based Human Resource Management Processing Systems for Detecting Personal Stress. 6th International Conference on Contemporary Computing and Informatics (IC3I), 2421-2426.

Bowen, J., & Morosan, C. (2018). Beware hospitality industry: The robots are coming. *Worldwide Hospitality and Tourism Themes*, *10*(6), 726–733. doi:10.1108/WHATT-07-2018-0045

Bowyer, K. W. (2004). Face recognition technology: Security versus privacy. *IEEE Technology and Society Magazine*, *23*(1), 9–19. doi:10.1109/MTAS.2004.1273467

Buhalis, D., Harwood, T., Bogicevic, V., Viglia, G., Beldona, S., & Hofacker, C. (2019). Technological disruptions in services: Lessons from tourism and hospitality. *Journal of Service Management*, *30*(4), 484–506. doi:10.1108/JOSM-12-2018-0398

Çeltek, E., & İlhan, İ. (2020). *Big Data*. Artificial Intelligence, and Their Implications in the Tourism Industry.

Colque, J., Manoharan A., Thomson Fredrik, E., Kumar, N., & Torres-Cruz, F. (2024). A Deep Learning Approaches for Natural Language Processing and Sentiment Analysis in Social Media. *6th International Conference on Contemporary Computing and Informatics (IC3I),* (pp. 1746-1750). IEEE.

Deviprasad, S., Madhumithaa, N., Vikas, I. W., Yadav, A., & Manoharan, G. (2023). The Machine Learning-Based Task Automation Framework for Human Resource Management in MNC Companies. *Engineering Proceedings*, *59*(1), 63.

Dogru, T., Line, N. D., Mody, M., Hanks, L., Abbott, J., Acikgoz, F., Assaf, A. G., Bakir, S., Berbekova, A., Bilgihan, A., Dalton, A. N., Erkmen, E., Geronasso, M., Gomez, D., Graves, S., Iskender, A., Ivanov, S., Kizildag, M., Lee, M., & Zhang, T. C. (2023). Generative Artificial Intelligence in the Hospitality and Tourism Industry: Developing a Framework for Future Research. *Journal of Hospitality & Tourism Research (Washington, D.C.)*, 10963480231188663. doi:10.1177/10963480231188663

Du, H., Sun, W., Jiao, Y., Li, J., & Liu, L. (2022). Countermeasures for the Development of Data Integration of the Internet Ice and Snow Tourism Industry under the Background of Artificial Intelligence. *Applied Bionics and Biomechanics*, *2022*, 2022. doi:10.1155/2022/8496766 PMID:35528531

Fang, W. (2022). Cultural Tourism Industry Feature Extraction Based on Multiscale Feature Fusion Algorithm and Artificial Intelligence. *Mathematical Problems in Engineering*, *2022*, 1–8. doi:10.1155/2022/5946166

García-Madurga, M., & Grilló-Méndez, A. (2023). Artificial Intelligence in the Tourism Industry: An Overview of Reviews. *Administrative Sciences*, *13*(8), 172. doi:10.3390/admsci13080172

Goel, R., Singh, T., Baral, S. K., Sahdev, S. L., & Gupta, S. (2022). The Era of Artificial Intelligence Reforming Tourism Industry in Society 5.0. *2022 10th International Conference on Reliability, Infocom Technologies and Optimization (Trends and Future Directions) (ICRITO)*, (pp. 1-4). IEEE.

Gretzel, U. (2011). Intelligent systems in tourism: A social science perspective. *Annals of Tourism Research*, *38*(3), 757–779. doi:10.1016/j.annals.2011.04.014

Gretzel, U., Sigala, M., Xiang, Z., & Koo, C. (2015). Smart tourism: Foundations and developments. *Electronic Markets*, *25*(3), 179–188. doi:10.1007/s12525-015-0196-8

Jabeen, F., Zaidi, S. A., & Dhaheri, M. H. (2021). Automation and artificial intelligence in hospitality and tourism. *Tourism Review*.

Kannan, P., & Bernoff, J. (2019). The future of customer service is AI-Human collaboration. *MIT Sloan Management Review*.

Kong, H., Wang, K., Qiu, X., Cheung, C., & Bu, N. T. (2022). 30 years of artificial intelligence (AI) research relating to the hospitality and tourism industry. *International Journal of Contemporary Hospitality Management.*

Kumar, S., Kumar, P., Ahmad, S. S., Jayasaradadevi, P., Rajeyyagari, S., Manoharan, G., & Radhakrishnan, V. (2024). A Novel Approach for IoT-Based Cloud Computing Technology and its Impact on Business Entrepreneurship. *International Journal of Intelligent Systems and Applications in Engineering*, *12*(10s), 624–628.

Kunekar, P., Manoharan, G., Mekala, S., Bhuvana, M., Brat Gupta, D., & Bhatt, V. (2024). Natural Language Processing and Deep Learning Techniques to Improve Sentiment Analysis in Social Media Texts. *6th International Conference on Contemporary Computing and Informatics (IC3I),* (pp. 1751-1755). IEEE.

Laurent, P., Chollet, T., & Herzberg, E. (2015). *Intelligent automation entering the business world.* Deloitte. www2.deloitte.com/content/dam/Deloitte/lu/Documents/operations/lu-intelligent-automation business-world.pdf.

Li, J. J., Bonn, M. A., & Ye, B. H. (2019). Hotel employee's artificial intelligence and robotics awareness and its impact on turnover intention: The moderating roles of perceived organizational support and competitive psychological climate. *Tourism Management*, *73*, 172–181. doi:10.1016/j.tourman.2019.02.006

Lommatzsch, A. (2018). A next generation Chatbot-Framework for the public administration. *International Conference on Innovations for Community Services.* Springer. 10.1007/978-3-319-93408-2_10

Lourens, M., Raman, R., Vanitha, P., Singh, R., Manoharan, G., & Tiwari, M. (2022). *Agile Technology and Artificial Intelligent Systems in Business Development.* 2022 5th International Conference on Contemporary Computing and Informatics (IC3I), Uttar Pradesh, India. 10.1109/IC3I56241.2022.10073410

Manoharan, G., Ashtikar, S., Nithya, P., & Maheshwari, V. (2023). Social media marketing influence on usage as a brand choice towards users in varied district. *BioGecko*, *12*(2), 2234-2242.

Manoharan, G., Durai, S., Ashtikar, S. P., & Kumari, N. (2024). Artificial Intelligence in Marketing Applications. In Artificial Intelligence for Business (pp. 40-70). Productivity Press.

Manoharan, G., Durai, S., Rajesh, G. A., Razak, A., Rao, C. B., & Ashtikar, S. P. (2023). A study of postgraduate students' perceptions of key components in ICCC to be used in artificial intelligence-based smart cities. In *Artificial Intelligence and Machine Learning in Smart City Planning* (pp. 117–133). Elsevier. doi:10.1016/B978-0-323-99503-0.00003-X

Manoharan, G., Durai, S., Rajesh, G. A., Razak, A., Rao, C. B., & Ashtikar, S. P. (2023). A study on the perceptions of officials on their duties and responsibilities at various levels of the organizational structure in order to accomplish artificial intelligence-based smart city implementation. In *Artificial Intelligence and Machine Learning in Smart City Planning* (pp. 1–10). Elsevier. doi:10.1016/B978-0-323-99503-0.00007-7

Manoharan, G., & Narayanan, S. (2021). A research study to investigate the feasibility of digital marketing strategies in advertising. *PalArch's Journal of Archaeology of Egypt/Egyptology, 18*(09), 450-456.

Manoharan, K. G., Nehru, J. A., & Balasubramanian, S. (2021). *Artificial Intelligence and IoT*. Springer. doi:10.1007/978-981-33-6400-4

Meenaakumari, M., Jayasuriya, P., Dhanraj, N., Sharma, S., Manoharan, G., & Tiwari, M. (2022, December). Loan Eligibility Prediction using Machine Learning based on Personal Information. In *2022 5th International Conference on Contemporary Computing and Informatics (IC3I)* (pp. 1383-1387). IEEE. 10.1109/IC3I56241.2022.10073318

Mohd Shith Putera, N. S., Saripan, H., Mohd Bajury, M. S., & Ya'cob, S. N. (2022). *Artificial Intelligence in the Tourism Industry: A privacy impasse*. Environment-Behaviour Proceedings Journal.

Murphy, J., Hofacker, C., & Gretzel, U. (2017). Dawning of the age of robots in hospitality and tourism: Challenges for teaching and research. *European Journal of Tourism Research, 15*, 104–111. doi:10.54055/ejtr.v15i.265

Nagar, R., Singh, Y., Gobinath, R., & Manoharan, G. (2022). Aspects of medical tourism in India: A review. *AIP Conference Proceedings, 2418*, 020030. doi:10.1063/5.0093282

Ponduri, S. B., Ahmad, S. S., Ravisankar, P., Thakur, D. J., Chawla, K., Chary, D. T., & Sharma, S. (2024). A Study on Recent Trends of Technology and its Impact on Business and Hotel Industry. *Migration Letters : An International Journal of Migration Studies, 21*(S1), 801–806.

Razak, A., Nayak, M. P., Manoharan, G., Durai, S., Rajesh, G. A., Rao, C. B., & Ashtikar, S. P. (2023). Reigniting the power of artificial intelligence in education sector for the educators and students competence. In *Artificial Intelligence and Machine Learning in Smart City Planning* (pp. 103–116). Elsevier. doi:10.1016/B978-0-323-99503-0.00009-0

Reddy, R. (2006). Robotics and intelligent systems in support of society. *IEEE Intelligent Systems, 21*(3), 24–31. doi:10.1109/MIS.2006.57

Rogers, E. M. (2010). *Diffusion of innovations*. Simon and Schuster.

Satpathy, A., Samal, A., Gupta, S., Kumar, S., Sharma, S., Manoharan, G., Karthikeyan, M., & Sharma, S. (2024). To Study the Sustainable Development Practices in Business and Food Industry. *Migration Letters : An International Journal of Migration Studies, 21*(S1), 743–747. doi:10.59670/ml.v21iS1.6400

Shameem, A., Ramachandran, K. K., Sharma, A., Singh, R., Selvaraj, F. J., & Manoharan, G. *The Rising Importance of AI in Boosting the Efficiency of Online Advertising in Developing Countries.* 2023 3rd International Conference on Advance Computing and Innovative Technologies in Engineering (ICACITE), Greater Noida, India. 10.1109/ICACITE57410.2023.10182754

Sobhani, S. R., Armaghan, N., Haghir, S., & Garmaroodi, A. A. (2022). The Impact of Interactive technology by using Artificial Intelligence on the Formation of Social Interactions: A Study in Tourism Industry 4.0. *2022 IEEE 28th International Conference on Engineering, Technology and Innovation (ICE/ITMC) & 31st International Association For Management of Technology (IAMOT) Joint Conference*, (pp. 1-7). IEEE.

Solakis, K., Katsoni, V., Mahmoud, A.B., & Grigoriou, N. (2022). Factors affecting value co-creation through artificial intelligence in tourism: a general literature review. *Journal of Tourism Futures.*

Thavamani, S., Mahesh, D., Sinthuja, U., & Manoharan, G. (2022, May). Crucial attacks in internet of things via artificial intelligence techniques: The security survey. In AIP Conference Proceedings (Vol. 2418, No. 1). AIP Publishing.

Theam, T. S., Veloo, P., Hussain, N. H., & Luu, Y. K. (2021). *Travellers' Satisfaction on the Applications of Artificial Intelligence in Malaysia's Tourism and Hospitality Industry.* Asia Proceedings of Social Sciences.

Tripathi, M. A., Tripathi, R., Effendy, F., Manoharan, G., John Paul, M., & Aarif, M. (2023). An In-Depth Analysis of the Role That ML and Big Data Play in Driving Digital Marketing's Paradigm Shift. *2023 International Conference on Computer Communication and Informatics (ICCCI)*, Coimbatore, India. 10.1109/ICCCI56745.2023.10128357

Tussyadiah, I., & Miller, G. (2019). Perceived impacts of artificial intelligence and responses to positive behaviour change intervention. In *Information and communication technologies in tourism 2019* (pp. 359–370). Springer. doi:10.1007/978-3-030-05940-8_28

Wang, G., Dong, T., Chu, Y., Shi, D., Ding, J., & Chen, C. (2021). The Integrated Development Evaluation of Tourism Industry from the Perspective of Global Tourism Based on Artificial Intelligence Model. *2021 3rd International Conference on Artificial Intelligence and Advanced Manufacture.*

# Chapter 5
# A Review of the Pre- and Post-COVID-19 Effects on the Tourism and Entertainment Industries:
## Innovative Methods and Predicted Challenges

**Saumendra Das**
https://orcid.org/0000-0003-4956-4352
*GIET University, India*

**N. V. J. Rao**
*GIET University, India*

**Dwipanita Mishra**
*GIET University, India*

**Rohit Bansal**
https://orcid.org/0000-0001-7072-5005
*Vaish College of Engineering, India*

## ABSTRACT

*The outbreak of the deadly coronavirus (SARS-CoV-2) miserably ruined the desire and expectations of everyone in the entire world. The severity of the virus not only affected the health of an individual but also pushed the world economy into disaster. Most of the countries subsided it through temporary lockdown and partially secured human life by employing vaccines and other remedies. However, the impact of Covid-19 was considered a challenge for many in terms of survival and sustainability. Hence this chapter has attempted to identify several issues about the impact of Covid-19 and provided some intelligent solutions for sustainable recovery. In this regard, the study has chosen two industries, i.e. tourism and entertainment, which contribute to a balanced economy for the growth and development of any nation. The impact study of Covid-19 will be helpful for academicians, researchers, and policymakers to identify the problems and to overcome the challenges associated with the epidemic through intelligent solutions.*

DOI: 10.4018/979-8-3693-1978-9.ch005

## INTRODUCTION

The deadly coronavirus was initially detected in the city of Wuhan, China during the last week of December 2019. This disease was identified as a primary form of pneumonia that caused damage to the respiratory organ, lungs, liver and other major areas of the human body. On 31st January 2020, the World Health Organization (WHO) confirmed Covid-19 as an epidemic and on 11th March 2020 considered a global pandemic according to the harshness of the disease spread. Due to the severity of the virus's spread, the impact of Covid-19 has shut down the entire globe for around eight months and destroyed the world economy. Many industries have closed their production and supply which directly hit the employment and revenue across the globe. The multi-stage mutation of the deadly coronavirus has changed the hopes and aspirations of individuals (Das et al, 2022). The partial lockdown, social distancing, therapeutic medicines, mask and sanitization may have provided some relief but not controlled the spread of the virus completely. As of 8th July 2022, the spread of coronavirus is affected 228 countries with 559,860,508 confirmed cases and 6,371,761 death cases worldwide. The inception of the Covid-19 vaccine has controlled the spread and around 532,851,614 people recovered from the disease (Debata et al, 2020). Figure 1 exhibited the top ten countries confirmed death cases till 8th July 2022.

*Figure 1. Top ten countries with highest confirmed and death cases*
*Source: https://www.worldometers.info/coronavirus/*

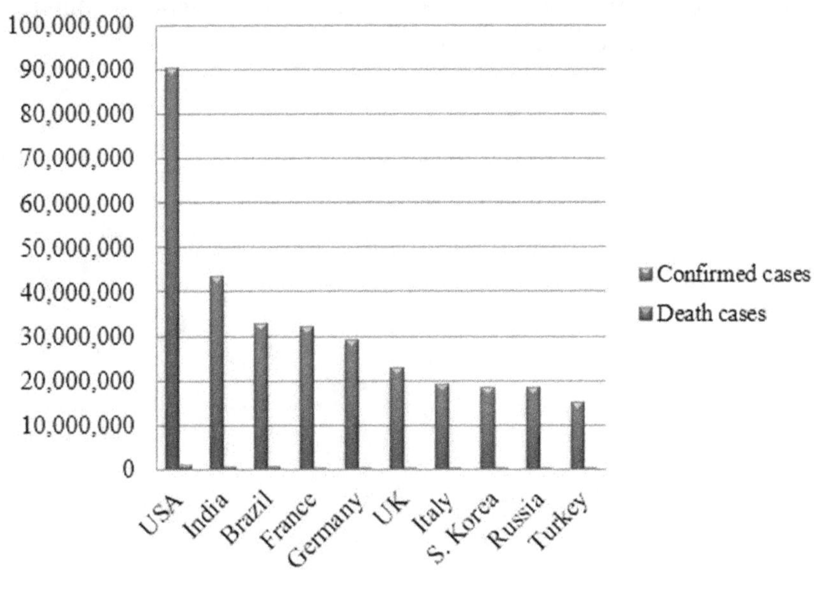

The outbreak of the pandemic has exaggerated a sense of fear and uncertainty among people in terms of job and pay loss. The countrywide lockdown triggered the trade and business into a cut short and forced the bread earners to stay at the home. The impact of the pandemic pushed the revenue down and affected major industries such as tourism, hotels, aviation, entertainment, manufacturing, start-ups etc. The outbreak of Covid-19 not only affected the industries but also destroyed the people's expectations, environment and economy. Most of the migrant workers have returned to their homes due to curfew restrictions imposed by the government. The schools, colleges and religious places have been closed and restrictions initiated on travel. The skies became clear with a 71 per cent decrease in nitrogen dioxide level and indicated purified water in the river Ganga. The Covid-19 pandemic disrupted the world economy as production and consumption were scaled down. A developing country like India was not resistant to such kind of external shock also. The Indian tourism, hotel and aviation industries have suffered a loss of 5 lakh crore, 30,000 crores and 8,200. The agricultural sector has also been affected hugely. There is an acceleration in demand observed for wheat, vegetable and other kinds of crops during that period. The aforesaid counterattacks of Covid-19 on export and import business have also been noticed (Ghosh et al, 2020). Hence it could be observed that the impact of Covid-19 severely destroyed the economy and human life but significantly improved the environment from pollution (Nayak et al, 2022). The Covid-19 crisis has not only distressed human life but also created massive disruption across the world. In their study, the authors have articulated the possible impact of Covid-19 on six different industries such as education, tourism, publishing, automobiles, food and supply and agriculture and provided strategic steps for the revival and recovery of those industries (Brem et al, 2021). Figure 2 exhibited the major industries affected due to Covid-19.

*Figure 2. Major industries affected due to Covid-19*
*Source: https://www.ilo.org*

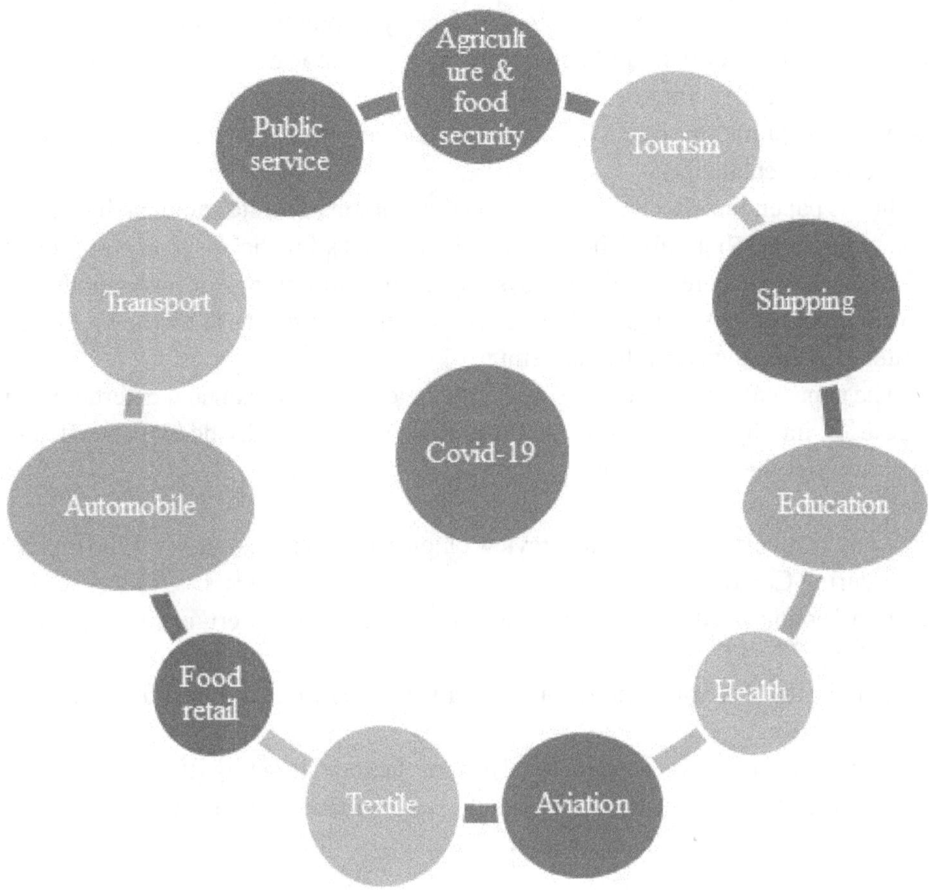


The unprecedented growth of this coronavirus spread made everyone discouraged and disgusting. Many kinds of research, innovations and discovery have taken place to reduce the diseases spread across the world. Many academic researchers have also suggested early recovery and detection of the virus through tests and precautionary measures. Particularly the advancement of technologies like artificial intelligence (AI), big data, data mining, machine learning (ML) etc. could be advanced level forecasting techniques where early detection is possible to stop the virus spread. There are some life-saving and health-improving technologies like 3D printing, flexible manufacturing, big data analytics and smart healthcare wearable, distance education, e-gaming videoconferencing, cashless payment, internet streaming, e-commerce etc. could be a possible way to make new normalcy (Siriwardhana et al, 2020). The application of 5G technology, IoT and other forms of technologies can also be utilized in the areas of transport management, smart cities, telehealth services, self-isolation, contact tracing, online education systems, retail and supply chains networks, smart manufacturing and factory automation system, e-governance and media and e-tourism and entertainment as an innovative prevention measure (Umair et al, 2021; Singh et al, 2021). Therefore, innovative technologies could identify the problems faced by the individual and provide a better solution to overcome the challenges.

In this paper, the effect of Covid-19 on the tourism and entertainment industries is emphasized elaborately. The issues and challenges for the survival and growth of these industries are highlighted systematically through recent innovations and developments in technologies. Further, a thorough analysis has drawn and provided strategic inputs to govern the pandemic.

The paper entitles "An impact study of Covid-19 on tourism and entertainment industries: intelligent solutions and future challenges" have divided into 5 different sections after the introduction:

Section- 2 articulated a systematic review of tourism industries' survival and growth during Covid-19;

Section 3 emphasized the review of issues and challenges of entertainment industries during Covid-19;

Section 4 provided some inputs on innovative technologies to face the pandemic challenges;

Section 5 depicted the critical analysis of factors affecting the tourism and entertainment industries, and finally, a systematic conclusion has drawn on suggestions and future direction.

## IMPACT OF COVID-19 ON TOURISM INDUSTRY

The term tourism is articulated as a means of travel by people to various places either in locally or globally for holiday or entertainment. Tourism emerged as the pillar of growth and development of any nation in terms of employment, income, foreign earnings or any indigenous growth of the particular locality. The tourism industry is not only improving the social cause but also enhancing the economic motive. Tourism development is considered to be potential for economic growth. Therefore, most countries are striving towards tourism research, hospitality management or destination management to attract visitors. Often the visitors are extremely exaggerated by coups, protests, warfare or political strikes which have a direct or indirect impact on tourism. The revenue will be directly hit by such consequences, but the emergences of Covid-19 have drastically changed the situation for the worse. The lockdown impact and severity of the coronavirus made world tourism inoperative. The travel restrictions across the world have reduced international tourist arrival to different places. Covid-19 has not left any scope of growth and development of the tourism industry either religious, medical or leisure. Kashmir valley which is recognized as the beauty of India and a symbol of nature was also a victim of Covid-19 with a loss of around US$ 160 million and a decline of 93 per cent in tourist flow (Singh et al, 2021). Covid-19 has directly affected the tourism industry and its vulnerability in terms of employment loss, production or income generation across the world. Most countries have suffered from lockdowns and restrictions imposed by the government that hit the tourism industry (Škare et al, 2021; Duro,et al, 2021; Knight et al, 2020). Figure 3 exhibited the different types of tourism sectors and their impact after Covid-19.

*Figure 3. Different types of tourism sectors and its impact after Covid-19*
*Source: Authors' own contribution*

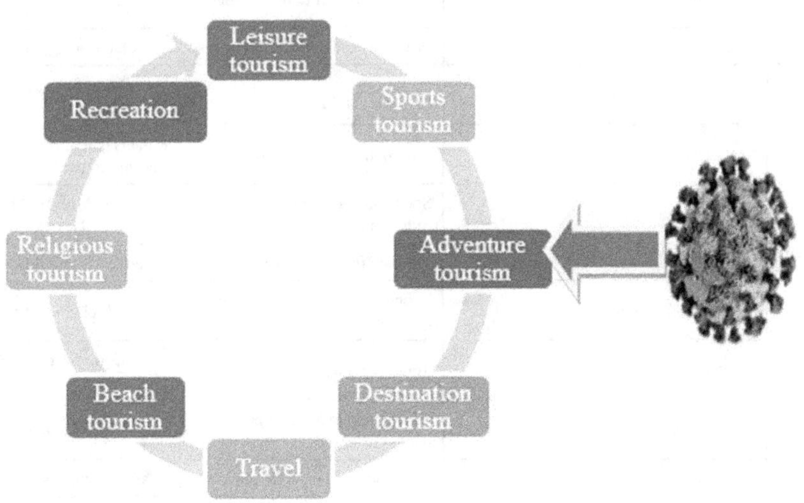


The outbreaks of the Covid-19 pandemic have significant impact on economic activities worldwide, especially on the tourism industry. The international travel restriction and government policies to mitigate the crises have resulted in a record loss of $80 billion in receipts and 100 million jobs were at risk (Khalid et al, 2021). Therefore, a perfect tour plan and revolutionary reformation could attract the tourist in many ways. Certainly, the accommodation or relaxation for 5 to 7 days in the same place could plan to avoid the risk of the pandemic (Uglis et al, 2022; Brouder,

2020). Further, the complexity of the pandemic became a challenge for public health measures. The reduction in inbound tourism became a major concern for all where some safety measures could be beneficial to attract the tourist and avoid loss (Beh & Lin, 2022). Therefore, inbound tourism could be developing through foreign exchange earnings (FEE) with some stringent initiation to attract foreigners (Jaipuria, Parida & Ray, 2021). The negative impact of Covid-19 on tourism has also influenced the stock market of China (Wu et al, 2021). According to several academic kinds of literature, it could be found that travel restrictions have directly declined the tourism flow and economy. Table 1 depicted some major contributions to the survival and growth strategy of the tourism industry.

*Table 1. Major contribution on tourism survival strategies*

| Sl No. | Major contributions | Findings | Authors |
|---|---|---|---|
| 1 | Tourism recovery | Interrelatedness of various departments should be focussed | Shih-Shuo Yeh |
| 2 | Rural tourism | Development of domestic tourist | Antonín Vaishar & Milada Šťastná |
| 3 | Sustainable tourism | Proximity tourism in local areas | Francesc Romagosa |
| 4 | Hospitality and tourism | Human rights | Tom Baum & Nguyễn Thị Thanh Hải |
| 5 | Sustainable tourism | Environmental sustainability | Rafał Nagaj & Brigita Žuromskaite |
| 6 | Tourism recovery | Social and economic dimensions of tourism | Mercyann Mukami Muragu et al. |
| 7 | Sustainable tourism | Tourism recovery in Spain | Libertad Moreno-Luna et al. |
| 8 | Hospitality and tourism | Economic & social impact on tourism | Habiba Mohammed et al. |
| 9 | Sustainable tourism | Tourism policy | Noga Collins-Kreiner & Yael Ram |
| 10 | Tourism recovery | Sustainable tourism in post pandemic era | Utkarsh & Marianna Sigala |
| 11 | Sustainable tourism | Strategies for business tourism | Asad A. Aburumman |
| 12 | Tourism recovery | Tourist perception and the risk of transmission | Alba Viana-Lora & Marta Gemma Nel-lo-Andreu1 |
| 13 | Sustainable tourism | E-Tourism | Raza Mohsin et al |
| 14 | Tourism recovery | Work on creating professional networks and plans | Bekë Kuqi et al |
| 15 | Sustainable tourism | Uncertain economy | Martina Aronica et al |

Source: Author's own contribution

## MAJOR IMPACT OF COVID-19 ON ENTERTAINMENT INDUSTRIES

Most of the entertainment industries like movies, TV shows, theatre and sporting activities were partially shut down during the pandemic period. The majority of the movies have not been released in proper time due to the unprecedented spread of Coronavirus. The uncertainty of the global crisis is abundantly shutting down the global box office revenue to 50 per cent from the pre-pandemic time. As per the reports motion picture, combined ticket sales around the world reached $21.3 billion in 2021, an improvement over 2020 sales ($11.8 billion). However, the sale of the ticket in 2019 was $42.3 billion. In India, the pandemic completely shuttered the Indian cinema by April 2020. After the reopening in October 2020, only 50 per cent of seats were allowed by the authority. It has been considered the worst period in the history of the Indian cinema Industry. In 2020, only 75 films were released compare to 1800 in 2019. The impact of Covid-19 has restricted TV shows suiting and delayed 60 per cent of scripted TV programmes. However, the online TV and movie shows of Netflix or Amazon prime have increased their profits up to 200 per cent. Covid-19 has drastically disrupted the entertainment industries across the world. Conventional theatres have closed abundantly in many places causing the loss of jobs of many professionals and declining the economy from conventional tickets. However, the growth of online streaming programmes and over-the-top (OTT) media services such as Disney plus hot-star and Netflix has offered many scopes for viewers via the internet. As the cost of these media was very low, the users were ready to accept the entertainment (Sihombing et al, 2022). Further, the residual impact of Covid-19 has destroyed the entertainment sectors such as music, television and special events which forced to drop of multibillion-dollar businesses in global entertainment. Particularly companies like Walt Disney and Box office suffered a huge loss during that period and threatened their employees with job loss. Further the pandemic interrupted both the demand and supply side of the business in the entertainment sector resulting in the postponement or cancellation of festivals and film production (Nhamo et al, 2020). The alarming rate of risk and pressure from employment in short term has affected musicians. The pandemic has made the future dark for many musicians. Therefore, it is a question for all of us to mitigate the policy to employ musicians (Crosby, & McKenzie, 2022). Further, the importance of leisure and entertainment industries like hotels or amusement parks was discussed by many authors from time to time (Lin & Falk, 2022). Table 2 depicted the major contributions of the entertainment industry during Covid-19.

*Table 2. Major contributions of entertainment industry during pandemic*

| Sl No. | Major contributions | Findings | Authors |
|---|---|---|---|
| 1 | Sustainable entertainment | Commercialization of music festivals, stadium rock and mainstream pop | Xin Gu et al |
| 2 | Sustainable entertainment | Digital entertainment | Sheetal Mahendher et al |
| 3 | Sustainable entertainment | Digital data practice in museum | Lukas Noehrer et al |
| 4 | Survival strategies | Entertainment industry's technological adaptation and innovation | Michael Johnson Jr |
| 5 | Survival strategies | Socio and economic development of entertainment | V.O Eze et al |
| 6 | Survival strategies | Rebuilding music industry by precarity & creative justice | Catherine Strong & Fabian Cannizzo |
| 7 | Sustainable entertainment | OTT played a major role for sustainable development | Divya Madnani et al |
| 8 | Sustainable entertainment | Digital entertainment unploughed | Sarah Moon |
| 9 | Sustainable entertainment | Book publishing improved | Cliff Guren et al |
| 10 | Survival strategies | Digital entertainment | S. Sunitha & S. Sudha |
| | | | |

Source: Author's own contribution

## THE IMPACT OF TECHNOLOGY IN COVID-19

The growing impact of Covid-19 has made the world challenging in terms of survival and sustainability. Most industries adopted the latest technological innovation for their survival. Social distancing, self-isolation or limiting the crowd several technologies like artificial intelligence, IoT, 5G, machine learning etc have been implemented in many industries. Particularly, these forecasting technologies will be helpful to identify the problems in the early stage to prevent disruption (Das, Nayak, & Naik, 2023). The adoption of technology in industry 4.0 is also an emerging step where the latest technologies like AI, CPS, IoT, robotics, cloud computing and big data analytics have reshaped the hospitality and tourism industry during the pandemic (Osei et al, 2020). In the same way, the role of web 4.0 and 5.0 will strengthen the tourism industry's sustainability (Duy et al, 2020). It is also observed that service quality could be enhanced through SEM and ANN in the tourism and hospitality industry (Leong et al, 2015). Technology like ANN, SVM, DBMS and deep learning can also be applied in business intelligence (BI) to understand the behaviour of people and management of festivals (Vajirakachorn & Chongwatpol, 2017; Hasan et al, 2021). To understand the proximity of the virus spread, the adoption of technologies could provide some relief from loss of employment or economy without disruptions. Figure 4 exhibited the adoption of technology during Covid-19.

*Figure 4. Technology adoption and Covid-19*
*Source: Author's own contribution*

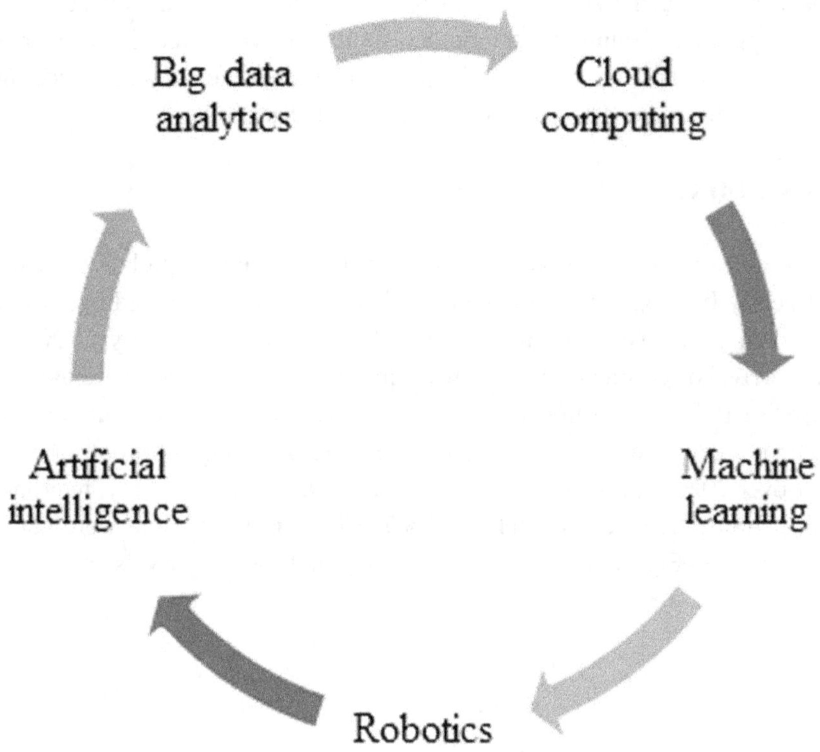


## CRITICAL ANALYSIS

A systematic analysis has done after a review of several academic articles published from 2019 to 2022. Various databases such as science direct, web of science, Pubmed, JOSTR, j-gate etc. have been used to gather the articles since 2019. Almost 250 articles are reviewed to understand the possible impact of Covid-19 on various industries. The impact of Covid-19 on the tourism and entertainment industries is specially analysed because both industries contribute almost 50 per cent of revenue to the economy. The industries like education, entertainment, tourism and manufacturing have declined their source of revenue due to the severity of the pandemic (Nayak et al, 2022; Das, Nayak & Naik, 2022). A country like India is also affected miserably during the pandemic. Although, the government of India implemented a countrywide lockdown in late March 2020 to fight the spread of the novel coronavirus still India has more than 5.73 million positive cases which was the second highest number of cases in the world. Further, it observed that in the initial quarter of the financial year 2021 India's Gross Domestic Product was slashed by 23.9 per cent. The pandemic has made many businesses, industries and services such as manufacturing, real estate, hospitality, mining etc. temporary shutdown which recorded its sharpest drop in 41 years. This analysis may help to overcome the challenges faced during the pandemic by various business houses and industries at large.

## Analysis on tourism industry

The pandemic harshly impacted the travel and tourism sectors globally causing the loss of nearly US$ 4.5 trillion. Domestic visitor spending declined by 45% while international visitor spending reduced to 69.4% compared to the year 2019. Just after the arrival of vaccination and new normal condition, the international arrivals increased to 182 per cent in Q1 of 2022. However, international tourism remains below 61 per cent. There is a growth of international receipt of around 4 per cent in 2021 over 2020, but low as 62 per cent in 2019. In the same way, international passenger transport receipts reached US$ 713 billion in 2021 but were below 61 per cent in 2019. Figure 5 depicted the international tourist arrivals.

*Figure 5. International tourist arrivals*
*Source: World tourism organization*

| | World | Europe | Asia pacific | America | Africa | Middle east |
|---|---|---|---|---|---|---|
| 2022 | -61% | -43% | -93% | -46% | -61% | -59% |
| 2021 | -71% | -62% | -94% | -62% | -73% | -75% |

Despite waiver of lockdown or shut down the international tourist flow has declined proportionately. According to the contribution made in academic research 47 per cent of papers have emphasized tourism sustainability, 33 per cent said tourism recovery, 13 per cent articulated hospitality and tourism and finally, 7 per cent emphasized the development of rural tourism. Therefore, it can be analysed that tourism sustainability through technology or other means of innovation could be helpful to improve the tourism industry. Figure 6 exhibited the major contribution to the tourism industry.

*Figure 6. Major contributions on tourism industry*
*Source: Author's own contribution*

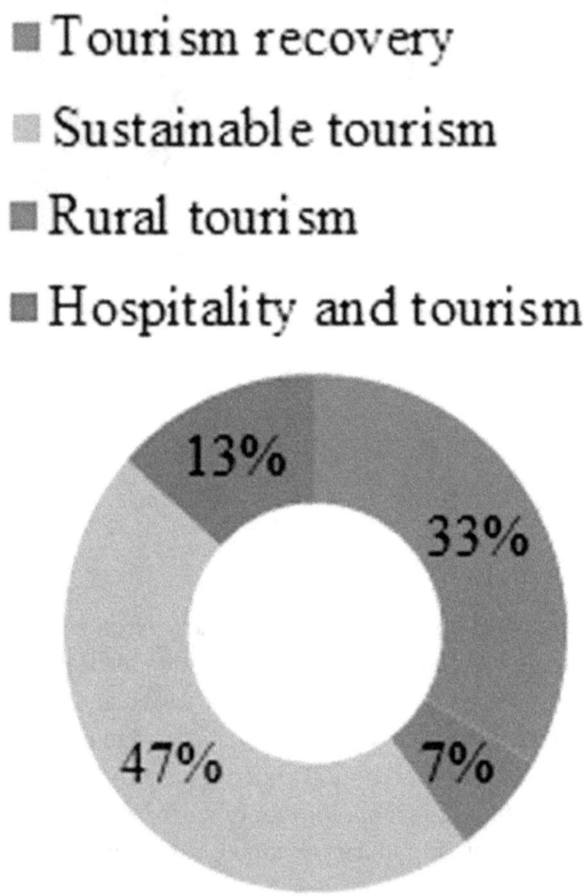


Tourism sustainability or recovery can be done with various perspectives such as economic environment, travel restrictions, higher transportation & accommodation, vaccination rollout, low consumer confidence, lack of coordination with other countries, or other factors that are importantly responsible for tourism sustainability. Figure 7 exhibited the factors responsible for international tourism recovery.

*Figure 7. International tourism recoveries*
*Source: World tourism organization*

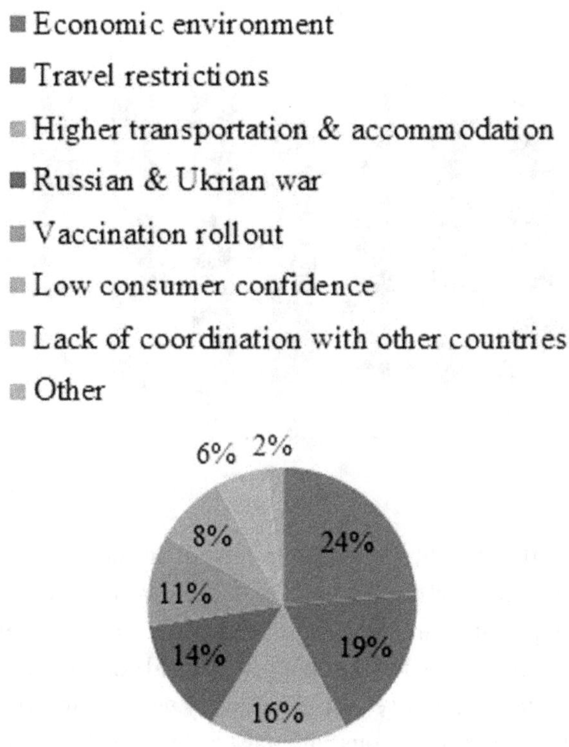


## Analysis on Entertainment Industry

The entertainment industry like the movie, theatre, sporting events, books, recreation clubs etc. have destroyed its position in Covid-19. Even after the reopening of the industry, there were no changes have recorded so far. The international box office releases declined 50 per cent, and the sale of tickets has not improved the situation. However, the digital demands of internet service coupled with OTT have surged to a 281 per cent increase in revenue.

The theatres have closed and opened with 50 per cent of seats impacted more on the release of movies across the world. Figure 8 exhibited the released movie in US and Canada between 2011 to 2021 [30].

*Figure 8. Movie released in US and Canada during 2011-2021*
*Source: https://www.statista.com/statistics*

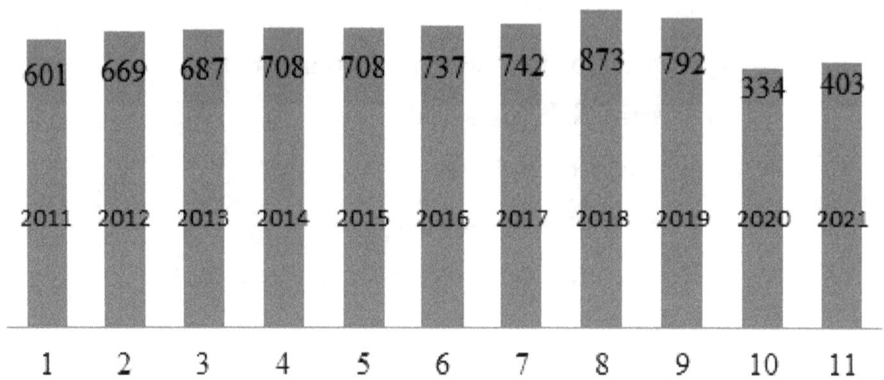


By considering the statistics of released movies in the US and Canada, a total of 403 movies released in 2021. But it remained low compared to 2019 data. In India the chief film production houses have been abandoned or indefinitely delayed, thousands of cinema halls shut down, supply chains and post-production interrupted, not to declare significant job losses. In India, every year around 1600 to 1800 films are produced collectively in various languages. Among these, 200 to 250 Hindi films alone are produced in a year. The yearly earnings of Bollywood's box office are stands at a little over 30 billion Indian rupees including Hindi films. During that period more than 70% of the box office big-budget movies released in multiplexes and smaller single screens are not having considerable earnings also. From 2019 to 2022, there are more than 100 articles published on the entertainment industry amid Covid-19 where 60 per cent of articles articulated the sustainable entertainment industry and 40 per cent of papers emphasized the survival of the entertainment industry after the pandemic. Figure 9 exhibited the major contribution of academic research to the entertainment industry.

*Figure 9. Major contribution of academic research on entertainment industry*
*Source: Authors' own contribution*

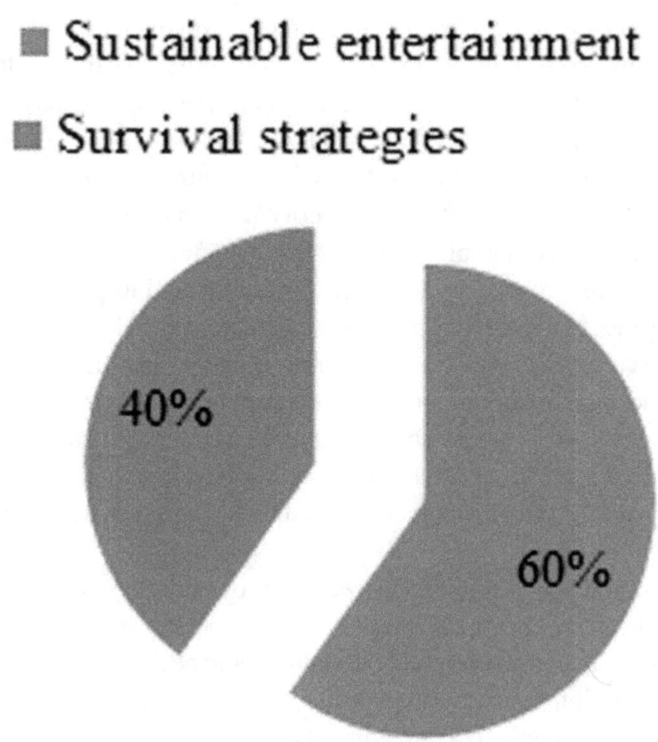


## Analysis on impact of technology on tourism and entertainment industry

The adoption of technology has improved the loss of life and employment in tourism and entertainment during Covid-19. Technology like artificial intelligence (AI), machine learning (ML), big data analytics, cloud computing, data mining, robotics etc is considered an important factor for the improvement and development of the tourism industry. Because of the digital age information transmissions become easy and understandable. The economy of the tourism industry was balanced through e-tourism and virtual travel. Technology like DBMS, SVM, robotics, data mining etc has controlled and managed the entertainment industries. The growth of internet usage and online TV shows and movies have proved to record earnings. Therefore, the adoption of the 5G network and IoT have changed the lifestyle of people and understanding of the behaviour of the individual.

## CONCLUSION

Tourism and entertainment are the deeds of every individual. Both the industry has a significant impact on human social and psychological needs. The impact of coronavirus has ruined all the expectations and hope of individuals who wish to travel or entertain themselves. The contagious virus spread has created fear among the people and depressed them mentally. The mode of relaxation has been abandoned completely and distressed the whole community. The fear of job loss, income and environment is a matter of concern during that period. Both the tourism and entertainment industries spill over their income after the new normal situation, however international tourist arrival is still low compared to pre-pandemic. Even after the emergence of technology in the tourism sector, the behaviour of individuals has not changed progressively. The entertainment sector also slightly improved just after the new normal, but not progressed compared to pre-pandemic. Now, there is no restriction by the government on travel or entertainment but could not ignite the hopes of people. Therefore, it can be suggested to incorporate huge computational technologies in all the people interacted industries to face such kinds of challenges in future.

The present paper is only emphasized the pros and cons of the tourism and entertainment industry during the pandemic. The emergence of technology is also articulated in the paper; however, several studies could be done on different forms of tourism and entertainment such as sporting tourism, event tourism, beach tourism, recreational entertainment, book reading habits etc. concerning the impact of Covid-19. The study has several limitations like Covid-19, tourism and entertainment and could be extended to various perspectives of business.

## REFERENCES

Beh, L. S., & Lin, W. L. (2022). Impact of COVID-19 on ASEAN tourism industry. *Journal of Asian Public Policy*, *15*(2), 300–320. doi:10.1080/17516234.2020.1871180

Brem, A., Viardot, E., & Nylund, P. A. (2021). Implications of the coronavirus (COVID-19) outbreak for innovation: Which technologies will improve our lives? *Technological Forecasting and Social Change*, *163*, 120451. doi:10.1016/j.techfore.2020.120451 PMID:33191956

Brouder, P. (2020). Reset redux: Possible evolutionary pathways towards the transformation of tourism in a COVID-19 world. *Tourism Geographies*, *22*(3), 484–490. doi:10.1080/14616688.2020.1760928

Crosby, P., & McKenzie, J. (2022). Survey evidence on the impact of COVID-19 on Australian musicians and implications for policy. *International Journal of Cultural Policy, 28*(2), 166–186. doi:10.1080/10286632.2021.1916004

Das, S., Nayak, J., & Naik, B. (2022). Impact of COVID-19 on Indian Education System: Practice and Applications of Intelligent Technologies. *In Future of Work and Business in Covid-19 Era: Proceedings of IMC-2021* (pp. 265-283). Springer Nature Singapore. 10.1007/978-981-19-0357-1_23

Das, S., Nayak, J., & Naik, B. (2023). An impact study on Covid-19 and tourism sustainability: Intelligent solutions, issues and future challenges. *World Review of Science, Technology and Sustainable Development, 19*(1-2), 92–119. doi:10.1504/WRSTSD.2023.127268

Das, S., Nayak, J., & Subudhi, S. (2022, April). An Impact Study on Covid-19 with Sustainable Sports Tourism: Intelligent Solutions, Issues and Future Challenges. *In International Conference on Computational Intelligence in Pattern Recognition* (pp. 605-624). Singapore: Springer Nature Singapore. 10.1007/978-981-19-3089-8_57

Debata, B., Patnaik, P., & Mishra, A. (2020). COVID-19 pandemic! It's impact on people, economy, and environment. *Journal of Public Affairs, 20*(4), e2372. doi:10.1002/pa.2372

Duro, J. A., Perez-Laborda, A., Turrion-Prats, J., & Fernández-Fernández, M. (2021). Covid-19 and tourism vulnerability. *Tourism Management Perspectives, 38*, 100819. doi:10.1016/j.tmp.2021.100819 PMID:34873568

Duy, N. T., Mondal, S. R., Van, N. T. T., Dzung, P. T., Minh, D. X. H., & Das, S. (2020). A study on the role of web 4.0 and 5.0 in the sustainable tourism ecosystem of Ho Chi Minh City, Vietnam. *Sustainability (Basel), 12*(17), 7140. doi:10.3390/su12177140

Ghosh, A., Nundy, S., & Mallick, T. K. (2020). How India is dealing with COVID-19 pandemic. *Sensors International, 1*, 100021. doi:10.1016/j.sintl.2020.100021 PMID:34766039

Hasan, M. R., Abdunurova, A., Wang, W., Zheng, J., & Shams, S. R. (2021). Using deep learning to investigate digital behavior in culinary tourism. *Journal of Place Management and Development, 14*(1), 43–65. https://www.statista.com/statistics/187122/movie-releases-in-north-america-since-2001/ https://www.worldometers.info/coronavirus/. doi:10.1108/JPMD-03-2020-0022

Jaipuria, S., Parida, R., & Ray, P. (2021). The impact of COVID-19 on tourism sector in India. *Tourism Recreation Research*, *46*(2), 245–260. doi:10.1080/02508281.2020.1846971

Khalid, U., Okafor, L. E., & Burzynska, K. (2021). Does the size of the tourism sector influence the economic policy response to the COVID-19 pandemic? *Current Issues in Tourism*, *24*(19), 2801–2820. doi:10.1080/13683500.2021.1874311

Knight, D. W., Xiong, L., Lan, W., & Gong, J. (2020). Impact of COVID-19: Research note on tourism and hospitality sectors in the epicenter of Wuhan and Hubei Province, China. *International Journal of Contemporary Hospitality Management*, *32*(12), 3705–3719. doi:10.1108/IJCHM-04-2020-0278

Leong, L. Y., Hew, T. S., Lee, V. H., & Ooi, K. B. (2015). An SEM–artificial-neural-network analysis of the relationships between SERVPERF, customer satisfaction and loyalty among low-cost and full-service airline. *Expert Systems with Applications*, *42*(19), 6620–6634. doi:10.1016/j.eswa.2015.04.043

Lin, X., & Falk, M. T. (2022). Nordic stock market performance of the travel and leisure industry during the first wave of Covid-19 pandemic. *Tourism Economics*, *28*(5), 1240–1257. doi:10.1177/1354816621990937

Nayak, J., Mishra, M., Naik, B., Swapnarekha, H., Cengiz, K., & Shanmuganathan, V. (2022). An impact study of COVID-19 on six different industries: Automobile, energy and power, agriculture, education, travel and tourism and consumer electronics. *Expert Systems: International Journal of Knowledge Engineering and Neural Networks*, *39*(3), e12677. doi:10.1111/exsy.12677 PMID:33821074

Nhamo, G., Dube, K., Chikodzi, D., Nhamo, G., Dube, K., & Chikodzi, D. (2020). Implications of COVID-19 on gaming, leisure and entertainment industry. *Counting the cost of COVID-19 on the global tourism industry*, 273-295.

Osei, B. A., Ragavan, N. A., Kandappan, B., & Mensah, H. K. (2020). Hospitality revolution 4.0: A literature review on a unified typology of IR 4.0 technologies for the tourism and hospitality industry in the era of COVID-19. *Asia-Pacific Journal of Innovation in Hospitality and Tourism*, *9*(1), 25–45.

Sihombing, L. H., Lestari, P., & Dante, J. (2022). The effects of COVID-19 pandemic towards conventional theaters and online streaming services in Indonesia. *International Journal of Communication and Society*, *4*(1), 153–162. doi:10.31763/ijcs.v4i1.337

Singh, A. L., Jamal, S., & Ahmad, W. S. (2021). Impact assessment of lockdown amid COVID-19 pandemic on tourism industry of Kashmir Valley, India. *Research in Globalization*, *3*, 100053. doi:10.1016/j.resglo.2021.100053

Siriwardhana, Y., De Alwis, C., Gür, G., Ylianttila, M., & Liyanage, M. (2020). The fight against the COVID-19 pandemic with 5G technologies. *IEEE Engineering Management Review*, *48*(3), 72–84. doi:10.1109/EMR.2020.3017451

Škare, M., Soriano, D. R., & Porada-Rochoń, M. (2021). Impact of COVID-19 on the travel and tourism industry. *Technological Forecasting and Social Change*, *163*, 120469. doi:10.1016/j.techfore.2020.120469 PMID:35721368

Uglis, J., Jęczmyk, A., Zawadka, J., Wojcieszak-Zbierska, M. M., & Pszczoła, M. (2022). Impact of the COVID-19 pandemic on tourist plans: A case study from Poland. *Current Issues in Tourism*, *25*(3), 405–420. doi:10.1080/13683500.2021.1960803

Umair, M., Cheema, M. A., Cheema, O., Li, H., & Lu, H. (2021). Impact of COVID-19 on IoT adoption in healthcare, smart homes, smart buildings, smart cities, transportation and industrial IoT. *Sensors (Basel)*, *21*(11), 3838. doi:10.3390/s21113838 PMID:34206120

Vajirakachorn, T., & Chongwatpol, J. (2017). Application of business intelligence in the tourism industry: A case study of a local food festival in Thailand. *Tourism Management Perspectives*, *23*, 75–86. doi:10.1016/j.tmp.2017.05.003

Wu, W., Lee, C. C., Xing, W., & Ho, S. J. (2021). The impact of the COVID-19 outbreak on Chinese-listed tourism stocks. *Financial Innovation*, *7*(1), 1–18. doi:10.1186/s40854-021-00240-6 PMID:35024277

# Chapter 6
# Managing Guest Expectations and Safety With AI and Smart Solutions

**Ruby Jindal**
*Department of Physics, School of Basic and Applied Sciences, K.R. Mangalam University, Gurugram, India*

**Harleen Kaur**
*Department of Applied Sciences, Baba Banda Singh Bahadur Engineering College, Fatehgarh Sahib, India*

## ABSTRACT

*In this chapter, the authors delve into the transformative impact of artificial intelligence (AI) and smart solutions on the hospitality sector. They examine how these technologies are not only meeting guest expectations, but also enhancing safety measures. Topics covered include AI-driven personalization, cutting-edge communication tools, safety innovations, and the invaluable insights gained from data analysis. This chapter serves as an essential guide for industry experts, scholars, and students as they navigate the ever-evolving landscape of guest management and safety in our digital era.*

## INTRODUCTION

In this chapter, we embark on a journey through the transformative landscape of the hospitality industry, driven by the fusion of human warmth and cutting-edge artificial intelligence (AI). The seismic shift in traveler expectations, influenced by the digital age, sets the stage for a discussion on the evolving nature of guest

DOI: 10.4018/979-8-3693-1978-9.ch006

management. The digital era has empowered travelers with unprecedented access to information and choices, pushing beyond conventional accommodation-centric services to a realm where guests seek unique, personalized experiences tailored to their individual tastes (Allam, 2016; Berezina et al., 2019; Bisoi et al., 2020; Limna, 2023; Prentice, Dominique Lopes, & Wang, 2020).

A key focal point emerges in the role of AI as the linchpin of this new era of personalization. AI's capacity to analyze extensive datasets enables the anticipation of guest needs and preferences, shaping a hospitality landscape where room amenities, dining options, and bespoke experiences are meticulously customized to elevate guest satisfaction and foster loyalty (Citak et al., 2021). The evolution extends to communication dynamics, where the era of wait times and missed calls makes way for instant, seamless interactions facilitated by AI-powered chatbots and virtual concierges. These intelligent tools bridge the digital gap between guests and hotel staff, offering swift responses to inquiries, facilitating efficient check-ins and check-outs, and providing valuable insights into local attractions and services.

However, the chapter also acknowledges the paramount concern of guest safety, particularly in a world shaped by global events. AI contributes significantly to this aspect through innovations like contactless check-ins, temperature screenings, and real-time monitoring of social distancing, reaffirming the industry's commitment to guest well-being.

The true power of AI, however, lies in its capacity to analyze data. This analytical prowess provides hoteliers and service providers with invaluable insights into guest preferences and safety trends, enabling real-time decision-making and rapid adaptation to changing circumstances. Yet, amidst the promises and potentials, the chapter does not shy away from highlighting the challenges inherent in this technologically-driven voyage. Data privacy concerns, ethical considerations, and the delicate equilibrium between technology and the enduring importance of the human touch in guest interactions demand thoughtful attention as the industry navigates this dynamic landscape.

Overall the synthesis of human hospitality and AI innovation defines a new era in guest management. This chapter serves as a guide through the complexities of this transformation, exploring the synergies between technology and hospitality, and advocating for a balanced approach to ensure a harmonious coexistence that enhances the guest experience.

## THE EVOLUTION OF GUEST EXPECTATIONS

The hospitality industry has witnessed a profound transformation in recent years, largely driven by the digital revolution and changing consumer behaviors.

Understanding the evolution of guest expectations is paramount in adapting to these shifts. In this section, we will explore the factors that have shaped and continue to shape guest expectations in the modern era:

## Digital Empowerment and Connectivity

The advent of the digital age has revolutionized the way travelers engage with the world, and within the hospitality industry (Drexler & Lapré, 2019), it has ushered in an era of digital empowerment and connectivity that fundamentally shapes guest expectations. Traditionally, travelers relied on travel agencies and guidebooks to plan their journeys, but the digital revolution has given rise to a new breed of travelers who are equipped with smartphones, travel apps, and immediate access to a wealth of information. The democratization of information has elevated travelers to the status of digital navigators, enabling them to make informed decisions and bookings in real-time. Social media platforms have emerged as potent influencers, exposing travelers to diverse experiences and fostering a desire for unique, shareable moments. User-generated content, in the form of online reviews and social media posts, has assumed a central role in shaping guest expectations, as potential travelers trust the firsthand experiences shared by their peers. Moreover, the digital age has instilled a culture of instant gratification and decision-making. Modern guests expect convenience at every turn, thanks to the availability of real-time services like ride-sharing apps and on-demand food delivery. This convenience has liberated travelers from rigid itineraries, empowering them to make spontaneous choices based on up-to-the-minute information. Central to this transformation is the empowerment of choice. Digital platforms have bestowed upon guests an array of options for accommodations, services, and activities, ushering in an era of personalization and customization. Guests now anticipate tailored experiences that align with their unique preferences, driven by the same level of personalization they encounter in other facets of their digital lives.

## The Influence of User-Generated Content

In the digital landscape of the hospitality industry, user-generated content (UGC) stands as a powerful force shaping guest expectations and choices. UGC encompasses the reviews, photos, and social media posts shared by travelers about their experiences. It has evolved into a vital influencer, guiding prospective guests in their decision-making process. Social media platforms, travel forums, and dedicated review websites have become hubs where travelers share their adventures, recommendations, and critiques. These platforms serve as a digital grapevine, allowing guests to access a trove of real-world experiences and insights from their peers. What distinguishes UGC is its authenticity. It offers a window into the unfiltered realities of a destination or accommodation, allowing potential guests to see beyond carefully curated marketing (Davenport et al., 2020) materials. Travelers rely on the candid accounts of fellow adventurers to gain a genuine sense of what to expect. UGC wields considerable influence, not only in shaping perceptions of destinations but also in swaying booking decisions. Prospective guests often place immense trust in the experiences shared by their peers. Positive reviews and captivating photos can inspire wanderlust and sway travelers toward a particular destination or accommodation. Conversely, negative reviews can deter bookings and prompt hospitality providers to address concerns promptly.

In essence, UGC has democratized travel information, allowing travelers to become both creators and consumers of content. For hospitality providers, understanding and harnessing the influence of UGC is pivotal in adapting to the digital age. It underscores the importance of providing exceptional guest experiences that are worth sharing, as satisfied guests become brand advocates in the interconnected world of the digital traveler.

## Personalization and Customization

The hospitality landscape has been fundamentally reshaped by the rise of personalization and customization, ushering in an era where guest experiences are crafted to cater to individual preferences and desires. In an age where consumers have grown accustomed to tailored content and recommendations, travelers expect nothing less than experiences that resonate uniquely with their tastes and lifestyles (Goel et al., 2022).

Artificial intelligence (AI) emerges as the driving force behind this transformation, adept at creating comprehensive guest profiles that encompass a wide array of data. From booking histories to preferences, dietary restrictions, special requests, and even social media interactions, AI weaves together a rich tapestry of guest information. It is through the analysis of these profiles that AI systems can anticipate and preempt guest needs and desires, often before guests articulate them. Personalization extends across all touch points of the guest journey. Upon arrival at a hotel, AI-driven systems can seamlessly suggest dining options, spa treatments, and local activities based on the guest's profile and current preferences. Smart rooms, embedded with AI, adjust lighting, temperature, and even the choice of artwork in response to individual guest preferences.

The booking process itself has undergone a transformation, with AI-powered chatbots and virtual assistants facilitating natural language interactions to assist guests in finding the ideal accommodations, checking availability, and making reservations. These chatbots provide instant responses to inquiries, eliminating wait times and enhancing the overall guest experience. Personalized marketing campaigns, enriched by AI, deliver tailored offers and promotions to guests based on their preferences and past behavior. Meanwhile, loyalty programs have evolved to offer personalized rewards and incentives that resonate with individual guests, fostering engagement and loyalty.

However, personalization comes with an ethical dimension. Guests' data privacy and consent must be respected, and there should be transparency regarding how data is used to personalize experiences. Striking the right balance between the benefits of personalization and ethical considerations is essential in crafting the guest experiences of the future.

So, personalization and customization have transcended from being optional extras to becoming the core of modern hospitality. AI serves as the enabler of this transformation, allowing hotels and service providers to not only meet but surpass guest expectations. It's a journey into the realm of guest-centricity, where technology enhances the art of hospitality, creating experiences that captivate and delight guests at every juncture of their journey.

## Convenience and Instant Gratification

In the contemporary landscape of travel and hospitality, the principles of convenience and instant gratification have risen to prominence, profoundly shaping guest expectations and experiences. Modern travelers place a premium on seamlessness, seeking experiences that are effortlessly efficient from start to finish. This inclination towards convenience extends beyond mere preference; it has become an expectation deeply rooted in the digital age. The journey towards convenience often commences with digital booking platforms that offer travelers an array of choices for accommodations, services, and activities (Ivanov & Webster, 2019; Koo et al., 2021). These platforms empower travelers to browse, compare, and book with unparalleled ease, eliminating the need for time-consuming visits to brick-and-mortar travel agencies. AI-powered chatbots and virtual assistants stand as champions of instant gratification, available 24/7 to address guest inquiries and requests promptly. These digital concierges transcend basic interactions, facilitating check-ins, and check-outs, thereby reducing front desk wait times and providing the convenience of keyless entry through mobile apps.

Travelers today expect real-time access to information and services, and AI-driven systems fulfill this expectation seamlessly. Guests receive updates on weather conditions, local events, nearby attractions, and can even make restaurant reservations via their preferred communication channels, all in the blink of an eye. This immediate access to information empowers travelers to make informed decisions, enhancing their overall experience.

The on-demand economy, which has become an integral part of modern life, has left a significant imprint on the hospitality industry. Travelers have become accustomed to the convenience of ordering food, transportation, and other services at the tap of a button. Hotels have adapted by incorporating smart technology, such as in-room tablets and mobile apps, enabling guests to request room service, housekeeping, or additional amenities effortlessly.

Moreover, traditional check-in and check-out processes have undergone a digital transformation to align with the convenience and efficiency that today's travelers expect. Mobile apps have revolutionized these transactions, allowing guests to complete them swiftly, reducing paperwork, and eliminating wait times.

Basically, convenience and instant gratification are no longer mere preferences but have evolved into the bedrock of modern travel. The digital age has cultivated a generation of travelers who anticipate experiences that are both hassle-free and deeply satisfying, from the moment they decide to book a stay to every interaction throughout their journey. Hospitality providers that embrace these principles are poised to not only meet but exceed guest expectations, creating experiences that are a testament to the art of effortless hospitality.

## Safety and Well-Being

In an era marked by global challenges and health crises, ensuring the safety and well-being of guests has become the cornerstone of the hospitality industry's mission. Recent global events have elevated concerns surrounding health and safety to unprecedented levels, prompting travelers to approach their journeys with heightened awareness. In response, the hospitality industry has transformed its approach, redefining its role beyond providing comfort and amenities. Now, it places an unequivocal emphasis on safeguarding guests, making safety and well-being not just a legal obligation but a central commitment.

At the heart of this transformation lies the pivotal role of artificial intelligence (AI). AI technologies have emerged as formidable tools in the industry's arsenal to enhance guest safety. From contactless check-ins and check-outs, minimizing physical interactions at front desks, to AI-driven thermal cameras that conduct temperature screenings, providing an additional layer of health safety for both guests and staff, AI has proven instrumental. Furthermore, AI systems monitor real-time adherence to social distancing guidelines in communal areas, detecting and alerting staff when necessary. They also analyze health-related data, like guest symptoms and medical history, to identify potential health risks proactively.

Safety measures, once practical considerations, have also become powerful marketing and reassurance tools. Communicating robust safety measures and AI-driven health protocols reassures guests and attracts bookings. Travelers are increasingly seeking accommodations that prioritize their health and well-being, and the industry's response to these concerns is now a significant factor in decision-making.

Nevertheless, AI's integration into safety measures raises ethical considerations, including data privacy, consent, and transparency. The handling of guests' personal health information and interactions must adhere to the highest standards of care and compliance with relevant regulations

## Sustainability and Social Responsibility

The modern hospitality industry has undergone a significant transformation with the integration of sustainability and social responsibility into its core values. Today, these aspects are not just buzzwords but fundamental principles guiding the industry's operations and shaping guest experiences. Sustainability has emerged as an imperative, with guests increasingly expecting environmentally conscious practices in the establishments they choose. This encompasses initiatives to reduce energy consumption, minimize waste, and engage in responsible sourcing of materials and food products. Hotels and resorts are embracing eco-friendly measures, such as energy-efficient lighting, water-saving systems, and robust waste recycling programs, to minimize their environmental footprint and align with the growing sustainability expectations of guests. Simultaneously, social responsibility has become an integral part of the industry's ethos. Hospitality providers recognize the importance of ethical sourcing and community engagement. Guests appreciate establishments that source products locally, support fair trade practices, and actively engage with the communities in which they operate. This not only fosters a sense of goodwill but also contributes to the enrichment of the local economy and culture.

Sustainability and social responsibility are no longer optional endeavors but essential commitments that complement the art of hospitality. As the industry continues to embrace these principles, it not only meets evolving guest expectations but also contributes positively to the global environment and communities it serves, creating a win-win scenario that embodies the spirit of responsible and ethical hospitality (Rosário & Dias, 2022).

## Seamless Integration of Technology

The seamless integration of technology has become a defining feature of modern hospitality, underpinning a transformation that has redefined guest experiences. This subsection explores how technology, when flawlessly woven into the fabric of hospitality, has the power to create unforgettable and streamlined experiences for guests.

Technology's role in hospitality is multifaceted, beginning with the initial stages of travel planning and booking. Guests today have come to expect the convenience of digital booking platforms that offer a plethora of choices for accommodations, services, and activities. These platforms empower travelers to make informed decisions and reservations at their convenience.

Once guests arrive at their chosen accommodations, technology continues to enhance their experience. Artificial intelligence (AI) takes center stage, often in the form of chatbots (Pillai & Sivathanu, 2020) and virtual assistants. These AI-driven systems are available around the clock, addressing guest inquiries, facilitating check-ins and check-outs, and even providing room service options through seamless, natural language interactions. The result is a frictionless stay that minimizes wait times and maximizes guest satisfaction.

Smart technology plays a pivotal role in enhancing the physical environment of guest rooms. Smart rooms, equipped with AI, adjust lighting, temperature, and even artwork based on guest preferences stored in their profiles. This level of personalization creates a sense of comfort and delight that was once unimaginable.

The benefits of technology extend beyond individual accommodations. Hotels and resorts employ data-driven insights to optimize their operations, from dynamic pricing strategies that respond to market demands to predictive analytics that forecast fluctuations in demand for specific services or accommodations. This not only maximizes revenue potential but also ensures competitive pricing that attracts cost-conscious travelers.

Moreover, technology has ushered in an era of contactless operations, responding to the heightened importance of safety and well-being. Keyless entry through mobile apps, contactless payments, and digital menus all contribute to a safer and more efficient guest experience.

However, the integration of technology is not without its challenges, including data privacy, algorithmic bias, and the delicate balance between automation and human touch. Yet, when harnessed thoughtfully and ethically, technology emerges as a powerful enabler that elevates the art of hospitality. In conclusion, the seamless integration of technology has become an essential aspect of modern guest experiences, transforming the industry and reshaping expectations, while offering a glimpse into a future where the convergence of technology and hospitality continues to redefine the boundaries of possibility.

## AI-POWERED PERSONALIZATION

### Tailoring Experiences to Delight Guests

In the dynamic landscape of hospitality, where guest expectations have reached new heights, personalization stands as the lodestar guiding the industry forward. Modern travelers don't merely seek a place to rest; they desire experiences that resonate with their unique tastes and preferences. In this section, we will delve into how artificial intelligence (AI) (Berezina et al., 2019; Bisoi et al., 2020; Citak et al., 2021) has emerged as the driving force behind personalization in the hospitality sector:

#### Understanding the Power of Personalization

In the dynamic landscape of modern hospitality, personalization has transcended from being a luxury to an expectation that underpins exceptional guest experiences. Personalization has evolved in response to the digital age, where customized content and recommendations are ubiquitous. Travelers today anticipate experiences that resonate with their individual preferences, desires, and needs. This shift in expectations has prompted the hospitality industry to embrace personalization as an essential strategy to meet the demands of discerning guests. At the forefront of personalization efforts stands artificial intelligence (AI) (Kumar et al., 2021), a formidable tool that creates intricate guest profiles. These profiles encompass a wide spectrum of data, ranging from historical booking data and preferences to dietary requirements, special requests, and even social media interactions. These profiles serve as the building blocks for anticipating and fulfilling guest desires, often pre-empting their needs and wants.

The core of personalization lies in the ability to provide tailored recommendations and experiences. Upon a guest's arrival at a hotel or resort, AI systems can seamlessly suggest dining options, spa treatments, and local activities, all based on the guest's profile and real-time preferences. Smart rooms, empowered by AI, fine-tune lighting, temperature, and even room aesthetics to align with guest preferences stored in their profile, ensuring that every aspect of their stay caters to their unique tastes.

Furthermore, the booking process itself has been transformed by AI-driven chatbots and virtual assistants. These digital concierges guide guests through the process, helping them find the ideal accommodations, check availability, and make reservations using natural language interactions. These AI systems go beyond inquiries; they facilitate check-ins and check-outs, reducing wait times and enhancing the convenience of the guest experience through features like keyless entry via mobile apps. Personalization extends its reach to marketing campaigns and loyalty programs, where AI enables providers to target guests with personalized offers and promotions based on their preferences and past behavior. Loyalty programs have evolved to offer customized rewards and incentives, fostering deeper engagement and encouraging repeat business. However, the power of personalization is not without ethical considerations. Guest data, the lifeblood of personalization efforts, must be handled with the utmost care, respecting guests' privacy, consent, and boundaries. Striking the balance between the capabilities of personalization and ethical considerations is integral to maintaining trust and delivering truly exceptional guest experiences..

## The Role of AI in Guest Profiling

The world of guest profiling in the hospitality industry has been revolutionized by the advent of artificial intelligence (AI). This section delves into the pivotal role that AI plays in the creation of intricate and dynamic guest profiles, redefining how hotels and resorts anticipate and meet the unique needs and preferences of their guests. In the digital age, a deluge of guest data flows in from various sources, including booking histories, preferences, dietary requirements, special requests, and even social media interactions. This data landscape is characterized by its abundance and complexity, making it an ideal domain for AI to thrive. Machine learning algorithms, at the heart of AI, possess the capability to process and analyze vast datasets with remarkable speed and precision, uncovering patterns and insights that would be beyond human capacity.

The result is the creation of comprehensive guest profiles that extend far beyond traditional data points. These profiles paint a holistic picture of each guest, capturing their preferences, habits, and tendencies. Armed with these profiles, hospitality providers gain a deeper understanding of their guests, allowing for tailored experiences that cater to individual needs and desires. As guests interact with a property, AI systems continuously update their profiles based on current behavior and preferences. This agility enables hotels and resorts to pivot quickly, offering recommendations and services that align precisely with a guest's immediate desires (Naumov, 2019; Prentice, Dominique Lopes, & Wang, 2020). AI doesn't stop at reacting to guest behavior; it excels in anticipation. By analyzing historical data and real-time inputs, AI can predict a guest's preferences for dining, activities, and even room configurations. This predictive power transforms the guest experience from one of passive service to proactive anticipation and fulfillment.

Beyond enhancing guest satisfaction, AI contributes to operational efficiency. By automating data collection and analysis, it streamlines the process of creating and updating guest profiles. Additionally, AI supports revenue optimization by identifying trends and demand patterns that inform pricing and marketing strategies. However, the use of AI in guest profiling also raises ethical considerations. Data privacy, consent, and transparency are paramount in this era of data-driven personalization. Striking a balance between the potential of AI and ethical considerations is vital for maintaining trust with guests.

Hence, AI's role in guest profiling has redefined the hospitality industry's approach to understanding and serving its guests. Through data-driven insights, AI empowers hotels and resorts to provide tailored experiences that anticipate and meet guest desires, setting a new standard for personalized hospitality. Yet, ethical considerations must accompany this transformation, ensuring that data is managed responsibly to preserve guest trust and privacy.

## Real-Time Recommendations and Customization

The hospitality industry (Ruel & Njoku, 2021) has undergone a remarkable transformation with the advent of real-time recommendations and customization, driven predominantly by technology, particularly artificial intelligence (AI). This section unravels the dynamic landscape of personalized experiences that adapt and evolve in real-time as guests engage with a property.

At the core of this evolution lies real-time responsiveness, a hallmark feature of modern hospitality. Guests today expect instantaneous recommendations and customization that cater to their immediate preferences and needs. This level of responsiveness has become feasible through the adoption of AI-driven systems capable of processing data swiftly and providing recommendations on the spot. AI assumes a pivotal role in realizing real-time customization. Advanced algorithms analyze a wealth of guest data, including historical behaviors, current choices, and even environmental factors, to offer personalized suggestions and adjustments. For instance, if a guest communicates a preference for a tranquil room, AI can promptly modify room settings like lighting and temperature to align with this preference. This real-time personalization extends to dining and activities, where AI systems take into account a guest's dietary preferences, past dining choices, and real-time availability to recommend suitable restaurant options. Similarly, when it comes to activities, AI can suggest nearby attractions, events, or recreational options based on a guest's interests and prevailing weather conditions. The advent of smart rooms, equipped with AI technology, elevates real-time customization to new heights. These rooms can autonomously adjust lighting, temperature, and even room aesthetics in response to the guest's preferences and real-time feedback. For example, if a guest desires a cooler room with dimmed lights, AI systems make these adjustments seamlessly, eliminating the need for manual intervention. Real-time customization extends beyond the in-stay experience; AI-powered chatbots and virtual assistants provide instant guidance and assistance, addressing queries, making reservations, and facilitating requests promptly. This level of responsiveness enhances the guest journey holistically, ensuring that guests feel valued and well-cared-for at every touch point. However, the implementation of real-time recommendations and customization is not without ethical considerations. Ensuring data privacy and obtaining informed consent from guests are paramount. Guests should have confidence that their data is used responsibly and transparently to enhance their experience, all while preserving their privacy.

## Streamlining the Booking Experience

The hospitality industry has witnessed a remarkable transformation in the way guests book accommodations, thanks to the integration of artificial intelligence (AI). This section illuminates how AI has redefined and streamlined the booking experience, making it not only more accessible but also more efficient and tailored to the individual preferences of each guest. In the contemporary travel landscape, travelers demand nothing short of convenience and efficiency when booking accommodations. AI-powered systems have risen to this challenge, simplifying the booking process through intuitive interfaces and natural language interactions. Chatbots and virtual assistants, at the forefront of this transformation, offer real-time assistance, guiding guests step-by-step through the booking process, promptly addressing queries, and providing personalized recommendations.

The true power of AI shines in the realm of personalized suggestions. These systems take into account a guest's past booking history, preferences, and even their current context to suggest accommodations, room types, and additional services that align with their unique preferences and needs. This level of personalization not only enhances the booking experience but also ensures that guests find the perfect match for their specific requirements. Real-time availability is paramount for guests seeking to secure their ideal accommodations, and AI plays a pivotal role in ensuring accuracy. AI systems continuously update room availability, guaranteeing that guests receive up-to-the-minute information, empowering them to make well-informed decisions. In cases of high demand or limited availability, AI-driven platforms can proactively suggest alternative dates or properties that align with guest preferences, ensuring flexibility.

Furthermore, AI streamlines the booking process through seamless integration with other systems and services. Guests can seamlessly access and book additional services such as airport transfers, restaurant reservations, and spa appointments during the booking process. This integration simplifies the planning stage, offering guests a comprehensive experience within a single platform.

Mobile accessibility is another cornerstone of the streamlined booking experience. AI-powered mobile apps provide guests with the flexibility to make reservations, check availability, and manage bookings on the go. Mobile check-in and keyless entry options further enhance the convenience of the booking process, reducing wait times and providing a seamless arrival experience.

However, as AI enhances the booking experience, it must do so within the bounds of ethical considerations. Data privacy and consent must be upheld, ensuring that guest information is used responsibly and transparently to enhance their booking journey, fostering trust in the process.

So, AI's integration has revolutionized the booking experience in the hospitality industry, aligning it with the expectations of modern travelers. Effortless booking, personalized suggestions, real-time availability, seamless integration, mobile accessibility, and ethical considerations collectively contribute to a booking process that is not only efficient and user-friendly but also tailored to the unique preferences of each guest. By harnessing the capabilities of AI while respecting ethical boundaries, hospitality providers offer guests a streamlined and stress-free path to securing their accommodations and experiences, setting a new standard in guest-centric booking experiences.

## Personalized Marketing and Loyalty Programs

In the ever-evolving landscape of hospitality, personalized marketing and loyalty programs have emerged as transformative tools for building guest loyalty and satisfaction. This subsection illuminates the central role of personalization in modern hospitality marketing, showcasing how technology, data analytics, and artificial intelligence (AI) have reshaped customer engagement and loyalty strategies.

Personalization has become synonymous with contemporary marketing, reflecting the expectation of guests for experiences that are tailored to their preferences and past interactions. The advent of AI and data analytics has empowered hospitality providers to craft marketing campaigns and loyalty programs that are finely tuned to the individual needs and desires of their guests.

At the heart of this transformation lies data-driven insights. AI-driven systems meticulously analyze guest data, encompassing factors like booking histories, preferences, and spending behaviors. These insights serve as the bedrock upon which personalized marketing efforts are built. By gaining a comprehensive understanding of guests on a granular level, hotels and resorts can create campaigns that target specific guest segments, delivering promotions and incentives that are not just relevant but resonate deeply with each individual.

Personalized marketing goes beyond generic offers; it facilitates tailored incentives and promotions. AI algorithms discern patterns and trends in guest behavior, allowing providers to extend discounts, package deals, and rewards that are precisely aligned with each guest's preferences and spending habits. This high degree of customization enhances the guest experience and, in turn, fosters loyalty.

In tandem with personalized marketing, loyalty programs have undergone a transformation of their own. They now offer personalized rewards and incentives, tailored to the preferences and behaviors of individual loyalty members. AI-driven systems analyze guest data to determine which rewards and benefits will be most appealing, enhancing engagement and encouraging repeat business and advocacy.

Personalized marketing doesn't confine itself to a single channel; it extends across multiple platforms, including email, social media, and mobile apps. AI-driven marketing automation ensures that guests receive consistent and relevant messages through these channels, promoting engagement and conversion. Guests encounter communication that resonates with their preferences and behaviors, increasing the likelihood of meaningful interaction.

Yet, amid the potential of personalization, ethical considerations loom large. Data privacy and consent are paramount. Guests must trust that their data is used responsibly and transparently to enhance their experience without compromising their privacy. In conclusion, personalized marketing and loyalty programs have emerged as indispensable tools for cultivating guest loyalty and satisfaction in the hospitality industry. Through AI-driven insights and customization, providers can create tailored experiences that resonate deeply with guests, fostering loyalty and advocacy. However, as the industry continues its journey toward personalization, ethical considerations must guide these efforts, ensuring the responsible use of guest data and the preservation of trust in the guest-provider relationship..

## The Ethical Dimension of Personalization

In the age of personalization within the hospitality industry, ethical considerations play an increasingly critical role in the quest to offer tailored experiences that resonate with guests while safeguarding their privacy and consent. At the foundation of this ethical dimension lies data privacy and security, recognizing that guests entrust hotels and resorts with a trove of personal information. It is imperative that this data remains protected from breaches and misuse through robust data security measures. This ensures not only the confidentiality of guest information but also that it is utilized exclusively for its intended purposes.

Informed consent emerges as another ethical linchpin in the realm of personalization. Guests deserve transparency regarding how their data will be utilized to enhance their experience. They must possess a clear understanding of the process and have the freedom to provide or withdraw consent at their discretion. Transparent communication surrounding data usage is essential, not only for building trust but also for enabling guests to make informed choices about their involvement in personalization programs.

Ethical personalization further entails the principle of data minimization, emphasizing that only data essential for enhancing the guest experience should be collected and retained. Collecting excessive or irrelevant guest data is both intrusive and unnecessary, a practice that ethical providers should avoid.

Respect for guest boundaries is another integral aspect of ethical personalization. Striking a delicate balance between customization and intrusiveness is imperative. Personalized experiences should never compromise guest privacy or make them feel uncomfortable. Guests should always have the option to limit the extent of personalization to a level that aligns with their comfort.

Transparency and accountability form the bedrock of ethical personalization. Hospitality providers must be transparent in their communication about how guest data is collected, used, and shared. Additionally, mechanisms of accountability should be in place to address any data breaches or misuse promptly. Such measures not only foster trust but also underscore responsible data handling practices.

Lastly, ethical personalization places a premium on guest empowerment. It empowers guests to exercise control over their data and their experience. This empowerment ensures that guests are active participants in the personalization process, able to customize their interactions with hospitality providers according to their preferences and comfort levels.

## ENSURING GUEST SAFETY

The modern hospitality industry faces a transformative challenge in the form of prioritizing guest safety, especially in a world marked by global uncertainties and health crises. Beyond a legal obligation, ensuring guest safety has become a core commitment for establishments seeking to instill confidence and trust among their visitors. Recent global events have profoundly influenced traveler perceptions, prompting heightened concerns regarding health and safety during their stays. In this context, artificial intelligence (AI) has emerged as a formidable tool in the industry's arsenal to enhance guest safety. AI-driven solutions have redefined the check-in and check-out processes, reducing physical interactions with contactless procedures and mobile apps, thereby minimizing potential exposure to health risks. Moreover, AI-equipped thermal cameras have found a vital role in performing temperature screenings, adding an extra layer of health security for both guests and staff.

AI extends its capabilities to real-time monitoring of social distancing within communal areas, a critical element in the current landscape. Through the analysis of video feeds and sensor data, AI systems promptly detect instances where social distancing guidelines are not being adhered to and alert staff for immediate intervention, thus reducing potential risks. Furthermore, AI's analytical prowess comes into play when examining health-related data, such as guest symptoms and medical histories. This data-driven approach enables hospitality providers to proactively identify potential health risks, allowing for swift and appropriate actions, such as isolation measures or the implementation of additional safety protocols.

Beyond practicality, safety measures have morphed into potent marketing and reassurance tools. The communication of robust safety protocols, underpinned by AI technologies, reassures guests and fosters trust, influencing booking decisions. Travelers now actively seek out accommodations and experiences that prioritize their health and well-being, making the industry's response to these concerns a pivotal factor in their choices.

Nevertheless, AI's integration into guest safety measures must be carefully balanced with ethical considerations. Upholding data privacy, obtaining informed consent from guests, and maintaining transparency in data usage are non-negotiable. Ensuring that guests' personal health information and interactions are handled with the utmost care and strict adherence to relevant regulations is essential for preserving trust and confidence.

Hence, guest safety has undergone a profound evolution from a regulatory requirement to an integral facet of the contemporary guest experience. AI, with its multifaceted capabilities, has emerged as a crucial ally in safeguarding guest well-being. In an era where the assurance of safety is paramount, AI stands as a powerful instrument in realizing the hospitality industry's commitment to providing secure and protected stays for travelers.

## HARNESSING DATA-DRIVEN INSIGHTS

In the age of information, data has emerged as a precious commodity in the hospitality industry, offering profound insights into guest behaviors, preferences, and trends. This section delves into the pivotal role of data-driven insights and how artificial intelligence (AI) serves as the catalyst for informed decision-making, enabling hospitality providers to elevate guest experiences: The wealth of data generated throughout a guest's journey—spanning from booking patterns and preferences to on-site behaviors and post-stay reviews—constitutes a treasure trove of information. AI possesses the analytical prowess to process these voluminous datasets, extracting valuable insights that inform nearly every aspect of hospitality operations. AI's capacity to discern patterns and trends enables hospitality providers to tailor their offerings with precision. It helps in understanding guest preferences, from room amenities to dining choices, allowing for personalized experiences that resonate with individual tastes. For instance, a guest who frequently chooses in-room dining over restaurant meals may receive menu recommendations that align with their preference for convenience and privacy.

Moreover, data-driven insights facilitate dynamic pricing strategies, responding in real-time to market demands and guest behavior. AI algorithms can adjust room rates based on factors such as occupancy levels, seasonal trends, and special events. This flexibility not only maximizes revenue potential but also ensures competitive pricing that attracts cost-conscious travelers. Predictive analytics, a powerful application of AI, enables hospitality providers to anticipate future trends and guest needs. By analyzing historical data, AI can forecast fluctuations in demand for specific services or accommodations, allowing providers to proactively allocate resources and staff accordingly. The utilization of AI in data analysis also extends to guest satisfaction measurement. Sentiment analysis tools can parse guest reviews and social media mentions, providing a nuanced understanding of what guests appreciate and where improvements are needed. This real-time feedback loop guides service enhancements and operational adjustments.

However, the responsible management of guest data remains a paramount concern. Data privacy and security are non-negotiable, and adherence to regulatory frameworks, such as GDPR, is imperative. Guests must have confidence that their information is handled with the utmost care and respect. Henceforth, data-driven insights powered by AI have become instrumental in shaping the guest experience. This multifaceted approach empowers hospitality providers to deliver not just tailored services but also to optimize pricing, anticipate trends, and enhance overall guest satisfaction. The responsible and ethical use of data is integral to maintaining trust and ensuring that guests continue to benefit from the intelligent insights that AI can offer in the realm of hospitality.

## CHALLENGES AND ETHICAL CONSIDERATIONS

The era of personalization in the hospitality industry, while promising transformative guest experiences, also presents a complex landscape of challenges and ethical considerations. At the forefront of these concerns is data privacy and security, where the safeguarding of guest information from breaches and misuse is paramount. Robust data security measures are not just essential; they are foundational to ensuring that guest data remains confidential and is employed solely for its intended purposes.

Informed consent stands as another pivotal ethical consideration. Transparency is key, as guests must fully understand how their data will be harnessed to enhance their experience. This comprehension is integral to informed consent, granting guests the freedom to provide or withdraw consent as they see fit. Transparent communication regarding data usage is not just a legal requirement; it is a means to build trust and enable guests to make informed choices about their participation in personalization programs. Data minimization is a principle that underscores ethical personalization. It underscores the importance of collecting only the data that is necessary for enhancing the guest experience, avoiding the collection of excessive or irrelevant information that could be intrusive or unnecessary. Respect for guest boundaries is central to ethical personalization. Achieving a delicate equilibrium between customization and intrusiveness is essential. Personalized experiences should never encroach upon guest privacy or make them feel uneasy. Ensuring that guests retain the option to limit the extent of personalization is vital, empowering them to customize their interactions to align with their comfort levels. Transparency and accountability are foundational ethical pillars. Hotels and resorts must be transparent in communicating how guest data is acquired, employed, and shared. Simultaneously, accountability mechanisms should be in place to address any breaches or misuse of data promptly. These measures not only underscore responsible data handling practices but also serve as safeguards to maintain guest trust.

Lastly, ethical personalization emphasizes guest empowerment. It grants guests the agency to exercise control over their data and their experience. This empowerment ensures that guests actively participate in the personalization process, enabling them to tailor their interactions with hospitality providers to their unique preferences and comfort levels.

In navigating the challenges and ethical considerations inherent in personalization, the hospitality industry (Knani, 2014) can set the standard for responsible and respectful guest engagement. By upholding data privacy, transparency, accountability, and guest empowerment, providers can harness the potential of personalization while preserving guest trust and ensuring that tailored experiences enrich the guest journey without compromising individual rights and preferences.

## REAL-WORLD EXAMPLES AND CASE STUDIES

Some real-world examples or case studies that provide practical insights into managing guest expectations and safety through the intersection of hospitality and technology:

**Marriott International's Use of Chatbots:** Marriott International implemented a chatbot named "ChatGuru" to enhance guest communication and satisfaction. This AI-driven tool assists guests in real-time, providing information about hotel services, local attractions, and answering frequently asked questions. The chatbot ensures instant and personalized responses, improving overall guest experience and managing expectations efficiently (Marketing Dive, n.d.).

**Hilton's Digital Key Technology**: Hilton introduced Digital Key technology, allowing guests to use their smartphones as room keys. This AI-powered feature enables a contactless check-in experience, enhancing both convenience and safety. Guests can bypass the front desk, access their rooms securely, and have greater control over their stay, aligning with the evolving expectations for seamless and secure interactions (Hilton Worldwide Holdings Inc, n.d.).

**Singapore's AI-Powered Cleaning Robots:** In response to the heightened focus on safety and cleanliness, hotels in Singapore have adopted AI-powered cleaning robots. These robots use sensors and AI algorithms to navigate through spaces, performing tasks such as sanitizing surfaces and monitoring cleanliness levels. This not only ensures a higher standard of safety for guests but also showcases the integration of AI in maintaining hygiene standards.

**Wynn Las Vegas' Implementation of AI for Personalization**: Wynn Las Vegas has implemented AI technologies to enhance guest personalization. Through the use of AI algorithms, the hotel analyzes guest preferences, behaviors, and past interactions to tailor services and recommendations. From personalized room settings to curated dining suggestions, Wynn's AI-driven approach exemplifies how technology can elevate the guest experience by meeting individual expectations.

**InterContinental Hotels Group (IHG) and AI-Driven Revenue Management:** IHG utilizes AI in its revenue management strategy to optimize pricing and room allocations based on demand patterns. By analyzing vast datasets in real-time, the AI system adapts pricing dynamically, ensuring that guests receive competitive rates while maximizing revenue for the hotel. This demonstrates how AI contributes to both guest satisfaction and business efficiency.

**The Ritz-Carlton's Use of IoT for Safety Monitoring:** The Ritz-Carlton implemented IoT devices for safety monitoring in guest rooms. These devices include sensors that can detect unusual activities or emergencies, such as sudden temperature changes or prolonged inactivity. AI algorithms analyze the data from these devices to enhance guest safety by alerting staff to potential issues promptly.

These real-world examples showcase the diverse applications of AI and technology in managing guest expectations and safety within the hospitality industry. From personalized interactions and contactless experiences to enhanced safety measures, these case studies provide practical insights into navigating the intersection of hospitality and technology for the benefit of both guests and hotel operations.

## CONCLUSION

In the ever-evolving landscape of the hospitality industry, the synergy between technology, particularly artificial intelligence (AI), and the age-old art of hospitality has ushered in a new era of guest experiences. This chapter has journeyed through the transformative impact of utilizing smart technology and AI in managing guest expectations, ensuring safety, and harnessing data-driven insights. It has also delved into the challenges and ethical considerations that accompany this technological transformation.

Guest expectations have transcended from mere accommodation to personalized, seamless, and secure experiences. AI-powered personalization has become the heartbeat of modern hospitality, enabling providers to anticipate and fulfill guest desires, offer tailored recommendations, and redefine the concept of guest-centricity.

Smart communication tools, driven by AI, have reshaped guest interactions, providing instant gratification, efficiency, and accessibility. From contactless check-ins to real-time assistance, these tools bridge the digital divide and create a more connected guest experience. Ensuring guest safety is now a paramount concern. AI, with its capabilities in contactless operations, temperature screening, real-time monitoring, and health data analysis, has emerged as a powerful ally in safeguarding guest well-being. It's not just about compliance; it's a commitment to providing secure and protected stays.

The insights gleaned from data-driven analytics, facilitated by AI, guide decision-making, enabling providers to tailor offerings, optimize pricing, anticipate trends, and enhance guest satisfaction. However, the responsible management of guest data and ethical considerations, such as privacy, consent, and transparency, are integral to maintaining trust. Yet, this technological revolution is not without its challenges and ethical dilemmas. Data privacy and security, algorithmic bias, and the delicate balance between automation and human touch all require careful navigation. Compliance with evolving regulations, technological integration, and educating guests about AI's role add to the complexity.

In conclusion, the integration of AI and smart solutions into hospitality represents a profound transformation, where technology and human warmth converge to create memorable and secure guest experiences. It's a journey guided by the commitment to meet evolving guest expectations, ensuring their safety, and harnessing the power of data-driven insights. As the hospitality industry continues to embrace these innovations, the promise of more personalized, efficient, and enriching guest experiences is on the horizon, setting a course for a future where technology elevates the art of hospitality to new heights.

## REFERENCES

Allam, S. (2016). The Impact of Artificial Intelligence on Innovation - An Exploratory Analysis. *International Journal of Creative Research Thoughts*, *4*(4), 810–814.

Berezina, K., Ciftci, O., & Cobanoglu, C. (2019). *Robots, Artificial Intelligence, and Service Automation in Restaurants. In Robots, Artificial Intelligence, and Service Automation in Travel, Tourism, and Hospitality*. Emerald Publishing Limited.

Bisoi, S., Mou Roy, D., & Samal, A. (2020). Impact of Artificial Intelligence in the Hospitality Industry. *International Journal of Advanced Science and Technology, 29*(5), 4265–4276.

Citak, J., Owoc, M. L., & Weichbroth, P. (2021). A Note on the Applications of Artificial Intelligence in the Hospitality Industry: Preliminary Results of a Survey. *Procedia Computer Science*, *192*, 4552–4559. doi:10.1016/j.procs.2021.09.233

Davenport, T., Guha, A., Grewal, D., & Bressgott, T. (2020). How Artificial Intelligence Will Change the Future of Marketing. *Journal of the Academy of Marketing Science*, *48*(1), 24–42. doi:10.1007/s11747-019-00696-0

Drexler, N., & Lapré, V. B. (2019). For Better or For Worse: Shaping the Hospitality Industry Through Robotics and Artificial Intelligence. Research in Hospitality Management, 9(2), 117-120. Springer.

Goel, P., Kaushik, N., Sivathanu, B., Pillai, R., & Vikas, J. (2022). Consumers' Adoption of Artificial Intelligence and Robotics in Hospitality and Tourism Sector: Literature Review and Future Research Agenda. *Tourism Review*, *77*(4), 1–16. doi:10.1108/TR-03-2021-0138

Hilton Worldwide Holdings Inc. (n.d.). Digital Transformation Strategies. *Global Data*. https://www.globaldata.com/store/report/hilton-worldwide-holdings-inc-enterprise-tech-analysis/)

Ivanov, S., & Webster, C. (2019). *Conceptual Framework of the Use of Robots, Artificial Intelligence and Service Automation in Travel, Tourism, and Hospitality Companies. Robots, Artificial Intelligence, and Service Automation in Travel, Tourism, and Hospitality*. Emerald Publishing Limited.

Knani, M. (2014). Ethics in the Hospitality Industry: Review and Research Agenda. *International Journal of Business and Management*, *9*(3), 1. doi:10.5539/ijbm.v9n3p1

Koo, C., Xiang, Z., Gretzel, U., & Sigala, M. (2021). Artificial Intelligence (AI) and Robotics in Travel, Hospitality, and Leisure. *Electronic Markets, 31*(3), 473–476. doi:10.1007/s12525-021-00494-z PMID:35603226

Kumar, S., Kumar, V., & Attri, K. (2021). Impact of Artificial Intelligence and Service Robots in Tourism and Hospitality Sector: Current Use & Future Trends. *Administrative Development: A Journal of HIPA, 8*(SI-1), 59-83.

Limna, P. (2023). Artificial Intelligence (AI) in the hospitality industry: A review article. *International Journal of Computing Sciences Research*, *7*, 1306–1317. doi:10.25147/ijcsr.2017.001.1.103

Marketing Dive. (n.d.). *Marriott makes more room for chatbots to enhance guest experiences.* https://www.marketingdive.com/news/marriott-makes-more-room-for-chatbots-to-enhance-guest-experiences/510117/

Naumov, N. (2019). *The Impact of Robots, Artificial Intelligence, and Service Automation on Service Quality and Service Experience in Hospitality. Robots, Artificial Intelligence, and Service Automation in Travel, Tourism, and Hospitality*. Emerald Publishing Limited.

Pillai, R., & Sivathanu, B. (2020). Adoption of AI-Based Chatbots for Hospitality and Tourism. *International Journal of Contemporary Hospitality Management*, *32*(10), 3199–3226. doi:10.1108/IJCHM-04-2020-0259

Prentice, C., Dominique Lopes, S., & Wang, X. (2020). The impact of artificial intelligence and employee service qualityon customer satisfaction and loyalty. *Journal of Hospitality Marketing & Management*, *29*(7), 739–756. doi:10.1080/19368623.2020.1722304

Rosário, A. T., & Dias, J. C. (2022). Sustainability and the Digital Transition: A Literature Review. *Sustainability (Basel)*, *14*(7), 4072. doi:10.3390/su14074072

Ruel, H., & Njoku, E. (2021). AI Redefining the Hospitality Industry. Journal of Tourism Futures, 7, 53-66. doi:10.1108/JTF-03-2020-0032

# Chapter 7
# Predictive Analytics for Heritage Site Visitor Patterns

**Aditi Nag**
https://orcid.org/0000-0002-0604-6945
*Birla Institute of Technology, India*

**Smriti Mishra**
https://orcid.org/0000-0001-7594-4960
*Birla Institute of Technology, India*

## ABSTRACT

*This study explores the relationship between predictive analytics and heritage site management, using a survey conducted across four Indian heritage cities involving 893 participants. The research uses advanced predictive modelling techniques and IoT technologies to understand visitor interactions at heritage sites. The study emphasises cultural sensitivity and the impact of diverse cultural backgrounds on visitor behaviours. It provides a comprehensive understanding of heritage site engagement, promoting long-term sustainability and informed strategic planning, conservation efforts, and community engagement initiatives. The research also explores climate change's impact on visitor patterns, integrating climate-related variables into predictive models to facilitate adaptive heritage site management. This study not only advances the theoretical understanding of predictive analytics in heritage site contexts but also offers practical, ethical, and culturally informed strategies for sustainable heritage management and safeguarding cultural heritage for future generations.*

DOI: 10.4018/979-8-3693-1978-9.ch007

## INTRODUCTION

Visitor demands and tastes have changed due to the tourism industry's dynamic character and advancements in media communications, transportation, and technology. These days, travellers want more engaging and memorable travel experiences rather than the traditional, mass-market "sea, sun, and sand" vacations *(OECD 2014; Timothy, 2011)*. The tourism sector has attempted to provide visitors with alternative or themed tourism experiences in response to visitor expectations *(Stamboulis & Skayannis, 2003)*. One such type of travel that has gained appeal is heritage tourism, which is also referred to as cultural tourism *(Richards & Wilson, 2006)*. The exodus of people to cultural attractions away from their usual residence to gather new knowledge and experiences to meet their cultural requirements is characterised as heritage tourism by *Richards (2001)*. Due to changes in consumer tastes and inclinations, there is an increasing demand for heritage tourism as visitors look for more varied, engaging, and thought-provoking experiences *(Timothy 2011)*. The demand from tourists for historical and cultural sites is significant; in 2007, as per *UNWTO (2010) and OECD (2009)*, 40% of all travel worldwide was related to historical and cultural sites *(Shore 2010)*. Heritage tourism is regarded as one of the tourist industry's fastest-growing segments and contributes significantly to the local and national economy.

Heritage sites, encompassing historical landmarks, cultural artefacts, and natural wonders, stand as windows to the past, preserving the rich tapestry of human history and heritage. For most heritage sites, visitor management is a significant concern *(Petr, 2002)*. Globally, the number of visitors to historical places is rising *(Gilmore, Carson, & Ascenção, 2007)*. Visitors now make up the most significant portion of the cultural audience *(Gombault & Petr, 2007; Boniface & Fowler, 1993)* and a highly targeted market *(Huang, Tsaur, & Yang, 2012; Jimura, 2011; Yang, Lin, & Han, 2010)* due to their growing attendance, particularly at foreign locations and events. Visitor studies are becoming increasingly important for everyone working in the tourism sector. Therefore, to better understand the unique expectations, attitudes, motives, and behaviours of visitors, both public and private administrators of cultural places and events seek to understand better *(Laing et al., 2014; Calver & Page, 2013; Kolar & Zabkar, 2010; Chen & Chen, 2010; Bourgeon-Renault et al., 2006)*. Policymakers and regional directors of destination marketing organisations work to promote heritage tourism in light of their economic worth *(Su & Lin, 2014; Choi et al., 2010; Ramsey & Everitt, 2008)*. In studies that specifically address visitors in the cultural domain, the tourism industry frequently highlights how tourists consume culture. There are two significant domains covered. According to the traditions of consumer behaviour, heritage and cultural practices are studied for reasons of satisfaction and to profile the distinctive features of heritage tourists in comparison to other tourists *(Petr, 2015; Caton & Santos, 2007; Poria, Reichel, & Biran, 2006; Ryans & Higgins, 2006; Poria, Butler, & Airey, 2004; Chandler, 2004; Huh & Uysal, 2003; Chandler & Costello, 2002; Kerstetter et al., 2001)*. In contrast, professionals in the fields of hospitality management and destination research aim to ascertain how tourist attractions and events draw visitors to a particular location and how this aids in the destination's positioning in the global tourism market *(Petr, 2015; Cuccia and Cellini, 2007; Flowers & Easterling, 2006; Quinn, 2006; Du Cros et al., 2005; Buckley, 2004; Colbert, 2003; Timothy & Boyd, 2003; Boyd, 2002; Hughes, 2001; Boniface & Fowler, 1993)*. While it is clear that visitors are essential to heritage sites, little is known about their microbehavioral patterns *(Holmes et al., 2006; Hughes, 2001)*. For instance, many visitors only enjoy sightseeing rather than monument visiting, never setting foot on the central monument *(Petr, 2009)*.

In recent years, the intersection of technology and heritage site management has opened new avenues for understanding visitor behaviours and optimising site experiences. Heritage sites hold profound significance as tangible links to cultural preservation and tourism. Culturally, these sites preserve the identity of nations, encapsulating historical traditions and societal roots. By safeguarding these sites, communities connect with their past, instilling a sense of pride and cultural continuity. Preservation efforts ensure that societies' artistic, architectural, and historical heritage is conserved for future generations, enriching their understanding of their ancestors' achievements and cultural expressions. Simultaneously, heritage sites are pivotal in driving tourism, acting as economic engines that stimulate local and national economies. The economic impact of heritage tourism is far-reaching, stimulating growth by channelling revenue into accommodations, dining, transportation, and local businesses. This financial influx creates employment opportunities, bolstering economic development in the surrounding areas. Moreover, tourism at heritage sites fosters cultural exchange between visitors and local communities. These interactions promote mutual understanding, tolerance, and appreciation of diverse cultures. Such exchanges contribute to cultural enrichment, breaking down stereotypes and fostering connections between different societies. Furthermore, heritage tourism promotes sustainable practices by setting examples for eco-friendly tourism. Managed responsibly, these sites emphasise conservation and encourage visitors to adopt environmentally conscious behaviours. This approach safeguards natural surroundings, preserves wildlife, and maintains ecological balance. Additionally, heritage sites serve as platforms for promoting local crafts and cuisine. Visitors can engage with local artisans, supporting traditional skills and purchasing authentic crafts. Similarly, they can savour regional cuisine, preserving culinary heritage and encouraging local culinary traditions. Culturally, tourism at heritage sites leads to a deeper appreciation of diverse traditions, customs, and rituals. By immersing visitors in the cultural fabric of the host community, heritage tourism fosters empathy, respect, and understanding. This cultural exchange enriches travellers' lives and contributes to global harmony, promoting a sense of shared heritage and fostering peaceful coexistence. In essence, the significance of heritage sites in cultural preservation and tourism underscores their pivotal role in shaping cultural identities, fostering economic development, promoting sustainability, and encouraging cross-cultural understanding.

This study delves into the domain of predictive analytics applied to heritage site visitor patterns, exploring its significance in enhancing heritage site management strategies. In heritage site research, several interconnected gaps persist, impeding a comprehensive understanding of visitor behaviours. One prominent void is the lack of cultural sensitivity in many studies. For instance, understanding how the preferences of visitors from diverse backgrounds, such as tourists from Eastern and Western cultures, influence their interactions with heritage sites remains underexplored. This cultural nuance is vital for tailoring site management strategies effectively. Additionally, studies often focus on specific phases of the visitor journey, such as analysing on-site interactions or post-visit feedback. Yet, comprehensive research capturing the entire spectrum of the visitor experience, including online engagement before the visit, is scarce. For instance, investigating how online discussions and social media interactions influence visitor expectations and behaviours can provide critical insights often missing from current analyses. Furthermore, while short-term predictions about visitor trends are standard, there is a notable gap concerning long-term sustainability planning. Considering the ancient city of Pompeii as an example, understanding how visitor patterns change over years or decades is essential for preserving delicate archaeological sites. Insights into prolonged visitor behaviours inform conservation efforts and long-term site management strategies. Climate change adds another layer of complexity. For instance, UNESCO World Heritage Sites like the Great Barrier Reef face shifting visitor patterns due to environmental changes. Integrating climate-related variables, such as water temperature and weather patterns, into predictive models is crucial to understanding visitor fluctuations caused by climate shifts. Despite their significance, ethical considerations concerning data privacy and responsible data practices are often overlooked. For example, ensuring that visitor data collected via mobile apps or sensors is anonymised and used responsibly is vital to maintaining visitor trust. Neglecting these ethical aspects can lead to privacy breaches and potential visitor reluctance to engage with heritage sites digitally. Additionally, emerging technologies like the Internet of Things (IoT) offer immense potential. For instance, IoT sensors at historical sites can track visitor movements and preferences in real time. However, integrating such technologies into predictive analytics frameworks is still in its infancy, limiting our understanding of their full potential in enhancing visitor experiences and site management. Lastly, theoretical advancements often fall short of translating into practical applications. For heritage sites like Machu Picchu, translating predictive models into real-time crowd management strategies during peak tourist seasons remains challenging. Bridging this gap between theoretical research and on-ground implementation is crucial for ensuring that heritage sites are preserved and enjoyed sustainably by visitors.

The study aims to integrate predictive analytics, cultural sensitivity, ethical considerations, and long-term sustainability to provide a comprehensive and responsible framework for understanding and managing visitor behaviours at heritage sites. By achieving this integration, the research aims to contribute to the theoretical understanding of heritage site management and develop practical strategies that promote cultural preservation and responsible visitor engagement. Understanding visitor patterns is pivotal for heritage site managers and conservationists. Predictive analytics, leveraging historical visitation data, demographic information, and environmental factors, provides a powerful toolset. By analysing these data points, site managers can anticipate visitor trends, enabling them to tailor preservation efforts and visitor experiences.

1. Optimizing Visitor Experiences: Predictive analytics enables the customisation of visitor experiences. By understanding peak visitation times, popular attractions, and visitor demographics, heritage site managers can design tailored exhibits and events, ensuring a more engaging and educational experience for visitors.
2. Preservation and Conservation: Preservation efforts can be optimised through predictive modelling. Anticipating visitor flow helps implement conservation measures strategically, ensuring that high-traffic areas are protected, and delicate artifacts are preserved without compromising the visitor experience.
3. Resource Allocation: Efficient resource allocation is essential for any heritage site. Predictive analytics aids in resource planning by forecasting visitor numbers. This information guides staffing, ticketing, and facility management, ensuring that resources are utilised optimally and sustainably.

In the context of this study, our research focuses on a selection of diverse heritage sites, each with its unique historical, cultural, and natural significance. These sites include ancient archaeological ruins, heritage museums, natural reserves, and culturally significant landmarks across different regions. For instance, one site might be a UNESCO World Heritage archaeological site with ancient ruins dating back centuries. At the same time, another could be a heritage museum housing a vast collection of artefacts from a specific historical era. Each site attracts a varied demographic of visitors, including tourists, historians, students, and residents, all seeking to engage with the heritage on offer. Understanding these sites' nuanced visitor behaviour patterns is critical for preserving authenticity, ensuring visitor satisfaction, and promoting sustainable tourism practices. We aim to uncover vital patterns for informed decision-making by applying predictive analytics to these sites. Through this study, we bridge the gap between heritage preservation and data-driven insights, paving the way for a more profound understanding of visitor dynamics and effective heritage site management.

Research Objectives:

1. To Develop Predictive Models: The primary objective of this research is to develop accurate and reliable predictive models using advanced analytics techniques. These models will forecast visitor patterns at heritage sites, considering historical visitation data, demographic information, and environmental variables.
2. To Optimize Visitor Experiences: Another key objective is to leverage the predictive models to enhance visitor experiences. By understanding visitor behaviour, the research aims to provide actionable insights to heritage site managers, enabling them to tailor exhibits, events, and facilities to meet their visitors' specific preferences and expectations.
3. To Inform Conservation Efforts: The research seeks to contribute to preserving and conserving heritage sites. By predicting visitor flow, the study aims to guide conservation efforts, ensuring that high-traffic areas are protected and delicate artefacts are preserved, thus striking a balance between visitor engagement and site preservation.
4. To Improve Resource Allocation: Efficient resource allocation is crucial for heritage site management. This research aims to provide insights that aid in optimal resource allocation. By forecasting visitor numbers, site managers can streamline staffing, ticketing, and facility management, maximising resource utilisation and sustainability.

Research Questions:

RQ1: What are the significant factors influencing visitor patterns at heritage sites?

- This question identifies critical variables, such as historical visitation data, demographic information, and environmental factors significantly impacting visitor patterns.

RQ2: Can predictive models accurately forecast visitor numbers and behaviours at heritage sites?

- This question assesses the effectiveness of the developed predictive models in forecasting visitor numbers and behaviours. It involves evaluating the accuracy and reliability of the models in different contexts.

RQ3: How can predictive analytics be leveraged to enhance visitor experiences at heritage sites?

- This question explores the practical applications of predictive analytics in tailoring visitor experiences. It involves understanding how insights derived from predictive models can be translated into actionable strategies to improve visitor satisfaction.

RQ4: In what ways can predictive analytics inform conservation efforts at heritage sites?

- This question investigates the role of predictive analytics in guiding conservation efforts. It explores how predicting visitor flow can help implement conservation measures strategically, ensuring the preservation of heritage sites.

RQ5: How does predictive analytics contribute to optimising resource allocation for heritage site management?

- This question focuses on the impact of predictive analytics on resource allocation. It examines how forecasting visitor numbers and behaviours can facilitate efficient staffing, ticketing, and facility management, maximising resource utilisation and sustainability.

By addressing these research questions, this study aims to advance the understanding of predictive analytics in heritage site management and provide valuable insights for site managers, conservationists, and policymakers.

Predicting visitor patterns is the linchpin of effective heritage site management and preservation, intricately connecting a web of advantages essential for the site's thriving existence. By delving into the intricate nuances of visitor behaviours, heritage site managers gain the invaluable ability to craft tailored, immersive experiences. Based on predictive insights, this personalisation allows for the meticulous arrangement of exhibits, events, and guided tours, ensuring that every visitor, whether a historian, a student, or a tourist, finds relevance and fascination within the site's historical narratives. Furthermore, these predictive analytics serve as guiding stars in conservation. They empower site custodians to orchestrate strategic preservation efforts, safeguarding fragile artefacts and ancient structures without impinging on the visitor experience. This delicate balance between conservation and visitor engagement is essential, preserving the site's authenticity while allowing visitors to connect intimately with the past. Predictive modelling is not merely a tool but the cornerstone of sustainable tourism practices. By foreseeing visitor trends, heritage sites can mitigate overcrowding, a menace threatening the visitor experience and the site's physical integrity. This foresight enables an environment where visitors can explore, learn, and appreciate without overwhelming the delicate historical fabric.

Yet, the impact of predictive analytics extends far beyond visitor experiences. It directly influences the efficient allocation of resources, from staffing levels to ticketing systems and facility management. This optimisation ensures that resources are utilised judiciously and contribute substantially to the financial sustenance of the heritage site. The revenue generated can be reinvested in crucial conservation endeavours, creating a self-sustaining preservation and visitor engagement cycle. Moreover, this predictive knowledge acts as a catalyst for educational initiatives. By understanding visitor demographics and preferences, educational programs can be curated to cater to the specific needs of diverse visitor segments. This targeted education enriches the visitor experience and cultivates a deep sense of understanding and appreciation for the site's cultural and historical significance. In the face of unforeseen challenges such as natural disasters, predictive analytics provides a shield of preparedness. By identifying low-visitor periods, site managers can plan vital maintenance and reinforce structures, fortifying the site's resilience against the unpredictable forces of nature. Additionally, predictive models inform policy formulation, shaping regulations that encourage responsible tourism and the ethical preservation of heritage sites. These policies become the guardians of the site's integrity, ensuring that it remains unscathed by the adverse impacts of unchecked tourism. Lastly, predictive analytics's influence permeates the community, fostering engagement and empowerment. The local economy is stimulated by strategically planning events and markets during peak visitor periods. This economic empowerment enhances the local population's sense of ownership and pride, establishing a symbiotic relationship between the heritage site and its surrounding community.

In essence, the ability to predict visitor patterns transcends beyond statistical algorithms; it forms the heart of a holistic approach to heritage site management. It harmonises the intricate dance between visitor experiences, conservation efforts, financial sustainability, education, disaster resilience, policy advocacy, and community engagement. Predictive analytics, therefore, is a tool and the essence of ensuring the heritage site's enduring legacy for generations.

## LITERATURE REVIEW

*Palmer (1999)* asserted that "the buzz" term of the 1990s was "heritage". Heritage tourism is seen via an economic lens by *Fyall & Garrod (1998)*, who propose that it is a process in which natural and sociocultural resources are employed to draw in tourists. But heritage tourism is "a subgroup of tourism, in which the main motivation for visiting a site is based on the place's heritage characteristics according to the tourists' perception of their own heritage," as described by *Poria, Butler, & Airey (2003)*. According to *Timothy (1997)*, there are four levels at which heritage visitor attractions (HVA) ought to be evaluated: (1) global, (2) national, (3) local, and (4) personal. HVA is an essential industry component and is frequently seen as a "pull" factor that draws visitors to a destination for various reasons *(Kempiak et al., 2017)*. Tourists visiting heritage places interact with three main spheres: Person basis, Space basis, and Situation basis. These variables interact to explain a tourist's intention to discover a monument. The interactive aspect of heritage experience and the importance of situational aspects have led researchers to accept a chronological and situation-driven presentation of variables explaining monument visits. Touring heritage sites involves rationale for discovery and in-situ reactions to consumption circumstances and cultural offers. The tourism industry and the heritage tourism sector are closely linked to the consumption of experiences, according to the core idea of the experience economy *(Pine & Gilmore, 1999; Chen & Chen, 2010)*. It is crucial to analyse how experience notions have evolved in light of the industry's dynamic character and technology advancements. As *Richards (2012)* noted, some have argued that the experience economy idea overemphasises the producer's involvement in generating experiences and undervalues the role of the customer in designing, modifying, and customising their own. According to *Richards (2012)*, co-creation and communities are important components of the evolutionary model of the tourism consumer experience. The co-creation process allows companies and consumers to work together. It encourages both to actively participate in the design and implementation of the experience, in contrast to the experience economy, where the emphasis is on staging the experience *(Prahalad & Ramaswamy, 2004)*. Although this study won't specifically address co-creation, it will attempt to investigate visitor behaviour at a local and national HVA. A visit to a heritage site entails engaging with a complex range of interrelated components, as suggested by *Dierking & Falk (1992)*. These components include the personal—an individual's characteristics, such as motivations and interests—the social—experience and behaviours that vary, such as according to the travelling party—and the physical—the heritage setting, such as exhibitions and atmospherics. "An experience occurs when a company intentionally uses services as the stage and goods as props to engage individual customers in a way that creates a memorable event," according to *Pine & Gilmore (1999)*. This concept emphasises key elements, including purposeful application, involvement, and a memorable experience. In addition, the writers distinguished four aspects of experiences—entertainment, education, aesthetics, and escapism—based on the type of experience and the degree of visitor engagement. The experience model's four realms imply that visitors seeking entertainment participate in the encounter only indirectly. However, it's important to remember that, as *Hughes & Benn (1995)* pointed out, entertainment is one of the most important components within the vast range of tourist offerings. However, when it comes to education, tourists want to learn something new; therefore, the process calls for more active participation and engagement, allowing visitors to broaden their knowledge. Additionally, absorption—a term that denotes the occupation of a visitor's attention by a certain experience—defines both characteristics *(Pine & Gilmore, 1999)*. The separation of entertainment and education is unquestionably noteworthy, particularly when considering cultural sites that seek to both amuse and educate visitors. More recent research has identified the emerging trend of edutainment, which aims to combine educational technologies and educational content to fully utilise their values and improve the visitor experience *(Hertzman, Anderson, & Rowley, 2008)*, considering that both are strong motivating factors. Additionally, the model suggests that the perception of the physical surroundings and passive appreciation of the location are related to the aesthetic component. According to *Oh, Fiore, & Jeoung (2007)*, the importance of aesthetics is seen in servicescape, which frequently influences users' decisions on whether to return to and promote the site to others. On the other hand, when people engage in escapism, they frequently "travel" into a new reality; as a result, they actively participate in the experience, which allows them to escape from their routine and everyday activities *(Che et al., 2022)*.

Prior studies on heritage consumption *(Daengbuppha, Hemmington, & Wilkes, 2006; Petr, 2002)* have shown that the factors that may influence the frequency of visits to monuments should be examined in a methodical and progressively context-specific sequence. The literature on predictive analytics in heritage site management weaves a comprehensive narrative, revealing a landscape rich with research and practical applications. Researchers have meticulously explored various facets, emphasising the pivotal role of predictive analytics in heritage sites. One prominent theme within this literature is the predictive modelling of visitor behaviour. Advanced statistical models and machine learning algorithms have been employed to anticipate visitor numbers, preferences, and patterns. Predictive analytics becomes instrumental in forecasting visitor influx by dissecting historical data alongside demographic information and external factors such as weather conditions. This foresight equips site managers with the ability to prepare for peak periods effectively, optimising staffing levels and ensuring overall visitor satisfaction. Beyond mere prediction, this analytical approach extends to customising visitor experiences. Predictive analytics empowers site managers to tailor exhibits, guided tours, and events based on anticipated visitor preferences. By discerning which artefacts or historical aspects are likely to capture attention, heritage sites can create personalised and captivating experiences. This customisation engages visitors profoundly and nurtures a deeper connection between the audience and the site's cultural significance. The application of predictive analytics isn't confined to visitor experiences alone; it permeates the domain of preservation and conservation efforts. Site managers can strategically implement conservation measures by accurately predicting visitor flow and pinpointing high-traffic areas. Delicate artefacts and vulnerable structures can thus be protected without compromising the visitor experience. This balanced approach ensures the long-term sustainability of heritage sites, allowing public access and appreciation while safeguarding historical treasures. Efficient resource allocation emerges as another critical area influenced by predictive analytics. Site managers leverage predictive models to optimise staffing, ticketing, and facility management. This strategic allocation enhances operational efficiency and contributes significantly to the financial sustainability of heritage sites. Such optimisation allows for further investments in conservation and site development, fostering a cycle of growth and preservation.

Moreover, integrating predictive analytics with cutting-edge technologies such as IoT and mobile applications marks a significant stride. Real-time data collection and analysis enable adaptive management strategies. Site managers are empowered to make data-driven decisions, promptly responding to changing visitor patterns and preferences. This integration transforms heritage sites into interactive and engaging spaces, enhancing the overall visitor experience. However, amidst the promising prospects, the literature also sheds light on challenges and ethical considerations. Issues related to data privacy, visitor tracking, and the need for interpretive balance are carefully addressed. Ethical frameworks underscore transparent communication with visitors and stakeholders, ensuring data collection methods respect individual privacy. The literature paints a vivid picture of predictive analytics as a transformative force in heritage site management. From predicting visitor behaviour to customising experiences, optimising resources, and integrating technology, this approach stands at the intersection of preserving cultural heritage and providing immersive, enriching visitor interactions. Researchers and practitioners, guided by ethical principles, continue to shape this landscape, contributing to the evolution of predictive analytics in the nuanced context of heritage site management.

Predicting visitor behaviours at heritage sites involves the application of various theories and models, each offering unique insights into the complex interplay of factors shaping visitor interactions. Here are some relevant theories and models commonly used in predicting visitor behaviours:

1. Theory of Planned Behavior (TPB): According to TPB, individual behaviour is determined by behavioural intentions, which are influenced by attitudes, subjective norms, and perceived behavioural control. In the context of heritage sites, attitudes towards the site, social norms related to visiting cultural landmarks, and perceived ease of access and enjoyment influence visitors' intentions. Predictive models incorporating TPB variables can anticipate visitor decisions and behaviours, aiding in designing targeted interventions to influence these factors *(Che et al., 2022; Petr, 2015; Cuccia and Cellini, 2007)*.
2. Push-Pull Theory: This model posits that tourists are pushed out of their home locations by specific factors (such as stress or routine) and pulled to a destination by different factors (such as cultural attractions or natural beauty).

Understanding the push factors (motivations to leave home) and pull factors (attractions at the destination) helps predict visitors' preferences and choices. Heritage sites can analyse these factors to predict the influx of visitors during specific periods *(Miah et al., 2017).*

3. Expectation-Confirmation Theory: This theory suggests that fulfilling their pre-visit expectations influences visitor satisfaction. Predictive models based on this theory incorporate online reviews, promotional materials, and prior visitor experiences to anticipate visitor satisfaction. By aligning actual experiences with visitor expectations, heritage sites can predict and enhance visitor satisfaction *(Che et al., 2022; Kempiak et al., 2017).*
4. Destination Lifecycle Model: This model categorises destinations into stages, such as exploration, involvement, development, consolidation, stagnation, and decline. Predictive analytics using this model can anticipate visitor behaviours based on the destination's current stage. For example, heritage sites in the exploration stage might experience different visitor behaviours than those in the consolidation stage. Understanding these stages helps predict visitor numbers and preferences *(Zhou & Chen, 2023; Oren, Poria, & Reichel, 2022).*
5. Machine Learning Algorithms: Machine learning models, including decision trees, random forests, and neural networks, are increasingly used in predictive analytics. These algorithms can handle large and complex datasets, identifying intricate patterns within visitor behaviour. Machine learning models can predict visitor behaviours, preferences, and even sentiment analysis from online reviews by analysing historical data, visitor demographics, and external variables *(Che et al., 2022).*
6. Time Series Analysis: Time series forecasting methods, such as Autoregressive Integrated Moving Average (ARIMA) and Seasonal-Trend decomposition using LOESS (STL), are essential for predicting visitor patterns over time. These models account for temporal trends and variations, allowing heritage sites to predict visitor numbers during specific time frames, which is crucial for staffing, resource allocation, and event planning *(Goulding & Pomfret, 2022).*
7. Social Network Analysis: Social network analysis explores visitor relationships and interactions. By understanding social dynamics within visitor groups, heritage sites can predict group behaviours. Analysing social networks also helps identify influential visitors, which can be leveraged for targeted marketing or personalised experiences *(Miah et al., 2017; Kempiak et al., 2017).*
8. Technology Adoption Models: Models such as the Technology Acceptance Model (TAM) and the Unified Theory of Acceptance and Use of Technology (UTAUT) focus on users' acceptance and adoption of technology. In the context of heritage sites, these models are valuable for predicting visitor behaviours

related to mobile apps, augmented reality guides, or interactive exhibits *(Md Khairi, Ismail, & Syed Jaafar, 2022)*.

Combining these theories and models with advanced data analytics techniques provides a robust foundation for predicting visitor behaviours at heritage sites. By understanding the psychological, sociological, and technological factors influencing visitors, heritage sites can anticipate, accommodate, and enhance visitor experiences, ultimately contributing to the sustainable management and preservation of these valuable cultural assets.

In the dynamic landscape of heritage site management, understanding visitor behaviours is pivotal for creating enriching experiences and preserving cultural treasures. This intricate exploration involves a sophisticated interplay of methodologies and techniques. Researchers study visitor behaviours at heritage sites using various methods and techniques. Surveys and questionnaires provide quantitative data, while qualitative approaches like interviews and focus groups provide nuanced insights into visitor experiences, motivations, and emotions *(Zhou & Chen, 2023)*. Observational studies record visitor movement interactions and exhibit engagement, yielding real-time data that informs site managers. Data mining techniques reveal intricate patterns within visitor behaviour, while machine learning algorithms forecast visitor behaviours based on historical data *(Md Khairi, Ismail, & Syed Jaafar, 2022)*. Spatial analysis, facilitated by Geographic Information Systems (GIS), optimises layouts and infrastructure, while social network analysis uncovers social dynamics shaping visitor behaviour *(Che et al., 2022)*. Mobile tracking technologies and Wi-Fi analytics offer real-time insights into visitor movements, guiding exhibit layouts and crowd management strategies. Sentiment analysis, a part of Natural Language Processing (NLP), gauges visitor satisfaction levels and pinpoints areas for improvement *(Oren, Poria, & Reichel, 2022)*. Time series analysis methods, like ARIMA and STL, predict visitor numbers over time, considering temporal patterns and variations. Experimental studies, like A/B testing, create controlled environments to assess interventions' impact on visitor behaviours *(Goulding & Pomfret, 2022)*. This interconnected web of methodologies and techniques helps researchers gain a multifaceted understanding of visitor behaviours, guiding site management strategies for personalised experiences, efficient resource allocation, and sustainable preservation of heritage sites.

In the ever-evolving landscape of heritage site management, a nuanced understanding of visitor behaviour is indispensable. Within the existing body of research, several critical gaps persist, forming the focal points of this study's exploration. One of these gaps lies in cultural sensitivity, where the rich tapestry of diverse cultural backgrounds often remains unexplored. This study endeavours to bridge this gap by integrating cultural nuances into predictive models, acknowledging the profound influence of cultural diversity on visitor behaviours. A notable void in the current research landscape involves the limited integration of cutting-edge technologies such as the Internet of Things (IoT) and mobile tracking systems. To fill this void, this study aims to comprehensively leverage these technologies, allowing for real-time data collection and refining predictive models with granular, up-to-the-minute insights. Such integration promises to enhance the accuracy and responsiveness of predictive analytics in understanding and forecasting visitor behaviours at heritage sites. Another significant gap lies in focusing on short-term visitor predictions at the expense of long-term sustainability considerations. The study addresses this by spotlighting the enduring impact of predictive analytics on heritage site preservation and conservation efforts. By extending the temporal horizon, the research aims to unravel strategies that ensure the longevity of heritage sites, balancing visitor engagement with preservation imperatives and community integration. Ethical considerations often emerge as an overlooked aspect in predictive analytics studies. Respect for visitor privacy and responsible data use is paramount. This study recognises this ethical gap and endeavours to embed principles of privacy and responsibility in its methodologies, ensuring that the insights gleaned are ethically sound and respect visitor confidentiality. Social dynamics and community involvement also represent underexplored dimensions in existing research. This study delves into these intricate webs, examining the influence of social networks and community-driven initiatives on visitor patterns. By unravelling these dynamics, the research aims to inform heritage site management strategies that are not only visitor-centric but also community-engaged, fostering a symbiotic relationship between the site and its local inhabitants. Additionally, the study acknowledges the pressing concern of climate change and its impact on visitor patterns, especially in outdoor heritage sites. Incorporating climate-related variables into predictive models becomes imperative for adaptive management. By considering these variables, the research aims to develop strategies for changing weather patterns, ensuring visitor safety and experience continuity in the face of climate-related challenges. Lastly, the study addresses the gap in tailored visitor education initiatives. By leveraging predictive analytics, the research aims to inform educational programs that resonate with diverse visitor segments. These programs, aligned with the varied interests and backgrounds of visitors, promise to enrich the visitor experience and foster a deeper understanding and appreciation of the heritage site's cultural significance. Through a holistic exploration of these interconnected gaps, this study aspires not only to advance the scholarly discourse on predictive analytics in heritage site management but also to provide pragmatic, culturally sensitive, and ethically robust solutions. In doing so, the research endeavours to shape a future where heritage sites are not only preserved and sustained but also become vibrant centres of engagement, education, and cultural celebration.

## METHODOLOGY

The research design and approach for this study involve a systematic and structured methodology to investigate the predictive analytics of visitor behaviours at heritage sites. This study employs a quantitative research design, focusing on numerical data and statistical analysis. A cross-sectional approach is utilised to collect data at a specific point in time, providing a snapshot of visitor behaviours. The research is observational and non-experimental, aiming to analyse existing patterns and trends rather than manipulating variables. The research approach integrates both primary and secondary data sources. Primary data is collected through surveys, interviews, and on-site observations of four heritage sites of India, aiming to capture visitor demographics, preferences, and behaviours directly. Secondary data, derived from scholarly articles, reports, and previous studies, supplements the primary data and provides a broader context for the analysis. The data collection involves structured surveys administered to visitors at selected heritage sites. These surveys include questions about visitor demographics, interests, reasons for the visit, and overall satisfaction levels. Interviews with site managers and staff provide qualitative insights into site management practices. On-site observations are conducted to gather real-time data on visitor movements, interactions, and engagement with exhibits. Quantitative data from surveys are analysed using statistical techniques such as descriptive statistics, regression analysis, and correlation analysis. These methods help identify patterns, correlations, and factors influencing visitor behaviours. Qualitative data from interviews and observations are thematically analysed to extract meaningful insights and enhance the quantitative findings. Ethical guidelines are followed throughout the research process. Informed consent is obtained from participants, ensuring their willingness to participate in surveys and interviews. The anonymity and confidentiality of participants are maintained, and the data is securely stored and accessed only by authorised researchers. The study acknowledges certain limitations, including potential response bias in surveys and the influence of external factors such as weather or special events on visitor behaviours. These limitations are considered during the data analysis and interpretation processes. By employing this comprehensive research design and approach, the study aims to provide valuable insights into the predictive analytics of visitor behaviours at heritage sites, contributing to enhancing visitor experiences and sustainable site management practices.

### Data Collection

The data collection process in studying visitor behaviours at heritage sites involves a meticulous approach, gathering diverse datasets to gain a comprehensive understanding of visitor patterns. The types of data collected encompass various categories, each providing unique insights into visitor behaviours:

1. Demographic Data: Demographic data includes information about visitors' age, gender, nationality, educational background, and occupation. Surveys and questionnaires are commonly employed methods to collect demographic data. Understanding the demographics of visitors helps in segmenting the audience and tailoring exhibits and events to specific groups.
2. Historical Visitation Data: Historical visitation data comprises records of past visitors, including entrance numbers, visitation frequency, peak hours, and popular exhibits or areas within the site. This data is typically obtained from site databases, visitor logs, or ticketing systems. Historical visitation patterns provide valuable insights into seasonal variations, visitor preferences, and site popularity.
3. Environmental Data (Weather, Seasons, Local Events): Weather data, including temperature, precipitation, and humidity, is collected from local meteorological sources. Additionally, information about local events, festivals, and public holidays that might influence visitor patterns is gathered. Understanding these environmental factors helps predict visitor turnout during specific weather conditions and planning events to coincide with local festivities.
4. Site Accessibility and Infrastructure Data: Data related to site accessibility, including transportation options, parking availability, and proximity to public transport, is collected. Information about site amenities such as restrooms, cafeterias, guided tours, and wheelchair accessibility is also essential. Site infrastructure data assists in analysing visitor comfort and determining areas for improvement.
5. Marketing and Outreach Data: Marketing and outreach data encompass the effectiveness of promotional campaigns, social media engagement, website traffic, and online reviews. Data from online platforms, visitor feedback, and surveys provide insights into visitor perceptions, expectations, and motivations. Analysing marketing data helps in assessing the impact of promotional efforts on visitor numbers and satisfaction levels.
6. Visitor Expectations and Feedback: Surveys, interviews, and online feedback forms collect visitor expectations, feedback, and suggestions. Qualitative data from these sources provide in-depth insights into visitor experiences, interests, and areas of improvement. Visitor feedback helps gauge visitor satisfaction and tailor future site offerings to meet visitor expectations.
7. Cultural and Historical Significance Data: Data related to the cultural and historical significance of artefacts, exhibits, or landmarks within the site are gathered. This information includes historical context, cultural importance,

and archaeological significance. Understanding the cultural and historical relevance of site elements aids in crafting meaningful narratives and educational experiences for visitors.

By systematically collecting and analysing these diverse data types, researchers and site managers can unravel complex visitor behaviours, enabling data-driven decision-making, personalised visitor experiences, and sustainable heritage site management practices.

In the pursuit of unravelling the intricate tapestry of visitor behaviours at heritage sites, the selection of predictive analytics techniques stands as a pivotal decision, shaping the depth and precision of insights gleaned from the data. Among the chosen methodologies, incorporating Artificial Neural Network (ANN) and Correlation Analysis represents a strategic fusion of computational complexity and foundational exploration. As heritage sites evolve into multifaceted domains, influenced by many interrelated factors, the application of ANN becomes indispensable. Its remarkable ability to discern intricate, non-linear patterns within data aligns seamlessly with the intricacies of visitor behaviours, allowing for a profound understanding of nuanced interactions. This complexity is further complemented by the simplicity and clarity offered by Correlation Analysis, serving as the initial beacon of exploration. The strength of Correlation Analysis lies in its capacity to identify key relationships, providing foundational insights that validate and refine the intricate patterns deciphered by ANN. Together, these techniques form a symbiotic alliance, offering a comprehensive approach to analysing visitor behaviours. ANN delves deep, capturing subtle nuances, while Correlation Analysis grounds the findings, ensuring their reliability and interpretability. This harmonious integration promises not only an in-depth exploration of the factors shaping visitor patterns but also a robust validation process, instilling confidence in the research outcomes. In heritage site management, where data-driven decisions hold the key to enriching visitor experiences, this fusion of advanced computational prowess and foundational analysis stands as a beacon, illuminating the path toward a profound understanding of the intricacies of visitor behaviours at heritage sites.

## Data Processing

In data analysis for understanding visitor behaviours at heritage sites, a meticulous data preprocessing process is the foundation for meaningful insights. The initial step involves cleaning the dataset addressing missing values, outliers, and duplicates. By ensuring data completeness and integrity, the subsequent analyses are built upon a reliable foundation. Outliers, if not handled, can distort the results significantly, making their identification and treatment crucial. Removing duplicates eliminates redundancy, streamlining the dataset for practical analysis. Following data cleaning, transformation becomes imperative to standardise the dataset. Normalisation and standardisation techniques are applied to numerical features, ensuring uniformity and comparability across scales. Categorical variables intrinsic to heritage site data are transformed into numerical format through one-hot encoding, making them suitable for machine learning algorithms. Additionally, feature engineering, where new variables are derived from existing data, captures nuanced insights. These new features, tailored to the specific context of heritage sites, enrich the dataset, providing a deeper understanding of visitor behaviours. Feature selection, guided by meticulous reasoning and domain expertise, plays a pivotal role in shaping the analytical framework. Correlation analysis uncovers relationships between variables and the target, identifying influential features. Features exhibiting strong correlations are crucial in predicting visitor behaviours and are thus prioritised. Recursive Feature Elimination (RFE) refines the selection process, systematically removing less significant features and enhancing the model's predictive power. Domain expertise acts as a guiding beacon, ensuring the inclusion of variables known to impact visitor behaviours at heritage sites profoundly. In this interconnected process, the power of Artificial Neural Networks (ANN) comes to the fore. ANN, with its innate ability to decipher complex patterns, simplifies feature selection by autonomously identifying pertinent variables crucial for predicting visitor behaviours. In the context of software, SPSS serves as the platform, providing a robust environment for data analysis, statistical modelling, and machine learning applications.

This systematic approach to data preprocessing guarantees that subsequent analyses are robust and reliable. Through these interconnected steps, the dataset is refined, transformed, and enriched, setting the stage for in-depth studies that unveil the intricate dynamics of visitor behaviours at heritage sites. The application of ANN, coupled with the utilisation of SPSS, adds a layer of sophistication and accuracy to the predictive models, ensuring a comprehensive understanding of visitor patterns.

## DATA ANALYSIS

The analysis of visitor influence is based on extracting influential variables (refer to Table 1), including demographics and environmental conditions. A thorough data collection process is then initiated to reveal subtle patterns and trends that define visitor behaviours. Advanced analytical techniques decode the impact of variables such as historical visitation data, demographic information, environmental factors, and site-specific features. The objective is to uncover the layers of visitor engagement, providing profound insights that underpin heritage site management strategies. Using cutting-edge predictive analytics, the collected data is used to forecast future visitor patterns. ANN and statistical methods form the backbone of our predictive models, offering glimpses into the future of heritage site visitation. This informs informed decision-making, preserving heritage authenticity and enhancing visitor experiences. The insights derived from data analysis and predictive analytics are translated into actionable strategies, allowing site managers and policymakers to optimise resource allocation, personalise visitor experiences, and strategic conservation efforts. Combining data-driven insights with heritage site management ensures a balance between visitor satisfaction, site preservation, and sustainable tourism practices.

*Table 1. Variable list influencing heritage site visitor pattern*

| Variables | Heritage site visitor pattern influencer | | References |
|---|---|---|---|
| Historical Visitation Data | Total visitor numbers per day/week/month/year | HV1 | *(Miah et al., 2017; Kempiak et al., 2017)* |
| | Visitor patterns during specific events or exhibitions | HV2 | |
| | Trends in repeat visitors vs. new visitors | HV3 | |
| Demographic Information | Age groups (children, teenagers, young adults, middle-aged, seniors) | D1 | *(Zhou & Chen, 2023; Che et al., 2022; Petr, 2015; Cuccia and Cellini, 2007).* |
| | Gender distribution (male, female, non-binary) | D2 | |
| | Nationalities and cultural backgrounds | D3 | |
| | Education levels (students, researchers, general public) | D4 | |
| Environmental Factors | Weather conditions (temperature, precipitation, humidity) | EV1 | *(Zhou & Chen, 2023; Oren, Poria, & Reichel, 2022)* |
| | Seasonal variations and their impact on visitor numbers | EV2 | |
| | Site accessibility (distance from urban centres, public transport availability) | EV3 | |
| | Natural factors (presence of flora and fauna, scenic beauty) | EV4 | |
| Site-Specific Features | Popularity of specific exhibits or artifacts | SS1 | *(Md Khairi, Ismail, & Syed Jaafar, 2022; Miah et al., 2017; Kempiak et al., 2017)* |
| | Availability of interactive displays or multimedia installations | SS2 | |
| | Special events, festivals, or temporary exhibitions | SS3 | |
| | Amenities (restrooms, cafeterias, souvenir shops, seating areas) | SS4 | |
| Online and Social Media Data | Social media engagement (likes, shares, comments) | OS1 | *(Md Khairi, Ismail, & Syed Jaafar, 2022; Goulding & Pomfret, 2022)* |
| | Online reviews and ratings (on platforms like TripAdvisor and Google Reviews) | OS2 | |
| | Website traffic and user behaviour (pages viewed, time spent) | OS3 | |
| | Social media influencers' impact on visitor numbers | OS4 | |
| Economic Factors | Ticket pricing strategies (regular, student, senior, group discounts) | EC1 | *(Goulding & Pomfret, 2022; Miah et al., 2017; Kempiak et al., 2017)* |
| | Economic conditions of the local area (income levels, employment rates) | EC2 | |
| | Accessibility of the heritage site about transportation costs | EC3 | |
| | Economic impact of the heritage site on the local community | EC4 | |
| Marketing and Promotion | Effectiveness of marketing campaigns (online ads, brochures, billboards) | MP1 | *(Zhou & Chen, 2023; Oren, Poria, & Reichel, 2022)* |
| | Collaborations with local businesses and hotels | MP2 | |
| | Partnerships with travel agencies and tour operators | MP3 | |
| | Social media marketing reach and engagement metrics | MP4 | |

*Continued on following page*

*Table 1. Continued*

| Variables | Heritage site visitor pattern influencer | | References |
|---|---|---|---|
| Visitor Behavior Data | Dwell time at specific exhibits or areas | VB1 | *(Che et al., 2022; Petr, 2015; Cuccia and Cellini, 2007)* |
| | Interaction frequency with guided tours or workshops | VB2 | |
| | Participation in educational programs or cultural events | VB3 | |
| | Purchases made at souvenir shops or cafes | VB4 | |
| Visitor Feedback | Survey responses regarding visitor experiences and satisfaction levels | VF1 | *(Che et al., 2022; Petr, 2015; Cuccia and Cellini, 2007).* |
| | Specific comments or suggestions provided by visitors | VF2 | |
| | Complaints or issues raised by visitors and resolutions offered | VF3 | |

A meticulous data collection process was undertaken through surveys conducted in four culturally diverse cities: Udaipur, Bishnupur, Ahmedabad, and Jaipur. These cities served as unique canvases, each showcasing distinct forms of heritage sites. In Udaipur, renowned for its palace heritage, visitors' interactions within regal residences were observed, capturing the essence of royal splendour and historical intrigue. Bishnupur, characterised by its temple heritage, provided insights into spiritual inclinations and architectural appreciation, offering a glimpse into the sacred world of ancient temples. In Ahmedabad, the survey focused on mining heritage, delving into the historical contexts and visitor engagement within mining sites, highlighting the city's industrial heritage. Meanwhile, Jaipur's rich tapestry included both memorial and palace heritage, providing a multifaceted perspective on visitor dynamics within commemorative spaces and regal palaces. Leveraging the demographic profiles of the selected heritage cities, our research recalibrated its approach. Utilising a calculated sample size of 893, determined at a 95% confidence level with a 5% error margin, the study embarked on a comprehensive survey strategy. This redirection became imperative due to the partial availability of historical visitation data. By tapping into the perceptions and experiences of visitors through surveys, the research aimed to bridge the data gap and extract valuable insights directly from the individuals engaging with the heritage sites. This methodological shift ensured a robust foundation for the study. Through carefully structured surveys, we captured various visitor perspectives, including demographics, preferences, and behaviours. This data-driven approach not only compensated for the limitations in historical data but also enriched the study with firsthand accounts from the heritage site visitors themselves. By adopting this survey-centric methodology, the research embraced the dynamic nature of visitor interactions within heritage sites. Visitors' responses, reflective of their motivations and experiences, became pivotal in shaping the study's analytical framework. This recalibration allowed us to draw meaningful conclusions, shedding light on visitor behaviours, preferences, and patterns within the unique context of the selected heritage cities. Thus, the study's redirection underscored the adaptability and resilience of the research methodology, ensuring the acquisition of valuable insights despite initial data constraints. In this study, on-site surveys and interviews were conducted with crucial assistance from heritage trusts and tour guides at all four sites. Additionally, separate support was provided by Udaipur and Jaipur charitable foundations. These collaborations allowed for the meticulous gathering of diverse and detailed data directly from the heritage sites. Working closely with these organisations, comprehensive surveys and interviews were structured, benefiting from the expertise of heritage trusts and tour guides. The involvement of Udaipur and Jaipur charitable foundations further enhanced the research, ensuring a comprehensive understanding of visitor behaviours across these culturally significant locations. The survey data of 893 visitors was meticulously organised and input into Excel, a crucial step in ensuring its systematic arrangement. Subsequently, the data was exported into SPSS for in-depth analysis. It's noteworthy that the collected data was primarily presented in verbal expression terms, aligning with the conventional format of survey forms. This approach was deliberately chosen to enhance participants' comprehension during the surveys, employing the Analytical Hierarchy Process (AHP) format. To facilitate comprehensive analysis, these verbal expressions were then meticulously converted into numeric representations. This conversion allowed for more efficient data handling, ensuring a seamless transition from the qualitative to the quantitative realm for precise analysis and interpretation. Following the initial data input, a rigorous cleaning process was employed to ensure accuracy and reliability. The research used correlation analysis to explore the relationships between variables and the interconnections among various factors. It aimed to uncover intricate patterns and associations within the dataset, providing insights into the complex dynamics of visitor behaviours at heritage sites. The Pearson correlation coefficient was used for variable analysis, allowing precise quantification of linear relationships between variables. This method provided a robust foundation for understanding the complex interplay among factors influencing visitor behaviours at heritage sites. Tables 2a and 2b provide a detailed analysis of the correlations between identified variables, providing a comprehensive understanding of their interdependencies. The tabular format of these tables enhances the interpretation of nuanced connections and patterns, providing a solid foundation for understanding the complex web of factors influencing visitor behaviours at heritage sites.

*Table 2a. Correlation matrix of identified variables in heritage site visitor behaviors (Part I)*

| | | EV1 | EV2 | EV3 | EV4 | SS1 | SS2 |
|---|---|---|---|---|---|---|---|
| EV1 | Pearson Correlation<br>Sig. (2-tailed)<br>N | 1<br>893 | -.044<br>.187<br>893 | -.159**<br>.000<br>893 | .019<br>.578<br>893 | .148**<br>.000<br>893 | 1.00**<br>.000<br>893 |
| EV2 | Pearson Correlation<br>Sig. (2-tailed)<br>N | -.044<br>.187<br>893 | 1<br>893 | .486**<br>.000<br>893 | -.257**<br>.000<br>893 | .027<br>.423<br>893 | -.044<br>.187<br>893 |
| EV3 | Pearson Correlation<br>Sig. (2-tailed)<br>N | -.159**<br>.000<br>893 | .486**<br>.000<br>893 | 1<br>893 | -.031<br>.348<br>893 | -.261**<br>.000<br>893 | -.159**<br>.000<br>893 |
| EV4 | Pearson Correlation<br>Sig. (2-tailed)<br>N | .019<br>.578<br>893 | -.257**<br>.000<br>893 | -.031<br>.348<br>893 | 1<br>893 | .094**<br>.005<br>893 | .019<br>.578<br>893 |
| SS1 | Pearson Correlation<br>Sig. (2-tailed)<br>N | .148**<br>.000<br>893 | .027<br>.423<br>893 | -.261**<br>.000<br>893 | .094**<br>.005<br>893 | 1<br>893 | .148**<br>.000<br>893 |
| SS2 | Pearson Correlation<br>Sig. (2-tailed)<br>N | 1.00**<br>.000<br>893 | -.044<br>.187<br>893 | -.159**<br>.000<br>893 | .019<br>.578<br>893 | .148**<br>.000<br>893 | 1<br>893 |
| SS3 | Pearson Correlation<br>Sig. (2-tailed)<br>N | -.044<br>.187<br>893 | 1.00**<br>.000<br>893 | .486**<br>.000<br>893 | -.257**<br>.000<br>893 | .027<br>.423<br>893 | -.044<br>.187<br>893 |
| SS4 | Pearson Correlation<br>Sig. (2-tailed)<br>N | -.159**<br>.000<br>893 | .486**<br>.000<br>893 | 1.00**<br>.000<br>893 | -.031<br>.348<br>893 | -.261**<br>.000<br>893 | -.159**<br>.000<br>893 |
| OS1 | Pearson Correlation<br>Sig. (2-tailed)<br>N | .019<br>.578<br>893 | -.257**<br>.000<br>893 | -.031<br>.348<br>893 | 1.00**<br>.000<br>893 | .094**<br>.005<br>893 | .019<br>.578<br>893 |
| OS2 | Pearson Correlation<br>Sig. (2-tailed)<br>N | .148**<br>.000<br>893 | .027<br>.423<br>893 | -.261**<br>.000<br>893 | .094**<br>.005<br>893 | 1.00**<br>.000<br>893 | .148**<br>.000<br>893 |
| OS3 | Pearson Correlation<br>Sig. (2-tailed)<br>N | -.130**<br>.000<br>893 | .345**<br>.000<br>893 | .228**<br>.000<br>893 | -.297**<br>.000<br>893 | .050<br>.134<br>893 | -.130**<br>.000<br>893 |

*Continued on following page*

*Table 2a. Continued*

| | | EV1 | EV2 | EV3 | EV4 | SS1 | SS2 |
|---|---|---|---|---|---|---|---|
| OS4 | Pearson Correlation<br>Sig. (2-tailed)<br>N | .340**<br>.000<br>893 | .009<br>.779<br>893 | .002<br>.949<br>893 | .102**<br>.002<br>893 | -.071*<br>.033<br>893 | .340**<br>.000<br>893 |
| EC1 | Pearson Correlation<br>Sig. (2-tailed)<br>N | .036<br>.286<br>893 | .499**<br>.000<br>893 | .190**<br>.000<br>893 | -.037<br>.264<br>893 | .273**<br>.000<br>893 | .036<br>.286<br>893 |
| EC2 | Pearson Correlation<br>Sig. (2-tailed)<br>N | -.101**<br>.003<br>893 | .200**<br>.000<br>893 | .416**<br>.000<br>893 | -.077*<br>.021<br>893 | .097**<br>.005<br>893 | -.101**<br>.003<br>893 |
| EC3 | Pearson Correlation<br>Sig. (2-tailed)<br>N | -.015<br>.658<br>893 | -.135**<br>.000<br>893 | -.016<br>.635<br>893 | .423**<br>.000<br>893 | -.175**<br>.000<br>893 | -.015<br>.658<br>893 |
| EC4 | Pearson Correlation<br>Sig. (2-tailed)<br>N | .202**<br>.000<br>893 | .012<br>.717<br>893 | -.042<br>.210<br>893 | .124**<br>.000<br>893 | .431**<br>.000<br>893 | .202**<br>.000<br>893 |
| MP1 | Pearson Correlation<br>Sig. (2-tailed)<br>N | -.145**<br>.000<br>893 | .091**<br>.007<br>893 | .091**<br>.006<br>893 | -.163**<br>.000<br>893 | -.093**<br>.005<br>893 | -.145**<br>.000<br>893 |
| MP2 | Pearson Correlation<br>Sig. (2-tailed)<br>N | .245**<br>.000<br>893 | -.088**<br>.009<br>893 | -.078**<br>.019<br>893 | -.046<br>.170<br>893 | -.138**<br>.000<br>893 | .245**<br>.000<br>893 |
| MP3 | Pearson Correlation<br>Sig. (2-tailed)<br>N | .056<br>.096<br>893 | .478**<br>.000<br>893 | .228**<br>.000<br>893 | -.126**<br>.000<br>893 | .064<br>.056<br>893 | .056<br>.096<br>893 |
| MP4 | Pearson Correlation<br>Sig. (2-tailed)<br>N | -.033<br>.326<br>893 | .184**<br>.000<br>893 | .397**<br>.000<br>893 | .163**<br>.000<br>893 | -.060<br>.075<br>893 | -.033<br>.326<br>893 |
| VB1 | Pearson Correlation<br>Sig. (2-tailed)<br>N | -.021<br>.525<br>893 | -.066*<br>.050<br>893 | .028<br>.397<br>893 | .439**<br>.000<br>893 | .122**<br>.000<br>893 | -.021<br>.525<br>893 |
| VB2 | Pearson Correlation<br>Sig. (2-tailed)<br>N | .124**<br>.000<br>893 | .075*<br>.026<br>893 | -.077*<br>.021<br>893 | -.011<br>.749<br>893 | .453**<br>.000<br>893 | .124**<br>.000<br>893 |
| VB3 | Pearson Correlation<br>Sig. (2-tailed)<br>N | -.019<br>.573<br>893 | .252**<br>.000<br>893 | .209**<br>.000<br>893 | -.192**<br>.000<br>893 | .052<br>.118<br>893 | -.019<br>.573<br>893 |

*Continued on following page*

*Table 2a. Continued*

| | | EV1 | EV2 | EV3 | EV4 | SS1 | SS2 |
|---|---|---|---|---|---|---|---|
| VB4 | Pearson Correlation<br>Sig. (2-tailed)<br>N | .099**<br>.003<br>893 | .028<br>.396<br>893 | .182**<br>.000<br>893 | .149**<br>.000<br>893 | -.110**<br>.001<br>893 | .099**<br>.003<br>893 |
| VF1 | Pearson Correlation<br>Sig. (2-tailed)<br>N | -.090**<br>.007<br>893 | .087**<br>.010<br>893 | .014<br>.680<br>893 | .079*<br>.018<br>893 | .112**<br>.001<br>893 | -.090**<br>.007<br>893 |
| VF2 | Pearson Correlation<br>Sig. (2-tailed)<br>N | .035<br>.300<br>893 | .070*<br>.037<br>893 | .062<br>.063<br>893 | -.072*<br>.031<br>893 | .044<br>.187<br>893 | .035<br>.300<br>893 |
| VF3 | Pearson Correlation<br>Sig. (2-tailed)<br>N | .103**<br>.002<br>893 | -.040<br>.228<br>893 | -.092**<br>.006<br>893 | .005<br>.875<br>893 | -.064<br>.057<br>893 | .103**<br>.002<br>893 |

** Correlation is significant at the 0.01 level (2-tailed)
* Correlation is significant at the 0.05 level (2-tailed)

*Table 2b. Correlation matrix of identified variables in heritage site visitor behaviors (Part I)*

| SS3 | SS4 | OS1 | OS2 | OS3 | OS4 | EC1 |
|---|---|---|---|---|---|---|
| -.044<br>.187<br>893 | -.159**<br>.000<br>893 | .019<br>.578<br>893 | .148**<br>.000<br>893 | -.044<br>.187<br>893 | -.159**<br>.000<br>893 | .019<br>.578<br>893 |
| 1.00**<br>.000<br>893 | .486**<br>.000<br>893 | -.257**<br>.000<br>893 | .027<br>.423<br>893 | .345**<br>.000<br>893 | .009<br>.779<br>893 | .499**<br>.000<br>893 |
| .486**<br>.000<br>893 | 1.00**<br>.000<br>893 | -.031<br>.348<br>893 | -.261**<br>.000<br>893 | .228**<br>.000<br>893 | .002<br>.949<br>893 | .190**<br>.000<br>893 |
| -.257**<br>.000<br>893 | -.031<br>.348<br>893 | 1.00**<br>.000<br>893 | .094**<br>.005<br>893 | -.297**<br>.000<br>893 | .102**<br>.002<br>893 | -.037<br>.264<br>893 |
| .027<br>.423<br>893 | -.261**<br>.000<br>893 | .094**<br>.005<br>893 | 1.00**<br>.000<br>893 | .050<br>.134<br>893 | -.071*<br>.033<br>893 | .273**<br>.000<br>893 |
| -.044<br>.187<br>893 | -.159**<br>.000<br>893 | .019<br>.578<br>893 | .148**<br>.000<br>893 | -.044<br>.187<br>893 | -.159**<br>.000<br>893 | .019<br>.578<br>893 |
| 1<br>893 | .486**<br>.000<br>893 | -.257**<br>.000<br>893 | .027<br>.423<br>893 | .345**<br>.000<br>893 | .009<br>.779<br>893 | .499**<br>.000<br>893 |
| .486**<br>.000<br>893 | 1<br>893 | -.031<br>.348<br>893 | -.261**<br>.000<br>893 | .228**<br>.000<br>893 | .002<br>.949<br>893 | .190**<br>.000<br>893 |
| -.257**<br>.000<br>893 | -.031<br>.348<br>893 | 1<br>893 | .094**<br>.005<br>893 | -.297**<br>.000<br>893 | .102**<br>.002<br>893 | -.037<br>.264<br>893 |
| .027<br>.423<br>893 | -.261**<br>.000<br>893 | .094**<br>.005<br>893 | 1<br>893 | .050<br>.134<br>893 | -.071*<br>.033<br>893 | .273**<br>.000<br>893 |
| .345**<br>.000<br>893 | .228**<br>.000<br>893 | -.297**<br>.000<br>893 | .050<br>.134<br>893 | 1<br>893 | -.086*<br>.010<br>893 | .196**<br>.000<br>893 |
| .009<br>.779<br>893 | .002<br>.949<br>893 | .102**<br>.002<br>893 | -.071*<br>.033<br>893 | -.086*<br>.010<br>893 | 1<br>893 | .127**<br>.000<br>893 |
| .499**<br>.000<br>893 | .190**<br>.000<br>893 | -.037<br>.264<br>893 | .273**<br>.000<br>893 | .196**<br>.000<br>893 | .127**<br>.000<br>893 | 1<br>893 |
| .200**<br>.000<br>893 | .416**<br>.000<br>893 | -.077*<br>.021<br>893 | .097**<br>.005<br>893 | .382**<br>.000<br>893 | -.109**<br>.001<br>893 | .302**<br>.000<br>893 |

*Continued on following page*

*Table 2b. Continued*

| SS3 | SS4 | OS1 | OS2 | OS3 | OS4 | EC1 |
|---|---|---|---|---|---|---|
| -.135**<br>.000<br>893 | -.016<br>.635<br>893 | .423**<br>.000<br>893 | -.175**<br>.000<br>893 | -.125**<br>.000<br>893 | .192**<br>.000<br>893 | -.292**<br>.000<br>893 |
| .012<br>.717<br>893 | -.042<br>.210<br>893 | .124**<br>.000<br>893 | .431**<br>.000<br>893 | -.161**<br>.000<br>893 | .090**<br>.007<br>893 | .000<br>.988<br>893 |
| .091**<br>.007<br>893 | .091**<br>.006<br>893 | -.163**<br>.000<br>893 | -.093**<br>.005<br>893 | .395**<br>.000<br>893 | -.016<br>.623<br>893 | .064<br>.055<br>893 |
| -.088**<br>.009<br>893 | -.078**<br>.019<br>893 | -.046<br>.170<br>893 | -.138**<br>.000<br>893 | -.055<br>.101<br>893 | .398**<br>.000<br>893 | -.127**<br>.000<br>893 |
| .478**<br>.000<br>893 | .228**<br>.000<br>893 | -.126**<br>.000<br>893 | .064<br>.056<br>893 | .102**<br>.002<br>893 | -.063<br>.060<br>893 | .442**<br>.000<br>893 |
| .184**<br>.000<br>893 | .397**<br>.000<br>893 | .163**<br>.000<br>893 | -.060<br>.075<br>893 | -.031<br>.361<br>893 | .002<br>.945<br>893 | .221**<br>.000<br>893 |
| -.066*<br>.050<br>893 | .028<br>.397<br>893 | .439**<br>.000<br>893 | .122**<br>.000<br>893 | -.085*<br>.011<br>893 | -.011<br>.732<br>893 | -.119**<br>.000<br>893 |
| .075*<br>.026<br>893 | -.077*<br>.021<br>893 | -.011<br>.749<br>893 | .453**<br>.000<br>893 | .144**<br>.000<br>893 | .147**<br>.000<br>893 | .029<br>.388<br>893 |
| .252**<br>.000<br>893 | .209**<br>.000<br>893 | -.192**<br>.000<br>893 | .052<br>.118<br>893 | .424**<br>.000<br>893 | -.093**<br>.005<br>893 | .277**<br>.000<br>893 |
| .028<br>.396<br>893 | .182**<br>.000<br>893 | .149**<br>.000<br>893 | -.110**<br>.001<br>893 | -.112**<br>.001<br>893 | .153**<br>.000<br>893 | .090**<br>.007<br>893 |
| .087**<br>.010<br>893 | .014<br>.680<br>893 | .079*<br>.018<br>893 | .112**<br>.001<br>893 | -.018<br>.598<br>893 | -.022<br>.515<br>893 | .023<br>.499<br>893 |
| .070*<br>.037<br>893 | .062<br>.063<br>893 | -.072*<br>.031<br>893 | .044<br>.187<br>893 | .144**<br>.000<br>893 | .059<br>.078<br>893 | .049<br>.143<br>893 |
| -.040<br>.228<br>893 | -.092**<br>.006<br>893 | .005<br>.875<br>893 | -.064<br>.057<br>893 | .057<br>.089<br>893 | -.019<br>.575<br>893 | -.053<br>.112<br>893 |

*Table 2c. Correlation matrix of identified variables in heritage site visitor behaviors (Part II)*

| | | EC2 | EC3 | EC4 | MP1 | MP2 | MP3 |
|---|---|---|---|---|---|---|---|
| EV1 | Pearson Correlation | -.101** | -.015 | .202** | -.145** | .245** | .056 |
| | Sig. (2-tailed) | .003 | .658 | .000 | .000 | .000 | .096 |
| | N | 893 | 893 | 893 | 893 | 893 | 893 |
| EV2 | Pearson Correlation | .200** | -.135** | .012 | .091** | -.088** | .478** |
| | Sig. (2-tailed) | .000 | .000 | .717 | .007 | .009 | .000 |
| | N | 893 | 893 | 893 | 893 | 893 | 893 |
| EV3 | Pearson Correlation | .416** | -.016 | -.042 | .091** | -.078* | .228** |
| | Sig. (2-tailed) | .000 | .635 | .210 | .006 | .019 | .000 |
| | N | 893 | 893 | 893 | 893 | 893 | 893 |
| EV4 | Pearson Correlation | -.077* | .423** | .124** | -.163** | -.046 | -.126** |
| | Sig. (2-tailed) | .021 | .000 | .000 | .000 | .170 | .000 |
| | N | 893 | 893 | 893 | 893 | 893 | 893 |
| SS1 | Pearson Correlation | -.097** | -.175** | .431** | -.093** | -.138** | .064 |
| | Sig. (2-tailed) | .004 | .000 | .000 | .005 | .000 | .056 |
| | N | 893 | 893 | 893 | 893 | 893 | 893 |
| SS2 | Pearson Correlation | -.101** | -.015 | .202** | -.145** | .245** | .056 |
| | Sig. (2-tailed) | .003 | .658 | .000 | .000 | .000 | .096 |
| | N | 893 | 893 | 893 | 893 | 893 | 893 |
| SS3 | Pearson Correlation | .200** | -.135** | .012 | .091** | -.088** | .478** |
| | Sig. (2-tailed) | .000 | .000 | .717 | .007 | .009 | .000 |
| | N | 893 | 893 | 893 | 893 | 893 | 893 |
| SS4 | Pearson Correlation | .416** | -.016 | -.042 | .091** | -.078* | .228** |
| | Sig. (2-tailed) | .000 | .635 | .210 | .006 | .019 | .000 |
| | N | 893 | 893 | 893 | 893 | 893 | 893 |
| OS1 | Pearson Correlation | -.077* | .423** | .124** | -.163** | -.046 | -.126** |
| | Sig. (2-tailed) | .021 | .000 | .000 | .000 | .170 | .000 |
| | N | 893 | 893 | 893 | 893 | 893 | 893 |
| OS2 | Pearson Correlation | -.097** | -.175** | .431** | -.093** | -.138** | .064 |
| | Sig. (2-tailed) | .004 | .000 | .000 | .005 | .000 | .056 |
| | N | 893 | 893 | 893 | 893 | 893 | 893 |
| OS3 | Pearson Correlation | .382** | -.125** | -.161** | .395** | -.055 | .102** |
| | Sig. (2-tailed) | .000 | .000 | .000 | .000 | .101 | .002 |
| | N | 893 | 893 | 893 | 893 | 893 | 893 |
| OS4 | Pearson Correlation | -.109** | .192** | .090** | -.016 | .398** | -.063 |
| | Sig. (2-tailed) | .001 | .000 | .007 | .623 | .000 | .060 |
| | N | 893 | 893 | 893 | 893 | 893 | 893 |
| EC1 | Pearson Correlation | .302** | -.292** | .000 | .064 | -.127** | .442** |
| | Sig. (2-tailed) | .000 | .000 | .988 | .055 | .000 | .000 |
| | N | 893 | 893 | 893 | 893 | 893 | 893 |
| EC2 | Pearson Correlation | 1 | .071* | -.316** | .254** | .080* | .208* |
| | Sig. (2-tailed) | | .034 | .000 | .000 | .017 | .000 |
| | N | 893 | 893 | 893 | 893 | 893 | 893 |

*Continued on following page*

*Table 2c. Continued*

| | | EC2 | EC3 | EC4 | MP1 | MP2 | MP3 |
|---|---|---|---|---|---|---|---|
| EC3 | Pearson Correlation | .071* | 1 | .060 | -.030 | -.135** | .035 |
| | Sig. (2-tailed) | .034 | | .073 | .367 | .000 | .299 |
| | N | 893 | 893 | 893 | 893 | 893 | 893 |
| EC4 | Pearson Correlation | -.316** | .060 | 1 | -.082* | .070* | .010 |
| | Sig. (2-tailed) | .000 | .073 | | .014 | .036 | .769 |
| | N | 893 | 893 | 893 | 893 | 893 | 893 |
| MP1 | Pearson Correlation | .254** | -.030 | -.082* | 1 | .529** | .005 |
| | Sig. (2-tailed) | .000 | .367 | .014 | | .000 | .892 |
| | N | 893 | 893 | 893 | 893 | 893 | 893 |
| MP2 | Pearson Correlation | .080* | -.135** | .070* | .529** | 1 | -.091** |
| | Sig. (2-tailed) | .017 | .000 | .036 | .000 | | .006 |
| | N | 893 | 893 | 893 | 893 | 893 | 893 |
| MP3 | Pearson Correlation | .208* | .035 | .010 | .005 | -.091** | 1 |
| | Sig. (2-tailed) | .000 | .299 | .769 | .892 | .006 | |
| | N | 893 | 893 | 893 | 893 | 893 | 893 |
| MP4 | Pearson Correlation | .258* | -.031 | .015 | .082* | -.091** | .174** |
| | Sig. (2-tailed) | .000 | .359 | .664 | .015 | .006 | .000 |
| | N | 893 | 893 | 893 | 893 | 893 | 893 |
| VB1 | Pearson Correlation | -.048 | .385** | .054* | -.138** | -.002 | -.212** |
| | Sig. (2-tailed) | .152 | .000 | .108 | .000 | .946 | .000 |
| | N | 893 | 893 | 893 | 893 | 893 | 893 |
| VB2 | Pearson Correlation | .016 | .125** | .494** | .131** | .140** | .027 |
| | Sig. (2-tailed) | .634 | .000 | .000 | .000 | .000 | .415 |
| | N | 893 | 893 | 893 | 893 | 893 | 893 |
| VB3 | Pearson Correlation | .213** | -.067* | .014 | .397** | -.069** | .488** |
| | Sig. (2-tailed) | .000 | .045 | .675 | .000 | .039 | .000 |
| | N | 893 | 893 | 893 | 893 | 893 | 893 |
| VB4 | Pearson Correlation | .085* | -.073* | -.044 | .014 | .196** | -.033 |
| | Sig. (2-tailed) | .012 | .029 | .191 | .671 | .000 | .320 |
| | N | 893 | 893 | 893 | 893 | 893 | 893 |
| VF1 | Pearson Correlation | -.073* | .005 | .035 | -.081* | -.052 | .042 |
| | Sig. (2-tailed) | .029 | .892 | .293 | .016 | .119 | .209 |
| | N | 893 | 893 | 893 | 893 | 893 | 893 |
| VF2 | Pearson Correlation | .172** | .077* | -.058 | .086* | .115** | .011 |
| | Sig. (2-tailed) | .000 | .022 | .086 | .010 | .001 | .751 |
| | N | 893 | 893 | 893 | 893 | 893 | 893 |
| VF3 | Pearson Correlation | .053 | .245** | .007 | .058 | .074* | .007 |
| | Sig. (2-tailed) | .116 | .000 | .827 | .083 | .027 | .841 |
| | N | 893 | 893 | 893 | 893 | 893 | 893 |

*Continued on following page*

*Table 2d. Correlation matrix of identified variables in heritage site visitor behaviors (Part II)*

| MP4 | VB1 | VB2 | VB3 | VB4 | VF1 | VF2 | VF3 |
|---|---|---|---|---|---|---|---|
| -.033<br>.326<br>893 | -.021<br>.525<br>893 | .124**<br>.000<br>893 | -.019<br>.573<br>893 | .099**<br>.003<br>893 | -.090**<br>.007<br>893 | .035<br>.300<br>893 | .103**<br>.002<br>893 |
| .184**<br>.000<br>893 | -.066*<br>.050<br>893 | .075*<br>.026<br>893 | .252**<br>.000<br>893 | .028<br>.396<br>893 | .087**<br>.010<br>893 | .070*<br>.037<br>893 | -.040<br>.228<br>893 |
| .397**<br>.000<br>893 | .028<br>.397<br>893 | -.077*<br>.021<br>893 | .209**<br>.000<br>893 | .182**<br>.000<br>893 | .014<br>.680<br>893 | .062<br>.063<br>893 | -.092**<br>.006<br>893 |
| .163**<br>.000<br>893 | .439**<br>.000<br>893 | -.011<br>.749<br>893 | -.192**<br>.000<br>893 | .149**<br>.000<br>893 | .079*<br>.018<br>893 | -.072*<br>.031<br>893 | .005<br>.875<br>893 |
| -.060<br>.075<br>893 | .122**<br>.000<br>893 | .453**<br>.000<br>893 | .052<br>.118<br>893 | -.110**<br>.001<br>893 | .112**<br>.001<br>893 | .044<br>.187<br>893 | -.064<br>.057<br>893 |
| -.033<br>.326<br>893 | -.021<br>.525<br>893 | .124**<br>.000<br>893 | -.019<br>.573<br>893 | .099**<br>.003<br>893 | -.090**<br>.007<br>893 | .035<br>.300<br>893 | .103**<br>.002<br>893 |
| .184**<br>.000<br>893 | -.066*<br>.050<br>893 | .075*<br>.026<br>893 | .252**<br>.000<br>893 | .028<br>.396<br>893 | .087**<br>.010<br>893 | .070*<br>.037<br>893 | -.040<br>.228<br>893 |
| .397**<br>.000<br>893 | .028<br>.397<br>893 | -.077*<br>.021<br>893 | .209**<br>.000<br>893 | .182**<br>.000<br>893 | .014<br>.680<br>893 | .062<br>.063<br>893 | -.092**<br>.006<br>893 |
| .163**<br>.000<br>893 | .439**<br>.000<br>893 | -.011<br>.749<br>893 | -.192**<br>.000<br>893 | .149**<br>.000<br>893 | .079*<br>.018<br>893 | -.072*<br>.031<br>893 | .005<br>.875<br>893 |
| -.060<br>.075<br>893 | .122**<br>.000<br>893 | .453**<br>.000<br>893 | .052<br>.118<br>893 | -.110**<br>.001<br>893 | .112**<br>.001<br>893 | .044<br>.187<br>893 | -.064<br>.057<br>893 |
| -.031<br>.361<br>893 | -.085*<br>.011<br>893 | .144**<br>.000<br>893 | .424**<br>.000<br>893 | -.112**<br>.001<br>893 | -.018<br>.598<br>893 | .144**<br>.000<br>893 | .057<br>.089<br>893 |
| .002<br>.945<br>893 | -.011<br>.732<br>893 | .147**<br>.000<br>893 | -.093**<br>.005<br>893 | .153**<br>.000<br>893 | -.022<br>.515<br>893 | .059<br>.078<br>893 | -.019<br>.575<br>893 |
| .221**<br>.000<br>893 | -.119**<br>.000<br>893 | .029<br>.388<br>893 | .277**<br>.000<br>893 | .090**<br>.007<br>893 | .023<br>.499<br>893 | .049<br>.143<br>893 | -.053<br>.112<br>893 |
| .258*<br>.000<br>893 | -.048<br>.152<br>893 | .016<br>.634<br>893 | .213**<br>.000<br>893 | .085*<br>.012<br>893 | -.073*<br>.029<br>893 | .172**<br>.000<br>893 | .053<br>.116<br>893 |

*Continued on following page*

*Table 2d. Continued*

| MP4 | VB1 | VB2 | VB3 | VB4 | VF1 | VF2 | VF3 |
|---|---|---|---|---|---|---|---|
| -.031<br>.359<br>893 | .385**<br>.000<br>893 | .125**<br>.000<br>893 | -.067*<br>.045<br>893 | -.073*<br>.029<br>893 | .005<br>.892<br>893 | .077*<br>.022<br>893 | .245**<br>.000<br>893 |
| .015<br>.664<br>893 | .054*<br>.108<br>893 | .494**<br>.000<br>893 | .014<br>.675<br>893 | -.044<br>.191<br>893 | .035<br>.293<br>893 | -.058<br>.086<br>893 | .007<br>.827<br>893 |
| .082*<br>.015<br>893 | -.138**<br>.000<br>893 | .131**<br>.000<br>893 | .397**<br>.000<br>893 | .014<br>.671<br>893 | -.081*<br>.016<br>893 | .086*<br>.010<br>893 | .058<br>.083<br>893 |
| -.091**<br>.006<br>893 | -.002<br>.946<br>893 | .140**<br>.000<br>893 | -.069**<br>.039<br>893 | .196**<br>.000<br>893 | -.052<br>.119<br>893 | .115**<br>.001<br>893 | .074*<br>.027<br>893 |
| .174**<br>.000<br>893 | -.212**<br>.000<br>893 | .027<br>.415<br>893 | .488**<br>.000<br>893 | -.033<br>.320<br>893 | .042<br>.209<br>893 | .011<br>.751<br>893 | .007<br>.841<br>893 |
| 1<br>893 | .176**<br>.000<br>893 | -.210**<br>.000<br>893 | .088**<br>.009<br>893 | .546**<br>.000<br>893 | .210**<br>.000<br>893 | .073*<br>.029<br>893 | -.040<br>.238<br>893 |
| .176**<br>.000<br>893 | 1<br>893 | .017<br>.602<br>893 | -.194**<br>.000<br>893 | -.191**<br>.000<br>893 | .374**<br>.000<br>893 | .011<br>.735<br>893 | -.038<br>.259<br>893 |
| -.210**<br>.000<br>893 | .017<br>.602<br>893 | 1<br>893 | .080*<br>.017<br>893 | -.248**<br>.000<br>893 | .013<br>.703<br>893 | .424**<br>.000<br>893 | .015<br>.647<br>893 |
| .088**<br>.009<br>893 | -.194**<br>.000<br>893 | .080*<br>.017<br>893 | 1<br>893 | -.028<br>.403<br>893 | -.098**<br>.003<br>893 | .056<br>.095<br>893 | .078*<br>.020<br>893 |
| .546**<br>.000<br>893 | -.191**<br>.000<br>893 | -.248**<br>.000<br>893 | -.028<br>.403<br>893 | 1<br>893 | .168**<br>.000<br>893 | -.141**<br>.000<br>893 | .063<br>.058<br>893 |
| .210**<br>.000<br>893 | .374**<br>.000<br>893 | .013<br>.703<br>893 | -.098**<br>.003<br>893 | .168**<br>.000<br>893 | 1<br>893 | -.058<br>.085<br>893 | -.216**<br>.000<br>893 |
| .073*<br>.029<br>893 | .011<br>.735<br>893 | .424**<br>.000<br>893 | .056<br>.095<br>893 | -.141**<br>.000<br>893 | -.058<br>.085<br>893 | 1<br>893 | .077*<br>.022<br>I893 |
| -.040<br>.238<br>893 | -.038<br>.259<br>893 | .015<br>.647<br>893 | .078*<br>.020<br>893 | .063<br>.058<br>893 | -.216**<br>.000<br>893 | .077*<br>.022<br>I893 | 1<br>893 |

The analysis revealed positive correlations among variables overall, indicating general interdependence. However, within specific variable domains, negative correlations were more prevalent, suggesting nuanced and contrasting relationships within those categories. This intricate pattern underscores the complexity of visitor behaviours at heritage sites, showcasing the need for a nuanced understanding of how different factors interact within distinct contexts. Due to the absence of a singular form of relationship observed in the Pearson correlation test, a more sophisticated analysis was conducted. The dataset was subjected to Multilayer Perceptron Neural Network (ANN) analysis in SPSS. This advanced technique was employed to capture the intricate and nonlinear interactions among the variables; by utilising ANN, the research aimed to create a complex model capable of discerning subtle patterns and relationships within the data, offering a deeper understanding of the multifaceted dynamics of visitor behaviours at heritage sites. Table 3 provides a comprehensive overview of the ANN case processing, utilising a training dataset comprising 70% of the data and a testing dataset with the remaining 30%. It outlines the network information, encompassing factors, covariates, hidden layers, and the dependent variable. Additionally, the table presents the model's relative error, offering insights into the accuracy and precision of the neural network model in capturing the complex relationships among the variables.

*Table 3. Multilayer perceptron neural network (ANN) analysis summary*

| **Case Processing Summary** | | | |
|---|---|---|---|
| | | N | Percent |
| Sample | Training | 625 | 70.0% |
| | Testing | 268 | 30.0% |
| Valid | | 893 | 100.0% |
| Excluded | | 0 | |
| Total | | 893 | |
| **Network Information** | | | |
| Input Layer | Factors | 1 | SS1 |
| | | 2 | OS1 |
| | | 3 | EC1 |
| | | 4 | VF1 |
| | | 5 | MP3 |
| | | 6 | EC4 |
| | | 7 | VB4 |
| | Covariates | 1 | SS3 |
| | | 2 | EV1 |
| | | 3 | EV2 |
| | | 4 | OS3 |
| | | 5 | EC2 |
| | | 6 | MP1 |
| | | 7 | MP2 |
| | | 8 | VB3 |
| | | 9 | SS2 |
| | | 10 | OS2 |
| | | 11 | VF3 |
| | | 12 | OS4 |
| | | 13 | VF2 |
| | | 14 | EC3 |
| | | 15 | MP4 |
| | | 16 | VB2 |
| | | 17 | EV3 |
| | | 18 | EV4 |
| | | 19 | SS4 |
| | Number of Units[a] | | 54 |
| | Rescaling Method for Covariates | | Standardised |
| Hidden Layer(s) | Number of Hidden Layers | | 1 |
| | Number of Units in Hidden Layer 1[a] | | 10 |
| | Activation Function | | Hyperbolic tangent |

*Continued on following page*

*Table 3. Continued*

| | | | |
|---|---|---|---|
| Output Layer | Dependent Variables | 1 | VB1 |
| | Number of Units | | 1 |
| | Rescaling Method for Scale Dependents | | Standardised |
| | Activation Function | | Identity |
| | Error Function | | Sum of Squares |
| a. Excluding the bias unit | | | |

**Model Summary**

| | | |
|---|---|---|
| Training | Sum of Squares Error | 28.695 |
| | Relative Error | .092 |
| | Stopping Rule Used | 1 consecutive step(s) with no decrease in error[a] |
| | Training Time | 00:00:00.250 |
| Testing | Sum of Squares Error | 44.259 |
| | Relative Error | .336 |
| Dependent Variable: VB1 | | |
| a. Error computations are based on the testing sample. | | |

The variables were systematically categorised into factors and covariates based on their level of influence on each other, as determined through Pearson correlation analysis. Specifically, these factors and covariates were assessed in relation to the dependent variable, VB1 (Dwell time at specific exhibits or areas). The analysis results indicated a relative training error of 0.92 and a relative testing error of 0.336. Notably, a relative error close to 0, as observed in this case, signifies a highly accurate model structure. In essence, the model's negligible inaccuracy suggests a nearly perfect alignment between the predicted outcomes and the actual data. This level of precision underscores the effectiveness of the organised variables in explaining the complexities of visitor behaviours, particularly their dwell time at specific exhibits or areas within the heritage sites.

A multitude of factors influences visitor dwell time at specific exhibits or areas within heritage sites. The popularity of particular exhibits or artefacts (SS1) captivates visitors, drawing them to spend more time exploring these attractions. Social media engagement (OS1) plays a role, with online interactions shaping visitor expectations and interests. Ticket pricing strategies (EC1), catering to various visitor demographics with regular, student, senior, and group discounts, impact visitor decisions on how long to engage with the exhibits. Survey responses (VF1) reflecting visitor experiences and satisfaction levels provide critical insights, guiding heritage site managers in enhancing visitor engagement. Partnerships with travel agencies and tour operators (MP3) influence the flow of visitors, potentially affecting dwell times. Additionally, the economic impact of the heritage site on the local community (EC4) and visitor spending at souvenir shops or cafes (VB4) create a financial ecosystem, which indirectly affects visitor engagement durations. These interconnected variables collectively shape the visitor experience, determining the duration visitors spend at specific exhibits or areas within heritage sites. A diverse set of covariates intricately influences the dwell time at specific exhibits or areas within heritage sites, each playing a distinct role in shaping the overall visitor experience. Special events, festivals, or temporary exhibitions (SS3) are pivotal as they create unique attractions, drawing visitors for extended periods. Weather conditions (EV1) and seasonal variations (EV2) directly impact visitor numbers and engagement, with favourable weather often leading to longer exploration times. Online interactions, including website traffic and user behaviour (OS3) and online reviews and ratings (OS2), serve as crucial covariates. They significantly influence visitor expectations and decision-making, affecting the time visitors spend at specific exhibits or areas. Economic conditions of the local area (EC2) and accessibility factors like transportation costs (EC3) indirectly influence dwell times, as visitor affordability and convenience play essential roles. The effectiveness of marketing campaigns (MP1) and collaborations with local businesses and hotels (MP2) shape visitor flow, impacting engagement durations. Visitor feedback, including specific comments or suggestions (VF2) and complaints or issues raised (VF3), directly guides site management and visitor satisfaction, thus affecting dwell times. Social media influencers' impact (OS4) and social media marketing reach and engagement metrics (MP4) indirectly influence visitor numbers and engagement durations. Interaction frequency with guided tours or workshops (VB2) and participation in educational programs or cultural events (VB3) directly enhance visitor engagement. Additionally, site amenities (SS4) and site accessibility (EV3) contribute significantly to the overall visitor experience, potentially prolonging dwell times due to increased visitor comfort and convenience. These variables are considered covariates because they are not the primary focus of the study but are controlled or observed due to their potential influence on dwell times. Their diverse roles collectively create a multifaceted environment, influencing the duration visitors choose to spend at specific exhibits or areas within heritage sites.

## RESULTS AND DISCUSSION

The study's findings offer valuable insights for heritage site management, highlighting the importance of understanding factors such as exhibit popularity, social media engagement, ticket pricing strategies, visitor satisfaction, partnerships with travel agencies, local economic impact, on-site spending patterns, and collaborative efforts. These factors can guide targeted marketing and promotional efforts, attracting and retaining audiences. Interpreting visitor satisfaction surveys and addressing specific suggestions can foster a proactive approach. Economic impact analysis helps create mutually beneficial relationships between heritage sites and local communities, enabling support and a sense of ownership. Understanding visitor spending patterns at on-site facilities allows for optimising resource allocation, such as placing souvenir shops and cafes, enhancing visitor convenience, and potentially increasing revenue. Adaptive pricing strategies, including discounts for students, seniors, and group visitors, bridge accessibility, increasing visitor numbers and overall revenue. Collaborative partnerships with travel agencies, local businesses, and hotels strengthen the site's market presence. Joint promotional activities and package deals can incentivise tourists, benefiting the heritage site and the local economy. Educational initiatives, such as workshops and guided tours, are crucial in extending visitor engagement. Understanding visitor interests and participation frequency allows site managers to craft educational experiences that enrich visitors' understanding and appreciation of the site's heritage. These insights can inform site development efforts by aligning new exhibits, interactive displays, and amenities with visitor preferences, addressing accessibility challenges, and providing enriching experiences for visitors from diverse backgrounds. By integrating these insights into their strategies, heritage sites can preserve their cultural legacy while providing inclusive experiences.

Predictive analytics is a powerful tool that can revolutionise visitor experiences and site operations at heritage sites. By analysing visitor behaviour patterns, it allows sites to tailor exhibits, guided tours, and events to cater to specific demographics, enhancing visitor engagement. Predictive models can forecast visitor numbers, helping sites anticipate peak periods and potential overcrowding, ensuring a comfortable and enjoyable experience for visitors. This also aids in optimising staff allocation and facility management during high-traffic periods. Resource optimisation is another benefit of predictive analytics. By matching resources with visitor demand, sites can minimise wastage, reduce operational costs, and enhance sustainability. Understanding visitor demographics allows for targeted marketing efforts, attracting the right audience and increasing visitor numbers. Preservation and conservation are also benefits of predictive analytics. By identifying high-traffic areas prone to wear and tear, site managers can strategically implement conservation efforts without disrupting visitor experiences. This delicate balance between preservation and engagement is crucial for maintaining the site's authenticity. Data-driven decision-making is another benefit of predictive analytics. Site managers can base decisions on empirical evidence, ensuring resource utilisation judiciously and continually improving visitor experiences. Proactive problem-solving is another benefit of predictive analytics. By analysing historical data, predictive analytics can identify potential challenges or issues, enhancing visitor satisfaction and fostering positive reviews and recommendations. In essence, predictive analytics is a guiding light towards improved visitor experiences and efficient site operations.

Understanding visitor behaviours at heritage sites through predictive analytics requires acknowledging inherent limitations and potential sources of bias. Historical visitation data may exhibit inconsistencies in quality and completeness, potentially impacting the accuracy and reliability of predictive models. Sampling bias may arise from selecting specific heritage sites, limiting the applicability of findings to a broader context. Technological limitations, such as the choice of advanced analytics techniques like Artificial Neural Networks, may restrict the depth and complexity of the analysis. Ethical considerations are also crucial, as the risk of unintentional identification remains, raising ethical dilemmas. Balancing detailed analysis with ethical obligations towards visitor privacy presents a challenge. Temporal factors and external influences pose further challenges, as seasonal changes, holidays, and local events often influence visitor behaviours. Failure to account for these fluctuations could confound the results, impacting the accuracy of predictive insights. Response bias, where visitors alter their behaviours when aware of being observed, introduces complexity and requires meticulous approaches to minimise its impact on the study's conclusions. Acknowledging these limitations and biases is not just a formality but a crucial step in ensuring the transparency and integrity of the research. By understanding and openly addressing these challenges, researchers can refine their methodologies and interpretations, fortifying the study against potential pitfalls and reinforcing the credibility of their findings.

In heritage site management and predictive analytics, comparing our findings with existing literature provides valuable insights into the consistency and novelty of our results. Several key themes and trends emerge when aligning our research outcomes with prior studies in the field. One recurring theme evident in our findings and existing literature is the significance of visitor demographics. Studies conducted in heritage sites globally have consistently highlighted the impact of age, cultural background, and interests on visitor behaviours. Our research reaffirms these trends, emphasising the importance of tailored experiences for diverse visitor segments. The alignment of these findings underscores the universal nature of demographic influences on visitor patterns. Furthermore, our study resonates with prior research concerning the role of technology, specifically social media engagement. Contemporary literature emphasises the profound influence of online platforms on visitor decision-making processes. Our findings, indicating a positive correlation between social media engagement and visitor behaviours, echo these observations. This alignment underscores the enduring relevance of online platforms in shaping heritage site visitation patterns. Contrastingly, our research introduces a nuanced perspective on the impact of economic factors. While existing studies predominantly focus on visitor spending, our findings delve deeper into the financial repercussions for the local community. By exploring the economic impact of heritage sites on the surrounding area, our study offers a broader understanding of the symbiotic relationship between heritage tourism and local economies. This unique contribution expands the existing discourse on the economic dimensions of heritage site management. Additionally, our research sheds light on the influence of collaborative efforts, such as partnerships with travel agencies and local businesses. While some literature acknowledges the importance of collaborative initiatives, our study provides specific insights into the effectiveness of these partnerships. By demonstrating their positive correlation with visitor engagement, our findings underscore the practical implications of fostering such alliances for heritage site managers.

In summary, our study not only aligns with established trends in existing literature but also introduces novel perspectives. By delving into the economic dimensions and evaluating the efficacy of collaborative partnerships, our research extends the discourse on heritage site management. This synthesis of traditional themes and innovative insights contributes to a more comprehensive understanding of predictive analytics in heritage site visitor patterns, positioning our study within the broader scholarly landscape.

## CONCLUSION

The study on heritage site visitor patterns revealed significant insights for management and preservation. It highlighted the impact of demographics, such as age, cultural background, and interests, on visitor behaviours. This highlights the need for tailoring experiences to specific demographic segments to improve visitor satisfaction and engagement. The economic dynamics of heritage tourism revealed a symbiotic relationship between heritage sites and local economies, with collaborative initiatives with travel agencies, local businesses, and social media influencers driving visitor engagement. The study also highlighted the importance of strategic partnerships with travel agencies, tour operators, and local businesses in enhancing visitor numbers. Social media platforms also play a crucial role in shaping visitor perceptions and driving site visitation. The study also identified factors that enhance visitor contentment, such as interactive displays, educational programs, and amenities. These findings offer a comprehensive roadmap for heritage site managers, allowing them to create tailored experiences, foster economic sustainability, and cultivate a positive visitor environment, ensuring the preservation and thriving legacy of cultural treasures. By understanding these factors, heritage site managers can create enriching and memorable experiences for visitors.

This research stands as a significant milestone in the realm of heritage site management and preservation. Its contribution to the field is multifold and transformative. Firstly, by unravelling the intricate interplay of visitor demographics, economic dynamics, collaborative initiatives, social media engagement, and visitor satisfaction, this study provides a comprehensive understanding of heritage site visitor behaviours. This holistic perspective equips heritage site managers with invaluable insights, enabling them to tailor experiences, optimise resource allocation, and enhance visitor engagement. Secondly, the research pioneers a nuanced exploration of the economic dimensions of heritage tourism. Uncovering the symbiotic relationship between heritage sites and local economies emphasises the pivotal role these sites play in fostering economic sustainability in their communities. This insight not only enriches the economic discourse of heritage tourism but also provides actionable strategies for stakeholders and policymakers. Thirdly, the study sheds light on the power of collaboration in heritage site management. By identifying the effectiveness of partnerships with travel agencies, local businesses, and social media influencers, the research underscores the transformative potential of collective efforts. These insights serve as a roadmap for fostering strategic alliances, thereby bolstering the cultural and economic impact of heritage sites. Fourthly, in an age dominated by digital interactions, the research underscores the enduring influence of social media platforms. By emphasising the positive correlation between social media engagement and visitor behaviours, the study highlights the need for heritage sites to craft compelling online narratives. This finding is a guiding principle for digital marketing strategies, ensuring heritage sites remain relevant and enticing to a global audience. Lastly, the study places visitor satisfaction and experience at the core of heritage site management. By identifying the pivotal role of interactive displays, educational programs, and accessible amenities, the research offers practical insights for enhancing visitor contentment. These insights are a foundation for creating immersive, educational, and memorable experiences, fostering a deeper connection between visitors and heritage sites. This research not only advances the academic understanding of heritage site management but also provides actionable, real-world strategies for site managers, policymakers, and industry stakeholders. Its contribution lies not only in enriching scholarly discourse but also in shaping the future trajectory of heritage tourism, ensuring the preservation, appreciation, and sustainable management of our cultural heritage for generations to come.

Practical applications:

1. Visitor Experience Enhancement: Implement personalised visitor experiences based on demographic data, ensuring tailored exhibits, guided tours, and events that resonate with specific visitor segments. Utilise social media insights to design engaging online campaigns, fostering a global audience and encouraging visitation.

2. Resource Optimization: Optimize staffing, ticketing, and facility management through predictive analytics, ensuring efficient resource allocation during peak visitation periods. This can lead to reduced operational costs and enhanced visitor satisfaction.
3. Community Engagement: Foster collaborations with local businesses, hotels, and social media influencers to stimulate the local economy. Encourage partnerships that promote responsible tourism, benefiting both the heritage site and the surrounding community.
4. Conservation and Preservation: Utilize predictive analytics to strategically plan conservation efforts, protecting high-traffic areas and delicate artefacts. Allocate resources judiciously, ensuring the preservation of heritage sites for future generations.

Future research directions:

1. Longitudinal Studies: Conduct longitudinal studies to observe visitor patterns over extended periods. Long-term data analysis can reveal evolving trends and visitor behaviour changes, providing a more comprehensive understanding of heritage site visitation dynamics.
2. Technological Integration: Explore integrating emerging technologies such as augmented reality (AR) and virtual reality (VR) to enhance visitor experiences. Investigate how these technologies influence visitor engagement and satisfaction, shaping the future of heritage site interactions.
3. Cultural Impact Studies: Investigate the cultural impact of heritage sites on visitors, including their perceptions, learning experiences, and emotional connections. Explore how heritage sites contribute to cultural understanding and preservation of cultural heritage.
4. Climate Change Resilience: Study the impact of climate change on heritage sites and visitor behaviours. Analyse how changing weather patterns influence visitor numbers and preferences, leading to informed strategies for climate change resilience in heritage site management.
5. Sustainable Tourism Practices: Research sustainable tourism practices, including eco-friendly initiatives, waste management strategies, and community-based tourism programs. Explore how these practices contribute to heritage site preservation, visitor satisfaction, and long-term environmental sustainability.
6. Visitor Sentiment Analysis: Utilize natural language processing (NLP) techniques to analyse visitor reviews and sentiments shared on online platforms. Understand visitor opinions, preferences, and criticisms to tailor future strategies for improving visitor experiences.
7. Accessibility and Inclusivity: Investigate the accessibility of heritage sites for people with disabilities and diverse cultural backgrounds. Explore

how inclusive practices can enhance visitor engagement, ensuring that heritage sites are accessible and welcoming to all visitors.

Exploring these practical applications and future research directions will not only enrich the field of heritage site management but also contribute to the holistic understanding of visitor behaviours, sustainable tourism, and the preservation of cultural heritage in a rapidly evolving world.

## FUTURE APPLICATIONS

Heritage site management is poised at the intersection of tradition and innovation, with the potential to redefine visitor experiences, conservation efforts, and community engagement. Integrating immersive technologies like augmented and virtual reality can create interactive and educational backgrounds, transporting visitors back in time and fostering a deep connection with the past. Artificial intelligence and machine learning enable predictive analytics, allowing heritage site managers to anticipate visitor patterns, tailor exhibitions, and optimise resource allocation in real time. Sustainable tourism is gaining momentum, focusing on eco-friendly practices, waste reduction, and community empowerment. Future applications in heritage site management involve implementing green technologies, renewable energy sources, and conservation initiatives to preserve cultural significance and natural surroundings. Community engagement is critical, with partnerships with local artisans, businesses, and educational institutions offering authentic cultural experiences. Digital platforms and social media will continue to play a pivotal role in heritage site management, allowing sites to reach a global audience, share engaging content, and facilitate virtual tours. By embracing these innovative applications, heritage sites can preserve their historical legacy while creating dynamic, inclusive, and immersive experiences that resonate with visitors across generations.

## FUNDING

The Department of Science and Technology-Inspire [Grant number IF210191, 2022], Ministry of Science and Technology, Government of India, provided funding for this work.

## REFERENCES

Boniface, P., & Fowler, P. (2002). *Heritage and tourism in the global village*. Routledge. doi:10.4324/9780203033685

Bourgeon-Renault, D., Urbain, C., Petr, C., Le Gall-Ely, M., & Gombault, A. (2006). An experiential approach to the consumption value of arts and culture: The case of museums and monuments. *International Journal of Arts Management*, 35–47. https://www.jstor.org/stable/41064896

Boyd, S. (2002). Cultural and heritage tourism in Canada: Opportunities, principles and challenges. *Tourism and Hospitality Research*, *3*(3), 211–233. doi:10.1177/146735840200300303

Buckley, R. (2004). The effects of World Heritage listing on tourism to Australian national parks. *Journal of Sustainable Tourism*, *12*(1), 70–84. doi:10.1080/09669580408667225

Calver, S. J., & Page, S. J. (2013). Enlightened hedonism: Exploring the relationship of service value, visitor knowledge and interest, to visitor enjoyment at heritage attractions. *Tourism Management*, *39*, 23–36. doi:10.1016/j.tourman.2013.03.008

Caton, K., & Santos, C. A. (2007). Heritage tourism on Route 66: Deconstructing nostalgia. *Journal of Travel Research*, *45*(4), 371–386. doi:10.1177/0047287507299572

Chandler, J. A. (2004). Comparing visitor profiles at heritage tourism destinations in Eastern North Carolina. *Journal of Travel & Tourism Marketing*, *16*(1), 53–63. doi:10.1300/J073v16n01_06

Che, Y., Cao, Y., Wu, R., Liu, J., Chen, L., & Wu, J. (2022). Spatio-Temporal Pattern of World Heritage and Its Accessibility Assessment in China. *Sustainability (Basel)*, *14*(5), 3033. doi:10.3390/su14053033

Chen, C. F., & Chen, F. S. (2010). Experience quality, perceived value, satisfaction and behavioral intentions for heritage tourists. *Tourism Management*, *31*(1), 29–35. doi:10.1016/j.tourman.2009.02.008

Choi, A. S., Ritchie, B. W., Papandrea, F., & Bennett, J. (2010). Economic valuation of cultural heritage sites: A choice modeling approach. *Tourism Management*, *31*(2), 213–220. doi:10.1016/j.tourman.2009.02.014

Colbert, F. (2003). Company profile: the Sydney opera house: an Australian icon. *International Journal of Arts Management*, 69–77. doi:10.1080/09669580408667225

Cuccia, T., & Cellini, R. (2007). Is cultural heritage really important for tourists? A contingent rating study. *Applied Economics*, *39*(2), 261–271. doi:10.1080/00036840500427981

Daengbuppha, J., Hemmington, N., & Wilkes, K. (2006). Using grounded theory to model visitor experiences at heritage sites: Methodological and practical issues. *Qualitative Market Research*, *9*(4), 367–388. doi:10.1108/13522750610689096

Dierking, L. D., & Falk, J. H. (1992). Redefining the museum experience: The interactive experience model. *Visitor Studies*, *4*(1), 173–176.

Du Cros, H., Bauer, T., Lo, C., & Rui, S. (2005). Cultural heritage assets in China as sustainable tourism products: Case studies of the Hutongs and the Huanghua section of the Great Wall. *Journal of Sustainable Tourism*, *13*(2), 171–194. doi:10.1080/09669580508668484

Flowers, J., & Easterling, K. (2006). Growing South Carolina's tourism cluster. *Business and Economic Review*, *52*(3), 15–20.

Fyall, A., & Garrod, B. (1998). Heritage tourism: At what price? *Managing Leisure*, *3*(4), 213–228. doi:10.1080/136067198375996

Gilmore, A., Carson, D., & Ascenção, M. (2007). Sustainable tourism marketing at a World Heritage site. *Journal of Strategic Marketing*, *15*(2-3), 253–264. doi:10.1080/09652540701318930

Gombault, A., & Petr, C. (2007). *La réputation des musées et des monuments superstars* (No. halshs-00260154).

Goulding, P., & Pomfret, G. (2022). Managing temporal variation at visitor attractions. In *Managing visitor attractions* (pp. 213–233). Routledge. doi:10.4324/9781003041948-15

Hertzman, E., Anderson, D., & Rowley, S. (2008). Edutainment heritage tourist attractions: A portrait of visitors' experiences at Storyeum. *Museum Management and Curatorship*, *23*(2), 155–175. doi:10.1080/09647770802012227

Holmes, K., Jones, P., Lockwood, A., Miller, G., Scarles, C., Szivas, E., & Tribe, J. (2006). An eclectic agenda for Tourism and Hospitality Research. *Tourism and Hospitality Research*, *7*(1), 76–82. doi:10.1057/palgrave.thr.6050035

Huang, C. H., Tsaur, J. R., & Yang, C. H. (2012). Does world heritage list really induce more tourists? Evidence from Macau. *Tourism Management*, *33*(6), 1450–1457. doi:10.1016/j.tourman.2012.01.014 PMID:32287738

Hughes, H. (2013). *Arts, entertainment and tourism*. Taylor & Francis. doi:10.4324/9780080499468

Hughes, H. L., & Benn, D. (1995). *Entertainment: its role in the tourist experience*. Leisure Studies Association.

Huh, J., & Uysal, M. (2004). Satisfaction with cultural/heritage sites: Virginia historic triangle. *Journal of Quality Assurance in Hospitality & Tourism*, *4*(3-4), 177–194. doi:10.1300/J162v04n03_12

Jimura, T. (2011). The impact of world heritage site designation on local communities–A case study of Ogimachi, Shirakawa-mura, Japan. *Tourism Management*, *32*(2), 288–296. doi:10.1016/j.tourman.2010.02.005

Kempiak, J., Hollywood, L., Bolan, P., & McMahon-Beattie, U. (2017). The heritage tourist: An understanding of the visitor experience at heritage attractions. *International Journal of Heritage Studies*, *23*(4), 375–392. doi:10.1080/13527258.2016.1277776

Kerstetter, D. L., Confer, J. J., & Graefe, A. R. (2001). An exploration of the specialization concept within the context of heritage tourism. *Journal of Travel Research*, *39*(3), 267–274. doi:10.1177/004728750103900304

Kolar, T., & Zabkar, V. (2010). A consumer-based model of authenticity: An oxymoron or the foundation of cultural heritage marketing? *Tourism Management*, *31*(5), 652–664. doi:10.1016/j.tourman.2009.07.010

Laing, J., Wheeler, F., Reeves, K., & Frost, W. (2014). Assessing the experiential value of heritage assets: A case study of a Chinese heritage precinct, Bendigo, Australia. *Tourism Management*, *40*, 180–192. doi:10.1016/j.tourman.2013.06.004

Md Khairi, N. D., Ismail, H. N., & Syed Jaafar, S. M. R. (2022). Knowledge of tourist spatial behaviour to improve Melaka world heritage site management. *International Journal of Tourism Cities*, *8*(1), 88–106. doi:10.1108/IJTC-01-2021-0018

Miah, S. J., Vu, H. Q., Gammack, J., & McGrath, M. (2017). A big data analytics method for tourist behaviour analysis. *Information & Management*, *54*(6), 771–785. doi:10.1016/j.im.2016.11.011

OECD. (2009). *The Impact of Culture on Tourism*. OECD Publishing.

OECD. O. (2014). OECD Tourism trends and policies 2014. OECD Publishing.

Oh, H., Fiore, A. M., & Jeoung, M. (2007). Measuring experience economy concepts: Tourism applications. *Journal of Travel Research*, *46*(2), 119–132. doi:10.1177/0047287507304039

Oren, G., Poria, Y., & Reichel, A. (2022). The positive role of negative emotions in heritage-site visits: The case of Auschwitz Death Camp. *Journal of Heritage Tourism, 17*(2), 158–173. doi:10.1080/1743873X.2021.1937186

Palmer, C. (1999). Tourism and the symbols of identity. *Tourism Management, 20*(3), 313–321. doi:10.1016/S0261-5177(98)00120-4

Petr, C. (2002). Tourist apprehension of heritage: A semiotic approach to behaviour patterns. *International Journal of Arts Management*, 25–38. https://www.jstor.org/stable/41064753

Petr, C. (2009). Fame is not always a positive asset for heritage equity! Some clues from buying intentions of national tourists. *Journal of Travel & Tourism Marketing, 26*(1), 1–18. doi:10.1080/10548400802656694

Petr, C. (2015). How heritage site tourists may become monument visitors. *Tourism Management, 51*, 247–262. doi:10.1016/j.tourman.2015.05.018

Pine, B. J., & Gilmore, J. H. (1999). *The Experience Economy: Work is Theatre and Every Business a Stage*. Harvard Business School Press.

Poria, Y., Butler, R., & Airey, D. (2003). The core of heritage tourism. *Annals of Tourism Research, 30*(1), 238–254. doi:10.1016/S0160-7383(02)00064-6

Poria, Y., Butler, R., & Airey, D. (2004). Links between tourists, heritage, and reasons for visiting heritage sites. *Journal of Travel Research, 43*(1), 19–28. doi:10.1177/0047287504265508

Poria, Y., Reichel, A., & Biran, A. (2006). Heritage site perceptions and motivations to visit. *Journal of Travel Research, 44*(3), 318–326. doi:10.1177/0047287505279004

Prahalad, C. K., & Ramaswamy, V. (2004). Co-creating unique value with customers. *Strategy and Leadership, 32*(3), 4–9. doi:10.1108/10878570410699249

Quinn, B. (2006). Problematising 'festival tourism': Arts festivals and sustainable development in Ireland. *Journal of Sustainable Tourism, 14*(3), 288–306. doi:10.1080/09669580608669060

Ramsey, D., & Everitt, J. (2008). If you dig it, they will come!: Archaeology heritage sites and tourism development in Belize, Central America. *Tourism Management, 29*(5), 909–916. doi:10.1016/j.tourman.2007.11.002

Richards, G. (2001). The experience industry and the creation of attractions. In *Cultural attractions and European tourism* (pp. 55–69). Cabi Publishing. doi:10.1079/9780851994406.0055

Richards, G. (2012). An overview of food and tourism trends and policies. In *Food and the tourism experience: The OECD-Korea workshop* (pp. 13–46). The OECD Tourism Studies. doi:10.1787/9789264171923-3-en

Richards, G., & Wilson, J. (2006). Developing creativity in tourist experiences: A solution to the serial reproduction of culture? *Tourism Management*, *27*(6), 1209–1223. doi:10.1016/j.tourman.2005.06.002

Ryan, C., & Higgins, O. (2006). Experiencing cultural tourism: Visitors at the Maori arts and crafts institute, New Zealand. *Journal of Travel Research*, *44*(3), 308–317. doi:10.1177/0047287505279002

Shore, S. (2010). Cultural and heritage tourism-international. *Travel & Tourism Analyst*, 8.

Stamboulis, Y., & Skayannis, P. (2003). Innovation strategies and technology for experience-based tourism. *Tourism Management*, *24*(1), 35–43. doi:10.1016/S0261-5177(02)00047-X

Su, Y. W., & Lin, H. L. (2014). Analysis of international tourist arrivals worldwide: The role of world heritage sites. *Tourism Management*, *40*, 46–58. doi:10.1016/j.tourman.2013.04.005

Timothy, D. J. (1997). Tourism and the personal heritage experience. *Annals of Tourism Research*, *24*(3), 751–754. doi:10.1016/S0160-7383(97)00006-6

Timothy, D. J. (2011). *Cultural heritage and tourism: An introduction* (Vol. 4). Channel View Publications. doi:10.21832/9781845411787

Timothy, D. J., & Boyd, S. W. (2003). *Heritage tourism*. Pearson Education.

UNWTO. (2010). *World Tourism Barometer January 2010*. UNWTO.

Yang, C. H., Lin, H. L., & Han, C. C. (2010). Analysis of international tourist arrivals in China: The role of World Heritage Sites. *Tourism Management*, *31*(6), 827–837. doi:10.1016/j.tourman.2009.08.008 PMID:32287732

Zhou, X., & Chen, Z. (2023). Destination attraction clustering: Segmenting tourist movement patterns with geotagged information. *Tourism Geographies*, *25*(2-3), 797–819. doi:10.1080/14616688.2021.2006769

# Chapter 8
# Exploring the Prospects of Artificial Intelligence in the Tourism Sector

**Mandeep Kaur**
*Lovely Professional University, India*

**Uma Pandey**
https://orcid.org/0000-0002-8817-1546
*Lovely Professional University, India*

## ABSTRACT

*Travel and tourism businesses heavily rely on AI-powered products and services for various operations, from planning trips to booking accommodations. At the moment, the travel and tourism sector heavily rely on AI-powered goods and services for a range of tasks, from planning vacations to sharing travel experiences. The travel and hospitality industries have incorporated AI into a variety of tasks and processes to provide travelers with comfort, serenity, and unsurpassed happiness. This chapter discusses how artificial intelligence (AI) is developing in the travel and tourism industry and considers possible long-term effects. This chapter explores several important areas of integrating AI, such as chatbots, predictive analytics, smart infrastructure, and personalized suggestions. This chapter will provide an overview of how AI could be used in the tourism sector. Secondary sources are used to obtain the information. This chapter offers insightful information to stakeholders who want to fully utilize AI to influence the direction of the tourism sector.*

DOI: 10.4018/979-8-3693-1978-9.ch008

## INTRODUCTION

The tourism industry is at the forefront of a shift, spurred by the rapid integration of AI technologies(El-Moffock, 2023a). As nations around the globe become more linked, organizations in the tourism industry are leveraging AI to alter how they operate, interact with clients, and manage locations. AI, a branch of computer science, studies the creation and application of intelligent technologies(Ting et al., 2021) It includes the intelligence displayed by software or computers. AI is applied in many aspects of our lives, although it originated in the computer sciences as a vague idea.(Saariluoma & Karvonen, 2023). Due to its unique perspectives on difficult issues, it has captured the curiosity of academics. At the forefront of technological advancement, AI has the potential to significantly alter many facets of our daily lives. Artificial intelligence's primary attribute is its capacity for reasoning and making decisions to maximize the likelihood of accomplishing a given objective.

## Types of AI

Artificial intelligence can be categorized into one of four types.

### Reactive AI

-Algorithms are used by reactive AI to maximize outcomes given a set of inputs.(Abdul-Rahman et al., 1995). AIs that play chess, for instance, are reactive systems that maximize the optimal move to win. Reactive AI is typically quite static and incapable of picking up new skills or changing with the times. It will therefore yield the same result when given identical inputs. Reactive AI, sometimes referred to as rule-based or deterministic AI, uses pre-established sets of algorithms and rules to decide what to do given particular inputs. Reactive AI reacts to inputs in a rigid and deterministic way as opposed to more adaptive or learning-based AI approaches, which learn or grow over time. Tasks where the decision-making process can be precisely outlined and described are especially well-suited for this kind of AI (Landgrebe & Smith, 2022).

### Restricted Memory

-In the context of artificial intelligence, "restricted memory" refers to systems that may not remember information for a long time and have a limited ability to update themselves based on fresh observations or data(Al-Amri et al., 2021) .Although kids can learn from experiences right away, their memory and learning capacity is frequently limited and prioritize short-term learning over long-term retention.

AI can update itself depending on fresh observations or data or adjust to previous experiences (Cappelli et al., 2018) .Frequently, there is little to no updating (hence the name), and the memory is not very long. For example, autonomous cars are capable of "reading the road" and "learning" from previous experiences to adjust to unfamiliar circumstances (Agrawal et al., 2019).

### Theory of Mind

-AI is completely adaptable and possesses a vast memory for prior encounters. The ability of a system to comprehend and interpret the thoughts, intentions, and feelings of others is referred to as a "Theory of Mind" in artificial intelligence(Wortham, 2018) .AI might have seen significant advancements, like making sophisticated chatbots that can interact like humans but it is crucial to acknowledge that these lack genuine emotions and self-awareness. These chatbots possess the ability to adapt to various conversational scenarios by leveraging their repositories of past interactions to generate contextually suitable responses(Chaves & Gerosa, 2019). However, instead of possessing genuine awareness or consciousness, their adaptability and memory primarily stem from their programming and training material. Instances of this type of AI include sophisticated chatbots capable of completing the Turing Test and deceiving individuals into believing they are interacting with a human. These AIs are highly impressive and advanced, although they do not possess self-awareness (Stewart et al., 2019).

### Self-Aware AI

-As the name implies, self-aware AI develops sentience and awareness of their existence. Some scientists, still in the realm of science fiction, think that AIs will never become conscious or "alive". Science fiction has contributed significantly to the popularisation of the idea of self-aware AI, which describes AI systems that are not only capable of highly developed cognitive functions but also have some degree of consciousness and knowledge of their own existence(Galanos, 2023) .The creation of genuinely self-aware AI is still mostly theoretical and speculative at this point. Many scientists and researchers contend that it is extremely difficult, if not essentially impossible, to achieve true awareness in artificial intelligence(Kottum Elmar, 2019).

## Essential Elements of AI

AI is a vast field that includes several subfields, each of which focuses on a distinct aspect of intelligent systems. Some of the key subfields are discussed below:

## Deep Learning

Deep learning is a specialised branch of machine learning that uses multi-layered neural networks, or artificial neural networks, to handle extremely complicated tasks with exceptional effectiveness. Deep learning systems automatically build hierarchical data representations from raw inputs, in contrast to typical machine learning models that could need feature engineering and explicit programming(Sarker, 2021). This strategy has changed the face of technology and produced breakthroughs in several fields. A subset of machine learning that analyses many aspects of data by employing multi-layered neural networks. Natural language processing, computer vision, and gaming have all been transformed by deep learning. (Taye, 2023)

## Natural Language Processing (NLP)

At the forefront of the development of AI is Natural Language Processing (NLP), which aims to decipher the nuances of human language and provide robots with the ability to engage with it meaningfully. This multidisciplinary field aims to narrow the communication gap between humans and machines by utilizing linguistics, machine learning, and computational linguistics(Basha et al., 2023). NLP is a specific field within the realm of artificial intelligence that focuses on the analysis and understanding of computer-based language usage. It enables machines to generate, understand, and interpret human language in practical ways with applications such as sentiment analysis, chatbots, translation, and others that exemplify many uses (Mahato, 2021). Sentiment analysis is a widely used application of NLP that employs automated techniques to extract and evaluate textual attitudes. It aids organizations in comprehending their customers' viewpoints and making decisions based on data. Another revolutionary application is chatbots, which utilize NLP algorithms to engage in human-like dialogues and promptly and individually address customer service inquiries, hence enhancing user experiences. Machine translation, enabled by NLP, effectively eliminates language barriers by providing accurate and automatic translation across different languages(Dabre et al., 2020).

## Computer Vision

It is a new field of AI that makes machines that can see, process, and make sense of the visual data that is encountered by them daily. The technology is about providing computers with visual processing abilities that can act like human vision and cognition also the ability to understand and interpret visual data(Frintrop et al., 2010) .This requires algorithms and models that can collect useful information from visual media. It has a wide range of applications like autonomous cars, object detection, and picture identification. These developments have the potential to transform many aspects of our daily lives. It is also used in applications including picture recognition, object detection, and autonomous vehicles (Mah et al., 2022).

### Reinforcement Learning

In reinforcement learning, you show models how to reach a goal by making them make a series of choices in a certain situation. A branch of machine learning called reinforcement learning teaches models how to make a set of choices or actions in a certain situation in order to reach a goal (Naeem et al., 2020)There are a lot of striking parallels between the paradigm and how other living things learn from their mistakes. When agents get input from their environment in the form of rewards or punishments based on what they do, this is called reinforcement learning. The agent needs to figure out a plan or approach that will get them the most money over time. This is one way a virtual person could learn new skills (Vaughan et al., 2016).

## ARTIFICIAL INTELLIGENCE AND TOURISM SECTOR

AI is slowly becoming part of our daily lives. In the tourism sector also, AI is used in various ways (Filieri et al., 2021a). By 2032, the travel and tourism industry is projected to reach a staggering $14.6 trillion, accounting for an astonishing 11.3% of the world economy. To achieve this, it is essential to incorporate more products and services that are powered by AI. As such, AI has already been partially used in several tourism-related industries (Zlatanov & Popesku, 2019). One of the significant applications is in travel-related decision-making. AI can help travelers in decision-making. It can gather and analyze data about their preferences and impact their next information searches by providing personalized results which ranges from booking hotels to creating itineraries. Other AI technologies include forecasting tools, autonomous agents, recommendation systems, customization methods and systems, conversation systems (chatbots and voice assistants), language translation apps, and smart tourist destinations. It is important to note that, even though we examine each system independently, tourists typically engage with technology that incorporates many systems. A visitor might converse with a robot that incorporates a conversational system, recommender system, personalization method, or autonomous agent, based on their needs (Bulchand-Gidumal, 2020). Tourism in India has a lot of potential to grow, and the country's travel industries are embracing new technologies like virtual reality (Kumar, Dhiraj, Shah, et al., 2023) and augmented reality as well as popular AI approaches like deep learning and artificial neural networks for predictive analytics and robotics. Due to this technical adaption, their services are now much better, dynamic pricing is now possible, and smart customer experience management is now possible. (Dey Sharmistha, 2022).

The tourism sector is at a point of dramatic change, with Artificial Intelligence (AI) emerging as a driving force transforming the very core of travel(Hassan Editor, 2022) .AI is changing the tourism industry drastically, from personalized experiences to operational efficiency, ushering in an era of unrivaled innovation and response which is discussed below.

## Personalization of Travel Experiences

AI can examine large datasets and detect patterns in tourist behavior. This ability is revolutionizing the way travel experiences are tailored to individual preferences(Zhang et al., 2019) .AI is changing the way we travel by providing personalized recommendations through virtual assistants who can record their preferences and give recommendations(Kabassi, 2010) .The literature review highlights AI applications, employing sophisticated algorithms and machine learning models, to construct a customized travel environment that accommodates the unique interests and preferences of individual traveller.

## Dynamic Pricing and Inventory Management

AI can also play a role in inventory management. AI algorithms utilize real-time data and predictive analytics(Singh, 2023). This ability allows companies to adjust pricing under demand fluctuations. This helps the companies to enhance revenue management while also guaranteeing that passengers may access the most competitive and contextually relevant pricing, contributing to a more efficient and consumer-friendly pricing ecosystem.

## Chatbots and Virtual Assistants Enhancing Customer Interaction

The implementation of AI-driven chatbots and virtual assistants is transforming customer communication in the tourism sector (Cheriyan, 2021).These intelligent systems, fueled by Natural Language Processing (NLP), provide real-time assistance, respond to queries, and facilitate smooth communication, as documented in the literature. Chatbots are increasingly essential tools for enhancing consumer engagement and satisfaction, whether they are assisting tourists in navigating the reservation procedure or delivering travel-related information(Ukpabi et al., 2019).

## Predictive Analytics and Demand Forecasting

To predict future demand, demand forecasting requires historical demand data as well as forecasting techniques. Gathering pertinent information on the many elements such as product attributes, marketing campaigns, upcoming occasions, weather, and overall economic conditions—that affect consumer demand for retail items is the first phase in the process.(Punia & Shankar, 2022). Retailers may effectively plan and manage their sales by using the business knowledge that comes from knowing how these factors affect demand.

## Augmented Reality (AR) Enhancing Tourist Experiences

The integration of Artificial Intelligence (AI) and Augmented Reality (AR) is revolutionizing how passengers see and engage with their destinations (El-Moffock, 2023). AR applications enhance the whole travel experience by offering real-time information about historical sites, cultural landmarks, and local attractions(Han et al., 2019).The integration of AI and AR not only provides valuable educational information but also transforms the act of touring into an engaging and interactive experience.

# METHODOLOGY

To achieve the goal of this study, a thorough analysis of the current literature was carried out. This thorough literature analysis helps readers understand the boundaries of the field and the present level of knowledge about it. It is also possible to gain insight into the underlying theories of the issue by analyzing relevant literature, which helps to define the research topic more precisely.

*Figure 1. Research data collection process*
*(Developed by Authors)*

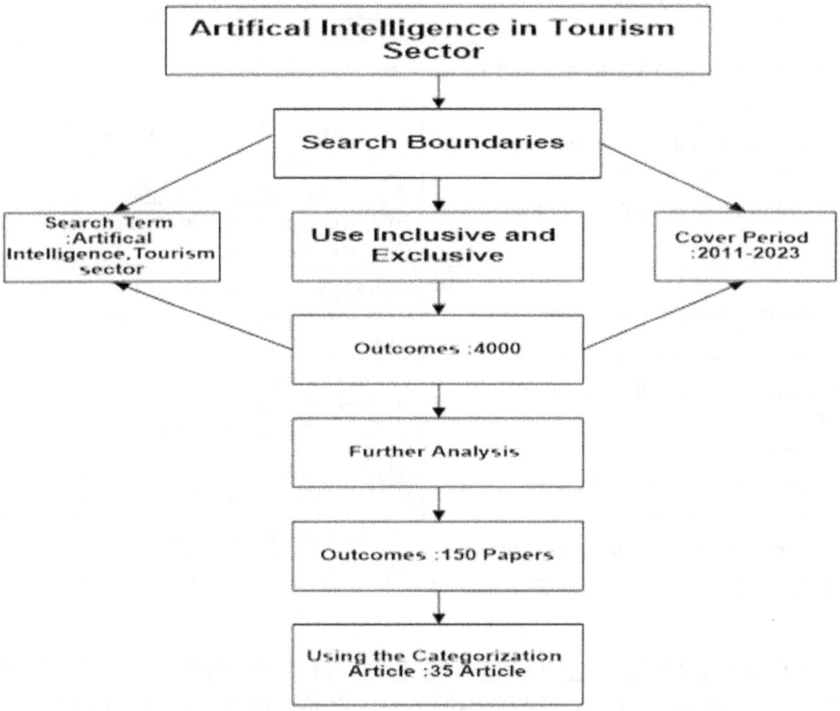


## RESULTS AND DISCUSSIONS

We provide a thorough overview of the 35 research publications that were analyzed in this part. Following our analysis, seven main themes emerged, which are shown in the table below.

*Table 1. Key themes in implications of artificial intelligence in tourism*

| Key Themes | Sources |
|---|---|
| **Customized Itineraries & Planning for Trips** | (Filieri et al., 2021b),(Kazak et al., 2020) , (Lisi & Esposito, 2015),(Rodríguez et al., 2012) (ÇOLAK, 2023) |
| **Improved Booking and Accommodation Selection** | (Gupta et al., 2023a),(Sekhon & Ahuja, 2023) ,(Kar et al., 2023),(Deshpande et al., 2022) |
| **Augmented Reality (AR) and Virtual Reality (VR)** | (Huang et al., 2022),(van Nuenen & Scarles, 2021),(Deshpande et al., 2022), (Jung et al., 2016) (Nayyar et al., 2018) |
| **Immersion in Language and Culture** | (Divekar et al., 2022) , (Frey & Briviba, 2021), (Bearse & de Jong, 2008), (Nero, 2009), (Mccalla, 2000) |
| **Utilizing Predictive Analytics to Forecast Demand:** | (Sun et al., 2021), (Xu et al., 2020), (Ratten et al., 2019), (Li et al., 2020), (Wang et al., 2016) .(Fronzetti Colladon et al., 2019) |
| **Enhanced Safety and Security Measures** | (D Buhalis, 2018), (Beriša & Zorić, 2019), (Gaur et al., 2021), (McA Baker, 2015), (Gupta et al., 2023) |
| **Customized Tours and Culinary Experiences** | (Milton, 2023),(Chiang & Huang, 2015), (Kariru, 2023),(Kariru, 2023) |

## ARTIFICIAL INTELLIGENCE APPLICATIONS AND THEIR USE IN THE TRAVEL AND TOURISM SECTOR IN THE FUTURE

### Customised Itineraries and Planning for Trips

Travelers often encounter the difficult task of sifting through an overwhelming amount of information to plan their vacations in the fast-paced environment of the twenty-first century. Systems propelled by AI have the potential to revolutionize this process by delivering a streamlined and personalized travel planning experience.

#### User Interests

AI algorithms will consider various factors such as gastronomic exploration, historical sites, cultural interactions, and adventure pursuits, among other preferences of the traveler. By analyzing a user's professed interests and previous travel patterns, the AI is capable of generating an itinerary that is precisely tailored to the individual.

## Optimization of Budget

Artificial intelligence will consider the financial decisions of the traveler, acknowledging the importance of financial constraints. It guarantees a comprehensive and cost-effective vacation by providing recommendations for lodging, dining, and activities that remain within the designated budget.

## Real-Time Information and Advice

The AI-driven system will consistently evaluate data provided by users, weather conditions, traffic reports, and nearby occurrences during the course of the voyage. To provide a dynamic and adaptable travel experience, the itinerary will be dynamically modified to accommodate unanticipated circumstances or opportunities that arise.

## Integration With Local Experts and Guides

The utilization of AI may facilitate instantaneous correspondence with local authorities and advisers who possess extensive expertise about specific regions, historical sites, or cultural encounters. This enables a more profound examination and comprehension of the historical significance and allure of Punjab.

## Multi-Lingual Support

AI-driven platforms will offer seamless communication through multilingual support, recognizing the diverse linguistic landscape that travelers traverse. The addition of translation services will enable guests to actively participate in community affairs and gain a comprehensive understanding of the local culture.

## Geo-Position and Contextual Recommendations

AI will provide real-time recommendations grounded in the traveler's location, utilizing GPS technology (Kumar, Dhiraj, & Rani, 2023). When a visitor approaches a historic site, for instance, the AI may suggest nearby restaurants or other points of interest.

## Feedback and Learning Loop

In the post-journey phase, AI platforms will collect feedback from travelers, thereby facilitating continuous development. As subsequent iterations are developed using the collective experiences of previous visitors as a foundation, they will inevitably become ever more individualized and refined.

## Improved Booking and Accommodation Selection:

The procedure for selecting and reserving lodging is an essential element of any journey. The implementation of AI-driven solutions holds the capacity to revolutionize this process by offering patrons a more streamlined and tailored approach to selecting the most suitable hotel.

### Personalized Recommendations

AI algorithms will consider the distinct preferences of individual travelers, encompassing factors such as preferred accommodation options (hotel, guesthouse, or homestay), desired locations, desired amenities, and financial constraints. By analyzing previous reservations and expressed preferences, AI can generate a personalized inventory of options that perfectly suit the user.

### Real-Time Availability and Pricing

The AI system will provide instantaneous notifications regarding the availability and expenses of accommodation through the application of predictive analytics. This ensures that individuals access the latest information, empowering them to make informed decisions.

### Multi-Faceted Search Filters

Platforms propelled by AI will offer advanced search filters that enable users to zero in on specific attributes, such as the dimensions of the area, proximity to notable landmarks, accessibility features, and more. This feature empowers tourists to find accommodations that precisely fulfill their requirements.

### Analysis of User Reviews and Ratings

By examining customer reviews and ratings, artificial intelligence can provide valuable insights regarding the quality and reputation of lodging establishments. Visitors can ensure a pleasant and distress-free sojourn by making informed decisions based on the provided information.

### Dynamic Pricing Optimisation

AI algorithms will leverage historical data, external variables (such as vacations or regional events), and demand trends to optimize pricing strategies. Thus, budget-friendly accommodations and exclusive promotions that appeal to the preferences and purchasing power of travelers are accessible to them.

### Integration With Extra Services

The capabilities of the AI-powered platform extend beyond mere accommodation selection. It could also include cuisine suggestions, recommendations for local activities, and alternative modes of transportation in order to provide a more comprehensive travel planning experience.

### Safe and Easy Booking Procedure

The platform enabled by AI will facilitate a secure and user-friendly booking process. Investing confidence in the transactions of travelers will be ensured through the secure and efficient management of their payment information.

### Integration With Loyalty Programmes

Lodging providers' loyalty programs may be integrated with AI-powered platforms, allowing visitors to accrue rewards and benefits for future stays. Fostering a reciprocal alliance between lodging providers and visitors promotes revisits.

## Immersion in Language and Culture

One of the most enlightening aspects of travel is the opportunity to interact with local communities, acquire an understanding of their way of life, and share in their culture. By providing cultural context and bridging language barriers, AI may fundamentally transform meaningful relationships.

### Real-Time Translation Services

AI-powered translation solutions provide seamless communication between travelers and locals who may speak different languages. These technologies' quick and accurate translations will enhance the smoothness of conversations. This fosters cultural exchange and inclusiveness, hence enhancing the overall travel experience.

## Diverse Language Support

AI-driven systems will be capable of accommodating a wide range of languages, effectively catering to the linguistic requirements of both local populations and visitors. By facilitating effective communication among individuals with diverse linguistic origins, obstacles are dismantled, fostering an inclusive work environment.

## Contextual Understanding

Advanced AI systems consider the context of the discussion, in addition to translating individual words. This enables translations to achieve a higher level of precision and sophistication, ensuring that cultural intricacies and subtleties are faithfully conveyed.

## Learning and Adaptation

AI-powered translation systems have the ability to learn from user interactions and adapt to various accents, dialects, and slang expressions. Over time, the system enhances its sensitivity to the nuances of the local language, resulting in translations that are increasingly accurate.

## Local Accents and Dialects

Artificial intelligence (AI) will undergo training to recognize and adapt to different regional accents and dialects, facilitating effective communication even in regions with unique linguistic characteristics. This ensures that tourists have the opportunity to engage with a diverse range of communities.

## Contextual Information and Cultural Perspectives

AI will provide visitors with not only language translation but also valuable cultural insights about Punjab. These details may encompass information regarding regional traditions and customs, the historical importance of prominent locations, and etiquette guidance. Prior knowledge of the subject will improve the visitor's experience and promote a deeper understanding of the region's cultural heritage.

## Guided Cultural Experiences

AI-driven platforms might offer guided cultural experiences led by well-informed locals, who would provide insights into the historical and cultural significance of specific locales. These interactions will be deeply engaging and educational due to the inclusion of relevant background information and instantaneous translation.

### Improved Connections With Locals

AI-driven translation services will facilitate more profound connections between tourists and locals by eliminating linguistic obstacles. This may lead to stronger connections, mutual experiences, and an increased recognition of the warm and generous nature of hospitality.

### Preserving Local Languages

The preservation of local languages can be facilitated by AI through the provision of translation services, hence safeguarding endangered or less often used languages. This ensures that the linguistic diversity of the region is respected and protected.

### Accessibility for All Visitors

The utilization of AI-driven language and cultural immersion technologies will enhance accessibility for tourists with diverse linguistic backgrounds and varying degrees of proficiency, hence promoting a more welcoming and inclusive environment for everyone.

## Experiences with Augmented Reality (AR) and Virtual Reality (VR)

The integration of AI-driven augmented reality (AR) and virtual reality (VR) technology has immense potential to revolutionize the visitor experience in Punjab. These interactive gadgets can transport tourists to historical locations, cultural landmarks, and natural marvels in ways that were previously unattainable.

### Historical Site Reconstructions

Augmented Reality (AR) and Virtual Reality (VR) technologies may accurately reconstruct historical landmarks, allowing tourists to experience time travel and see important events in history. Through the utilization of interactive simulations, individuals have the opportunity to investigate and examine old ruins, palaces, and forts, so gaining a more profound understanding and admiration for the region's extensive historical background.

## Virtual Reality (VR) and Augmented Reality Experiences

Utilizing virtual reality (VR), individuals can partake in tours of historical sites that may have limited accessibility or attract minimal visitors. This includes ancient temples, forts, palaces, and other architecturally remarkable structures that hold immense cultural and historical importance.

## Cultural Heritage in 3D

Through the utilization of augmented reality (AR) and virtual reality (VR) technologies, historical structures and objects can be animated in three-dimensional form, providing tourists with a simulated environment to actively explore and interact with them. Users can engage in a dynamic and educational experience that beyond mere visual or textual content.

## Interactive Learning Environments

Augmented reality (AR) and virtual reality (VR) can enhance educational settings by providing contextual information and specific insights into the cultural and historical significance of particular locations. This interactive learning technique enhances visitor engagement, hence amplifying the impact and memorability of the material.

## Time Travel Simulation

Through the utilization of Augmented Reality (AR) and Virtual Reality (VR), individuals can be transported to various historical epochs and witness historical events, architectural structures, and cultural traditions as they were in the past. This comprehensive time-travel experience provides a unique perspective on the evolving history.

## Natural Wonders and Ecotourism

Virtual reality (VR) can offer virtual tours of Punjab's diverse natural landscapes, encompassing its rivers, forests, and wildlife reserves. By utilizing this technology, tourists can have a comprehensive understanding of the ecological variety in the region, thereby fostering environmental consciousness and preservation.

### Cultural Events, Performances, and Festivals

By utilizing augmented reality (AR) and virtual reality (VR), visitors may experience the vibrancy and excitement of festivities (Kumar, Dhiraj, & Hassan, 2023). This immersive experience may encompass several forms of artistic expression, including traditional dance, music, and other art forms.

### Accessibility and Inclusivity

People with physical or mobility impairments can now enjoy Punjab's historical and cultural places virtually thanks to AR and VR technologies. This guarantees that everyone can participate in the cultural adventure, irrespective of physical capability.

### Personalized Experiences

AI can modify augmented reality (AR) and virtual reality (VR) experiences according to the individual user's specific preferences and interests. For example, those with a profound fascination for architecture can be provided with exclusive excursions that focus on historic structures and their intricate details.

### Advancing Cultural Travel

Utilizing AR and VR technology can serve as powerful marketing tools to promote tourism in Punjab by enticing potential visitors to explore the region's rich historical and cultural sites. Immersive virtual tours may motivate tourists to include these sites in their travel plans.

## Utilising Predictive Analytics to Forecast Demand

Accurately predicting and understanding the actions of travelers is crucial for businesses to thrive in the fast-evolving and dynamic tourism industry. The integration of AI-powered predictive analytics is set to revolutionize demand forecasting in the tourism industry. This advancement will not only provide valuable insights to enhance operational efficiency but also elevate the overall guest experience.

### Historical Data Analysis

AI systems will analyze extensive collections of previous data, encompassing visitor demographics, travel trends, booking behaviors, and seasonal fluctuations. Businesses can have a comprehensive understanding of the factors that have historically attracted travelers by researching past trends and patterns.

## Real-Time Data Integration

AI-powered systems will consistently examine up-to-the-minute data, such as current booking prices, foot traffic at popular attractions, and weather conditions, alongside historical data. This dynamic strategy ensures that businesses will consistently have access to the latest insights, enabling them to make well-informed decisions.

## Trend Identification and Seasonal Variations

AI systems can readily detect recurring patterns and trends. By discerning seasonal patterns, businesses can anticipate periods of heightened activity and make adjustments to their resources and products accordingly. This enables them to strategize for periods of low demand and capitalize on seasons characterized by high demand.

## Customer Segmentation

By utilizing AI-powered predictive analytics, travellers can be classified into specific categories based on several criteria including behavior, preferences, and demographics. By employing segmentation, businesses may tailor their products and marketing strategies to certain consumer groups, thereby providing customers with a personalized and appealing experience.

## Optimising Pricing Strategies

Companies can implement dynamic pricing strategies by understanding the fluctuations in demand. AI-powered systems can optimize pricing for accommodations, excursions, and other services by considering current demand, so maximizing revenue while ensuring competitiveness.

## Staffing and Resource Allocation

Businesses can efficiently allocate resources by predicting fluctuations in demand. To ensure the highest level of service, additional personnel may be allocated during periods of high demand, while resources may be adjusted or reduced during slower periods to minimize costs.

### Inventory Management

Predictive analytics can assist in making informed decisions regarding inventory for organizations operating in the accommodation or guided tour industry. Businesses may align hotel availability, tour dates, and other items with projected demand levels by accurately forecasting demand (Dhiraj, et al., 2023)

### Optimizing Marketing Campaigns

Companies have the ability to fine-tune their marketing tactics by leveraging predictive analytics insights. This involves targeting specific markets or demographics that are expected to have greater demand and allocating the advertising money in a highly efficient manner to achieve the best potential results.

### Improving the Visitor Experience

Companies can ensure they are prepared to meet the needs and desires of tourists by accurately predicting demand. This involves ensuring an adequate workforce, maintaining hygienic facilities, and implementing a streamlined reservation process.

## Enhanced Safety and Security Measures

AI-driven surveillance systems will enhance safety protocols by offering live monitoring in densely populated regions and popular tourist spots. Utilizing predictive analytics will enable authorities to forecast probable hazards, hence safeguarding the welfare of visitors. Surveillance systems equipped with artificial intelligence (AI) capabilities represent a significant advancement in security and safety standards. These technologies employ cutting-edge artificial intelligence algorithms to monitor high-traffic roadways and popular tourist destinations in real-time. This enables the proactive detection and mitigation of potential hazards or security risks. One of the primary benefits of AI-powered surveillance is its ability to efficiently and dependably handle substantial volumes of data. The vast volume of data produced in densely populated areas may exceed the capacity of conventional monitoring systems to manage. In contrast, AI has the capability to evaluate video feeds, sensor data, and other inputs at a scale and speed that would be unfeasible for humans to do independently.

Given the circumstances, the significance of predictive analytics is substantial.

AI systems may detect patterns and deviations in historical data, which may indicate potential security threats. For example, the system has the capability to recognize acts or situations that have a statistical correlation with security incidents, allowing authorities to respond promptly. These AI systems can also be employed in conjunction with other technologies, such as license plate recognition and facial recognition. This allows for the immediate recognition of individuals or vehicles associated with security concerns, providing law enforcement with vital information necessary for an appropriate response.

The utilization of AI in surveillance has benefits that extend beyond the immediate identification of potential dangers. To optimize resource allocation, authorities can employ time-series analysis to detect patterns and hotspots based on the data collected. To address the underlying reasons behind consistently high incidence of minor incidents in specific areas, additional measures can be implemented.

Moreover, the very presence of AI-driven surveillance can act as a deterrent on its own. Prospective offenders are less inclined to initiate unlawful activities when they are aware of being under surveillance by sophisticated and intelligent technologies. Overall, the integration of AI-powered surveillance systems has greatly enhanced the capabilities of modern security infrastructure. The integration of predictive analytics and real-time monitoring enables authorities to enhance the security and safety of tourist spots and areas with high levels of traffic.

## Personalized Culinary Experiences and Guided Tours

The hotel and tourism industry are being revolutionized by the progress in artificial intelligence, which is changing how organizations cater to their customers. By employing AI-driven data analysis, these organizations can acquire invaluable insights into the preferences and inclinations of their clients. This allows companies to offer highly personalized experiences, such as meticulously curated eating options and meticulously designed tours that cater to each individual's specific preferences. The ability of AI to efficiently process and analyze vast amounts of data is one of its primary advantages in this context. Businesses can acquire extensive client information from several sources, such as social media engagements, online reviews, and booking records. AI systems excel at efficiently analyzing this data, identifying patterns, and drawing meaningful inferences. They are capable of discerning common interests, such as specific culinary preferences, popular tourist spots, or levels of physical activity.

Businesses can utilize the abundance of information available to them to create personalized and impactful experiences for each visitor. For example, a restaurant may utilize AI to analyze a recurrent customer's past dining preferences, dietary limitations, and allergies to develop a customized menu. Similarly, a tour operator can utilize AI to recommend certain destinations, events, and travel plans based on the previous preferences and interests of tourists.

AI has the potential to enhance booking and reservation procedures, further increasing their convenience and user-friendliness. Intelligent recommendation engines can utilize a visitor's established preferences to provide personalized itineraries or packages. This ensures that every aspect of the experience aligns with the individual's preferences, while also optimizing time efficiency. Customized experiences offer benefits that extend beyond catering to specific interests. Companies that excel in delivering personalized services are more inclined to foster a loyal customer base and receive favorable recommendations through word-of-mouth. A satisfied customer is likely to become a repeat customer and may even refer the company to others, thus enhancing its success further.

In summary, companies in the hotel and tourism industries may now offer unparalleled customized experiences through the utilization of AI-powered data analysis. By leveraging the wealth of easily accessible knowledge, they can craft customized culinary excursions and guided tours that cater specifically to individual preferences and interests. This enhances customer satisfaction and drives corporate success in an increasingly competitive industry.

## ETHICAL CONSIDERATIONS OF AI IN THE TOURISM INDUSTRY

The extensive incorporation of AI in the tourism industry presents substantial ethical considerations and notable obstacles. An essential factor to take into account is the ethical management of personal data. Artificial intelligence relies heavily on data analytics, necessitating the collection and analysis of vast amounts of user data. Regarding data privacy and security, significant challenges arise that require the deployment of robust protective measures to prevent unauthorized access and misuse of personal data. The displacement of workers is an additional ethical quandary linked to the incorporation of AI. There is concern that traditional job responsibilities may become outdated as automation and AI technology simplify operating procedures. This concern is quite rational. Implementing proactive measures such as extensive staff development programs and reskilling initiatives is crucial for maintaining ethical responsibility and reducing the potential negative impact on employment. Moreover, openness is a crucial ethical concern when it comes to AI systems. The lack of transparency in advanced AI systems leads to questions about responsibility and fairness, especially when these systems have an impact on decisions that significantly affect people's lives. Guaranteeing openness in the functioning of AI algorithms and addressing biases within them are crucial steps in the endeavor to ethically use AI. The extensive integration of artificial AI in the tourism sector requires a delicate balance between leveraging the benefits of technical progress and safeguarding personal data, job security, and overall well-being of persons. Attaining this balance is crucial to facilitate the conscientious and enduring integration of artificial intelligence into the dynamic tourism industry.

To promote sustainable growth, responsible AI adoption requires giving priority to user privacy, impartiality, and transparency. Establishing explicit criteria for ethical data usage, ensuring algorithmic transparency, and correcting biases are key factors in fostering a more responsible AI ecosystem. Preventive solutions, such as workforce development efforts and reskilling programs, aim to address concerns about job displacement by building a technologically capable and resilient workforce. By upholding ethical values and supporting societal well-being, the tourism industry may efficiently harness the transformative potential of AI while also advancing sustainable development.

## CONCLUSION

AI applications are already being used in the tourism industry. These applications show immense potential to transform the tourism sector. This chapter has investigated the impact that AI is expected to have on the industry, offering a full understanding of its consequences, practical applications, and the ethical challenges that come with this technological advancement. Undoubtedly, the incorporation of AI technology holds immense potential to revolutionize the traveler's experience. AI enhances travelers' involvement by providing tailored suggestions and effortless interactions facilitated by chatbots and virtual assistants. This chapter also emphasizes the ability of AI to tailor services based on changing travelers' preferences, which improves service quality and client happiness. Furthermore, the research highlights the crucial role that AI plays in improving decision-making processes through data insights and analytics. Utilizing large datasets allows firms to quickly adapt to changing market dynamics and emerging consumer preferences. Analytical skills play a vital role in the travel industry's efforts to implement a customer-centric and adaptable approach. This ensures the ongoing efficacy of services while also accommodating the diverse needs of modern tourists. A significant aspect of the research focuses on investigating how destination management may integrate predictive analytics and intelligent destination technologies. This signifies a fundamental change in the way tourism ecosystems are developed and maintained. The proficient application of artificial intelligence has enabled the creation of robust and enduring destinations, systems for controlling population, and the effective distribution of resources. This development has implications that go beyond immediate operational benefits, as it significantly contributes to the broader discussion on environmentally sustainable tourism practices and conservation.

However, like any scientific progress, the research thoroughly investigates the ethical consequences that come from the widespread use of AI in the tourism industry. The issues of data privacy, security, and potential employment displacement require careful and thorough thought. This study emphasizes the immediate necessity for politicians, industry participants, and researchers to directly address these ethical quandaries and collaborate in order to create solutions that promote the conscientious and enduring incorporation of artificial intelligence. The study's findings offer a comprehensive comprehension of the varied impacts that AI has on the tourism industry. This article serves as a guide for navigating the always evolving landscape of technology-driven changes. It encourages relevant parties to take a practical approach to this major upheaval, carefully assessing both the benefits and drawbacks. The knowledge and conclusions presented in this research will have a significant impact on shaping policies, refining strategies, and fostering an industry that embraces technological advancements while adhering to ethical principles and sustainable development in the ongoing integration of AI into the tourism sector.

## LIMITATIONS AND FUTURE RECOMMENDATIONS

This study is grounded in a critical analysis of secondary data. When assembling our references, we restricted our search to papers released after 2011 and used the Google Scholar database. Subsequent studies with an alternative methodology may be capable of discussing the issues we ran into. An extensive analysis utilizing original data from many stakeholders as well as an alternative quantitative or qualitative methodology for the investigation of Future adjustments can be made for better, more precise outcomes.

This study focuses primarily on the benefits of using artificial intelligence in the travel and tourist industry including how it will enhance the national economy, standards of goods and services provided, data handling and security, and tourism operations. Thus, future research should examine the primary challenges or drawbacks that artificial intelligence brings to the travel industry and assess how they affect travel operations.

## REFERENCES

Abdul-Rahman, K. H., Shahidehpour, S. M., & Daneshdoost, M. (1995). AI APPROACH TO OPTIMAL VAR CONTROL WITH FUZZY REACTIVE LOADS. In 88 lEEE Transactions on Power Systems. IEEE.

Agrawal, A., Gans, J., & Goldfarb, A. (2019). *The economics of artificial intelligence : an agenda*.

Al-Amri, R., Murugesan, R. K., Man, M., Abdulateef, A. F., Al-Sharafi, M. A., & Alkahtani, A. A. (2021). A review of machine learning and deep learning techniques for anomaly detection in iot data. In Applied Sciences (Switzerland). MDPI AG. doi:10.3390/app11125320

Baker, D. (2015). *Tourism and Terrorism: Terrorists Threats to Commercial Aviation Safety & Security*.

Basha, M. J., Vijayakumar, S., Jayashankari, J., Alawadi, A. H., & Durdona, P. (2023). Advancements in Natural Language Processing for Text Understanding. *E3S Web of Conferences, 399*. doi:10.1051/e3sconf/202339904031

Bearse, C., & de Jong, E. J. (2008). Cultural and linguistic investment: Adolescents in a secondary two-way immersion program. *Equity & Excellence in Education, 41*(3), 325–340. doi:10.1080/10665680802174817

Beriša, H., & Zorić, O. (2019). *Safety Culture Of Touris M S Ector In The Function Of S Strengthening The Security Culture Of Citizens*.

Buhalis, D. (2018). *Technological disruptions in Services: lessons from Tourism and Hospitality*. Manuscript Central. http://mc.manuscriptcentral.com/josm

Bulchand-Gidumal, J. (2020). Impact of Artificial Intelligence in Travel, Tourism, and Hospitality. In *Handbook of e-Tourism* (pp. 1–20). Springer International Publishing. doi:10.1007/978-3-030-05324-6_110-1

Cappelli, P., Tambe, P., & Yakubovich, V. (2018). Artificial Intelligence in Human Resources Management: Challenges and a Path Forward. SSRN *Electronic Journal*. doi:10.2139/ssrn.3263878

Chaves, A. P., & Gerosa, M. A. (2019). *How should my chatbot interact? A survey on human-chatbot interaction design*. Taylor & Francis. doi:10.1080/10447318.2020.1841438

Cheriyan, J. (2021). *Consumer Acceptance towards AI-enabled Chatbots; case of Travel and Tourism Industries*. Journal PPW. http://journalppw.com

Çolak, O. (2023). The Role of Generative Pre-trained Transformers (GPT) in Recreational Tourism: An Interview with ChatGPT. *Spor Bilimleri Araştırmaları Dergisi, 8*(3), 733–748. doi:10.25307/jssr.1341967

Dabre, R., Chu, C., & Kunchukuttan, A. (2020). A Survey of Multilingual Neural Machine Translation. *ACM Computing Surveys*, *53*(5), 1–38. doi:10.1145/3406095

Deshpande, M., Munje, P., Zilpelwar, T., Narnawre, V., Sharma, A. K., Thakre, B., & Purohit, N. (2022). *An AI Integrated Online Hotel Management System*. https:// doi.org/ doi:10.37591/JoWET

Dey Sharmistha, S. D. (2022). *Analytical study on use of AI techniques in tourism sector for smarter customer experience management.*

Dhiraj, A., Kumar, S., Rani, D., Grima, S., & Sood, K. (2023). Blockchain Payment Services in the Hospitality Sector: The Mediating Role of Data Security on Utilisation Efficiency of the Customer. *Data*, *8*(8), 123. doi:10.3390/data8080123

Divekar, R. R., Drozdal, J., Chabot, S., Zhou, Y., Su, H., Chen, Y., Zhu, H., Hendler, J. A., & Braasch, J. (2022). Foreign language acquisition via artificial intelligence and extended reality: Design and evaluation. *Computer Assisted Language Learning*, *35*(9), 2332–2360. doi:10.1080/09588221.2021.1879162

El-Moffock, N. (2023a). *Economic Studies Digital Transformation and AI in Tourism: Trends*. Challenges, and Successful Experiences.

El-Moffock, N. (2023b). *Economic Studies Digital Transformation and AI in Tourism: Trends*. Challenges, and Successful Experiences.

Filieri, R., D'Amico, E., Destefanis, A., Paolucci, E., & Raguseo, E. (2021a). Artificial intelligence (AI) for tourism: An European-based study on successful AI tourism start-ups. *International Journal of Contemporary Hospitality Management*, *33*(11), 4099–4125. doi:10.1108/IJCHM-02-2021-0220

Filieri, R., D'Amico, E., Destefanis, A., Paolucci, E., & Raguseo, E. (2021b). Artificial intelligence (AI) for tourism: An European-based study on successful AI tourism start-ups. *International Journal of Contemporary Hospitality Management*, *33*(11), 4099–4125. doi:10.1108/IJCHM-02-2021-0220

Frey, B. S., & Briviba, A. (2021). A policy proposal to deal with excessive cultural tourism. *European Planning Studies*, *29*(4), 601–618. doi:10.1080/09654313.2021.1903841

Frintrop, S., Rome, E., & Tech, G. (2010). Computational Visual Attention Systems and their Cognitive Foundations. *ACM Transactions on Applied Perception*, *7*(1), 1–39. doi:10.1145/1658349.1658355

Fronzetti Colladon, A., Guardabascio, B., & Innarella, R. (2019). Using social network and semantic analysis to analyze online travel forums and forecast tourism demand. *Decision Support Systems*, *123*, 113075. Advance online publication. doi:10.1016/j.dss.2019.113075

Galanos, V. (2023). Expectations And Expertise. *In Artificial Intelligence: Specialist Views And Historical Perspectives On Conceptualisation, Promise, And Funding*.

Gaur, L., Afaq, A., Singh, G., & Dwivedi, Y. K. (2021). Role of artificial intelligence and robotics to foster the touchless travel during a pandemic: A review and research agenda. *International Journal of Contemporary Hospitality Management*, *33*(11), 4079–4098. doi:10.1108/IJCHM-11-2020-1246

Gupta, S., Modgil, S., Lee, C. K., & Sivarajah, U. (2023a). The future is yesterday: Use of AI-driven facial recognition to enhance value in the travel and tourism industry. *Information Systems Frontiers*, *25*(3), 1179–1195. doi:10.1007/s10796-022-10271-8 PMID:35529102

Gupta, S., Modgil, S., Lee, C. K., & Sivarajah, U. (2023b). The future is yesterday: Use of AI-driven facial recognition to enhance value in the travel and tourism industry. *Information Systems Frontiers*, *25*(3), 1179–1195. doi:10.1007/s10796-022-10271-8 PMID:35529102

Han, D., Weber, J., Bastiaansen, M., Mitas, O., & Lub, X. (2019). *Virtual and Augmented Reality Technologies to enhance the visitor experience in cultural tourism*.

Hassan Editor, A. (2022). *Handbook of Technology Application in Tourism in Asia*.

Huang, A., Chao, Y., de la Mora Velasco, E., Bilgihan, A., & Wei, W. (2022). When artificial intelligence meets the hospitality and tourism industry: An assessment framework to inform theory and management. *Journal of Hospitality and Tourism Insights*, *5*(5), 1080–1100. doi:10.1108/JHTI-01-2021-0021

Jung, T., Tom Dieck, M. C., Lee, H., & Chung, N. (2016). *Effects of Virtual Reality and Augmented Reality on Visitor Experiences in Museum*. 621–635. https://doi.org/ doi:10.1007/978-3-319-28231-2-45

Kabassi, K. (2010). Personalizing recommendations for tourists. In Telematics and Informatics, 27(1), 51–66. doi:10.1016/j.tele.2009.05.003

Kar, A. K., Choudhary, S. K., & Ilavarasan, P. V. (2023). How can we improve tourism service experiences: Insights from multi-stakeholders' interaction. *Decision (Washington, D.C.)*, *50*(1), 73–89. doi:10.1007/s40622-023-00338-z

Kariru, D. (2023). Contemporary Trends and Issues in The Hospitality and Tourism Industry. *International Journal of Research and Innovation in Social Science*, *VII*(IV), 970–986. doi:10.47772/IJRISS.2023.7481

Kazak, A. N., Chetyrbok, P. V., & Oleinikov, N. N. (2020). Artificial intelligence in the tourism sphere. *IOP Conference Series. Earth and Environmental Science*, *421*(4), 042020. Advance online publication. doi:10.1088/1755-1315/421/4/042020

Kottum Elmar, C. (2019). *Charting Artificial Intelligence in Reality and Fiction.*

Kumar, S., Dhiraj, A., & Hassan, S. C. C. (2023). Metaverse and Cultural Marketing in Hospitality and Tourism. In *Cultural Marketing and Metaverse for Consumer Engagement* (pp. 224–233). IGI Global. doi:10.4018/978-1-6684-8312-1.ch016

Kumar, S., Dhiraj, A., & Rani, D. (2023). Challenges and Advantages of Location-Based Services in Tourism Industries. In *Enhancing Customer Engagement Through Location-Based Marketing* (pp. 66–76). IGI Global. doi:10.4018/978-1-6684-8177-6.ch006

Kumar, S., Dhiraj, A., Shah, M. A., & Rani, D. (2023). Application of Metaverse in the Hospitality Industry. In *Influencer Marketing Applications Within the Metaverse* (pp. 178–194). IGI Global. doi:10.4018/978-1-6684-8898-0.ch011

Landgrebe, J., & Smith, B. (2022). *Why Machines will Never Rule the World; Artificial Intelligence without Fear.*

Li, H., Hu, M., & Li, G. (2020). Forecasting tourism demand with multisource big data. *Annals of Tourism Research, 83*, 102912. doi:10.1016/j.annals.2020.102912

Lisi, F. A., & Esposito, F. (2015). An AI application to integrated tourism planning. Lecture Notes in Computer Science (Including Subseries Lecture Notes in Artificial Intelligence and Lecture Notes in Bioinformatics), 9336 LNCS, 246–259. Springer. doi:10.1007/978-3-319-24309-2_19

Mah, P. M., Skalna, I., & Muzam, J. (2022). Natural Language Processing and Artificial Intelligence for Enterprise Management in the Era of Industry 4.0. *Applied Sciences (Basel, Switzerland)*, *12*(18), 9207. doi:10.3390/app12189207

Mahato, R. (2021). *Artificial Intelligence Language Learning And Communication: Exploring The Intersection Of Technology And Education*. Research Gate. https://www.researchgate.net/publication/371830162

Mccalla, G. (2000). The Fragmentation of Culture, Learning, Teaching and Technology: Implications for the Artificial Intelligence in Education Research Agenda in 2010. In International Journal of Artificial Intelligence in Education, 11.

Milton, T. (2023). *Artificial Intelligence in Tourism-A review of Trends Opportunities and Challenges*. Chandigarh Philosophers. www.chandigarhphilosophers.com

Naeem, M., Rizvi, S. T. H., & Coronato, A. (2020). A Gentle Introduction to Reinforcement Learning and its Application in Different Fields. *IEEE Access : Practical Innovations, Open Solutions*, *8*, 209320–209344. doi:10.1109/ACCESS.2020.3038605

Nayyar, A., Mahapatra, B., Le, D., & Suseendran, G. (2018). Virtual Reality (VR) & Augmented Reality (AR) technologies for tourism and hospitality industry. [). www.sciencepubco.com/index.php/IJET]. *IACSIT International Journal of Engineering and Technology*, *7*(2).

Nero, S. (2009). Inhabiting the other's world: Language and cultural immersion for us-based teachers in the dominican republic. *Language, Culture and Curriculum*, *22*(3), 175–194. doi:10.1080/07908310903203066

Punia, S., & Shankar, S. (2022). Predictive analytics for demand forecasting: A deep learning-based decision support system. *Knowledge-Based Systems*, *258*, 109956. doi:10.1016/j.knosys.2022.109956

Ratten, V. Álvarez-García, J., & Río Rama, M. de la C. del. (2019). Entrepreneurship, Innovation and Inequality : Exploring Territorial Dynamics and Development. Routledge.

Rodríguez, B., Molina, J., Pérez, F., & Caballero, R. (2012). Interactive design of personalised tourism routes. *Tourism Management*, *33*(4), 926–940. doi:10.1016/j.tourman.2011.09.014

Saariluoma, P., & Karvonen, A. (2023). Theory languages in designing artificial intelligence. *AI & Society*. doi:10.1007/s00146-023-01716-y

Sarker, I. H. (2021). Deep Learning: A Comprehensive Overview on Techniques, Taxonomy, Applications and Research Directions. In SN Computer Science, 2(6). Springer. doi:10.1007/s42979-021-00815-1

Sekhon, G., & Ahuja, S. (2023). Review Machine Learning Models for Managing Hotel Cancellations in the Tourism Industry. *2023 3rd International Conference on Intelligent Technologies, CONIT 2023*. IEEE. 10.1109/CONIT59222.2023.10205827

Sen Chiang, H., & Huang, T. C. (2015). User-adapted travel planning system for personalized schedule recommendation. *Information Fusion*, *21*(1), 3–17. doi:10.1016/j.inffus.2013.05.011

Singh, N. (2023). AI in Inventory Management: Applications, Challenges, and Opportunities. *International Journal for Research in Applied Science and Engineering Technology*, *11*(11), 2049–2053. doi:10.22214/ijraset.2023.57010

Stewart, S. L. K., Wright, C., & Atherton, C. (2019). Deception Detection and Truth Detection Are Dependent on Different Cognitive and Emotional Traits: An Investigation of Emotional Intelligence, Theory of Mind, and Attention. *Personality and Social Psychology Bulletin*, *45*(5), 794–807. doi:10.1177/0146167218796795 PMID:30264653

Sun, S., Li, Y., Guo, J.-E., & Wang, S. (2021). *Tourism Demand Forecasting: An Ensemble Deep Learning Approach.*

Taye, M. M. (2023). Understanding of Machine Learning with Deep Learning: Architectures, Workflow, Applications and Future Directions. In Computers, 12(5). MDPI. doi:10.3390/computers12050091

Ting, S.-H., Ng, Y.-J., & Neelam, M. (2021). *Aspects of Artificial Intelligence*. Research Gate. https://www.researchgate.net/publication/358119068

Ukpabi, D. C., Aslam, B., & Karjaluoto, H. (2019). Chatbot adoption in tourism services: A conceptual exploration. In Robots, Artificial Intelligence and Service Automation in Travel, Tourism and Hospitality (pp. 105–121). Emerald Group Publishing Ltd. doi:10.1108/978-1-78756-687-320191006

van Nuenen, T., & Scarles, C. (2021). Advancements in technology and digital media in tourism. *Tourist Studies*, *21*(1), 119–132. doi:10.1177/1468797621990410

Vaughan, N., Gabrys, B., & Dubey, V. N. (2016). An Overview of Self-Adaptive Technologies Within Virtual Reality Training. In *Computer Science Review*. https://www.oculus.com

Wang, X., Li, X. R., Zhen, F., & Zhang, J. H. (2016). How smart is your tourist attraction?: Measuring tourist preferences of smart tourism attractions via a FCEM-AHP and IPA approach. *Tourism Management*, *54*, 309–320. doi:10.1016/j.tourman.2015.12.003

Wortham, R. (2018). *Using Other Minds: Transparency as a Fundamental Design Consideration for Artificial Intelligent Systems*. Taylor & Francis.

Xu, F., Nash, N., & Whitmarsh, L. (2020). Big data or small data? A methodological review of sustainable tourism. *Journal of Sustainable Tourism*, *28*(2), 147–166. doi:10.1080/09669582.2019.1631318

Zhang, K., Chen, Y., & Li, C. (2019). Discovering the tourists' behaviors and perceptions in a tourism destination by analyzing photos' visual content with a computer deep learning model: The case of Beijing. *Tourism Management*, *75*, 595–608. doi:10.1016/j.tourman.2019.07.002

Zlatanov, S., & Popesku, J. (2019). *Current Applications of Artificial Intelligence in Tourism and Hospitality*. 84–90. doi:10.15308/Sinteza-2019-84-90

# Chapter 9
# The Future Prospect of Online Travel Agencies in Hotel Bookings

**Jagjit Singh**
https://orcid.org/0000-0001-9753-4866
*Chandigarh University, India*

**Shikha Sharma**
https://orcid.org/0009-0001-3680-3556
*Chandigarh University, India*

## ABSTRACT

*The internet's history goes back to the 1950s and 1960s with the invention of computers. Its brief existence has spawned several businesses, one of which is online travel agencies (OTAs). It has transformed travelers' requirements into "one-stop shops" for all our travel needs. The online travel business did not begin on a particular day. However, we can conclude that consumer attitudes and behaviors regarding travel reservations have shifted during the last five years. The conventional "brick and mortar" travel agency was phased out in favor of internet trip booking. Instead of relying on travel agencies to arrange their travels, travelers want to book and see their itinerary themselves. The passengers want direct access to the rates. A travel portal is a highly integrated booking engine that connects providers in the travel and hospitality industries with customers on a single screen.*

DOI: 10.4018/979-8-3693-1978-9.ch009

# INTRODUCTION

## Introduction to Online Travel Agencies (OTAs)

Convenience comes first. Customers may book hotel rooms, airline tickets, and car rentals from their home or office using their smartphone or tablet (Ho et al., 2011). Customers may easily change or cancel online bookings since many sites provide free cancellations and changes. Finalize client evaluations. Customers' reviews of hotels, restaurants, and airlines may also be found online. TripAdvisor is a great place to browse user reviews on flights, hotels, excursions & activities, restaurants, and transportation. With the help of travel websites, you can compare prices and get great deals. Before making a reservation or planning a vacation, use your network to read reviews and interact with locals (Valva, 2014).

A single traveler, a family, or even a small group will benefit from flexibility. Sites offering last-minute savings and internet connections to obtain a passport, insurance, and weather report are common. Streamlined Booking In the hotel traveler programme, you may earn points and receive lower prices if you are a regular customer. Second, online purchases are safe. Many travel sites compete to provide consumers with the best discounts and deals, which we are taking advantage of. Consumers can save money compared to purchasing via online travel agencies, which will charge a booking fee. Another benefit of online Booking is the safe and secure credit card payment option. To remain in business, online travel firms offer great travel offers to consumers. When compared to conventional travel companies, these websites provide lower hotel rates, flights, and transportation. Consumers can compare the prices of travel portals and other trip booking websites and their different packages and special offers (Budarick, 2004).

## Online Travel Agencies (OTAs) in India

On the cutting edge, India has quickly learned and adapted to developed nation methods. Travel boom, internet expansion, e-commerce acceptance, and low-cost airlines have aided the sector's growth (Nghiem-Phu, 2019). Additionally, online travel portals have boosted tourism in India. Consumers increasingly recognize the importance and benefits of technology in trip planning. Online travel companies allow customers to be their travel agents. The customer can book flights, cruises, hotels, and car rentals with a few mouse clicks. Travel planning used to take hours but now takes just minutes. If a visitor does not want to spend time looking for hundreds of plane ticket costs and hotel locations, a website will work for them. The traveler also gets weather updates, flight status, tour guides, and suggestions. A travel portal is a brand that accepts bookings 24 hours a day (Ospina-Pinillos et al., 2018). As India's largest e-commerce sector, internet travel is dynamic and complex. Indigenous online travel firms continue to dominate the industry despite the growing presence of prominent international brands in online travel.

## Indian Tourism and Hospitality Industry

Among the major growing sectors in India, the Indian tourism and hospitality industry has emerged as one of the driving forces (Sarmah et al., 2018). India's tourism industry has a major opportunity because of the nation's rich cultural and historical legacy, varied ecological environments, varied terrains, and breathtaking sites of natural beauty that can be found throughout the country. Tourism is also a major source of foreign currency for the nation and may generate huge jobs. Almost 39 million jobs are associated with the tourism industry in India in FY20, which is around 8% of the total number of jobs in the nation. About 53 million employments are anticipated to be accounted for by 2029. India was rated 10th out of 185 nations in terms of the overall contribution of travel & tourism to GDP in 2019, according to WTTC (Penela et al., 2019) . Travel and tourism make up around 6.8% of GDP, equivalent to Rs. 13,68,100 crore (US$ 194.3 billion).

## Fact and Figures

*Figure 1. Co-occurrence maps with keywords*

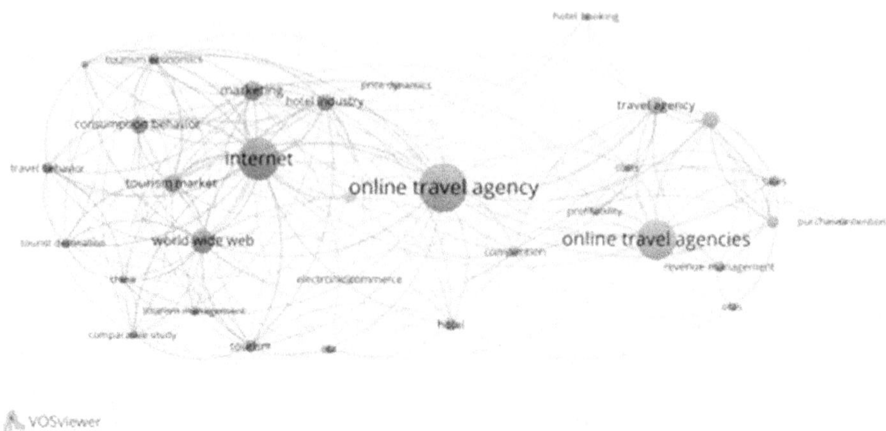


Figure 1 illustrates the most often used keywords by various authors and articles from multiple nations. It reveals that out of 115 articles, which is gather from Scopus Data base the most often used terms are Online Travel Agency and agencies, followed by the Internet and various other words, as shown in Figure 2. Consumer purchasing behavior toward internet bargains is still minimal. It is obtained via the use of the VOSviewer Software.

*Figure 2. Top twenty country-wise publications*

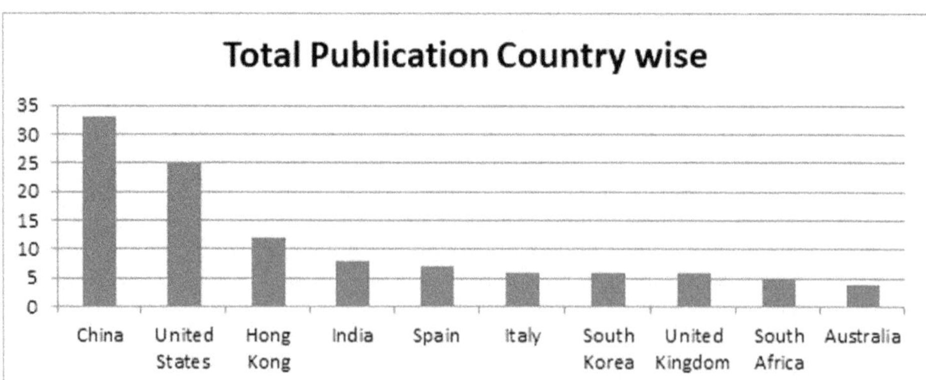

Figure 2 illustrates the total number of publications per nation. As seen in the above Bar Chart, China is the market leader in terms of consumer purchasing behavior when it comes to hotel selection through OTAs, followed by the United States, Hong Kong, and India. It demonstrates India's obligation to act on such issues to elevate the subject. The Scopus database was used to get the data. It also shows very less study on an Online Hotel Booking is done in India.

*Figure 3. Total publications from 2008 to 2021*

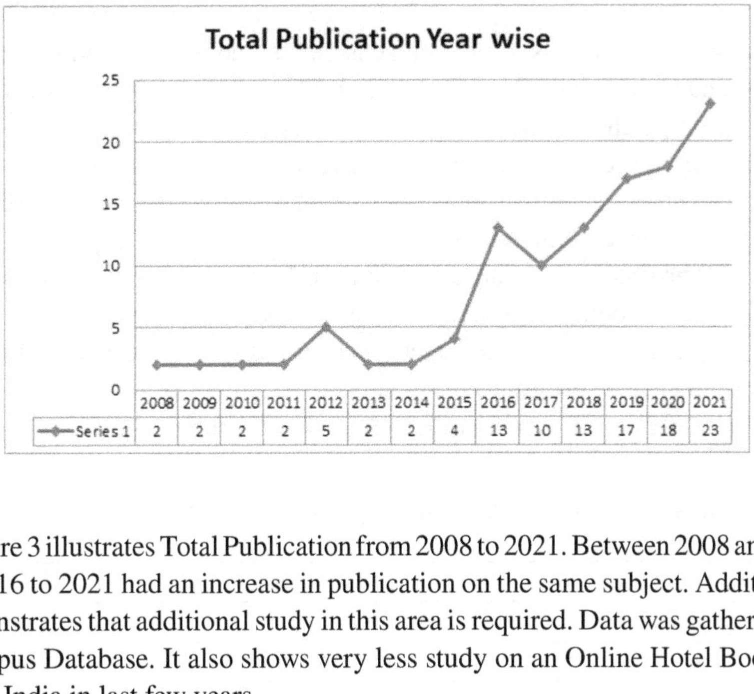


Figure 3 illustrates Total Publication from 2008 to 2021. Between 2008 and 2015, only 2016 to 2021 had an increase in publication on the same subject. Additionally, it demonstrates that additional study in this area is required. Data was gathered from the Scopus Database. It also shows very less study on an Online Hotel Booking is done in India in last few years.

## STATEMENT OF THE PROBLEM

Now a day's Consumers are informed and encouraged to conduct comprehensive pricing research and comparisons before making a final purchasing choice. Understanding online customer behavior is critical for building effective marketing tactics in this highly competitive arena. Numerous previous researches have examined customer buying intentions when it comes to internet purchasing. However, just a little amount of study has been conducted on customer behavior in the deal-purchasing market. Even though these impressive statistics demonstrate the tremendous extent of online trip booking, research on consumers' deal-purchasing behavior is lacking. Lack of published scholarly research about customer behavior concerning online travel agencies when searching and purchasing discounted products have been detailed. There are still unanswered questions concerning the things that inspire people to search for hotel discounts online and why they cause them to book. In short, this research's current approach is to bridge this research gap and then provide insights for marketing professionals who study the hospitality industry.

## Purpose of Study

The purpose of this study is to ascertain customers' motivations and intentions for searching hotel booking deals via online travel agencies. To better understand the causes of deal-purchasing behavior in the tourist business. A quantitative study technique will be used to assess the cognitive, emotional, and social aspects that affected motivation and the way motivation mediated these elements in the direction of booking intention. Additionally, customers' penchant for deal-purchasing wills significantly impacted by their capacity to obtain information through sales promotions and comparison shopping. To assist consumers in navigating the site and determining the value of products, online travel agencies may address the website's information quality, usability, and performance. As a result, customers' positive views and self-confidence may grow, favorably influencing their buy intention.

*Table 1. Market cap of top online travel agency*

| | |
|---|---|
| Booking.com (United States) | 78,171 |
| Airbnb (United States) | 54,137 |
| Trip.com (China) | 22,076 |
| Expedia (United States) | 13,674 |
| MakeMyTrip (India) | 2,902 |
| Webjet (Australia) | 1,606 |
| Edreams Odigeo (Spain) | 514 |
| Trivago (Germany) | 487 |
| Despegar.com (Argentina) | 340 |
| On the Beach (United Kingdom) | 313 |
| Holidaycheck (Germany) | 264 |
| Lastminute.Com (Netherlands) | 242 |
| Hostelworld (Ireland) | 163 |
| Travelzoo (United States) | 55 |

The table above displays the top online travel firms globally by market capitalization as of December 2022, measured in millions of U.S. dollars. The data is collected and analyzed by GP Bullhound and S&P Capital IQ. The survey period concluded on December 31, 2022 and included the global region. As of December 2022, Booking.com holds the top position among the largest online travel companies globally, with a market worth of around 78.2 billion US dollars. Following that, Airbnb, Trip.com, and Expedia were included in the sequence. The market capitalization of Airbnb was at around 54.1 billion US dollars.

## CONCLUSION

Due to smartphones and high-speed internet, it is now possible for customers to schedule a hotel in another country without leaving their home. Even international online travel agencies make it simple to visit hotels that were previously obscure to residents. It also functions as a voice for locals, as many hotels and homestays are owned by families who are unable to provide global branding and have therefore struggled to succeed in business. Currently, everyone has access to a smartphone and high-speed internet. It has opened a variety of doors, and we can anticipate more in the future.

## REFERENCE

Budarick, B. (2004). Rest and relaxation in Coffs Harbour. *Civil Engineers Australia, 76*(8), 62. https://www.scopus.com/inward/record.uri?eid=2-s2.0-4344568624&partnerID=40&md5=9a3264e11a136260bd6cec8e2d91cb59

Ho, L.-H., Lu, M.-H., Ho, H.-Y., & Peng, T.-F. (2011). A Study of Website Optimization Strategy and Implementation. In William, Z and Xiong, F (Ed.), COMPUTATIONAL MATERIALS SCIENCE, PTS 1-3. doi:10.4028/www.scientific.net/AMR.268-270.829

Nghiem-Phu, B. (2019). What determines the loyalty of airline passengers? Findings of a quantitative data-mining study. *MARKET-TRZISTE, 31*(1), 23–37. doi:10.22598/mt/2019.31.1.23

Ospina-Pinillos, L., Davenport, T. A., Ricci, C. S., Milton, A. C., Scott, E. M., & Hickie, I. B. (2018). Developing a Mental Health eClinic to Improve Access to and Quality of Mental Health Care for Young People: Using Participatory Design as Research Methodologies. *Journal of Medical Internet Research*, *20*(5), e188. doi:10.2196/jmir.9716 PMID:29807878

Penela, D., Estevao, J., & Gregory, A. (2019). Accounting and financial antecedents of corporate spin-offs in the lodging industry. *International Journal of Hospitality Management*, *83*, 151–158. doi:10.1016/j.ijhm.2019.05.007

Sarmah, B., Kamboj, S., & Kandampully, J. (2018). Social media and co-creative service innovation: An empirical study. *Online Information Review*, *42*(7), 1146–1179. doi:10.1108/OIR-03-2017-0079

Valva, P. (2014). Shared Living and Sustainability: Emerging Trends in the Tourism Industry. *Almatourism-Journal Of Tourism Culture And Territorial Development*, *5*(3, SI), 1–18.

# Chapter 10
# AI-Powered Marketing Strategies in the Tourism and Hospitality Sector

**Rina Daline**
https://orcid.org/0000-0002-1979-0781
*Christ University, India*

**Joby Thomas**
https://orcid.org/0000-0002-4493-1048
*Christ University, India*

## ABSTRACT

*A highly competitive environment with increased demand for personalized services drives the tourism and hospitality industry to embrace immersive and intelligent technologies. Smart technologies like artificial intelligence (AI) and virtual reality (VR) assist in promotions, marketing brands, customer analysis, and ultimately leading to sustainable businesses. Marketing research is an inevitable element for any businesses that helps in understanding their customers, catering their needs, and turning them into loyal customers. Marketing strategies incorporated with smart technologies are gaining high importance in the tourism and hospitality industries due to three major outcomes such as experience enhancement, revenue improvement and effective operations. Artificial intelligence revamped the hospitality industry with customized services and tailored recommendations based on a wholesome of customer data. Virtual reality technology provides high immersive experience to boost tourism, to enhance customer experience, to influence positive travel decisions.*

DOI: 10.4018/979-8-3693-1978-9.ch010

## INTRODUCTION

Smart technologies are gradually transforming everything around us on a global perspective leading to a tech-friendly future. Gen Y and Gen Z are quite adaptive and welcoming towards smart technologies due to its availability at one's touch point. Various industries, organizations, companies have added smart technologies into their operations to obtain sustainable benefits on a long run. Incorporation of smart technologies in many industries bestows energy cost reduction and builds stronger brand image. In line with that, tourism and hospitality industry who are at the vanguard of adopting smart technologies have pivoted many of their business practices to enhance guest experiences, mitigate risks, market products and increase revenue. Smart technologies afford a range of services such as smart room controls, smart parking, smart booking, virtual tours, energy management, virtual reality marketing, Virtual reality stimulated training in the hospitality and tourism industry (Flame Analytics, 2023).

Information and Technology (ICT) has improvised the marketing research in various field leading to digital marketing. Digital Marketing is a technology-enabled one in which service providers collaborates with customers, partners to enable a sustainable value to all stakeholders (Kannan & Li, 2017). A good number of studies have been recorded on analysing the influence of technologies such as internet, social network on market research (Brady et al., 2008; Kannan & Li; 2017). The digital marketing gives space to e-commerce era which is one of the most successful applications of digital marketing. E-commerce/ E-retail (i.e.) online buying and selling (Dennis et al., 2004) started to rule to the world in the Asian and Eastern European markets (Neilsen 2017) while their growth faces downfall in the North American and Western European markets (Statista, 2017a). With the progressing side of digital marketing, advanced immersive technologies (Extended Reality) started to integrate in the marketing world giving rise to V-commerce (virtual commerce) (Nguyen et a., 2016). Extended Reality(XR) which is an umbrella term of virtual reality, augmented reality and mixed reality started to leverage the marketing aspects of global industries.

Several studies have predicted that these extended realities will have a greater impact on many dimensions of lives (Slater and Sanchez-Vives, 2016). For example, analysing customer needs, behaviour pattern, priority, will be hugely affected by these extended reality technologies. Incorporation of Artificial Intelligence and Extended Realities in businesses will interpret the customer activities, behavior, and their preferences towards a product (Grewal et al., 2017; Bailenson, 2008; Brohm et al., 2007).

Market researchers, practitioners are showing progressive interest in smart technologies like artificial intelligence, mixed reality, robotics, augmented reality and virtual reality due to their potential benefits that embellishes and bolsters the global market. Market researcher have proposed a framework on digital marketing where extended realities such as virtual reality, augmented reality and mixed reality emerges as the powerful technologies will novel marketing opportunities. Immersive technologies have been receiving great support in the field of marketing in order to devise astonishing strategies for effective decision making, winning customer support, establishing brand recognition, high returns on investment, increasing sales, etc. These technologies are showing sharp rise on the positive aspect because they are able to create satisfactory customer experiences (Alcañiz et al., 2019). Among these immersive technologies, Virtual Reality emerges to be a promising marketing tool due to unique experience and immersion associated with that technology (Pine & Gilmore, 2008).

Studies on marketing strategies related to digital technologies (You et al., 2015) have been explored in the previous studies (Babic Rosario et a., 2016) and the applications of extended reality marketing strategies have been discussed on various disciplines such as education, human resources, medicine, neuroscience, psychology, gaming, entertainment etc. (Bruer, 2008; Alcañiz et al., 2018; Chicchi Giglioli et al 2017; Teo et al., 2016). *This substantiates that there is a huge interest of market research revolving around extended reality and this book chapter will contribute exclusively on marketing strategies of smart technologies (Artificial Intelligence, Virtual Reality) in the tourism and hospitality industries an add-on to the existing research knowledge. Further, due to the evolving nature of the Virtual Reality, continuous research needs to be done on the incorporation of Virtual Reality and proper strategies needs to be devised to maximize the benefits of hospitality and tourism industry (Chigozie, 2020). This instigates the need to study the influence of Virtual Reality in the hospitality and tourism industry through exploratory research. Various pieces of literatures and blogs are reviewed to analyse the distinct AI-powered marketing strategies and various applications of Virtual Reality in the hospitality and Tourism industries.*

The Chapter highlights the potential of Artificial Intelligence and their services in the hospitality and tourism industries. Further, Virtual Reality and its role on marketing were analysed to identify the various AI- powered marketing strategies in hospitality and tourism industry through VR.

## GLIMPSE OF ARTIFICIAL INTELLIGENCE

Artificial Intelligence (AI) refers to the intelligent behaviours of machines or computers used to perform strenuous business tasks in a seamless way. Human Intelligence, technological innovations, automation, robotics acts as the most important factors that influences Artificial Intelligence (Jabeen et al., 2022). The AI is showing a great interest in the fields of tourism and hospitality to manage their operations effectively with less human errors and improved service quality. Tourism and hospitality being the service-oriented industry is greatly affected by the direct proportional of customer satisfaction and quality of service. It is an alarming situation for the service providers to cater to the needs of their customers. One of the major challenges in the service industry is understanding and quickly responding to the customer according to their needs. It is quite challenging because of its dynamic nature and also varies with customers to customers. In recent times, these issues are gradually vanishing with the presence of technologies. Artificial Intelligence marks an exceptional assistance in understanding customers, personalizing customer-oriented services, tailoring recommendations and training the employees to empathize with their customers. Big Data pays an exceptional role in learning the profile of the customers and AI helps in analysing the data and brings out the significant outcome related to each customer.

AI has the ability to handle both front office and back-office tasks for a seamless operation. It is highly recommended for critical, time-consuming tasks by humans and deliver it with high operational efficiency at minimal time. AI tops in empathizing customers as it maintains a separate meta data for each customer to records and analyse their likes, dislikes, purchase pattern in delivering exceptional services. Personalization has become quite easier with the intervention of technologies. A plethora of data is involved with the hospitality industry starting from point of sales, back office, property management system etc. AI emerges to the best manager for the effective management of these humongous data. It also analyses customer data and predict their needs based on their profile and previous purchase. This insight ultimately helps in streamlining hotel operations in line with the customers (Brohm et al., 2007).

Increased industrial competition, high return on investments, increased demand on skilled employees, customer empathy staffs, service quality, changing customer preferences drives the hospitality industry in embracing the artificial intelligence technologies (Kaur, 2023).

## Intelligent Services of AI in Hospitality Industry

Though the role of AI in the hospitality industry is still in its infancy stage it provides enormous applications. Hospitality industry used AI for three prime key outcomes such as increasing revenue, enhancing customer experience and improving operations (Revfine, n.d). The AI's intelligent services were grouped based on those prime features of AI in the hospitality industry.

### Enhancing Customer Experiences

AI has grown tremendously to provide in-person customer service to their customers. Hilton has launched AI robot "Connie" to interact with their customers regarding tourist information. AI also respond to innumerable queries from customers quickly using Chatbots and messaging systems. Handling huge data is quite hectic and time consuming which can be easily done through AI. It will analyse customer data and draws important conclusions regarding potential customers. Dorchester Collection Hotel chain has implemented "Metris AI platform" to analyse the data and conclude the overall performance of their hotels. Improvised version of responding to the customers is through voice digital assistance. The services can be done at the voice enabled devices to turn ON/OFF AC, TV or connect to the front desk (Flame Analytics, 2023).

### Devising Effective Operations

AI helps in performing sentiment analysis to understand customers attitude towards their brand. The user-generated content posted at hotel websites, social media acts as a forum to express customers feelings and emotions. This data will be processed by AI to find the tone of the customers and their opinion towards a particular hotel, hotel brand name or hotel chains. AI assist in identifying the optimal price of a product and the best channel to distribute the product. Large focus should be implemented on pricing and channel as it leads to the potential customers (Brohm et al., 2007).

### Improving Revenue

Room rates are dynamic in nature and its quite arduous for hoteliers to design rates based on various factors such as seasonality, demand, room categories etc. AI helps in analysing all those data and design real-time dynamic pricing structure that favours both hoteliers and customers at the same rate (Revfine, n.d). The requirements of the potential customers were taken into consideration while devising fares. Price related concerns such as over-pricing (affects customers) and low pricing (affects hoteliers) were effectively managed through AI.

## VIRTUAL REALITY

Immersive Technologies like Augmented Reality, Virtual Reality, Mixed Reality, Extended Reality are ruling the tourism and hospitality industry recently. Virtual Reality is one of the best immersive technologies and provides high immersive experience to the users. The AI plays a major part in enhancing user experience in virtual reality. Immersive experience, interaction and engagement in Virtual Reality applications are provided exclusively by Artificial Intelligence (Mattan, 2023).

Virtual Reality is a key immersive technology (Fritz et al., 2005) in which a three-dimensional stimulated environment is created by computers (Hobson & Williams, 1995). It creates a virtual world for the users and transmit people from real to virtual one through immersive experience (Desai et al., 2014). Immersion and Presence are the two major components of virtual reality (Slater and Sanchez-Vives, 2016). Immersion is an objective feature which is not influenced by personal feelings or beliefs while presence is subjective and influenced by person's feelings and opinions. VR includes engagement, interaction in the virtual environment (Guttentag, 2010) which creates an interactive environment for the users. Along with immersion and interaction VR allows users to access information form the virtual environment (Kounavis et al., 2012). The computer stimulated environment in VR (Mitchell, 2020) will change the user-technology interface by expressive information (Erenay & Hashemipour, 2003).

Virtual Reality has great potential in various aspects of the tourism industry like education, marketing, cultural heritage, and Sustainability (Bruer, 2008). It stands out from other immersive technologies as it provides immersive and interactive experiences along with dissemination of information which is lacking in other technologies (Yung &Khoo-Lattimore, 2019).

## Role of Virtual Reality in Marketing

Marketing is the essential and prominent part of hospitality and tourism as it helps tremendously in reaching out potential customers. Lot of resources, time, research, investment are required to create more personalized and tailored services based on large data. Smart technologies step into marketing to ease the marketing processes and helps in creating more tailored experiences by analysing the large dataset of user generated contents.

It is quite challenging for tourism and hospitality industry to build interest and optimistic approach towards tourism and hospitality products in the post-pandemic period. Traditional marketing strategies have become less impactful to attract the customers in the current scenario. This situation pays ways to immersive technologies like Virtual Reality to build stronger relationship with customer through Virtual Reality Marketing. This new trend of marketing gains advantage over other methods and intensifies with its impact on the target audience (Yung et al., 2021).

Marketers are showing massive interest in Virtual Reality due to the long-term future benefits, value creation with customers, strong brand engagement (Cowan & Ketron, 2019). Virtual Reality has revamped the marketing network of tourism and hospitality industries and bestows many sustainable benefits. Hospitality industry has incorporated Virtual Reality in their operations, marketing strategies, training, etc. because they provide a competitive advantage over others (Brazdauskas & Gaigalaite, 2015). The tourism industry adopts Virtual Reality in their marketing strategies to develop positive travel decisions, positive customer relations and establish brand name of the organization (Hudson et al., 2016).

## AI-Powered Marketing Strategies in Hospitality Industry by VR

Hospitality is going through tech-transformation with the intervention of smart technologies such as Artificial Intelligence, Virtual Reality, Robotics, IoT etc. Virtual Reality is reshaping the industry a way different from that it remembered to be. Virtual Reality have marked a new milestone in the areas of marketing and outperformed its traditional ways. An amalgamation of Artificial Intelligence, Information and Communication Technologies, Virtual Reality have revitalized the overall hospitality industry to the next level. They are able to provide an experience-oriented information and other concierge services to the customers (Guttentag, 2010). While Artificial Intelligence systematically handles the daily hotel operations (Lau, 2020) on one end, Robotics are highly recommended to handle cumbersome check-in and check-out processes (Tuo et al., 2021). VR is one of the best technologies in hospitality industry as it provides a unique way of sharing knowledges through experiences (Beck & Egger, 2018). Artificial Intelligence has played a crucial role in carrying out daily operations seamlessly

### Customer Empathy

Hospitality being a highly competitive industry needs to invest in establishing uniqueness from its peer competitors. One of the major Unique Selling Propositions (USPs) of a hotel from another would be the quality of service and no compromise is recommended on this factor as this led to loosing potential customers. Personalized services are receiving high importance from the customers and its high time for the hoteliers to empathize with their customers. Empathy plays a vital role in attracting new customers and holding potential customers and upgrading them to the loyal ones. Empathizing customers is a crucial task and would reap enormous benefits as long as one masters it. It is equally important for hoteliers to maintain emotional connect with the customers. This connection will help them to position their brand in the market as well as in the minds of the customers. Brand Positing is the major differentiating factors among the competitive hoteliers and customer empathy will fulfil this task (Ciapponi, n.d.). Customers come to a hotel with a lot of expectations and their service has to be addressed to satisfy their needs. To Tacke this condition, employees need to have a better understanding of their customers. Empathy is the best option to win customers as it helps in creating telepresence experiences (Kober & Neuper, 2013) and VR experiences are expected to improve customer empathy and helps them to deliver high quality services towards the customers. Hilton, one of the biggest hotel chains has launched a unique Virtual Reality Program to train their employees. They are given a range of real-time scenario in the virtual environment and train them how to react in that situation. This helps their decision-making ability and customer handling in a better way when they encounter critical situations with the customers. VR experiences train and shape the employees to deliver high end exceptional services (Carter, 2020).

## VR Hotel Tours

Hospitality industry has been witnessing a change in the conventional booking practices of hotel rooms. Virtual Reality generates a new opportunity to experience a room and then come to a productive decision. Studies have proven that a hotel enabled with VR tours have higher probabilities of preferring over the normal ones (Carter, 2020). Many hotels have used VR hotel tour as a marketing tool to improve their bookings. Hilton, Mariott International, Hyatt Hotels are some of the leading hospitality players who have invested in Virtual Reality technology to market their products ("Virtual Reality (VR) in Travel & Tourism Industry", 2021). Hilton have devised a marketing strategy of virtual reality hotel tours which is completely accessed and controlled by smartphones (Samuely, 2017).

VR experiences provided by hoteliers are of two types (i.e.) monoscopic and stereoscopic in nature ("VR for tourism", 2019). The distinct feature between these tours is interactive component which makes the virtual more realistic and engaging. Customers while experiencing VR hotel tours would be leveraged by interaction with the virtual environment (Kounavis et al., 2012) which makes their experience exhilarating.

The hoteliers market their property through a range of features such as 360 degree tours, VR tours, presentations developed in VR, Audio Video guides etc which narrates and provide experiential information in the virtual environment (Samuely, 2017). Key feature of this VR tour marketing is personalized messages when the customer enter a particular area say lobby.

Virtual tours have surpassed the marketing promotions of hotels through Ads, pictures and videos. Gen Y and Gen Z encourages pre-booking experiences rather than the traditional way of booking. Hotel Reservations were revamped with the successful implementation of virtual reality. Customers are given a complete immersive experience of a hotel covering all the dimensions of a property even before they enter the hotel or make a booking (Yoon et al., 2021). Marketing a hotel property through Virtual Reality is gradually attracting the attention of the customers lately.

## Explore the World From Hotel Room

To create a memorable stay and unique experience Marriot had launched virtual tours to their customers from their room. It emerges as an add on to the stay allowing them to explore the distinct places of the world through VR technology. Marriot had adopted VR as their marketing strategy to entice the customers and position their brand (Carter, 2020).

## Strengthening Company's Brand

Brand is arguably one of the important assets of a company and it reflects company's image, identity. It strives towards encouraging customers to purchase from that company and support their employees and actions on a long run (Decker 2023). Hoteliers aims to position their brand effectively on the marketplace ahead of their peer competitors. Hilton had collaborated with Facebook and Oculus on embracing Virtual Reality Technology to boost their company's brand.

## Strengthening Employee Branding

Employee Branding is a marketing strategy that motivates the employees to have a positive optimistic impression about their company. It acts as an internal and external strategy to turn norma employees into an effective brand ambassador (Tsang, 2022). Employee Branding can be achieved with the help of virtual reality as well. It helps in enabling better situation to employees at their hotel premises. Educating them and training them to be effective ambassadors is the biggest step towards employee branding. Hilton implemented VR training programme to their employees to upgrade themselves and improve their ability to handle miscellaneous situations on real-time. Hilton had partnered with Sweet Rush to provide a complete VR hotel experience for their employees, corporate team members who are new to the hotel experience (Carter, 2020). The training programme works in creating a Virtual Reality environment and allows employees to tarin and experience various situations. Critical situations, guest handling was created in a stimulated environment and they are trained with that environment which will help them in handling real-time situations. Self-improvement as a result of VR training leads to strong employee branding with the company.

## AI- Powered Marketing Strategies in Tourism Sector by Virtual Reality

### Virtual Reality Tours

The concept of virtual reality tours started to gain recognition during the pandemic period where the travel restrictions were imposed throughout the world. People were locked inside doors due to the outbreak of the COVID-19. It enabled as a supplementary way of travel when the world is not safe.

Tours are marketed through an immersive technology say Virtual Reality, to enhance image of a destination and to satisfy the wanderlusts. India and other many other countries had marketed their country's attractions such as museums, zoos, national parks, UNESCO's World Heritage sites, destinations through virtual tours (Kemska, 2021). Google Arts and Culture had marketed famous museums on an application built by the support of augmented and virtual reality (The Indian Express, 2020). TourHQ marketed the most important cities of the world (more than 100) through virtual reality except the continent Antarctica (Kapur, 2020).

Many countries have created virtual tours to their famous tourist destinations and allowed people to experience the places from their abode. Global leading travel brands Thomas Cook, MakemyTrip, TourHQ, Viator and ToursByLocals rolls out virtual tours to notable tourist destinations in the year 2020 (Ahaskar, 2020). Since destination image and tourists satisfaction being the crucial elements of the tourism industry, tourist destinations were recreated in the virtual platform. Higher customer satisfaction towards a destination leads to high destination loyalty (Kusdibyo, 2021). MakeMyTrip had marketed both domestic and international tours at pocket-friendly prices in order to attract more customers. Tour prices were fixed at INR99 for domestic tours and INR799 international tours. A normal family tour to Egypt will cost around $150 which would be reduced to $30 if they took a virtual tour. Pricing is the biggest advantage of virtual tour marketing over the traditional one (Ahaskar, 2020).

### Experience Based Booking

Travel tickets are perishable in nature and one cannot save it for later. It is equally important for everyone to know whether the money they had spent for tickets is worth the value and experience promised. Amadeus had launched Virtual Reality booking system that allows the customers to explore the flight seat or a hotel room in a virtual stimulated environment and book based on their experiences. As soon as a customer wears VR headset, he/she will enter into a simulated environment which is created replica of a flight or a hotel room. The customer can look around, experience, and gather information about the product. The customer can make a booking or reservation based on the interaction within the virtual environment. This type of experience-based bookings increases positive travel and room bookings. VR booking experiences are found to be more engaging, immersive and new way of booking to the customers. Transformative booking systems changed the customers attitude towards booing and they are more interested to spend on products who allows VR bookings (Yoon et al., 2021).

## Enhancing Product Life Cycle

Amusement parks are one of the great sources of entertainment in the tourism industry. Tourists visits theme/amusement parks because of the exhilarating rides they offer. Here the tourism products such as land rides, water rides remain the same for a longer time and henceforth, lack of innovation arises as a major drawback. Amusement parks rides growth occurs rapidly from introduction to growth and later on reaches to maturity. They reach the saturation point on a faster rate. The existing older rides gets older and older and becomes outdated with the tourists. However, technology revitalizes the existing rides by extending their product life cycle. An existing roller coaster can have an overlay with VR and thus preventing the ride to go abandoned or enter into declination stage (Malcolm, 2019). Revamping the older ride with immersive technology will entice the tourists and increases the ride's life cycle as well. Additionally huge cost would be required for constructing a new one leading to financial risk whereas demolishing the older ride puts additional pressure on the environment causing environmental risk. Those risks can be avoided by strategically incorporating VR into the amusement parks (Burt & Louw, 2019).

## Experiential Marketing

Attitude of visitors towards amusement parks seems dwindling in recent times as many competitors like game arcades, PlayStation, VR game centres offers amusement park rides in a different level. This diminishes the market value of amusement parks creating an alarming situation to look at this issue. Amusement Park gradually started to incorporate VR technology and started marketing immersive experiences. Countries like Dubai, China, US are the pioneers and successful experiential marketers of the VR amusement parks. The use of interactive VR projects in amusement parks changes the visitor attitude towards them. Technologies used in the amusement/ theme parks can be broadly classified into two major categories (i.e.) experiential technologies and supporting technologies. The supporting technologies comprises of ticketing, in-park transportation and intelligent services while the experiential technologies points to Schmitt's strategic experiential modules. The experience by sense, relate, think, feel act contribute to Schmitt's modules. Visitors found those experiential technology more engaging and favourable than the supporting technologies (Zhang et al., 2022).

Amusement parks markets VR at all three phases of experience (i.e.) Pre-VR experience, During VR experience and Post-VR experience. Pre-VR experience points to the waiting time and During VR experience contributes to the holistic factors associated with VR experience such as content, quality, immersion, technology, synchronization, settings etc while Post-VR experience confines to the emotional connect. During VR experience is the significant stage where visitors degree of enjoyment elevates and turn into loyal visitors (Hyejo & Miyoung, 2022)

## Destination Marketing

Marketing tourist destinations is important as it aims to enhance the beauty of a destination making it more attractive, boost the number of people travelling to that destination and also to support the local transportation, livelihood of the host community. Destination marketing create awareness about a destination which leads to increase in demand and subsequently uplift the overall image of destination. Marketing destinations through Virtual Reality leverages the destination image than a traditional way. The crux of this immersive technology is that it stimulates a tourist destination in the virtual environment which would be replica of the same destination in the same world. Marketing destinations through Virtual Reality creates a memorable and immersive experience to the viewers (Schmitt 1999). The destination experienced through VR will be stored in the minds of the viewers. Destination Management Organizations strive towards promoting tourist destinations and virtual tours acts a catalyst for proactive promotion.

A destination can be promoted to attract travellers and increase the demand of that destination. A destination which is less explored or at the introduction stage needs promotion to gain recognition among the visitors. In that scenario, virtual reality promotions comes in handy as it will recreate the destination emphasizing the hidden beauty of that destination (Luhar, 2021). Additionally, one can reach out to wider audience through Virtual Reality technology with less marketing expenses. These promotions happen during the pre-trip phase of a traveller and successful promotion leads to favourable decision (i.e.) the destination will be welcomed by new group of visitors by increasing demand and positive image of that destination (Luhar, 2021). Visiting deadly destinations as a matter of thrill or excitement is a part of tourism more precisely termed as "Dark Tourism". It is visiting historical places related to tragedy or death. Tourists who are captivated by dark experiences associated with horror or paranormal activity will act as a major driving force to visit such places (Lewis et al., 2022). The most dangerous sites are re-created with the help of Virtual reality technology. This new medium of traveling has been identified as a new opportunity to explore more in the area of dark tourism (Fisher, 2018). Dark tourism is a niche area and is gradually receiving recognition from the travellers. Virtual Reality act as an influencer to promote niche areas where tourism needs to be flourished.

Spain had adopted unique marketing strategy to promote their destinations. They have developed a game with the help of virtual reality and augmented reality. This game will portray the important places of Valladolid and enables user to learn the places through gaming (Zarzuela, 2013). Marketing destinations through VR/AR gaming is a novel strategy to let users familiarise with the destinations.

## Influences Travel Decisions

Virtual Reality tours are used wisely in the pre-trip planning phase to attract the customers. They will be given a pre-experience how the destinations would be and what are the things they could be engaged with the destination. Exposed to an experience before purchasing a tour wins customers confidence and lessen their financial risk associated with the tour. Destination promotions through Virtual Reality tours in the pre-trip phase are closely associated with decision making processes (Familmaleki et al., 2015). Positive impression towards a destination will contribute to positive travel decision to that place and this cycle will eventually contribute to influx of tourists (Luhar, 2021). During pandemic, a distinct range of virtual tours are provided by global providers and museum virtual tour found to be popular destination among all other VR tours. This implies that people there exists a positive travel motivation to visit those museums in the real world. A positive travel decision has emerged due to influence of VR tours (El-Said, 2021).

Virtual tours reduce the anticipation about a destination and other risks associated within it. Basically, it provides complete information about a destination to the tourists well in prior so that they can come outside from their doubt and trust the destination is safer and valuable to travel. Virtual tours acts as a ambassador or endorsing element for a tourist destination that aims to influence customers in visiting that destination. Travel intention, motivation have been created through virtual reality promotional tours (Io & Peralta, 2022).

Virtual Tours emerged to be a stress reliver during the times of lockdown in 2020 (Yang, 2021). It motivates them to visit the same places in real once it is safer back to travel. Telepresence, the presence which is enabled by technology such as Virtual Reality are proved to be great factor of motivation compared to the normal travel and greatly influences traveler's travel decision towards positivity (Tussyadiah, 2017).

## In-Store VR Experiences

Virtual Reality can be used to replace the normal shopping experience with a complete in-store VR experience. Travel information, brochures, itineraries cane be replaced by virtual experiences at the trave fair, trave trade or exhibitions related to travel and tourism ("VR for tourism", 2019). Travel information delivered through virtual reality experiences will stay longer in the minds of the people than the contemporary methods. Destination images will be clearly captured and saved as an experience with them. Selling tour packages through experiential marketing will be a breakthrough in the tourism industry as it would win customers confidence to purchase the tour product.

On the other hand, replacing the store and providing a complete virtual store experience to the customers. Virtual stores are still in its infancy and will grow in time. Virtual stores will emerge gradually in the marketplace coexisting with the contemporary channel of distribution. A virtual store channel will offer customers to interact virtually with the sellers and experience the products virtually. Information related to products can be gathered from the virtual environment and also with the virtual seller. Virtual stores will change the future methods of shopping providing a complete at-home customer experience shifting from in-store experience (Verhoef et al., 2015). However, virtual store shopping needs improvement in the areas of sensory factors to create a realistic shopping experience. Virtual stores and physical stores may bring up a new omni channel in the future merging the benefits of both stores (Neslin et al., 2006)

# CONCLUSION

Smart technologies such as Artificial Intelligence, Virtual Reality have impacted many aspects of the hospitality and tourism industries. They hugely target the consumer behaviour patterns by collaborating artificial intelligence with extended reality technologies. This study has focused on AI-powered Virtual Reality marketing strategies in the hospitality and tourism industries and the benefits they bestow to them. Artificial Intelligence helps in streamlining hotel operation by tailoring personalized customer services, training employees, enhancing service quality, and analysing customer data. AI has been used holistically in the hospitality industry for many competitive advantages however, the study has found out main three reasons for using AI such as to increase revenue, to enhance customer experience and to improve operations. One of the extended realities, Virtual Reality were discussed extensively in this study and they emerge to be the best marketing technologies in the areas of hospitality and tourism. The study substantiated the marketing potential of Virtual Reality through various applications in hospitality industry like VR hotel tours, VR bookings, Company Branding, Employee Branding, VR training, smart applications etc. Virtual Reality supports tourism industry predominately on the areas of marketing, promotions, experiential economy. Marketing strategies like increasing tourism product life cycle, experiential marketing, in-store VR experiences, travel decisions influencer, experiential booking and VR tours are incorporated in the tourism industry. Virtual Reality is like a double-edged in tourism industry as it has the potential to favour and disfavour the situation. It can bring both positive and negative changes to the tourism industry. Virtual Reality are used to promote destinations to boost tourism while on the other end people anticipate that it may lessen their interest to visit that place again in the real world. Virtual Reality is an evolving technology and market researchers are showing great keen in these immersive technologies. Due to its evolving nature, constant research has to be done to maximize its potential in the tourism and hospitality industry.

Tourism and Hospitality researchers and practitioners are showing great interest in adopting smart technologies to their businesses. A high-competitive environment with increased demand on personalized services drives the tourism and hospitality industry to embrace immersive and intelligent technologies. In the generation of fast evolving technological advancements, the tourism and hospitality industries are welcoming artificial intelligence in most of their operations. In future they may become an inevitable part of the tourism and hospitality industries. Experience enhancement, personalized services, and guest satisfaction drive the service-oriented industries towards smart technologies (Artificial Intelligence, Virtual Reality). Artificial Intelligence has already revolutionized hospitality industry through customer services, marketing, hotel operations, management operations and will advance further in the future.

The hospitality and tourism industries will go through a major transformation with the relentless evolution of artificial intelligence. Their major contributions will focus on leveraging efficiency, personal customization and satisfying the potential customers. Big Data and Data science will contribute a huge profit to those service-oriented industries to understand their customer in a better way than earlier. Customer related offers, discounts, loyalty programs, recommendations will take a major shift with the help of advanced artificial intelligence. The AI can design and recommend offers and individual services based on their preferences. Data plays a very significant role in knowing their customers better way. Subsequently most complex jobs will be replaced by AI in the future for seamless operations.

## REFERENCES

Ahaskar, A. (2020, July 10). Virtual tours over Zoom call keep tourists, guides happy amid COVID disruption. *Mint*. https://www.livemint.com/news/india/virtual-tours-over-zoom-call-keep-tourists-guides-happy-amid-covid-disruption-11594382679649.html

Alcañiz, M., Bigné, E., & Guixeres, J. (2019). Virtual Reality in Marketing: A Framework, Review, and Research Agenda. *Frontiers in Psychology*, *10*, 1530. doi:10.3389/fpsyg.2019.01530 PMID:31333548

Analytics, F. (2023, March 17). 7 Ways smart technology is reshaping the hotel industry. *Flame Analytics*. https://flameanalytics.com/en/blog/7-ways-smart-technology-is-reshaping-the-hotel-industry/#:~:text=With%20smart%20EMS%2C%20hotel%20staff,a%20much%20more%20costly%20one

Babić Rosario, A., Sotgiu, F., De Valck, K., & Bijmolt, T. H. (2016). The effect of electronic word of mouth on sales: A meta-analytic review of platform, product, and metric factors. *JMR, Journal of Marketing Research*, *53*(3), 297–318. doi:10.1509/jmr.14.0380

Bailenson, J. (2018). *Experience on Demand: What Virtual Reality Is, how it Works, and what it Can Do*. W. W. Norton & Company.

Brady, M., Fellenz, M. R., & Brookes, R. (2008). Researching the role of information and communications technology (ICT) in contemporary marketing practices. *Journal of Business and Industrial Marketing*, *23*(2), 108–114. doi:10.1108/08858620810850227

Brohm, D., Domurath, N., Glanz-Chanos, V., & Grunert, K. G. (2017). In L. W. S. Loijens (Ed.), *"Future trends of augmented reality," in Augmented Reality for Food Marketers and Consumers* (pp. 1681–1685). Wageningen Academic Publishers.

Burke, R. (2018). Virtual reality for marketing research. In L. Moutinho & M. Sokele (Eds.), Innovative Research Methodologies in Management (pp. 63–82). Palgrave Macmillan. doi:10.1007/978-3-319-64400-4_3

Burt, M., & Louw, C. (2019). Virtual reality enhanced roller coasters and the future of entertainment – audience expectations. *World Leisure Journal*, *61*(3), 183–199. doi:10.1080/16078055.2019.1639274

Burt, M., & Louw, C. (2019). Virtual reality enhanced roller coasters and the future of entertainment – audience expectations. *World Leisure Journal*, *61*(3), 183–199. doi:10.1080/16078055.2019.1639274

Carter, R. (2020, November 13). *Hilton Hotels and How VR is Changing Hospitality*. XR TODAY. https://www.xrtoday.com/virtual-reality/hilton-hotels-and-how-vr-is-changing-hospitality/

Chicchi Giglioli, I. A., Pravettoni, G., Sutil Martín, D. L., Parra, E., & Raya, M. A. (2017). A novel integrating virtual reality approach for the assessment of the attachment behavioral system. *Frontiers in Psychology*, *8*, 959. doi:10.3389/fpsyg.2017.00959 PMID:28701967

Chigozie, O. (2020). Tourism and virtual reality (VR) in developing nations. *African Journal of Hospitality, Tourism and Leisure*. doi:10.1080/01629778.2018.1455719

Ciapponi, D. (n.d.). *Why empathy skills are crucial for hoteliers*. EHL Insights. https://hospitalityinsights.ehl.edu/empathy-skills-crucial-hoteliers

Cowan, K., & Ketron, S. (2019). Prioritizing marketing research in virtual reality: Development of an immersion/fantasy typology. *European Journal of Marketing*, *53*(8), 1585–1611. doi:10.1108/EJM-10-2017-0733

Decker, A. (2023, March 15). *What is Branding? Understanding its Importance in 2023*. Hubspot. https://blog.hubspot.com/marketing/branding#:~:text=Your%20brand%20is%20arguably%20one,and%20brings%20your%20employees%20pride

Desai, P. R., Desai, P. N., Ajmera, K. D., & Mehta, K. (2014). A Review Paper on Oculus Rift-A Virtual [IJETT]. *International Journal of Engineering Trends and Technology*, *13*(4), 175–179. doi:10.14445/22315381/IJETT-V13P237

El-Said, O., & Aziz, H. (2021). Virtual Tours a Means to an End: An Analysis of Virtual Tours' Role in Tourism Recovery Post COVID-19. *Journal of Travel Research*. doi:10.1177/0047287521997567

Erenay, O., & Hashemipour, M. (2003). Virtual Reality in Engineering Education: A CIM Case Study. *The Turkish Online Journal of Educational Technology*, *2*(2), 51–56. http://www.tojet.net/articles/v2i2/228.pdf

Familmaleki, M., Aghighi, A., & Hamidi, K. (2015). Analyzing the Influence of Sales Promotion on Customer Purchasing Behavior. *International Journal of Economics and Management Sciences*, *4*(4). doi:10.4172/2162-6359.1000243

Grewal, D., Roggeveen, A. L., & Nordfält, J. (2017). The future of retailing. *Journal of Retailing*, *93*(1), 1–6. doi:10.1016/j.jretai.2016.12.008

Guttentag, D. A. (2010). Virtual reality: Applications and implications for tourism. *Tourism Management*, *31*(5), 637–651. doi:10.1016/j.tourman.2009.07.003

Hobson, J. S. P., & Williams, A. P. (1995). Virtual Reality: A new horizon for the tourism industry. *Journal of Vacation Marketing*, *1*(2), 125–135.

Jabeen, F., Al Zaidi, S., & Al Dhaheri, M. H. (2022). Automation and artificial intelligence in hospitality and tourism. *Tourism Review*, *77*(4), 1043–1061. doi:10.1108/TR-09-2019-0360

Kannan, P. K., & Li, H. A. (2017). Digital marketing: A framework, review and research agenda. *International Journal of Research in Marketing*, *34*(1), 22–45. doi:10.1016/j.ijresmar.2016.11.006

Kapur, M. (2020, August 21). Indians holiday around the world during the pandemic—from inside their living rooms. *Quartz India*. https://qz.com/india/1893473/indians-take-online-holidays-on-tourhq-viator-amid-covid-19/

Kaur, J. (2023, March 21). *RPA for Reservation in Travel and Hospitality Industry*. Xenonstack. https://www.xenonstack.com/insights/rpa-in-travel-hospitality

Kemska, A. S. (2021). Virtual tourism in Ukraine - Features and prospects. Polit. *Challenges of science Today*. http://fmv.nau.edu.ua/wp-content/uploads/2021/04/%D0%9F%D0%BE%D0%BB%D1%96%D1%82-2021.pdf#page=274

Kober, S. E., & Neuper, C. (2013). Personality and presence in virtual reality: Does their relationship depend on the used presence measure? *International Journal of Human-Computer Interaction*, *29*(1), 13–25. doi:10.1080/10447318.2012.668131

Kusdibyo, L. (2021). *Tourist loyalty to hot springs destination: the role of tourist motivation, destination image, and tourist satisfaction*. Leisure/Loisir. doi:10.1080/14927713.2021.1986420

Lau, A. (2020). New technologies used in COVID-19 for business survival: Insights from the Hotel Sector in China. *Information Technology & Tourism*, *22*(4), 497–504. doi:10.1007/s40558-020-00193-z

Lewis, H., Schrier, T., & Xu, S. (2022). Dark tourism: Motivations and visit intentions of tourists. *International Hospitality Review*, *36*(1), 107–123. doi:10.1108/IHR-01-2021-0004

Luhar, H. (2021). An Analytical Study on Economy Upliftment through Virtual Tourism with special reference to Vasai Virar City. *Palarch's Journal Of Archaeology Of Egypt/Egyptology 18*(7).

Mattan, M. (2023). *The Role of Artificial Intelligence in Augmented Reality and Virtual Reality*. Barnd XR. https://www.brandxr.io/the-role-of-ai-in-augmented-and-virtual-reality#:~:text=AI%20significantly%20enhances%20the%20user,the%20learner's%20progress%20and%20understanding

Neslin, S. A., Grewal, D., Leghorn, R., Shankar, V., Teerling, M. L., Thomas, J. S., & Verhoef, P. C. (2006). Challenges and opportunities in multichannel customer management. *Journal of Service Research*, *9*(2), 95–112. doi:10.1177/1094670506293559

Nguyen, B., Pantano, E., Dennis, C., & Gerlach, S. (2016). *Internet Retailing and Future Perspectives*. Routledge.

Pine, B. J., & Gilmore, J. H. (1998). Welcome to the experience economy. *Harvard Business Review*, *76*(4), 97–105. PMID:10181589

Revfine. (n. d.). *How to use Artificial Intelligence in the Hospitality Industry*. Revfine. https://www.revfine.com/artificial-intelligence-hospitality-industry/

Shin, H. H., & Jeong, M. (2022). Does a virtual trip evoke travelers' nostalgia and derive intentions to visit the destination, a similar destination, and share?: Nostalgia-motivated tourism. *Journal of Travel & Tourism Marketing*, *39*(1), 1–17. doi:10.1080/10548408.2022.2044972

Slater, M., & Sanchez-Vives, M. V. (2016). Enhancing Our Lives with Immersive Virtual Reality. *Frontiers in Robotics and AI*, *3*, 1–47. doi:10.3389/frobt.2016.00074

Teo, W.-P., Muthalib, M., Yamin, S., Hendy, A. M., Bramstedt, K., Kotsopoulos, E., Perrey, S., & Ayaz, H. (2016). Does a combination of virtual reality, neuromodulation and neuroimaging provide a comprehensive platform for neurorehabilitation? – a narrative review of the literature. *Frontiers in Human Neuroscience*, *10*, 284. doi:10.3389/fnhum.2016.00284 PMID:27445739

Tsang, S. (2022, April 27). What's Employee Branding and How to Build It. *Fond*. https://www.fond.co/blog/whats-employee-branding-and-how-to-build-it/#:~:text=Employee%20branding%20is%20an%20internal,being%20part%20of%20your%20organization

Tuo, Y., Ning, L., & Zhu, A. (2021). How Artificial Intelligence Will Change the Future of Tourism Industry: The Practice in China. In W. Wörndl, C. Koo, & J. L. Stienmetz (Eds.), *Information and Communication Technologies in Tourism*. Springer. doi:10.1007/978-3-030-65785-7_7

Tussyadiah, I. P., Wang, D., & Jia, C. (2017). Virtual Reality and Attitudes Toward Tourism Destinations. In R. Schegg & B. Stangl (Eds.), *Information and Communication Technologies in Tourism 2017*. Springer. doi:10.1007/978-3-319-51168-9_17

Um, S., Chon, K., & Ro, Y. H. (2006). Antecedents of revisit intention. *Annals of Tourism Research*, *33*(4), 1141–1158. doi:10.1016/j.annals.2006.06.003

Verhoef, P. C., Kannan, P. K., & Inman, J. J. (2015). From multi-channel retailing to omni-channel retailing: Introduction to the special issue on multi-channel retailing. *Journal of Retailing*, *91*(2), 174–181. doi:10.1016/j.jretai.2015.02.005

Yang, T., Lai, I., Fan, Z. B., & Mo, Q. M. (2021). The impact of a 360° virtual tour on the reduction of psychological stress caused by COVID-19. *Technology in Society*, *64*, 101514. doi:10.1016/j.techsoc.2020.101514 PMID:33424061

Yoon, S., Erdem, M., Schuckert, M., & Lee, P. C. (2021). Revisiting the impact of VR applications on hotel bookings. *Journal of Hospitality and Tourism Technology*, *12*(3), 489–511. doi:10.1108/JHTT-04-2019-0057

You, Y., Vadakkepatt, G. G., & Joshi, A. M. (2015). A meta-analysis of electronic word-of-mouth elasticity. *Journal of Marketing*, *79*(2), 19–39. doi:10.1509/jm.14.0169

Yung, R., & Khoo-Lattimore, C. (2019). New realities: A systematic literature review on virtual reality and augmented reality in tourism research. *Current Issues in Tourism*, *22*(17), 2056–2081. doi:10.1080/13683500.2017.1417359

Yung, R., Khoo-Lattimore, C., & Ellen Potter, L. (2021). Virtual reality and tourism marketing: Conceptualizing a framework on presence, emotion, and intention. *Current Issues in Tourism*, *24*(11), 1505–1525. doi:10.1080/13683500.2020.1820454

Zarzuela, M. M., Pernas, F. J. D., Calzón, S. M., Ortega, D. G., & Rodríguez, M. A. (2013). Educational Tourism through a Virtual Reality Platform. *Procedia Computer Science*, *25*, 382–388. doi:10.1016/j.procs.2013.11.047

Zhang, T., Li, B., Milman, A., & Hua, N. (2022). Assessing technology adoption practices in Chinese theme parks: Text mining and sentiment analysis. *Journal of Hospitality and Tourism Technology*, *13*(1), 195–213. doi:10.1108/JHTT-05-2020-0126

# Chapter 11
# Enhancing Competitive Advantages Through Virtual Reality Technology in the Hotels of India

**Milan Sharma**
https://orcid.org/0000-0002-3320-8129
*Lovely Professional University, India*

**Amrik Singh**
https://orcid.org/0000-0003-3598-8787
*Lovely Professional University, India*

## ABSTRACT

*VR, or virtual reality, has developed into one of the latest and most well-liked technical advancements and could have an effect regarding the hospitality and tourism industry. "Incredible India," a 360-degree virtual reality film produced in 2018 in collaboration between the Indian Ministry of Tourism and Google India, portrayed India as a multifaceted getaway. The utilisation of VR technology shows great promise in increasing competitive advantages within the hotel industry. Comprehensive research on VR technology's impact on the hotel business is necessary, as its adoption in India has been limited. The study intends to close this gap by investigating the advantages of integrating technology of VR in Indian hotels. Finding the main competitive benefits of VR technology adoption in hotel industry is the aim of this study. The methodology includes interviews with industry professionals and a review of the literature. According to the research, virtual reality technology can boost competitiveness by offering immersive experiences and raising customer engagement.*

DOI: 10.4018/979-8-3693-1978-9.ch011

## INTRODUCTION

Virtual reality (VR), being a widely acknowledged technological advancement, possesses the capacity to impact the travel and tourism industry. "Virtual reality" is the term used to describe a interface generated by computers, multidimensional, graphical, virtual world that utilises a diverse range of interface devices (Vishwakarma, P et al.,(2020). Ranasinghe et al., (2020) claim that tourism is a social phenomenon of great significance and one of the globe's largest and most rapidly growing industries. Numerous nations recognise tourism as a key driver of economic expansion (Aslan et al., 2021). Prior to the pandemic, the sector produced 1.5 trillion USD in revenue in 2019 (UNWTO, 2020).

Due to government-imposed laws restricting access to communities, which allowed people to visit vacation destinations, the tourism industry was primarily impacted by the pandemic. As a result, players in the tourism sector must employ alternative marketing techniques to imaginatively promote their goods. Among these strategies is virtual reality marketing, or VRM for short. According to Tussyadiah et al. (2018), the hotel and tourism industries stand to gain greatly from the development of VR marketing technology.

### Virtual Reality in Hospitality

As per the study of Subawa et al., (2020) is to examine the virtual reality marketing strategies used in the Bali tourism industry. The outcome demonstrated hegemony in the use of advanced technology in VRM i.e. Virtual Reality Marketing between the targeted customer and tourists. It is generally accepted that Virtual Reality (VR) represents an extremely attractive advancement in tourism and hospitality businesses. It has the remarkable ability to deceive the senses into seeing a virtual world as real, achieved through the creation of environment that is simulated by computer in 3D interactive sessions. Such are prototypes may accurately portray any site or visitor area using 3D visuals. They are operated by high-performance computers that generate a comprehensive Virtual Environment (VE). Virtual Environment (VE) is a computer-generated digital space that, when experienced with virtual reality (VR) technology, creates a sensation of being physically present within it. A comprehensive Virtual Reality (VR) phase is considered as intermediary among users in the physical world and the Virtual Environment (VE).

There are various display technologies regarding the virtual reality which are Stereoscopic imagery, Field of view (FOV), Interpupillary distance (IPD), HMD Resolution, On-Board Processing and Operating System (Ghandour, A et al., 2021). When choosing VR equipment, the primary consideration to choose a device that is easy for the user to operate, meaning it should be comfortable to wear, easy to operate, and capable of providing a visually immersive experience with a decent sense of depth and dynamic virtual environment. A fierce competition is underway among various developers specialising in virtual reality (VR) gear and software, with VR technological advancing at such a quick pace that the current technical specifications mentioned at the point of words, this information could have become obsolete by the time of publishing..

Virtual reality (VR) has greatly influenced the tourism and hospitality sector, resulting in an increase in both the availability and popularity of these immersive experiences. Prior debates have encompassed the question of whether virtual reality (VR) poses a danger to the industry (Cheong, 1995) or if it exists as a tangible reality or simply a figment of imagination (Williams and Hobson, 1995). Present concerns mostly focus on the enhancement of its capacity as a marketing instrument (Skard et al., 2021). VR technologies are presently employed to augment the travel experience for individuals by creating immersive digital environments prior to, during, and after their journey. These technologies are also giving rise to a novel form of tourism, known as virtual tourism (VT), which involves experiencing genuine tourism landscapes in an immersive online setting (Bogicevic et al., 2019; Zhang et al., 2022).

## Significance of VR in Enhancing Competitive Advantages for Hotels in India

Virtual Reality (VR) possesses the capacity to greatly enhance the competitive advantages of hotels in India. Through Implementing virtual reality (VR) systems, hotels have the ability to offer captivating experiences and distinctive marketing prospects, allowing them to stand out from their rivals. Virtual reality technology provides a unique opportunity for customers to explore hotel facilities and nearby attractions from the comfort of their own homes. This immersive experience empowers them to make well-informed decisions when booking their accommodations. In addition, VR can be utilised for virtual destination marketing, providing guests with immersive glimpses of local culture and one-of-a-kind experiences. In addition, utilising VR video can help set a hotel apart from its competitors, showcasing the property as innovative and progressive, thereby offering a distinct benefit within the market. Also, furthermore, VR technology has the potential to revolutionise employee training, create unforgettable events, and offer guests a range of virtual reality entertainment options. This not only sets the hotel apart from others, but also elevates the overall guest experience (de Lurdes Calisto, M., & Sarkar, S. 2024).

The objective of the study is to find the main competitive benefits of using VR technology in Hotel Industry. The study analysed the previous researches to find the Various technologies used in VR and what is the scope of VR in Hospitality for further implementation in Hotels.

The importance of VR in the hospitality industry stems from its potential to completely transform the customer experience, enhance customer engagement, and offer a more captivating and authentic means for customers to explore various destinations, cuisines, and activities. As a result, there can be a boost in travel, tourism, and sales of food and beverages. Through the use of immersive and lifelike experiences, virtual reality has the power to revolutionise the hospitality sector. It can elevate service standards and elevate guest experiences, resulting in higher levels of customer satisfaction and loyalty (Nayyar, A et al., 2018). Previous investigations concerning Virtual Reality in Hospitality has been lacking in terms of detailed knowledge, theoretical foundations, and conceptual frameworks.

## LITERATURE REVIEW

Virtual Reality used as 360-degree video technology has become a sought-after tool within the sector of tourism and hospitality, allowing people to gain virtual travel experiences through Virtual Reality (VR). This technology offers users the opportunity to explore a new horizon of destinations via their personal comfortable abode homes, providing an immersive and lifelike way to encounter various aspects of travel, including flights, arrivals, and notable landmarks (de Lurdes Calisto, M., & Sarkar, S. 2024). VR has been used to create virtual recreations of various travel components, offering users an engaging and interactive experience that can enhance their understanding of different destinations, foods, and activities. (Nayyar, A et al., 2018).

According to Zhang et al. (2022), virtual tourism involves immersing oneself in incredibly realistic scenes within a virtual environment using advanced visualisation technologies like virtual reality (VR) and augmented reality (AR). As per the study by Subawa S N. et al., (2020) The comprehensive interviews were carried out, the result shows virtual reality used as marketing tool and can be integrated with recreation business as a connecting link in the tourist chain and Hospitality establishments. Exploring the tourism industry, particularly in consideration of the pandemic, has sparked an interest in investigating the intersection of tourism, marketing, and economics. The study conducted by Newsome (2020) examined the rise of online perspectives as a reflection of the tourism industry. The findings of further investigation are focused on marketing, specifically on the examination of competitive advantages, which are analysed using VRM. Therefore, it is crucial to discuss competitive advantage in this literature review.

## VR as a Marketing Tool

According to Miller et al. (2020), a customer-centric iterative approach to product development is necessary to adapt to the constantly changing market environment. These studies analysed the market demand as a potential opportunity that has not yet been fully utilised, while emphasising the technology benefits. In a recent study, Wen et al. (2020) highlighted the severe impact of the pandemic on the tourism and hospitality sectors worldwide. Tourism has exerted a substantial influence on individuals' behaviour and attitudes how they live, travel, and make choices. It has influenced their preferences and consumption habits, leading to a rise in self-guided, high-end, and wellness-focused travel experiences. Based on a recent study by Jiang and Wen (2020), the pandemic had a significant impact on the marketing and management practices of hotels, particularly in relation to service trends.

Virtual Reality (VR) technology presents exciting marketing prospects and a competitive edge for hotels in India and globally. Through the use of VR technology, hotels can offer captivating and lifelike experiences that distinguish them from their rivals, resulting in heightened customer involvement and contentment. VR technology has a broad spectrum of applications, consist of hotel tours via virtual mode, virtual restaurant tours, and immersive emotions related to travelling through 360-degree video technology as depicted in Figure 1. These experiences can assist hotels in highlighting their facilities and distinctive locations, offering potential customers a deeper insight into the property and its offerings. VR technology offers customers the opportunity to fully immerse themselves in realistic experiences, giving them the sensation of actually being present at the destination. This can lead to an elevated level of consumer satisfaction and engagement, as individuals are more inclined to recall and value the virtual experiences they have encountered. In addition, VR technology has the potential to revolutionise employee training, create unforgettable events, and offer guests a wide range of virtual reality entertainment options. This will set the hotel apart from others and greatly enhance the overall guest experience. In addition, VR Tech features depicted in Figure 1. possesses the capacity to enhance virtual destination advertising through provision guests with deep and involved glimpses into local life and unforgettable experiences. Highlighting the distinct qualities of a location allows hotels to appeal to a larger audience and set themselves apart from rivals as shown in Figure 1. In addition, Virtual reality (VR) tech can be employed to offer simulated experiences hotel tours, giving potential customers the opportunity to virtually experience hotel facilities and nearby attractions. This allows them to make more informed decisions when booking their accommodations. Utilising VR technology can give the hotel a significant edge over competitors, resulting in higher bookings and revenue. The Figure 1 shows various features of VR technology ie. 360-degree view, Hotel virtual tours, Virtual Experiences which assist the hospitality professionals to provide personalised services to customers. All three-dimensional (3D) virtual environments (like a hotel lobby) that users may explore and potentially engage with are referred to as virtual environments (VE) or mediated environments' (Martínez-Mol′es et al., 2022). In the VE, "navigate" means to be able to travel around and discover new areas.

*Figure 1. Figure by author*

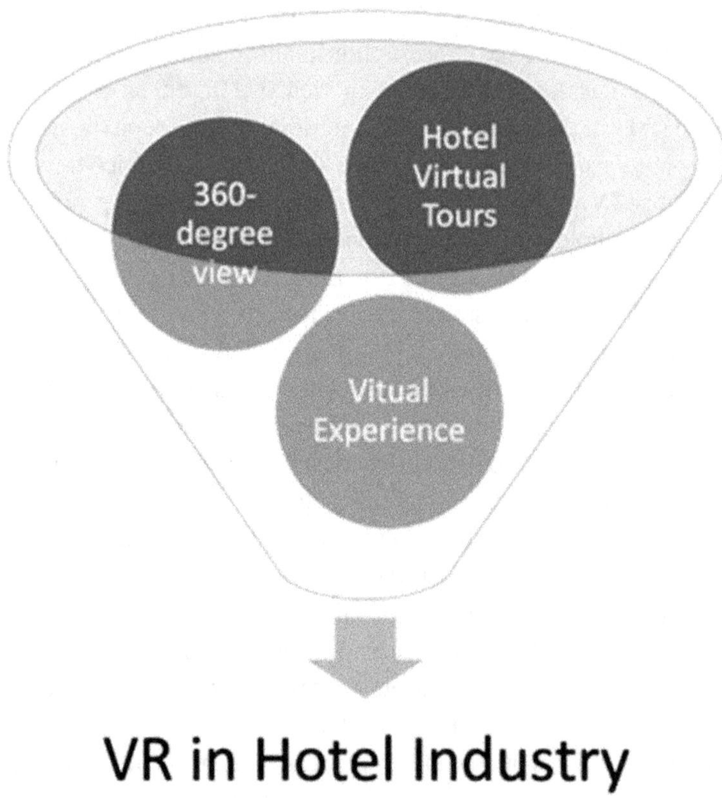


The comprehension and expertise in integrating both augmented reality (AR) and virtual reality (VR) are utilised as promotional instruments tool to enhance total customer experience and establish a conducive atmosphere, ultimately impacting the intention of customers to revisit. The achievement of an innovative tourism service is defined by its adoption growth at which customers adapt to it and their continuously evolving needs, sometimes through a rewarding system. In the coming years, an increasing number of hotels will offer the opportunity to virtually experience aspects of their services before arrival. This includes features such as online check-in, exploring hotel facilities, and discovering area attractions to get a feel of the whole hotel experience (Balasubramanian, K et al.,2022)

## Impact of VR on Consumer Preference

Demand for advanced virtual reality and its advocacy motives were both boosted by social distancing during the pandemic. Additionally, consumers who exhibited lower threat protection behaviours during the pandemic (and possibly in other risky contexts) were found to be more likely to keep taking personally tours for as much time as possible (Itani and Hollebeek, 2021)

Overall, people felt positively about VT throughout the pandemic, according to Zhang et al. (2022), but that feeling faded as the crisis passed. Motive, convenience, and the price are the drive factors in travel. Quality of expertise, on the other hand, plays a pivotal mediating role between VT project design and the appealing qualities of the location, which are pull factors (Zhang et al. 2022). Before going on a vacation, about half of all Indian tourists look up information about their destinations online (Phocus wire, 2016). Therefore, it is a common practice for contemporary tourists to research their destinations online by viewing photos and videos. Also, since most Indian visitors bring their families along on vacations, they naturally care about making sure everyone has a good time and is safe.

Virtual reality (VR) technology can provide consumers with a fresh method to view and feel the trip, which is appealing to their desire for novelty when researching vacation places. Virtual reality (VR) increases the probability that a user will actually visit a tourist area, according to Berger et al. (2007). Many well-known international and domestic travel businesses have an online presence in India. Brands like these use the visual content to market their destinations. Brands may increase conversion rates by incorporating virtual reality (VR) material of locations into their platforms. This allows potential tourists to experience the destination without ever leaving the site.

## DISCUSSION

This study involves the collection and analysis of secondary data and Interviews. This study utilised a qualitative descriptive approach. The utilisation of technology in this field is highly beneficial for managerial and professional purposes. The data collection technique involved conducting in-depth interviews, as well as observing online activities and studying virtual documents related to the use of virtual realities in the Indian hospitality industry. The informants include individuals working in the hospitality sector in different roles. The informants were chosen through purposive sampling, taking into account their level of engagement, expertise, years of background, and acquaintance with virtual reality applications in the hospitality sector. The Marketing through the virtual reality emerges as a new pattern of Marketing. This Pattern of Marketing advance the competitive advantage of hospitality as it enhance the Sustainable Tourism, Economic Growth and Guest engagement. In a recent study, Adachi et al. (2020) proposed the utilisation of virtual reality (VR) as a means to boost tourism and attract more visitors to specific locations. Their findings highlight VR's possibilities in promoting tourist activities. In their study, Gibson and O'Rawe (2018) highlighted the extensive use of VR in marketing, where it serves as a substitute for traditional promotional materials like brochures. They emphasised its ability to create immersive sensory experiences that captivate tourists and shape consumer decision-making. Recently, the Crown Plaza hotel in Noida, India, has embraced in conjunction with VR technology to showcase the various activity and offerings. Amidst the rapid advancements in VR technologies, the hospitality industry is witnessing a radical change in how individuals perceive & engage with the services. By utilising VR tech, businesses within the hotel sector can offer one-of-a-kind experiences that set them apart from their rivals. This improves interaction with customers and also provides a personalised touch with other benefits as shown in figure 2.

In Figure 2 the key benefits which provide the offering for guests more lifelike and engaging experiences, virtual reality (VR) technology has the potential to revolutionise the way Indian hotels serve their customers.

*Figure 2. Key benefits of using VR in hospitality industry*

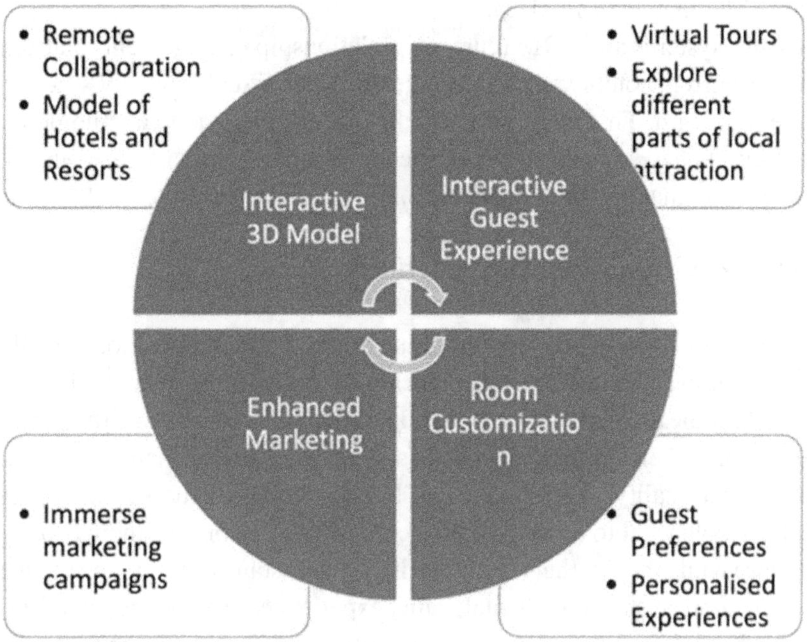


## Challenges in Adopting VR

Investment in VR is always the major concern for Hotels as Managers need more data to back their VR investment decisions because there are many VR technology possibilities ranging from less immersive to more immersive, and the characteristics of the VR systems, as discussed, greatly impact its effectiveness. Virtual reality (VR) technology requires an initial investment that can be rather high. This includes the cost of hardware, software, and the cost of creating content. It might be difficult for many hotels, particularly smaller ones, to set aside funds for virtual reality implementation. Perceived physical risk is a significant factor in the adoption behaviour of high-tech items, according to the extant literature.

There is shortage of knowledge in the hotel business when it comes to virtual reality (VR) implementation and management. Knowledge of how to incorporate virtual reality (VR) into pre-existing marketing and operational strategies is part of this, as is the technical expertise required to create and manage VR experiences (Barten Martijn, 2024).

Although virtual reality (VR) provides exciting and novel experiences, customers' views and opinions on the technology are still developing, especially as it pertains to the hotel sector. Both attracting prospective visitors and keeping the expectations of existing ones in check when it comes to virtual reality content might be difficult for hotels (Matthias Fuchs, 2023).

Bookings systems and CRM (customer relationship management) platforms are examples of current hotel systems and procedures that virtual reality (VR) technology must integrate with. This integration can be difficult. It is quite a struggle to make sure that guests have a smooth experience when they interact with your business through both online and offline channels.

## VR in Improving Guest Experience

Virtual reality (VR) enables prospective customers to experience thorough 3D tours of hotel rooms, event venues, and suites prior to making a reservation, giving them a greater feel for the area, its layout, and its key amenities. Because of this, guests can feel better about their booking decisions and have more information to work with.

With virtual reality (VR), hotels can build compelling marketing experiences that make people want to book a trip to a certain location or give them a taste of the local culture while they're there. This can help hotels stand out from the competition and bring in more customers. Virtual reality experiences provide for enhanced brand interaction by making a memorable and one-of-a-kind impression on guests. Virtual reality tours of hotels, in contrast to static photos, let viewers feel as though they are actually there, which has a profound effect on them. Guests can enjoy educational, entertaining, and relaxing experiences through the usage of virtual reality. While participating in wellness programmes and exploring a variety of locations, guests can unwind with meditation.

Virtual reality (VR) enhanced booking provides novel, immersive booking experiences, which foster customer loyalty and excitement for the business.

## CONCLUSION

The worldwide pandemic and lockdown seem to significantly affected the technology industry. Businesses are now embracing emerging capabilities of augmented and virtual reality to provide consumers with entertainment, engagement, and connection. Additionally, these companies are using these technologies so that they may establish a solid reputation for their brand and become industry leaders. Highlighting the possibility impact of VR technology on the Indian hotel and tourism sector, it becomes evident that hotels can gain a competitive edge by providing unique and immersive experiences. The study discuss the various obstacles and possibilities that come with adopting VR technology in Indian hotels, including the financial burden, lack of expertise, and reluctance to embrace change. In addition, it has emphasise the immense potential of VR technology in elevating the overall customer experience, fostering greater customer engagement, and offering a truly immersive and lifelike means for customers to explore various destinations, cuisines, and activities.

The implementation of new marketing technologies will profoundly affect all areas of firms, including strategic goals and infrastructure. Hence, successful integration of virtual reality technology in the hotel industry necessitates a comprehensive comprehension of the top management's guidance and involvement, facilitated by a meticulously formulated strategy. The purpose of transformation is to strategically sustain and expand the organisation, while avoiding the stage of closure. Currently, an increasing number of hotels are using virtual reality (VR) components into their customer experience interactions so that they can enhance their hotel experience to a diverse audience of market segments.

## Practical Implication

After carefully examining the results and conducting a thorough analysis, it was determined that several factors contribute to the implementation of VRM practice. The presence of state-of-the-art technological resources is crucial in delivering top-notch visuals and immersive audio experiences. The optimisation of VRM contributes to the competitive advancement of this industry and stimulates economic growth.

Despite the fact that further research is required in numerous areas mentioned earlier, this review offers valuable insights to practitioners who are interested in virtual reality applications in transportation and hospitality, based on the current state of research and technology. Based on what we've seen, virtual reality is a far better marketing tool than things like hotel websites, which are currently optimised. With the hope that customers will utilise the technology when deciding where to go on vacation, it has the potential to become an essential aspect of marketing communications operations.

In sum, the study shows how virtual reality (VR) might change the hotel business in India by providing guests with unique and exciting experiences that they won't find anywhere else. This study examines the present level of virtual reality (VR) technology adoption in Indian hotels, finds the main competitive advantages of VR adoption in the hospitality industry, looks into the possibilities and threats of VR implementation in the Indian hospitality sector, and finally suggests ways for VR integration in Indian hotels. The results show that virtual reality (VR) technology may boost competitiveness by making experiences more immersive, increasing consumer engagement, and creating new marketing possibilities. The report also notes that there are obstacles, including things like resistance to change, a lack of knowledge, and expensive implementation expenses. The study suggests options such as investing in staff training, establishing collaborations with technology companies, and marketing VR experiences to address these problems. Finally, the study shows that virtual reality has the ability to change the hospitality business in India by providing hotels with unique and exciting experiences. Hotels in India can take advantage of virtual reality technology to their benefit in the post-COVID age by applying the strategies and tackling the hurdles. This research fills a gap in our knowledge by examining the effects of virtual reality on India's hotel sector and provides useful direction for studies to come.

## REFERENCES

Adachi, R., Cramer, E. M., & Song, H. (2022). Using virtual reality for tourism marketing: A mediating role of self-presence. *The Social Science Journal*, *59*(4), 657–670. doi:10.1080/03623319.2020.1727245

Aslan, A., Altinoz, B., & Özsolak, B. (2021). The nexus between economic growth, tourism development, energy consumption, and CO 2 emissions in Mediterranean countries. *Environmental Science and Pollution Research International*, *28*(3), 3243–3252. doi:10.1007/s11356-020-10667-6 PMID:32910404

Balasubramanian, K., Kunasekaran, P., Konar, R., & Sakkthivel, A. M. (2022). Integration of Augmented Reality (AR) and Virtual Reality (VR) as Marketing Communications Channels in the Hospitality and Tourism Service Sector. In Marketing Communications and Brand Development in Emerging Markets Volume II: Insights for a Changing World (pp. 55-79). Cham: Springer International Publishing.

Berger, H., Dittenbach, M., Merkl, D., Bogdanovych, A., Simoff, S., & Sierra, C. (2007). Opening new dimensions for e-tourism. *Virtual Reality (Waltham Cross)*, *11*(2-3), 75–87. doi:10.1007/s10055-006-0057-z

Bogicevic, V., Seo, S., Kandampully, J. A., Liu, S. Q., & Rudd, N. A. (2019). Virtual reality presence as a preamble of tourism experience: The role of mental imagery. *Tourism Management*, *74*(5), 55–64. doi:10.1016/j.tourman.2019.02.009

Cheong, R. (1995). The virtual threat to travel and tourism. *Tourism Management*, *16*(6), 417–422. doi:10.1016/0261-5177(95)00049-T

de Lurdes Calisto, M., & Sarkar, S. (2024). A systematic review of virtual reality in tourism and hospitality: The known and the paths to follow. *International Journal of Hospitality Management*, *116*, 103623. doi:10.1016/j.ijhm.2023.103623

Ghandour, A., Kintonova, A., Demidchik, N., & Sverdlikova, E. (2021). Solving tourism management challenges by means of mobile augmented reality applications. [IJWLTT]. *International Journal of Web-Based Learning and Teaching Technologies*, *16*(6), 1–16. doi:10.4018/IJWLTT.293280

Gibson, A., & O'Rawe, M. (2018). Virtual reality as a travel promotional tool: Insights from a consumer travel fair. *Augmented reality and virtual reality: Empowering human, place and business*, 93-107.

Itani, O. S., & Hollebeek, L. D. (2021). Light at the end of the tunnel: Visitors' virtual reality (versus in-person) attraction site tour-related behavioral intentions during and post-COVID-19. *Tourism Management*, *84*, 104290. doi:10.1016/j.tourman.2021.104290 PMID:36530603

Martínez-Molés, V., Jung, T. H., Pérez-Cabañero, C., & Cervera-Taulet, A. (2022). Gathering pre-purchase information for a cruise vacation with virtual reality: The effects of media technology and gender. *International Journal of Contemporary Hospitality Management*, *34*(1), 407–429. doi:10.1108/IJCHM-04-2021-0500

Miller, C., Thomas, B. C., & Roeller, M. (2020). Innovation management processes and sustainable iterative circles: An applied integrative approach. *Journal of Work-Applied Management*, *12*(1), 69–90. doi:10.1108/JWAM-11-2019-0037

Nayyar, A., Mahapatra, B., Le, D., & Suseendran, G. (2018). Virtual Reality (VR) & Augmented Reality (AR) technologies for tourism and hospitality industry. *International journal of engineering & technology, 7*(2.21), 156-160.

Newsome, D. (2021). The collapse of tourism and its impact on wildlife tourism destinations. *Journal of Tourism Futures*, *7*(3), 295–302. doi:10.1108/JTF-04-2020-0053

Ranasinghe, R., Karunarathne, A. C. I. D., & Herath, J. (2021). After corona (COVID-19) impacts on global poverty and recovery of tourism based service economies: An appraisal. *International Journal of Tourism and Hospitality*, *1*(1), 52–64.

Skard, S., Knudsen, E. S., Sjåstad, H., & Thorbjørnsen, H. (2021). How virtual reality influences travel intentions: The role of mental imagery and happiness forecasting. *Tourism Management*, *87*, 104360. doi:10.1016/j.tourman.2021.104360

Subawa, N. S., Widhiasthini, N. W., Astawa, I. P., Dwiatmadja, C., & Permatasari, N. P. I. (2021). The practices of virtual reality marketing in the tourism sector, a case study of Bali, Indonesia. *Current Issues in Tourism*, *24*(23), 3284–3295. https://www.revfine.com/virtual-reality-hospitality-industry/. doi:10.1080/13683500.2020.1870940

Tussyadiah, I. P., Wang, D., Jung, T. H., & Tom Dieck, M. C. (2018). Virtual reality, presence, and attitude change: Empirical evidence from tourism. *Tourism Management*, *66*, 140–154. doi:10.1016/j.tourman.2017.12.003

UNWTO. (2020). *International tourism growth continues to outpace the global economy*. UN. https://www.unwto.org/ international-tourism-growth-continues-to-outpace-the-economy

Vishwakarma, P., Mukherjee, S., & Datta, B. (2020). Travelers' intention to adopt virtual reality: A consumer value perspective. *Journal of Destination Marketing & Management*, *17*, 100456. doi:10.1016/j.jdmm.2020.100456

Wen, J., Kozak, M., Yang, S., & Liu, F. (2021). COVID-19: Potential effects on Chinese citizens' lifestyle and travel. *Tourism Review*, *76*(1), 74–87. doi:10.1108/TR-03-2020-0110

Williams, P., & Hobson, J. P. (1995). Virtual reality and tourism: Fact or fantasy? *Tourism Management*, *16*(6), 423–427. doi:10.1016/0261-5177(95)00050-X

Wong, K. Y. (2021). Virtual Reality Marketing in Hospitality and Tourism. *University of South Florida M3 Center Publishing, 18*(9781732127586), 6.

Zhang, S. N., Li, Y. Q., Ruan, W. Q., & Liu, C. H. (2022). Would you enjoy virtual travel? The characteristics and causes of virtual tourists' sentiment under the influence of the COVID-19 pandemic. *Tourism Management*, *88*, 104429. doi:10.1016/j.tourman.2021.104429

# Chapter 12
# Embracing Technological Advancements:
## A Futuristic Approach to Hospitality Management

**Baljit Kaur**
https://orcid.org/0000-0001-6473-7704
*Maharishi Markandeshwar University, India*

**Sanjeev Kumar Kumar Saxena**
https://orcid.org/0000-0002-2139-9255
*Assam University, Silchar, India*

## ABSTRACT

*The chapter delves into futuristic trends in hospitality, propelled by artificial intelligence (AI), the internet of things (IoT), and blockchain. AI drives personalized guest interactions, IoT enables smart hotels, and blockchain ensures security. Data analytics personalize experiences, VR/AR engage guests, while contactless services address pandemic concerns. Sustainability aligns with eco-consciousness, and cybersecurity safeguards guest data. Embracing innovation is imperative for thriving in the evolving hospitality landscape.*

## INTRODUCTION TO FUTURISTIC TRENDS IN HOSPITALITY

The hospitality industry, once characterized by traditional practices and personalized guest services, is experiencing a profound transformation. This shift is driven by a confluence of technological advancements, evolving guest expectations, and

DOI: 10.4018/979-8-3693-1978-9.ch012

global events that have accelerated the adoption of innovative solutions. These factors collectively give rise to what can be termed "futuristic trends in hospitality management." In this chapter, we delve into the significance and implications of these trends, exploring how they are reshaping the industry in profound ways.

## The Significance of Futuristic Trends in the Hospitality Industry

The significance of futuristic trends in the hospitality industry cannot be overstated. In an era defined by rapid technological evolution, changing consumer expectations, and global events like the COVID-19 pandemic, embracing innovation is not just an option, but a necessity for businesses in this sector. These trends encompass a wide spectrum, from integrating cutting-edge technologies like AI, IoT, and blockchain to personalizing guest experiences through data analytics, promoting sustainability, and harnessing virtual and augmented reality.

The core significance lies in their collective potential to revolutionize guest experiences, streamline operations, and respond to environmental concerns. In a highly competitive marketplace, businesses that fail to adapt risk falling behind and are unable to meet evolving customer demands. Furthermore, the adoption of these trends is not only about staying relevant but also addressing ethical and ecological challenges and achieving long-term resilience. The ability to adapt to these innovations is thus a defining factor that separates industry leaders from laggards.

Ultimately, understanding and leveraging these trends is no longer a choice, but a strategic imperative. By embracing them, the hospitality industry not only meets the growing expectations of guests but also ensures its sustainability and competitiveness in an ever-evolving landscape.

# TECHNOLOGICAL INTEGRATION IN THE HOSPITALITY INDUSTRY

The hospitality industry is undergoing a profound transformation due to technological integration. With the advent of cutting-edge technologies, such as AI, IoT, and blockchain, the industry is finding innovative ways to enhance guest experiences, streamline operations, and manage data efficiently.

## Artificial Intelligence (AI) in Guest Experience

AI is ushering in a new era of guest experiences in the hospitality industry, offering unprecedented levels of personalization and convenience. By harnessing AI, hotels can create tailored, memorable experiences that go beyond traditional service.

AI-powered chatbots and virtual assistants are available 24/7 to address guest queries, handle bookings, and provide recommendations, enhancing engagement and efficiency (Buhalis et al., 2023). Moreover, AI-driven recommendation engines analyze guest preferences and past behavior to suggest everything from room upgrades to dining options, ensuring guests feel understood and catered to on an individual level (Buhalis et al., 2023).

The implementation of AI has transformative potential, as it not only streamlines operational processes but also nurtures guest loyalty and satisfaction. The ability to predict and fulfill guest needs and preferences showcases the industry's commitment to staying ahead in the age of technological innovation.

## The Internet of Things (IoT) in Operations in Smart Hotels

The IoT has revolutionized operations in smart hotels by enhancing guest experiences and streamlining efficiency. IoT technology enables a seamless and personalized guest journey, from check-in to check-out. In-room smart devices, such as thermostats, lights, and entertainment systems, can be controlled via smartphones, offering guests unprecedented convenience and control (Kakoulli, 2023).

Furthermore, IoT-connected sensors can monitor room occupancy and adjust energy consumption accordingly, optimizing resource utilization (Marinakis & Doukas, 2018). Smart hotels can also employ IoT for predictive maintenance, preventing equipment failures and minimizing downtime (Vashi et al., 2017). Additionally, IoT can improve security by monitoring access and providing real-time alerts in case of unauthorized entry (Zhou et al., 2017). Guest safety is enhanced through the deployment of IoT-enabled emergency response systems (Vashi et al., 2017).

In conclusion, IoT integration in smart hotels not only enhances guest satisfaction but also improves operational efficiency, cost-effectiveness, and security. This technological transformation marks a significant milestone in the hospitality industry.

Smart hotels are using IoT technology to cope with guest demand. IoT connects various devices and systems within a hotel, from climate control and lighting to security and inventory management. These connected systems allow for centralized control and monitoring, resulting in improved operational efficiency. For example, IoT sensors can adjust room temperatures based on occupancy, reducing energy consumption and costs (Kakoulli, 2023). They can also alert staff to maintenance issues before they lead to guest complaints, ensuring a seamless guest experience (Sigala, 2020).

### Blockchain for Security and Trust in Hospitality Industry

Blockchain technology is increasingly leveraged in the hospitality industry to enhance security and trust. It offers a transparent and tamper-proof ledger that can be applied in various ways, such as:

1. ***Identity Verification***: Blockchain can secure guest identity, streamline check-in processes, and protect personal information (Khanna et al., 2020).
2. ***Smart Contracts***: It enables automated and secure execution of agreements, such as reservations, ensuring trust and reducing the risk of disputes (Tasatanattakool & Techapanupreeda, 2018).
3. ***Supply Chain Management***: Tracking the origin and delivery of food and goods is made more transparent and trustworthy, reducing fraud and ensuring quality (Cole et al., 2019).
4. ***Guest Reviews***: Blockchain can authenticate guest reviews, mitigating fake or malicious feedback (Zohar, 2015).
5. ***Payment Security***: It can be used for secure, efficient, and cost-effective payment methods, reducing the risk of fraud (Iansiti & Lakhani, 2017).
6. ***Data Security***: Protecting sensitive data like guest preferences and payment information from cyber threats (Swan, 2015).

The adoption of blockchain technology in the hospitality industry contributes to increased security, trust, and the overall guest experience.

## PERSONALIZATION THROUGH DATA ANALYTICS IN THE HOSPITALITY INDUSTRY

Personalization in the hospitality industry has become a driving force for guest satisfaction and loyalty. Leveraging data analytics and machine learning, businesses can create tailored guest experiences, optimize services, and develop more effective marketing strategies. Here, we explore the significance of personalization through data analytics and its implications in the modern hospitality landscape.

### Leveraging Big Data for Personalization in the Hospitality Industry

The hospitality industry has undergone a remarkable transformation with the advent of Big Data analytics, allowing businesses to provide highly personalized experiences to their guests. Leveraging Big Data, hotels can collect, process, and analyze vast amounts of information from various touchpoints, including online booking platforms, mobile apps, and on-site interactions, to better understand guest preferences and behaviors (Xiang et al., 2017). This insight enables hotels to tailor services, such as room preferences, dining recommendations, and even personalized marketing offers, resulting in improved guest satisfaction and loyalty (Mariani & Baggio, 2022). Big Data analytics also helps hotels optimize pricing strategies by considering factors like demand, competitor rates, and historical data (Zhang et al., 2014).

Furthermore, by using guest data for operational enhancements, hotels can improve resource allocation, housekeeping efficiency, and energy conservation (Mariani & Baggio, 2022). This not only increases operational efficiency but also reduces costs.

In conclusion, the strategic application of Big Data in the hospitality industry empowers hotels to deliver personalized experiences, optimize pricing, and enhance operational efficiency, ultimately driving guest satisfaction and business success.

## Machine Learning for Predictive Personalization

Machine learning algorithms take personalization to the next level by predicting guest preferences and needs. These algorithms analyze historical data to predict what services, amenities, or offers a particular guest is likely to appreciate. For example, if a guest frequently orders room service breakfast, a hotel can proactively provide breakfast options or special promotions during their stay. This anticipatory approach not only enhances the guest experience but also boosts upselling opportunities and guest loyalty (Xiang et al., 2017).

## Enhancing Guest Satisfaction and Loyalty

The goal of personalization through data analytics is to provide guests with experiences that are tailored to their preferences. When guests feel that their needs and desires are understood and met, they are more likely to return and recommend the establishment to others. Personalization is closely linked to guest satisfaction and, by extension, loyalty. Satisfied guests are not only more likely to return but also to spend more during their stay and generate positive word-of-mouth (Zhang et al., 2014).

In conclusion, personalization through data analytics is a game-changer in the hospitality industry. By harnessing the power of big data and machine learning, hotels can create memorable, personalized experiences for their guests, leading to increased guest satisfaction and loyalty. It's not just about knowing your guests; it's about understanding them and delivering services that meet their individual needs and desires.

## THE RISE OF VIRTUAL REALITY (VR) AND AUGMENTED REALITY (AR) IN THE HOSPITALITY INDUSTRY

VR and AR are transforming the way the hospitality industry engages with its guests. These immersive technologies offer innovative approaches to enhancing guest experiences, marketing, and employee training.

### Virtual Reality (VR) in Guest Engagement in Hospitality Industry

VR has emerged as a powerful tool for enhancing guest engagement within the hospitality industry. By immersing guests in virtual environments, hotels can provide unique and memorable experiences. Guests can explore their chosen destinations, preview room options, and even participate in virtual tours before making reservations, leading to more informed and confident booking decisions (Spita et al., 2020). VR also allows guests to experience local attractions and activities, further personalizing their stay (Xiang et al., 2017). Additionally, VR-based training for hotel staff can enhance service quality and efficiency (Chathoth et al., 2016).

Moreover, VR can be employed for event planning and virtual conferences, extending hospitality services to the business sector (Laura et al., 2010). Integrating VR with in-room entertainment systems can also elevate the in-room guest experience (Correia Loureiro, 2022).

In conclusion, VR technology has the potential to redefine guest engagement by offering immersive, informative, and personalized experiences in the hospitality industry.

### Augmented Reality (AR) in Dining and Guest Services in Hospitality Services

AR is revolutionizing the hospitality industry, enhancing dining and guest services by creating immersive and interactive experiences. AR applications are transforming menus, allowing diners to visualize dishes through 3D models or holograms, helping in decision-making, and catering to dietary preferences (Nayyar et al., 2018). In-room AR devices can provide guests with information on local attractions, translate foreign menus, or offer virtual concierge services (ÖZKUL & Kumlu, 2019).

Moreover, AR enhances guest engagement through gamified experiences, like scavenger hunts, where diners and guests can explore the hotel's facilities or the city's landmarks (Buhalis et al., 2023). Staff training benefits from AR too, improving service quality and efficiency (Kontogianni & Alepis, 2020). However, privacy concerns (Han et al., 2019) and the need for high-quality AR hardware and software remain challenges (Xiang et al., 2017).

## CONTACTLESS AND REMOTE SERVICES IN THE HOSPITALITY INDUSTRY

In recent years, the hospitality industry has witnessed a significant transformation with the adoption of contactless and remote services. These technological advancements have not only enhanced the guest experience but also addressed safety concerns, especially in the wake of the COVID-19 pandemic.

### Contactless Check-In and Check-Out

Contactless check-in and check-out have become pivotal in the hospitality industry, providing guests with seamless, safe, and efficient processes. Guests can bypass traditional front desk procedures using mobile apps, self-check-in kiosks, or digital key cards, reducing physical contact and wait times (CAR & STIFANICH, 2020) This technology enhances guest convenience and aligns with the changing expectations of travelers. During the COVID-19 pandemic, it gained even more prominence due to its role in minimizing health risks (Hao & Chon, 2022). Contactless services are now a key component of the modern guest experience, offering both operational efficiency and improved safety (Fisher, Greg, and Beatson, 2002). These innovative solutions have transformed the way guests engage with hospitality services while also addressing health and hygiene concerns.

### Remote Concierge Services

Remote concierge services in the hospitality industry have gained prominence, offering guests a seamless and contactless experience. These services utilize technology to provide guests with information, assistance, and amenities through apps, chatbots, and virtual assistants (Gupta, 2019).

Guests can request room service, book activities, and receive recommendations from the convenience of their smartphones (Mccarty & Orientale, 2010). This approach enhances efficiency, reduces physical contact (Gosjen et al., 2022), and aligns with the evolving guest expectations for personalized and self-service options (Bharwani & Mathews, 2021). Key players in the industry, such as Marriott and Hilton, have embraced this trend, signaling its growing importance. Additionally, data security (Stephen C. Barth, 2017) and privacy concerns (Nwokorie & Igbojekwe, 2019) are essential considerations in implementing these services.

## Contactless Payments

Contactless payments have revolutionized the hospitality industry by offering seamless and secure transactions. This technology, which includes methods such as mobile wallets, contactless cards, and QR code payments, enhances guest experiences by minimizing physical contact and reducing transaction times (Popescul et al., 2016). It has become crucial during the COVID-19 pandemic, ensuring safety for both staff and customers. References supporting this transformation include (VISA, 2022), which reports a 6 times increase in contactless payments from December 2018 to December 2021; (Mastercard, 2021) Mastercard's study shows 40% of customers prefer contactless payments; (McKinsey & Company, 2020) highlighting the demand for digital payments; (Biscotti, 2023) on Forbes reported on QR code adoption in restaurants; (Statista, 2023) highlighted the statistics on mobile payment growth; (National Restaurant Association, 2022) insights from the National Restaurant Association highlighted the significance of contactless payments in the industry.

## In-Room Technology and Automation

In-room technology and automation have revolutionized the hospitality industry, enhancing guest experiences and operational efficiency. Smart thermostats (Eskerod et al., 2019) and lighting systems (Eskerod et al., 2019) allow guests to personalize their room environment, while voice-controlled assistants like Amazon's Alexa (Cao et al., 2022) provide quick access to services. Automated check-in and keyless entry (Kansakar et al., 2019) streamline the arrival process. In-room tablets (Lukanova & Ilieva, 2019) offer concierge services and information, reducing the need for physical staff presence. Furthermore, integrated systems can enable guests to control room settings from their smartphones (Lukanova & Ilieva, 2019), ensuring a seamless and convenient stay.

## Remote Work and Stay Packages

Remote work and stay packages in the hospitality industry have gained significant popularity because of the evolving work landscape. These packages offer professionals the opportunity to work from a different location while enjoying a change of scenery. Many hotels and resorts have adapted to this trend by providing attractive amenities, reliable Wi-Fi, and comfortable workspaces, creating a seamless workcation experience (Lukanova & Ilieva, 2019). These packages can cater to various preferences, from beachfront villas to cozy cabins in the mountains (Jelski, 2022). Furthermore, businesses can benefit from tax incentives by hosting meetings or conferences at such venues (Brown, 2020). This synergy between work and leisure is shaping the future of travel and hospitality (Singh, 2023).

## Safety and Hygiene

Contactless and remote services have proven crucial in maintaining safety and hygiene standards, particularly during the COVID-19 pandemic. Minimizing physical contact reduces the risk of virus transmission, making guests feel more secure during their stay (Popescul et al., 2016).

The adoption of contactless and remote services in the hospitality industry represents a significant shift in how hotels and resorts cater to their guests. These advancements offer convenience, safety, and efficiency while aligning with the changing expectations of modern travelers. As technology continues to evolve, the industry will likely see further integration of contactless and remote services to enhance the overall guest experience.

# SUSTAINABILITY AND GREEN HOSPITALITY

Sustainable hospitality management not only promotes eco-friendly practices but also future-proofs businesses in an era where sustainability is no longer a choice but a necessity (Kaur, 2021). Sustainability and Green Hospitality are two closely intertwined concepts that have gained increasing significance in the global hospitality industry. Green Hospitality refers to the practice of operating hotels and related establishments in an environmentally responsible and sustainable manner, with a primary focus on reducing negative environmental impacts. This approach involves implementing eco-friendly measures, such as energy and water conservation, waste reduction, and the use of renewable resources. Green hotels often seek eco-certifications like LEED or Green Key to validate their commitment to sustainability (Font & Harris, 2004).

Sustainability in hospitality extends beyond environmental aspects and encompasses social and economic dimensions. It involves not only minimizing the environmental footprint but also promoting social responsibility, ethical sourcing, and supporting local communities. Sustainable hospitality strives to strike a balance between the three pillars of sustainability: environmental, social, and economic (Hall et al., 2012).

Both Green Hospitality and sustainability align with changing consumer preferences and the industry's need to respond to global environmental challenges. Guests increasingly seek eco-conscious accommodations and experiences. Furthermore, adopting sustainable practices can lead to cost savings, operational efficiency, and a positive brand image, which is crucial for the long-term success of hospitality businesses (Mensah & Blankson, 2014).

In conclusion, Green Hospitality and sustainability are not only ethical imperatives but also strategic advantages for the modern hospitality industry. They are key to meeting consumer expectations, minimizing environmental impact, and ensuring long-term business resilience.

## CYBERSECURITY AND DATA PRIVACY IN THE HOSPITALITY INDUSTRY

The hospitality industry is increasingly reliant on technology and data-driven processes to enhance guest experiences. While this digital transformation offers numerous benefits, it also raises concerns regarding cybersecurity and data privacy. Protecting guest information and ensuring their privacy is a paramount responsibility for hospitality businesses.

### Data Security in Hospitality

Data security in the hospitality industry is of paramount importance to protect sensitive guest information and maintain trust. It involves safeguarding personal details, payment data, and reservation history from cyber threats, ensuring compliance with regulations like the General Data Protection Regulation (GDPR), Payment Card Industry Data Security Standard (PCI DSS), and Information Technology (IT) Act, 2000.

The GDPR is a comprehensive European Union (EU) data privacy law that was implemented in May 2018. It is designed to protect the personal data of EU citizens by regulating how organizations collect, process, and store this data. GDPR grants individuals' greater control over their personal information and imposes strict requirements on businesses and organizations to ensure data protection and privacy. It also includes provisions for data breach reporting and severe fines for non-compliance.

The PCI DSS is a global standard that applies to any entity that stores, processes, or transmits cardholder data. The PCI DSS is a set of security standards and requirements established to ensure the secure handling of payment card data, such as credit card and debit card information. It is designed to protect sensitive financial data and prevent data breaches in organizations that process, transmit, or store payment card information. The PCI DSS sets guidelines for data encryption, access controls, network security, and regular security assessments to safeguard payment card information and maintain the trust of consumers and the payment card industry. The PCI DSS is not legally binding and does not supersede any county, state, or local laws.

In India, the Information Technology (IT) Act, of 2000, Governs electronic data protection, and digital signatures, and prohibits unauthorized access.

Robust security measures, such as encryption, tokenization, and regular security audits, are essential to mitigate risks (Shabani & Munir, 2020). Training staff on data protection and implementing access controls helps prevent internal breaches (Shabani, 2017). By prioritizing data security, the hospitality sector can enhance its reputation and guest satisfaction while avoiding costly data breaches.

## Common Threats

The hospitality industry faces a myriad of cybersecurity threats that can compromise guest data and disrupt operations. Threats include data breaches through point-of-sale (POS) systems, and targeting payment card information, as seen in high-profile cases like the Marriott breach (Hollander, 2023; Shabani, 2017). Phishing attacks and ransomware can also paralyze hotel systems and compromise sensitive information (Buhalis et al., 2019). Insider threats, whether intentional or accidental, pose a significant risk (Shabani & Munir, 2020). To mitigate these challenges, the hospitality sector must invest in robust security protocols, employee training, and regular vulnerability assessments to safeguard guest data and maintain trust.

## Regulatory Compliance

Data protection regulations have evolved worldwide to safeguard individuals' data in the digital age. The European Union's General Data Protection Regulation(GDPR) (Tan, 1999), effective in 2018, has set a global benchmark for data protection. GDPR emphasizes transparency, consent, and the rights of data subjects. The California Consumer Privacy Act (Gamwell, 2022) and its successor, the California Privacy Rights Act (Gamwell, 2022), have bolstered data protection in the United States. Other countries, like Brazil with the Lei Geral de Proteção de Dados Pessoais (LGPD), (Hoffmann & Vargas, 2022) and India with the Personal Data Protection Bill (Government of India, 2023), have enacted or proposed comprehensive data protection laws. These regulations aim to balance the free flow of data with privacy rights, impacting businesses and technology sectors worldwide.

Implementing robust data encryption protocols and secure payment processing systems is crucial to protect sensitive guest information during online transactions and while it's stored in databases (Popescul et al., 2016).

## Employee Training and Awareness

In the hospitality industry, ensuring robust employee training and awareness regarding data protection is paramount (CAR & STIFANICH, 2020). Given the wealth of personal information collected from guests, staff must be well-versed in data security protocols. Regular training programs on handling sensitive data, recognizing phishing attempts, and compliance with relevant regulations (e.g., GDPR or PCI DSS) are essential. This not only mitigates the risk of data breaches but also builds trust with guests. An informed workforce safeguards customer privacy and minimizes legal and reputational risks for the organization.

## Guest Data Privacy

Guests expect their data to be handled responsibly and with respect for their privacy. Hospitality businesses must communicate their data privacy policies clearly and obtain consent for data usage (Shabani & Munir, 2020).

Cybersecurity and data privacy are paramount in the hospitality industry, given the sensitive information collected from guests. A breach of trust in these areas can have severe consequences. By implementing robust security measures, complying with regulations, and prioritizing data privacy, hospitality businesses can safeguard guest information and maintain a positive reputation in an increasingly digital world.

# FINDINGS

The hospitality industry is on the brink of a significant transformation, driven by a wave of futuristic trends that promise to reshape the way we experience travel, accommodation, and dining. These trends are a response to evolving consumer expectations, technological advancements, and sustainability concerns, which collectively push the boundaries of traditional hospitality.

Some of the most notable trends in the technological integration in the hospitality industry are Artificial Intelligence (AI), the Internet of Things (IoT), and the use of blockchain for security and trust.

Hotels and restaurants are increasingly leveraging AI-powered chatbots for seamless guest service and personalized recommendations. These findings are in line with the research (Ivanov & Webster, 2017) that supports that virtual concierges, like ChatGPT, can handle inquiries, make reservations, and even predict guest preferences based on past interactions.

Furthermore, the concept of “smart” hotels is gaining momentum. These establishments employ IoT technology to create an interconnected and convenient experience for guests. For instance, rooms equipped with IoT sensors can adjust temperature and lighting according to individual preferences and save energy when unoccupied.

In the hospitality industry, guest personalization has reached new heights through the strategic application of data analytics, harnessing the power of big data and machine learning methods. This dynamic combination enables businesses to delve into intricate guest preferences, behaviors, and trends, thereby tailoring their services, from room selection to dining options and amenities, to meet individual needs seamlessly. The result is a highly customized and memorable guest experience, fostering not only satisfaction but also brand loyalty, ultimately underlining the pivotal role of data-driven personalization in today's competitive hospitality landscape.

VR and AR are revolutionizing the hospitality industry by delivering immersive experiences. VR allows potential guests to explore hotel rooms and destinations, aiding in decision-making. Meanwhile, AR enhances the dining experience with interactive menus and offers wayfinding within the hotel. Both technologies create memorable, engaging encounters for guests, setting a new standard in the industry's approach to guest engagement and services.

Contactless and remote services have become pivotal in the hospitality industry, especially in the wake of the COVID-19 pandemic. They enable guests to check in, access room keys, make payments, and request services without physical contact. These technological innovations not only prioritize guest safety but also offer convenience and efficiency in an ever-evolving hospitality landscape.

Sustainability is another paramount trend in the hospitality sector. As travelers become more environmentally conscious, eco-friendly initiatives are becoming a necessity rather than a luxury. Some hotels now feature energy-efficient designs, zero-waste policies, and locally sourced, organic menus that reduce their carbon footprint.

Lastly, cybersecurity and data privacy are paramount in the hospitality industry. With the increasing digitization of services and guest data storage, protecting sensitive information is a top priority. Robust security measures safeguard guest data and payment details, ensuring trust, compliance with regulations, and maintaining the industry's reputation for reliability and safety.

In conclusion, the hospitality industry is amid a profound transformation driven by AI, IoT, Blockchain, personalization through data analytics, the use of VR and AR for enhancing guest experience, introducing contactless services, incorporating the concept of sustainability, and ensuring data privacy. These trends are not only shaping guest experiences but also redefining the very essence of hospitality in this futuristic era. Embracing these changes is not just a choice; it's a necessity for industry players to stay relevant in the evolving landscape.

## DISCUSSION

The complete discussion on the transformative traits within the hospitality industry highlights the imperative for industry stakeholders to embody technological innovations. As motels and restaurants navigate the evolving landscape marked with the aid of AI, IoT, data analytics, VR, AR, contactless offerings, sustainability, and cybersecurity, they're not merely adapting to alternate; they are pioneering a brand new era of hospitality. The insights gathered from this studies serve a manual for industry leaders, urging them to proactively integrate these technology to fulfill and exceed visitor expectations, thus making sure the continuing relevance and achievement in their establishments in an ever-evolving and tech-driven landscape.

## REFERENCES

Bharwani, S., & Mathews, D. (2021). Post-pandemic pressures to pivot: Tech transformations in luxury hotels. *Worldwide Hospitality and Tourism Themes*, *13*(5), 569–583. doi:10.1108/WHATT-05-2021-0072

Biscotti, L. (2023). Restaurants Face Backlash As QR Code Fatigue and Tech Costs Increase. *Forbes*. https://www.forbes.com/sites/louisbiscotti/2023/07/10/restaurants-face-tech-backlash-as-qr-code-fatigue-technology-costs-and-complexity-increase/?sh=1bc01c5b2552

Brown, J. (2020). The Tax Benefits of Hosting Business Events at Hotels and Resorts. *Forbes*. Https://Www.Forbes.Com/Sites/Jonathanbrown/2020/12/10/The-Tax-Benefits-Of-Hosting-Business-Events-At-Hotels-And-Resorts/?Sh=3e7ed6355741

Buhalis, D., Harwood, T., Bogicevic, V., Viglia, G., Beldona, S., & Hofacker, C. (2019). Technological disruptions in services: Lessons from tourism and hospitality. *Journal of Service Management*, *30*(4), 484–506. doi:10.1108/JOSM-12-2018-0398

Buhalis, D., O'Connor, P., & Leung, R. (2023). Smart hospitality: From smart cities and smart tourism towards agile business ecosystems in networked destinations. *International Journal of Contemporary Hospitality Management*, *35*(1), 369–393. doi:10.1108/IJCHM-04-2022-0497

Cao, D., Sun, Y., Goh, E., Wang, R., & Kuiavska, K. (2022). Adoption of smart voice assistants technology among Airbnb guests : A revised self-efficacy-based value adoption model (SVAM). *International Journal of Hospitality Management*, *101*, 1–20. doi:10.1016/j.ijhm.2021.103124

Car, T. & Stifanich, L. P. (2020). Mobile Technology: a Tool To Increase Hotel Sales and Revenue. *Economics Business and Organization Research*, 454–464.

Chathoth, P. K., Ungson, G. R., Harrington, R. J., & Chan, E. S. W. (2016). Co-creation and higher order customer engagement in hospitality and tourism services: A critical review. *International Journal of Contemporary Hospitality Management*, *28*(2), 222–245. doi:10.1108/IJCHM-10-2014-0526

Cole, R., Stevenson, M., & Aitken, J. (2019). Blockchain technology: Implications for operations and supply chain management. *Supply Chain Management*, *24*(4), 469–483. doi:10.1108/SCM-09-2018-0309

Correia Loureiro, S. M. (2022). Chapter 38 VIRTUAL REALITY, AUGMENTED REALITY AND TOURISM EXPERIENCE. In The Routledge handbook of tourism experience management and marketing (Issue 351, pp. 439–452). Routledge.

Eskerod, P., Hollensen, S., Morales-Contreras, M. F., & Arteaga-Ortiz, J. (2019). Drivers for pursuing sustainability through IoT technology within high-end hotels-An exploratory study. *Sustainability (Basel)*, *11*(19), 5372. doi:10.3390/su11195372

Fisher, Greg and Beatson, A. T. (2002). The impact of culture on self-service technnology adoption in the hotel indistry. *International Journal of Hospitality and Tourism Administration, 3*(3), 59–77. http://eprints.qut.edu.au/21114/1/c21114.pdf

Font, X., & Harris, C. (2004). Rethinking standards from green to sustainable. *Annals of Tourism Research*, *31*(4), 986–1007. doi:10.1016/j.annals.2004.04.001

Gamwell, B. (2022). *California Consumer Protection Act (CCPA): Narrowing CCPA Exemptions Will Ensur emptions Will Ensure Greater Priv eater Privacy Protections otections*. GGU Law Review Blog.

Gosjen, D. I., Haryadi, K. H., Nicholas, Gunawan, A. A. S., Djuwita, C. M., & Adiati, M. P. (2022). Nicholas, Gunawan, A. A. S., Djuwita, C. M., & Adiati, M. P. (2022). Implementation e-concierge in hotel. *Procedia Computer Science*, *216*, 485–498. doi:10.1016/j.procs.2022.12.161

Government of India. (2023). Digital Personal Data Protection Act 2023. *The Gazette of India, Dl.* https://www.meity.gov.in/writereaddata/files/Digital Personal Data Protection Act 2023.pdf

Hall, C. M., Gössling, S., Peeters, P., Hall, C. M., Ceron, J., & Dubois, G. (2012). Tourism and Water Use : Supply, Demand and Security – An International Review Tourism and water use : Supply, demand, and security. An international review. *Tourism Management*, *33*(1), 1–15. doi:10.1016/j.tourman.2011.03.015

Han, D.-I. D., Weber, J., Bastiaansen, M., Mitas, O., & Lub, X. (2019). Virtual and Augmented Reality Technologies to Enhance the Visitor Experience in Cultural Tourism. *Augmented Reality and Virtual Reality: The Power of AR and VR for Business*, 113–128. doi:10.1007/978-3-030-06246-0_9

Hao, F., & Chon, K. K. S. (2022). Contactless service in hospitality: Bridging customer equity, experience, delight, satisfaction, and trust. *International Journal of Contemporary Hospitality Management*, *34*(1), 113–134. doi:10.1108/IJCHM-05-2021-0559

Hoffmann, T., & Vargas, P. L. P. de M. (2022). LGPD Et Al. – Report on the Law of Data Disclosure in Brazil. SSRN *Electronic Journal, April*. doi:10.2139/ssrn.4082390

Hollander, J. (2023). *Marriott Data Breach FAQ: What Really Happened?* HotelTechReport. https://hoteltechreport.com/news/marriott-data-breach

Iansiti, M., & Lakhani, K. R. (2017). The truth about blockchain. *Harvard Business Review*, *2017*(January-February).

Ivanov, S., & Webster, C. (2017). Adoption of Robots, Aritificial Intelligence and Service Automation by Travel, Tourism and Hospitality Companies - A cost-benefit Analysis. *International Scientific Conference "Contemporary Tourism – Traditions and Innovations*. IEEE.

Jelski, C. (2022). Working during vacation: Hotels respond to bleisure's flipside. *Travel Weekly*. https://www.travelweekly.com/Travel-News/Hotel-News/The-flipside-of-bleisure-working-during-vacation

Kakoulli, M. S. P. and E. (2023). *IoT for Sustainable Hospitality: A Systematic Review of Opportunities and Challenges for the Hospitality Industry Revolution. 19th International Conference on Distributed Computing in Smart Systems and the Internet of Things (DCOSS-IoT)*, Pafos, Cyprus, 2023, 740–747. 10.1109/DCOSS-IoT58021.2023.00116

Kansakar, P., Munir, A., & Shabani, N. (2019). Technology in the Hospitality Industry: Prospects and Challenges. *IEEE Consumer Electronics Magazine*, *8*(3), 60–65. doi:10.1109/MCE.2019.2892245

Kaur, B. (2021). A Study of Barriers to Environmentally Sustainable Practices in Hotel Businesses in Punjab, India: Preliminary Findings. *Academica Turistica*, *14*(1), 71–86. doi:10.26493/2335-4194.14.71-86

Khanna, A., Sah, A., Choudhury, T., & Maheshwari, P. (2020). Blockchain Technology for Hospitality Industry. *Lecture Notes in Business Information Processing, 402*(November), 99–112. doi:10.1007/978-3-030-63396-7_7

Kontogianni, A., & Alepis, E. (2020). Smart tourism: State of the art and literature review for the last six years. *Array, 6*(September 2019), 100020. doi:10.1016/j.array.2020.100020

Laura, S. D., Verma, R., Ph, D., Clough, R., Gilman, G., Practices, E., & Llp, G. (2010). *How Travelers Use Online and Social Media Channels to Make Hotel-choice Decisions, 10*(11).

Lukanova, G., & Ilieva, G. (2019). Robots, artifiial intelligence, and service automation in hotels. In Robots, Artificial Intelligence and Service Automation in Travel, Tourism and Hospitality. Emerald. doi:10.1108/978-1-78756-687-320191009

Mariani, M., & Baggio, R. (2022). Big data and analytics in hospitality and tourism: A systematic literature review. *International Journal of Contemporary Hospitality Management, 34*(1), 231–278. doi:10.1108/IJCHM-03-2021-0301

Marinakis, V., & Doukas, H. (2018). An advanced IoT-based system for intelligent energy management in buildings. *Sensors (Basel), 18*(2), 610. doi:10.3390/s18020610 PMID:29462957

Mastercard. (2021). *Mastercard New Payments Index: Consumer Appetite for Digital Payments Takes Off.* Mastercard. https://www.mastercard.com/news/latin-america/en/newsroom/press-releases/pr-en/2021/may/mastercard-new-payments-index-consumer-appetite-for-digital-payments-takes-off/

Mccarty, K., & Orientale, P. (2010). Technology & Hospitality. *HOSTEUR, 19*(1), 1–43.

McKinsey & Company. (2020). The COVID-19 recovery will be digital: A plan for the first 90 days. McKinsey & Company.

Mensah, I., & Blankson, E. J. (2014). Commitment to Environmental Management in Hotels in Accra. *International Journal of Hospitality & Tourism Administration, 15*(2), 150–171. doi:10.1080/15256480.2014.901064

National Restaurant Association. (2022). *High-tech hospitality*. NRA. https://restaurant.org/education-and-resources/resource-library/high-tech-hospitality/

Nayyar, A., Mahapatra, B., Le, D. N., & Suseendran, G. (2018). Virtual Reality (VR) & Augmented Reality (AR) technologies for tourism and hospitality industry. *International Journal of Engineering and Technology(UAE)*, *7*(2), 156–160. doi:10.14419/ijet.v7i2.21.11858

Nwokorie, E. C., & Igbojekwe, P. (2019). Security challenges for the hotel industry. In Academica Turistica-Tourism and Innovation Journal.

Özkul, E., & Kumlu, S. T.ÖZKUL. (2019). Augmented Reality Applications in Tourism. *International Journal of Contemporary Tourism Research*, *3*, 107–122. doi:10.30625/ijctr.625192

Popescul, D., Diana, L., & Alexandru, R. (2016). Data Security in Smart Cities: Challenges and Solutions. *Informações Econômicas*, *20*(1), 29–38. doi:10.12948/issn14531305/20.1.2016.03

ShabaniN. (2017). *A study of cyber security in hospitality industry- threats and countermeasures: case study in Reno, Nevada* (Issue April). University of South Florida Sarasota. http://arxiv.org/abs/1705.02749

Shabani, N., & Munir, A. (2020). A Review of Cyber Security Issues in Hospitality Industry. *Advances in Intelligent Systems and Computing*, *1230 AISC*(July), 482–493. doi:10.1007/978-3-030-52243-8_35

Sigala, M. (2020). Tourism and COVID-19: Impacts and implications for advancing and resetting industry and research. *Journal of Business Research*, *117*(June), 312–321. doi:10.1016/j.jbusres.2020.06.015 PMID:32546875

Singh, A. (2023). *How Remote Work is Reshaping the Future of Tourism*. LinkedIn. https://www.linkedin.com/pulse/how-remote-work-reshaping-future-tourism-aastha-singh/

Spita, M., Peitzika, E., & Chatzi, S. (2020). Social media adoption among small and medium-sized Greek hotels: A survey about its antecedents and its impact on performance outcomes. *International Journal of Decision Sciences. Risk Management*, *9*(1/2), 23. doi:10.1504/IJDSRM.2020.110144

Statista. (2023). *Mobile payments in the United States - statistics & facts*. Statista. https://www.statista.com/topics/982/mobile-payments/#topicOverview

Stephen, C., & Barth, D. S. B. (2017). *Hospitality Law: Managing Legal Issues in the Hospitality Industry*. John Wiley & Sons, Ltd. https://books.google.co.in/books?hl=en&lr=&id=Z5VFEAAAQBAJ&oi=fnd&pg=PR13&dq=Data+Protection+and+Privacy+in+the+Hospitality+Industry&ots=RH_flR0pZ3&sig=layJuMY7zsqwPsCcrBj3VC-zGvc#v=onepage&q=Data Protection and Privacy in the Hospitality Industry&f=false

Swan, M. (2015). *Blockchain: Blueprint for a new economy*. O'Reilly Media, Inc. https://books.google.co.in/books?hl=en&lr=&id=RHJmBgAAQBAJ&oi=fnd&pg=PR3&dq=Blockchain:+Blueprint+for

Tan, D. R. (1999). Personal Privacy in the Information Age: Comparison of Internet Data Protection Regulations in the United Stats and European Union. *Loyola of Los Angeles International and Comparative Law Journal*, *21*(4), 661–684. http://heinonlinebackup.com/hol-cgi-bin/get_pdf.cgi?handle=hein.journals/loyint21&section=28

Tasatanattakool, P., & Techapanupreeda, C. (2018). Blockchain: Challenges and applications. *International Conference on Information Networking*, *24*(4), 473–475. 10.1109/ICOIN.2018.8343163

Vashi, S., Ram, J., Modi, J., Verma, S., & Prakash, C. (2017). Internet of Things (IoT): A vision, architectural elements, and security issues. *Proceedings of the International Conference on IoT in Social, Mobile, Analytics and Cloud, I-SMAC 2017, December*, (pp. 492–496). IEEE. 10.1109/I-SMAC.2017.8058399

VISA. (2022). *No TitleContactless payments witnessed a 6x growth in the last 3 years: Visa and Worldline India Whitepaper*. VISA. Https://Www.Visa.Co.In/About-Visa/Newsroom/Press-Releases/Contactless-Payments-Witnessed-A-6x-Growth-In-The-Last-3-Years-Visa-And-Worldline-India-Whitepaper.Html

Xiang, Z., Du, Q., Ma, Y., & Fan, W. (2017). A comparative analysis of major online review platforms: Implications for social media analytics in hospitality and tourism. *Tourism Management*, *58*(February), 51–65. doi:10.1016/j.tourman.2016.10.001

Zhang, H., Lu, Y., Gupta, S., & Zhao, L. (2014). What motivates customers to participate in social commerce? the impact of technological environments and virtual customer experiences. *Information & Management*, *51*(8), 1017–1030. doi:10.1016/j.im.2014.07.005

Zhou, J., Cao, Z., Dong, X., & Vasilakos, A. V. (2017). Security and Privacy for Cloud-Based IoT: Challenges. *IEEE Communications Magazine*, *55*(1), 26–33. doi:10.1109/MCOM.2017.1600363CM

Zohar, A. (2015). Bitcoin: Under the hood. *Communications of the ACM*, *58*(9), 104–113. doi:10.1145/2701411

## KEY TERMS AND DEFINITIONS

**Big Data:** Big data is large, complex, and diverse sets of data that keep on growing exponentially over time. Traditional data management systems are not compatible with storing, process, and analysing big data due to their large volume and complexity.

**Blockchains:** Blockchain derived its name from the way it stores the data in blocks which altogether form a chain. The blockchains grow with the number of transactions. Blocks also record the time and sequence of transactions. The data is stored across many computers to mitigate the chances of altering the records. Alteration will not work till the time the alteration is made in all the subsequent blocks.

**Concierge Services in Hotel:** A Concierge is a professional who is the first point of contact between guests and an organization. They answer inquiries, direct phone calls, and coordinate travel plans; in short, they work to make sure that every guest feels welcomed while always maintaining company culture.

**Internet of Things (IoT):** IoT is the network of physical devices that relate to sensors, software, and other technologies to connect and exchange data. Examples include gadgets connected to Alexa and control of electricity in a guest room with a key card.

**LEED-:** Leadership in Energy and Environmental Design (LEED) is the world's most widely used green building rating system. LEED certification is trustworthy for efficient, healthy, and cost-effective green buildings.

**Machine learning (ML):** ML is a branch of Artificial Intelligence (AI) that helps machines to learn from the collected data and past experiences. In ML, machines make predictions recognizing the similar pattern from the data.

**Robust data encryption protocols- these are secure and reliable methods of encoding data to protect it from unauthorized access or interception. They typically involve complex mathematical algorithms and encryption keys to encode the data:** making it unreadable without the appropriate decryption key. Robust encryption protocols are designed to withstand various types of attacks and provide a high level of security to safeguard sensitive information from potential threats and breaches.

# Chapter 13
# Artificial Intelligence in Human Resource Management in Hotels:
## A Qualitative Approach

**Partho Pratim Seal**
https://orcid.org/0000-0001-6867-8713
*Manipal Academy of Higher Education, India*

**Parul Gupta**
https://orcid.org/0009-0009-5709-817X
*Manipal Academy of Higher Education, India*

## ABSTRACT

*The advance in technology has influenced human beings and artificial intelligence (AI) is most discussed considering the similarity of human-like thinking process. AI has become inevitable in the hospitality industry both for the customers and the employees. Human resource management in hospitality has enormous challenges including high turnover rate, recruitment and retention, training, and development of the employees. A considerable gap is found between the expectations and the reality of artificial intelligence in human resource management. The study aims to find how human resource managers in hospitality effectively use artificial intelligence in their regular operations and in the well-being of the employees. The study takes a qualitative research approach to state how artificial intelligence is incorporated into regular functions of hospitality human resources and its impact on the organization. The findings of the study will state how AI will assist in redefining the role of hospitality human resources management in enhancing their efficiency and agility.*

DOI: 10.4018/979-8-3693-1978-9.ch013

## INTRODUCTION

In the era of digital technology adopting artificial intelligence (AI) has been essential as it provides new opportunities and challenges to all industries including hospitality. Researchers have defined AI differently, but commonly it is "stated to be a machine that performs tasks of humans or acts like human intelligence" (Jiang et al. 2018). AI is transforming the way individuals experience their lives, jobs, transportation, and interactions with big data, machine learning, mobile technology, the Internet of Things, geotagging, virtual reality, speech recognition, and biometrics which have been part of the Fourth Industrial Revolution (4IR) (Azadeh et al., 2018; Shank et al., 2019). AI-based solutions are sufficiently intelligent to entirely replace human tasks while enhancing the speed and precision of transactions. The leading hotels of the world have adopted AI as it enhances their operation in many ways (Zhou, 2019) which allows the guests to have a more innovative and memorable experience. Some of the hotels have adopted chatbot-based voice recognition systems that control the room temperature, and schedule and manage reservations and concierge services (Alexsoft, 2018). AI in hotels uses a facial recognition system for guest check-in and room check-in (Biron, 2019). AI uses analytics which leads to customer profiling for customized individual services, optimization of room occupancy, and energy consumption (Escobar, 2019). Other than strategic purpose AI provides several advantages which include cost reduction, an increase in efficiency, and an increase in revenue (Ransbotham et al., 2017). There is also uncertainty on the impact of AI which may bring in negative consequences. The most notable impact that AI can bring is the effect on the jobs that may replace people (Belanche et al., 2019).

Organizations that embrace data-centric and digital cultures rely on AI to innovate business models, transform processes, disrupt, and achieve competitive advantage (Ransbotham et al., 2020). AI's widespread implementation in the hospitality and tourism sector marks a pivotal phase in its digital evolution, holding significant promise for intelligent automation (Buhalis et al., 2019). AI in hospitality and tourism is used for planning, analysis, promotion, and service (Doborjeh et al., 2022). The hospitality industry is in a competitive environment with a saturation of new technologies and is also challenged by increasing costs. An organisation's success is dependent upon the ability of its employees, so it must be managed effectively by providing high-quality services, improving productivity leading to the profitability of the organisation. Hospitality, a labor-intensive industry must effectively utilize human resources to provide a competitive advantage to the hotel.

Human Resource Management (HRM) practices in an organisation do manage human resources to ascertain that the resources are utilized to meet the organisational objectives (Wright and Snell,1991). The HRM practices attract, develop, motivate, and retain employees so that the organisation and its members survives. The HRM practices include recruitment, selection, training and development and retention of employees in an organisation. Currently, HRM landscape is being dynamically redesigned by innovative technologies (Ancarani et al., 2019). Globally, HRM is undergoing a revolution in which administrative tasks are being replaced by more value-added activities. AI is now commonly used in HRM departments in various organisations due to the robust provision of information technology (IT) and the evolution of this knowledge. It is a trend that AI is being used by businesses and organisations across all industries and departments for which human resources department is not an exception when it comes to using AI. The application of AI has altered the various facets of human resource management, including hiring, employee management, and engagement (Sahoo & Mishra, 2023). The use of AI in HRM and recruiting has given rise to what is known as "the new age of HR," since it has replaced mundane duties previously carried out by human recruiters in the recruitment process (Upadhyay & Khandelwal, 2018). Traditional recruitment involves more than just considering a candidate's professional qualifications; appearance, words, deeds, attire, and so on, all affect the interview's objectivity and accuracy. In spite of using the most professional and authoritative quality evaluation model, some enterprises still select people who are not suitable for their organization, which results in recruitment failures. The use of artificial intelligence will extend beyond human resources into the fields of psychology, behavior, and so on in the future. AI-based algorithms and intelligent learning tools are available for evaluating candidates more directly and objectively, finding the best candidates, and evaluating the candidates during the quality evaluation process. Furthermore, AI can screen resumes quickly and match personnel based on their qualifications, eliminating prejudice, discrimination, and emotional factors (Jiang, et al. 2018). Numerous management and regular HRM jobs are being automated as AI and other cutting-edge technologies are used more widely (Larivière, et al. 2017). AI is changing the several roles that HRM plays. AI apps are a useful tool for managing several HRM operations, including training and development, performance management, procurement, selection, and employee engagement (Kovach, et al. 1999). The study discuss about how hospitality chain properties in India have adopted AI in HRM .

## LITERATURE REVIEW

The digital transformation of human resource management has been noted to be facilitated by advancements in the fields of information communication and technology .The use of AI technologies to support HR-related activities, functions, and procedures produced a new environment that led to the redesign of new resource management process workflows and related organisational consequences.

Innovative and cutting-edge technology are fundamentally redefining human resource management (Ancarani et al., 2019). Despite acting differently from humans, AI can simulate or imitate intelligent behaviours relevant to those of humans (Bhave et al., 2020). Machine learning and deep learning are among the research areas around AI applications in the workplace and can be applied to industries worldwide (Bhave et al., 2020). Aside from job replacement and human-AI collaboration, AI research in HRM encompasses training, decision-making, and recruiting within the arena of AI. Over the last five years, there has been a rise in AI scholarship in human resource management (HRM) (Budhwar et al., 2022; Edwards et al., 2022; Malik, Budhwar, & Kazmi, 2022; Chowdhury et al., 2023). For example, recent research has highlighted the advantages of using AI-based machine learning (ML) technologies to foster diversity (Daugherty et al., 2018), expanding the use of bots to improve the working environment for employees (Malik, Budhwar, Patel, & Srikanth, 2022), employee recruitment (Pan et al., 2022), aspects affecting HRM managers' adoption of AI (Suseno et al., 2022), the way AI is affecting job roles, duties, tasks, and the significance of work (Wilson et al., 2017). A recent review outlines how AI can facilitate HR analytics (Margherita, 2022), as well as its potential impacts on HRM processes (Pereira et al., 2023). According to Qamar and Samad (2021), several studies have demonstrated that HR analytics improve organizational performance. As HR professionals use HR analytics increasingly often around the world, they can make evidence-based and data-driven decisions instead of depending just on gut feelings. There is also evidence that it may result in unprofessional management decisions (Xue et al., 2022).

The usage of AI in HRM is in the initial stages (Sheila et al. 2018) with increasing interest. Past studies have also highlighted that IT has transformed the HR process (Nicastro, 2020). The usage of AI in HRM recruitment is the key area where many organizations have begun using AI as the organizations find important, measurable, and rapid responses that reduce the hiring time, raise recruiters' productivity, and improve the experience of the interviewees (Zeng, 2020). AI can also be useful in the selection process as it can scan, access, and shortlist prospective employees at a faster pace (Wislow, 2017). The selection process is enhanced by AI as it can analyse experience, skills, performance, and turnover rates while shortlisting candidates (Sithambaram & Tajudeen 2022). HRM does face an uphill task not only for recruitment but also for retaining employees as past studies state that 57 percent of organisations do consider retaining employees a laborious task (Ruby & Jayam, 2018). AI can also help in understanding individuals' outstanding values and performance and assist in career progression (Sindu, 2018).

Though AI has a lot of benefits for an organization, small or large but it still faces several challenges when it comes to its adoption. A survey conducted by McKinsey (2019), found that inadequate strategy formulation and execution, lack of skilled human resources, insufficient infrastructure, and a lack of data availability are the most significant challenges for acquiring and implementing AI. According to Tambe et al. (2019), there are four main obstacles to the use of AI for HRM: the intricacy of the HR phenomenon; limited data; ethical considerations; and employee resistance to the use of AI. Cubric (2020) study found that business organizations are still facing challenges related to economic, technological, and social factors in adopting of AI. The adoption of AI is being hampered also by a lack of knowledge about the technology, which calls for the establishment of appropriate goals, the determination of key performance metrics, and the monitoring of return on investment (Polachowska, 2019). AI-driven decision-making cannot be adopted blindly as this may lead to impersonal service and less human interaction.

Human resource differentiates itself from other departments where AI is used considering the complexity of HR roles and outcomes. HR is also criticized for metrics used for performance appraisal, their reliability and validity, and bias (Schoorman,1998). Many a time it becomes difficult to differentiate an individual's performance from group's performance. Considering the uncertainty of performance evaluations by humans AI can be trained for HRM by various AI algorithm which can scale up the arbitrary or outright discriminations due to human decisions(Tambe et al,2019).

For HR operations the tasks include the hiring process and other tasks which also involve a large amount of money. The Table1 lists the common tasks of HR along with the corresponding prediction tasks which are part of workforce analytics and are related to Human Resource life cycle (Tambe et al,2019)

*Table 1. The human resources life cycle*

| HumanResources Functions | Prediction Task |
|---|---|
| Recruitment | Identifying appropriate prospective employees |
| Selection | Offering a job to the right prospective employee |
| Training | Are proper interventions made for individuals to enhance their performance |
| Growth & Advancement | How will they perform in their senior roles |
| Retention | If we can know who will likely leave thereby |

Recruitment systems ease organisation and assist in saving the expenditure. Past research studies (Dickson & Nusair, 2010) state that usage of AI in recruitment process helps organisation to reach larger number of candidates with less paperwork and also assists to retrieve data even from social media sites thereby getting easy access to the values, attitude and personality traits. With AI recruiters can examine the personality traits before the job interview is conducted (Faliagka et al.2012) . AI also ensures that it is unbiased and provides equal opportunities to its applicants (Upadhyay & Khandelwal, 2018). Implementation of AI for manpower needs in hotel departments may reduce the staffing and free the staff for important task and create new job opportunities. The benefits obtained from AI is numerous along with potential savings and if not implemented may also lead to being behind the competitors. For the selection process, the examining of resumes is paramount as it involves identifying the necessary skills, experience, and qualifications for positions. Predictive analysis relies on historical data and AI algorithms to forecast successful candidates. AI can also conduct automated interviews via chatbots and virtual platforms, emphasizing applicants' skills and experience without human biases. AI can support the training and development of employees as employees' resumes could be electronically saved and an electronic inventory be maintained. It can also help to track skill shortages and develop personalized learning paths. AI algorithms can suggest appropriate learning resources, courses, and modules based on an employee's position, skill deficiencies, and career goals. AI can recommend training according to an individual's advancement to ensure the best possible learning journey for every employee based on an individual's progress. Further, it could also suggest online or virtual training which could be benefitted by both employees and the organisation. AI also assists HR managers in assessing training effectiveness and in decision-making about employees' competency including their emotional and intellectual aptitudes thereby assigning the right employees to the position as per their talent. The performance management tool enabled with AI can assist both employees and organisations in assessing and career advancement. A fuzzy multi-attribute decision making tool can identify employees who require necessary improvements and also the magnitude of improvement (Manoharan et al.,2011). The performance management tool can assist managers by providing employees with additional training and talent enhancement for career progression. AI can be effective in retaining employees as it can combine big data with machine learning along with a human touch. An organisation depending upon AI for retention of employees should balance between the technology and human role. With the availability of AI platforms the HRM team could analyse data from past and present employees to have insights into the factors that lead to the attrition of employees including job satisfaction, balancing work life, and career progression.

## METHODOLOGY

A qualitative approach was adopted for the study in which semi-structured interviews were held. Although exploratory the study aims to understand how human resource departments in hotels use AI in their operations. A total of 15 respondents from chain hotels both domestic and international brands located in major cities of India were considered. The respondents had at least 2 years of experience in HR in a supervisory or managerial role. After the design of the interview questions was prepared consent was obtained from all the respondents via e-mail before the telephonic interview was conducted. The personal information including telephone number and e-mail was kept confidential by the authors. The other details of the respondents and hotels is presented in Table - 2.

The interview questions were designed considering the roles the respondents had in the human resource department and their experience in working with AI in hotels. It takes into consideration what functions in HRM are used by the hotels to implement AI software and why? It also takes into consideration how various features of AI are used by the human resource department in a hotel. The interviews were conducted and then transcribed between August and September 2023. All interviews were conducted by telephone as traveling to all destinations was not feasible for the researchers. Each telephonic interview lasted between 30 to 45 minutes. The data obtained was analyzed by thematic analysis where the data was narrowed by coding the interviews and then categorized further into themes. To ensure the reliability and consistency of data adequate interviews were conducted considering that similar responses will be obtained. The process was conducted till the responses obtained reached a saturation point. All the respondent's points were considered and the outcome was reported.

*Table 2. Hotel and respondent background*

| Sl no | Hotel | Classification | City | Brand (Domestic/ International) | No of Rooms | Role of Interviewee | Years of Experience |
|---|---|---|---|---|---|---|---|
| 1 | H 1 | 5 Star | New Delhi | International | 240 | HR Executive | 3 yrs |
| 2 | H 2 | 5 Star | Gurgaon | International | 126 | HR Sr Manager | 5 yrs |
| 3 | H 3 | 5 Star | New Delhi | International | 270 | HR Executive | 2 yrs |
| 4 | H 4 | 4 Star | Noida | Domestic | 174 | HR Sr Manager | 6 yrs |
| 5 | H 5 | 4 Star | Mumbai | International | 207 | HR Executive | 2 yrs |
| 6 | H 6 | 5 Star | Mumbai | International | 170 | HR Sr Manager | 7 yrs |
| 7 | H 7 | 4 Star | Lucknow | International | 115 | HR Sr Manager | 5 yrs |
| 8 | H 8 | 5 Star | Jaipur | Domestic | 95 | HR Asst Manager | 7 yrs |
| 9 | H 9 | 5 Star | Bengaluru | International | 244 | HR Manager | 8 yrs |
| 10 | H10 | S Star | Hyderabad | Domestic | 167 | HR Executive | 3 yrs |
| 11 | H 11 | 5 Star | Bengaluru | International | 177 | HR Executive | 2 yrs |
| 12 | H 12 | 5 Star | Chennai | International | 210 | HR Sr Manager | 7yrs |
| 13 | H 13 | 5 Star | Pune | International | 138 | HR Executive | 2 yrs |
| 14 | H 14 | 4 Star | Kolkata | International | 175 | HR Asst Manager | 8yrs |
| 15 | H 15 | 5 Star | Kolkata | Domestic | 194 | HR Manager | 10 yrs |

## DATA ANALYSIS AND FINDINGS

The results show that hotels in India are using AI sparingly in HRM. The human resource managers of hotels stated that they believe AI will be used in recruitment, selection, training, advancement, and retention. It is been found that all 15 respondents were aware of AI in HRM and some have also been trained in the AI software but have not implemented it in their respective hotels.

### Recruitment

The data analysis of the 15 hotels on using of AI in recruitment process in HRM stated that only 10 hotels have trained their hotel staff for usage of AI in the recruitment process while 5 hotels have yet to train the employees though the employees said that they are aware of usage of AI. The 10 hotels where the staff were trained stated that they were aware that AI could help in screening a suitable applicant, assessing the applicant, and conducting the interview of the applicant. As the technology is new most of the managers are hesitant to use AI in the recruitment process.

" It is a boon for us as hotels in India have very high employee turnover and matching the resume with the job needs many times become tedious as man hours are used in to do it which AI can help to do faster. (H2, H3 stated it while H4, H5, H6, H7, H10, H11, H12, H13 also agreed for the same)

## Selection

During the selection process, the respondents were eager to use AI as all 15 respondents conveyed that the selection process involved many checkpoints with levels of evaluations for which AI could be the best path.

"As selection occurs after many levels of screening process AI could fasten the process with less human intervention. Although most of the respondents want to use AI but also stated without human intervention the selection may not be appropriate. (Mentioned by H4 an H12 and supported by H7)

## Training

On training, all the respondents stated that it was a Hercules task to identify the training needs of the staff though they felt that AI could at least reduce the gap. 13 of the 15 respondents stated that having an opportunity to use AI for training will make their work more focussed.

'Hotel employees work in various departments with different skills and knowledge and also differ in their retaining of training programs. The AI-generated training schedule will be appropriate for hospitality' (H2, H4, and H6 supported by H9 and H15).

## Advancement

Though all the 15 respondents when enquired regarding the usage of AI in career advancement were impressed none of them had an opportunity to use the same. Some respondents even believed that the AI application of performance ratings, skills, and experience matching for progression could be better than the human managers.

'Managers sometimes overlook the employee's experience and skills but AI can monitor the performance and accurately suggest the career path of all employees working in different operation departments by matching with the position available in the hotel' (H5, H9, H12, supported by H15)

## Retention

Turnover is a teething issue for HR managers as 12 of the 15 managers said that employees at all levels were not stable at a property. The respondents also stated that many times long working hours were also the trigger for employee departure.

' AI will monitor employee work patterns and understand their burnout and engagement. This will assist the managers in predicting employee dissatisfaction while suggesting remedial steps to minimize the turnover' (H1, H3, H5, H7 H9, supported by H12, H13, H14)

## DISCUSSION AND CONCLUSION

The findings from the current study state that in the Indian context AI tools have yet to be used in recruitment, selection, training, advancement, and retention. Some of the HR managers did admit that AI could help shortlist resumes from a pool and this can help HR select the right candidate in a short period. As the hospitality industry has a very high turnover it will be very helpful in identifying suitable candidates for a hotel. The findings derived from the study show that the usage of AI in hotels in the Indian context is still in its early stages though the importance of is understood, the acceptance of using AI in HRM in hotels must traverse longer.

Though AI has evolved as an inevitable technology in our lives the study findings do conclude that HRM practices with AI will have a positive influence on hotels though the usage of AI in HRM in hotels in India is rare. The outcome of the study does contribute to the literature that the usage of AI in HRM in hotels is still in the early stages as it relatively new perspective.

A research studies has its limitations, since though the authors used a structured qualitative research approach the findings may be restricted to the sample studied. Future studies may be replicated with more respondents and a wider representation of locations regarding AI adoption in the HRM of hotels. Longitudinal studies could also be conducted to provide considerable insights into the adoption of AI in HRM over a time frame.

## REFERENCES

Altexsoft. (2018). How the hospitality industry uses performance-enhancing artificial intelligence and data science. Altexsoft. https://www. altexsoft.com/blog/datascience/how-the-hospitality-industry-uses-performance-enhancing-artificial-intelligence-and-data-science/.

Ancarani, A., Di Mauro, C., & Mascali, F. (2019). Backshoring strategy and the adoption of Industry 4.0: Evidence from Europe. *Journal of World Business*, *54*(4), 360–371. doi:10.1016/j.jwb.2019.04.003

Azadeh, A., Yazdanparast, R., Abdolhossein Zadeh, S., & Keramati, A. (2018). An intelligent algorithm for optimising emergency department job and patient satisfaction. *International Journal of Health Care Quality Assurance*, *31*(5), 374–390. doi:10.1108/IJHCQA-06-2016-0086 PMID:29865961

Belanche, D., Casalo, L. V., Flavin, C., & Schepers, J. (2019). Service robot implementation: A theoretical framework and research agenda. *Service Industries Journal*.

Bhave, D. P., Teo, L. H., & Dalal, R. S. (2020). Privacy at work: A review and a research agenda for a contested terrain. *Journal of Management*, *46*(1), 127–164. doi:10.1177/0149206319878254

Budhwar, P., Malik, A., De Silva, M. T., & Thevisuthan, P. (2022). Artificial intelligence–challenges and opportunities for international HRM: A review and research agenda. *International Journal of Human Resource Management*, *33*(6), 1065–1097. doi:10.1080/09585192.2022.2035161

Buhalis, D., Harwood, T., Bogicevic, V., Viglia, G., Beldona, S., & Hofacker, C. (2019). Technological disruptions in services: Lessons from tourism and hospitality. *Journal of Service Management*, *30*(4), 484–506. doi:10.1108/JOSM-12-2018-0398

Chowdhury, S., Dey, P., Joel-Edgar, S., Bhattacharya, S., Rodriguez-Espindola, O., Abadie, A., & Truong, L. (2023). Unlocking the value of artificial intelligence in human resource management through AI capability framework. *Human Resource Management Review*, *33*(1), 100899. doi:10.1016/j.hrmr.2022.100899

Cubric, M. (2020). Drivers, barriers and social considerations for AI adoption in business and management: A tertiary study. *Technology in Society*, *101257*, 101257. doi:10.1016/j.techsoc.2020.101257

Daugherty, P. R., Wilson, H. J., & Chowdhury, R. (2018). Using artificial intelligence to promote diversity. *MIT Sloan Management Review Magazine*. https://sloanreview.mit.edu/article/using-artificial-intelligence-to-promote-diversity/

Doborjeh, Z., Hemmington, N., Doborjeh, M., & Kasabov, N. (2022). Artificial intelligence: A systematic review of methods and applications in hospitality and tourism. *International Journal of Contemporary Hospitality Management*, *34*(3), 1154–1176. doi:10.1108/IJCHM-06-2021-0767

Edwards, M. R., Charlwood, A., Guenole, N., & Marler, J. (2022). HR analytics: An emerging field finding its place in the world alongside simmering ethical challenges. *Human Resource Management Journal*, 1748-8583.12435. doi:10.1111/1748-8583.12435

Escobar, M. C. (2019). *IHG CEO discusses company's progress on loyalty, Concerto*. Hospitality Technology. https:// hospitalitytech.com/ihg-ceo-discusses-companys-progress-loyalty- concerto

Jiang, F., Du, C., Fu, T., & Xiao, R. (2018). Research on the application intelligence in human resource management. The *4th Annual 2018 International Conference on Management Science and Engineering (MSE2018)*. Francis Academic Press. https:// doi.org/ 10.25236/mse.2018.054

Kovach, K. A., & Cathcart, C. E. Jr. (1999). Human resource information systems (HRIS): Providing business with rapid data access, information exchange and strategic advantage. *Public Personnel Management*, *28*(2), 275–282. doi:10.1177/009102609902800208

Larivière, B., Bowen, D., Andreassen, T. W., Kunz, W., Sirianni, N. J., Voss, C., Wünderlich, N. V., & De Keyser, A. (2017). "Service Encounter 2.0": An investigation into the roles of technology, employees and customers. *Journal of Business Research*, *79*, 238–246. doi:10.1016/j.jbusres.2017.03.008

Malik, A., Budhwar, P., Patel, C., & Srikanth, N. R. (2022). May the bots be with you! Delivering HR cost-effectiveness and individualised employee experiences in an MNE. *International Journal of Human Resource Management*, *33*(6), 1148–1178. doi:10.1080/09585192.2020.1859582

Malik, A., Budhwar, P., & Srikanth, N. R. (2020). Gig economy, 4IR and artificial intelligence: Rethinking strategic HRM. In *Human & technological resource management (HTRM): New insights into revolution 4.0* (pp. 75–88). Emerald Publishing Limited. doi:10.1108/978-1-83867-223-220201005

Manoharan, T. R., Muralidharan, C., & Deshmukh, S. G. (2011). An integrated fuzzy multi-attribute decision-making model for employees' performance appraisal. *International Journal of Human Resource Management*, *22*(3), 722–745. doi:10.1 080/09585192.2011.543763

Margherita, A. (2022). Human resources analytics: A systematization of research topics and directions for future research. *Human Resource Management Review*, *32*(2), 100795. doi:10.1016/j.hrmr.2020.100795

McGovern, S. L., Pandey, V., Gill, S., Aldrich, T., Myers, C., Desai, C., & Balasubramanian, V. (2018). The new age: artificial intelligence for human resource opportunities and functions. Ey. com.

McKinsey. (2019). *How Artificial Intelligence will transform Nordic businesses.* McKinsey. https://www.mckinsey.com/featured-insights/artificial-intelligence/how-artificial-intelligence-will-transform-nordic-businesses

Nicastro, D. (2020). 7 ways artificial intelligence is reinventing Human Resources. *Digital workplace.* https://www.cmswire.com/digital-workplace/7-ways-artificial-intelligence-is-reinventing-human-resources/

Pan, Y., Froese, F., Liu, N., Hu, Y., & Ye, M. (2022). The adoption of artificial intelligence in employee recruitment: The influence of contextual factors. *International Journal of Human Resource Management, 33*(6), 1125–1147. doi:10.1080/09585192.2021.1879206

Pereira, V., Hadjielias, E., Christofi, M., & Vrontis, D. (2023). A systematic literature review on the impact of artificial intelligence on workplace outcomes: A multi-process perspective. *Human Resource Management Review, 33*(1), 100857. doi:10.1016/j.hrmr.2021.100857

Polachowska, K. (2019). *12 challenges of AI adoption.* Neoteric. https://neoteric.eu/blog/12-challenges-of-ai-adoption/

Qamar, Y., & Samad, T. A. (2022). Human resource analytics: A review and bibliometric analysis. *Personnel Review, 51*(1), 251–283. doi:10.1108/PR-04-2020-0247

Ransbotham, S., Khodabandeh, S., Kiron, D., Candelon, F., Chu, M., & LaFountain, B. (2020). *Expanding AI's impact with organizational learning.* MIT Sloan Management Review and Boston Consulting Group.

Ransbotham, S., Kiron, D., & Reeves, M. (2017). Research Report: Reshaping business with artificial intelligence. *MIT Sloan Management Review*, 1–17.

Sahoo, M., & Mishra, S. (2023). A Bibliometric Analysis of Artificial Intelligence and Human Resource Management. In *International Conference on ICT for Sustainable Development,* (pp. 33-40). Singapore: Springer Nature Singapore. 10.1007/978-981-99-5652-4_4

Schoorman, F. D. (1988). Escalation Bias in Performance Appraisals: An Unintended Consequence of Supervisor Participation in Hiring Decisions. *The Journal of Applied Psychology, 73*(1), 58–62. doi:10.1037/0021-9010.73.1.58

Shank, D. B., Graves, C., Gott, A., Gamez, P., & Rodriguez, S. (2019). Feeling our way to machine minds: People's emotions when perceiving mind in artificial intelligence. *Computers in Human Behavior, 98*, 256–266. doi:10.1016/j.chb.2019.04.001

Sithambaram, R. A., & Tajudeen, F. P. (2023). Impact of artificial intelligence in human resource management: A qualitative study in the Malaysian context. *Asia Pacific Journal of Human Resources, 61*(4), 821–844. doi:10.1111/1744-7941.12356

Suseno, Y., Chang, C., Hudik, M., & Fang, E. S. (2022). Beliefs, anxiety and change readiness for artificial intelligence adoption among human resource managers: The moderating role of high-performance work systems. *International Journal of Human Resource Management, 33*(6), 1209–1236. doi:10.1080/09585192.2021.1931408

Tambe, P., Cappelli, P., & Yakubovich, V. (2019). Artificial Intelligence in Human Resources Management: Challenges and a Path Forward. *California Management Review, 61*(4), 15–42. doi:10.1177/0008125619867910

Upadhyay, A. K., & Khandelwal, K. (2018). Applying artificial intelligence: Implications for recruitment. *Strategic HR Review, 17*(5), 255–258. doi:10.1108/SHR-07-2018-0051

Wilson, H. J., Daugherty, P., & Bianzino, N. (2017). The jobs that artificial intelligence will create. *MIT Sloan Management Review, 58*(4), 14. http://mitsmr.com/2odREFJ

Wright, P. M., & Snell, S. A. (1991). Toward an Integrative View of Strategic Human Resource Management. *Human Resource Management Review, 1*(3), 203–225. doi:10.1016/1053-4822(91)90015-5

Xue, M., Cao, X., Feng, X., Gu, B., & Zhang, Y. (2022). Is college education less necessary with AI? Evidence from firm-level labor structure changes. *Journal of Management Information Systems, 39*(3), 865–905. doi:10.1080/07421222.2022.2096542

Zeng, H. (2020). Adaptability of artificial intelligence in human resources management in this era. *International Journal of Sciences, 7*(1), 271–276.

Zhou, W. (2019). The impact of AI on the hospitality industry. *Towards Data Science.* https://towardsdatascience.com/the-impact-of -ai-on-the hospitality-industry-8ba7adb66be

# Chapter 14
# Implication of Artificial Intelligence in Hospitality Marketing

**Iva Rani Das**
https://orcid.org/0009-0006-9805-4331
*Daffodil Institute of IT, Bangladesh*

**Mohammad Badruddoza Talukder**
https://orcid.org/0000-0001-7788-2732
*Daffodil Institute of IT, Bangladesh*

**Sanjeev Kumar**
https://orcid.org/0000-0002-7375-7341
*Lovely Professional University, India*

## ABSTRACT

*The chapter investigates the impact of artificial intelligence (AI) on marketing strategies in the hospitality industry. It discusses how AI technologies like machine learning, natural language processing, and computer vision have transformed customer interactions. The chapter emphasizes the importance of AI in learning and adapting to customer behavior and standards, highlighting its significant role in the industry. This chapter explores the practical applications of AI in the hospitality industry, highlighting its potential in creating unique customer profiles and providing personalized tips. Predictive analytics reveals AI's ability to anticipate vacation patterns and enable dynamic pricing, enabling businesses to adapt to market changes. The chapter emphasizes the marketing significance of augmented and virtual reality, highlighting their potential to provide immersive experiences and influence customer decisions through virtual tours. The chapter concludes by highlighting the industry's progress in AI and the need for further research.*

DOI: 10.4018/979-8-3693-1978-9.ch014

## INTRODUCTION

Currently, the tourism and hotel sectors are undergoing a significant juncture. We are witnessing the dawn of a new era characterized by groundbreaking advancements and enhanced productivity, closely intertwined with the evolving capabilities of artificial intelligence (AI). The profound impact of AI technologies on marketing strategies—revolutionizing how businesses engage with customers, manage their operations, and make critical strategic decisions—is propelling this fundamental shift. According to research done by Sandeep et al. (2022), AI plays a more significant role in how people connect with brands, how businesses run, and how they make strategic decisions. This indicates that it plays a pivotal role in the industry's evolution. This chapter will thoroughly analyze the significant consequences of implementing AI-powered marketing tactics. It will be used for many things, like natural language processing, machine learning, chatbots, virtual helpers, predictive analytics, and the immersive worlds of augmented and virtual reality (Sayers et al., 2021).

Customers' desires for more interactive and tailored experiences have recently shifted significantly. Consequently, enterprises in the tourism industry must devise intelligent solutions to cope with these changes effectively. Rosário & Dias (2023) argue that AI is increasingly crucial in meeting evolving customer demands since it offers data-driven insights. Artificial intelligence (AI) is imperative in enhancing customer satisfaction and loyalty because it can expedite booking processes, offer predictive analytics-based anticipatory services, and generate customized recommendations. This introduction examines the potential impact of AI adoption on operational efficiency, cost-effectiveness, and strategic decision-making. It demonstrates how technology can align with company objectives (H. Li et al., 2021).

However, there are specific intrinsic obstacles to incorporating AI. Considerable challenges include worries about privacy and ethics and the necessity for companies to implement significant adjustments to stay up with the constantly evolving technology landscape (Talukder et al., 2023). This chapter aims to provide readers with a comprehensive understanding of the opportunities, challenges, and potential future trajectories that the hospitality industry may face in the era of artificial intelligence. It delves into the intricate network of outcomes associated with AI-driven marketing strategies. As we embark on this comprehensive examination, our primary goal is to offer insights beyond the immediate challenges, enabling enterprises to fully harness the potential of AI while addressing the ethical and operational considerations inherent in this transformative journey.

## OBJECTIVES

1. Assess the Impact of AI on Customer-Centric Experiences
2. Examine Operational and Ethical Implications of AI Adoption

## LITERATURE REVIEW

### The Rise of AI in Hospitality Marketing

Integrating Artificial Intelligence (AI) with the dynamic field of Hospitality marketing signifies remarkable and unparalleled change (Bulchand-Gidumal et al., 2023). As AI technologies advance, they become deeply integrated into the industry, transforming established models and bringing innovative approaches to attract customers, optimize operations, and guide strategic decision-making. The rise of AI in hospitality marketing is looked at in this study, which shows how it has changed the customer experience, operational efficiency, and the industry's general direction (Kumar et al., 2024).

### Evolution of AI Technologies

Artificial Intelligence (AI) is revolutionizing Hospitality marketing by fundamentally changing existing methods and presenting innovative solutions to industry obstacles. The advancement of AI technologies, such as machine learning, natural language processing (NLP), and computer vision, has been crucial in bringing about this significant change in perspective. Machine learning, a branch of artificial intelligence, has progressed from its early beginnings to advanced algorithms that can acquire knowledge from data and adjust to changing trends in the hospitality industry (Talukder & Hossain, 2020). This evolution is highly significant as it enables firms to utilize predictive analytics for forecasting client preferences and market trends. Utilizing machine learning in demand forecasting allows organizations to optimize inventory and services, resulting in a more agile and customized strategy to suit the needs of a constantly changing market.

The field of Natural Language Processing (NLP) has experienced substantial progress, augmenting its capacity to comprehend and manipulate human language. Within the Hospitality industry, this entails the utilization of advanced chatbots and virtual assistants that can interact with clients in a more conversational and contextually aware manner. Natural Language Processing (NLP) systems have become essential for delivering smooth customer service, facilitating booking procedures, and improving the overall user experience (Chiny et al., 2021). Computer vision, a fundamental aspect of artificial intelligence, has successfully addressed the distinctive obstacles in the field by facilitating visual marketing techniques. This progress is apparent in incorporating augmented reality (AR) and virtual reality (VR) apps for fully immersive destination experiences. Using computer vision, enterprises can provide virtual tours and simulations, enabling prospective tourists to investigate places before making judgments, consequently impacting their choices (Filieri et al., 2021). In conclusion, the progress of AI technologies in the Hospitality sector has seen machine learning, natural language processing, and computer vision adapt to the industry's specific demands. These technologies have advanced in complexity and have been applied practically to improve consumer experiences, optimize operations, and offer creative marketing solutions.

## The Changing Landscape of Customer Behavior

Amidst the substantial transformation of the hospitality business, it is crucial to comprehend and adjust to the changing patterns of client behavior. This section explores the analysis of changing consumer expectations and behaviors, emphasizing artificial intelligence's (AI) crucial role in understanding and adapting to these changes. The emergence of online platforms, social media, and mobile technology has given consumers unparalleled access to information, resulting in a discriminating and dynamic clientele in the Hospitality industry (Talukder, 2020b). Riaz et al. (2021) assert that an increasing desire for individualized and streamlined experiences distinguishes the abovementioned shifts in consumer behavior. Modern travelers desire more than a simple exchange; they strongly desire personalized suggestions, engaging encounters, and immediate, attentive assistance.

AI technologies, specifically machine learning and natural language processing, have become essential in understanding and addressing these changing consumer demands. Machine learning algorithms process large datasets to detect trends and preferences, allowing firms to provide customized suggestions for vacation destinations, lodgings, and activities (Guerra-Montenegro et al., 2021). This degree of customization corresponds to the aspiration for distinctive and customized encounters, augmenting client contentment and allegiance. Natural Language Processing (NLP) enhances firms' ability to adjust to evolving consumer habits. Chatbots and virtual assistants, which utilize natural language processing (NLP), have become essential in delivering round-the-clock customer service, managing questions, and streamlining booking procedures. These conversational interfaces, powered by artificial intelligence, are designed to accommodate the desire for immediate and easily accessible communication, thereby addressing the requirements of contemporary travelers (Buhalis & Moldavska, 2022).

To summarize, consumers' evolving behavior in the Hospitality industry is marked by a need for customized, smooth, and engaging experiences (Talukder, 2021). Through machine learning and natural language processing, AI has become essential to understanding and acting on these changes. Companies that utilize artificial intelligence (AI) have a strategic advantage in meeting the changing demands of clients. They may provide customized services and experiences that strongly appeal to modern travelers.

## AI-Driven Customer Personalization

AI-Driven Customer Personalization utilizes Artificial Intelligence (AI) technology, including machine learning and data analytics, to examine customer data and generate customized experiences. By analyzing large datasets, organizations can gain insights into individual preferences, which allows them to provide personalized services, recommendations, and interactions. Within sectors such as Hospitality, AI algorithms utilize predictive capabilities to anticipate and address customer behaviors, providing tailored trip suggestions, hotel choices, and activity recommendations (Lee et al., 2021). This strategy improves consumer pleasure, engagement, and loyalty by offering distinctive, focused experiences.

### Data-Driven Insights

As data-driven insights shape the Hospitality sector, organizations may improve consumer experiences, manage operations, and make strategic decisions. In a day when massive volumes of data are generated at every touchpoint, utilizing this information is critical for being competitive and responsive to changing passenger needs (Malik, 2023). Data-driven insights rely on applying sophisticated analytics tools and methodologies to extract significant patterns, trends, and correlations from various datasets. These observations are crucial for comprehending customer inclinations, actions, and market fluctuations within the tourism sector. Businesses can customize marketing campaigns and services by analyzing booking trends, reviews, and demographics (Chandra et al., 2022).

An exemplary utilization of data-driven insights lies in developing customized consumer profiles. By combining and analyzing data from multiple sources, organizations can create extensive consumer profiles for hyper-personalized suggestions, targeted marketing, and a more customized experience. Such customization amplifies customer contentment and cultivates brand allegiance and favorable word-of-mouth(Suo & Huang, 2023). Also, data-based ideas are constructive for making operational processes run more smoothly. By utilizing data, businesses may optimize workflows, minimize expenses, and enhance overall efficiency across several areas, such as resource allocation, inventory management, and predictive maintenance. Data analytics gives decision-makers a holistic view of market trends, letting them proactively adjust plans to changing consumer habits and industry dynamics. Data-driven insights are essential for hospitality success. Utilizing data analytics capabilities enables firms to comprehend their customers better, optimize processes, and maintain flexibility in a rapidly changing sector (Barlette & Baillette, 2022). As technology advances, the capacity to collect and interpret data will be a significant difference for hospitality organizations.

## Personalized Recommendations

In hospitality, personalized suggestions have become a game-changing strategy that improves each person's travel experience. With the help of advanced artificial intelligence and data analytics, organizations may explore extensive databases to identify distinct customer preferences, behaviors, and patterns (Verma et al., 2021). This level of comprehension enables the development of very tailored suggestions encompassing diverse aspects of travel, such as lodging, experiences, food, and additional options.

By utilizing these technologies, organizations can surpass routine offerings by providing travelers customized recommendations that harmoniously correspond to their preferences and needs. Whether it is proposing boutique hotels to a tourist who prefers intimate settings or adventurous activities to a thrill-seeker, personalized recommendations increase consumer engagement and pleasure. This individualized approach helps passengers make more informed decisions and fosters a sense of connection and devotion to the business (Cichy et al., 2021). Adopting personalized recommendations signifies a purposeful transition towards customer-centricity, recognizing the varied interests of contemporary travelers. As the industry increasingly adopts these technologies, personalized recommendations demonstrate the effectiveness of data-driven insights in providing highly tailored and unforgettable experiences in the tourist and hospitality sector.

## Chatbots and Virtual Assistants

Chatbots and virtual assistants are artificial intelligence (AI) systems that utilize natural language processing to interact with users. Chatbots are usually text- or voice-based programs that act as they chat with users while giving them information or helping them with their work (Rapp et al., 2021). Virtual assistants, in contrast, are highly advanced artificial intelligence entities capable of carrying out diverse duties, including responding to inquiries, performing commands, and even adapting to user preferences through machine learning. Both technologies strive to improve user experiences by providing efficient and interactive assistance in diverse applications, including customer service, information retrieval, and job automation.

## 24/7 Customer Support

In the ever-changing domain of hospitality, offering round-the-clock customer care has emerged as a crucial element in providing outstanding service. Recognizing the broad and often unpredictable nature of travel, organizations in the industry have adopted 24-hour customer service as a critical component of their commitment to passenger happiness. Utilizing developments in artificial intelligence and chatbot technologies, this continuous support model guarantees that travelers will obtain prompt assistance, direction, and resolution to any inquiries or problems, regardless of the time (Code & No, 2022).

The importance of round-the-clock customer care goes beyond resolving immediate concerns; it plays a role in establishing trust and improving the overall customer experience (Kamal & Himel, 2023). When a traveler needs help with a reservation, local information, or aid amid unanticipated events, having ongoing support available makes them feel safe and dependable. This dedication to accessibility is in line with the changing expectations of contemporary travelers, who demand effortless and immediate support during their trips. Using technology-based solutions, companies improve their operational performance and show that they care about their customers(Chi, 2021). A proactive approach to fulfilling the many demands of travelers and guaranteeing a satisfying and comforting experience at every point of their trip, round-the-clock customer service is becoming a strategic differentiation as the industry changes.

## Enhancing Booking Processes

The evolution of booking processes within the Hospitality sector has been significantly influenced by the integration of artificial intelligence (AI), transforming how travelers engage with services. Leveraging AI-driven virtual assistants, businesses can provide a seamless and efficient booking experience. These intelligent systems, powered by natural language processing and machine learning, offer real-time responses to customer inquiries, guiding users through the booking journey with unprecedented responsiveness and personalization.

As Sann et al. (2022) highlighted, implementing predictive analytics further enhances the booking process by anticipating and meeting customer preferences. Businesses can offer tailored recommendations by analyzing historical data and user behaviors, making decision-making more intuitive and efficient. Additionally, the automation capabilities of AI streamline various aspects of the booking process, reducing manual interventions and minimizing errors, as noted by (Boute et al., 2022). Incorporating AI in booking processes increases operational efficiency and caters to the growing demand for personalized and swift interactions in the modern travel landscape. As travelers increasingly prioritize convenience, businesses that harness the capabilities of AI to enhance booking processes position themselves as innovators in delivering a customer-centric approach.

## PREDICTIVE ANALYTICS FOR DEMAND FORECASTING

The integration of predictive analytics has emerged as a pivotal strategy in the Hospitality sector, revolutionizing demand forecasting and optimizing resource allocation. As elucidated by Bharatiya (2023), predictive analytics leverages advanced algorithms and data modeling to analyze historical patterns, user behaviors, and external factors, providing businesses with actionable insights into future demand trends. This proactive approach enables organizations to anticipate fluctuations in demand, optimize pricing strategies, and allocate resources effectively to meet the evolving needs of travelers. By harnessing the power of predictive analytics, businesses can go beyond reactive decision-making, adopting a more strategic and forward-looking stance (Feng et al., 2021). For instance, hotels can dynamically adjust room rates based on anticipated demand during peak periods, enhancing revenue optimization.

Similarly, travel agencies can tailor promotional campaigns in alignment with predicted high-demand periods, ensuring targeted marketing efforts. In conclusion, incorporating predictive analytics for demand forecasting in the Hospitality sector represents a transformative paradigm shift. Businesses embracing this technology gain a competitive edge by responding to current market dynamics and proactively shaping strategies to meet future demand, enhancing operational efficiency and overall performance (Allioui & Mourdi, 2023).

### Anticipating Travel Trends

AI and predictive analytics are pivotal in enabling businesses to anticipate travel trends and forecast demand patterns within the Hospitality sector. These technologies leverage historical data, user behaviors, and external factors to identify patterns and trends, providing insights into future travel preferences and demand fluctuations. Canhoto et al. (2021) emphasize the dynamic capabilities of predictive analytics in their research, showcasing how businesses can proactively align their services and offerings with emerging travel trends. Industry case studies demonstrate successful applications, illustrating how predictive analytics empowers businesses to make data-driven decisions, optimize resource allocation, and stay ahead of evolving customer expectations.

### Dynamic Pricing Strategies

Dynamic pricing strategies have become instrumental in the Hospitality sector, reshaping how businesses optimize revenue in response to varying market conditions. As Niaz (2022) discussed, this innovative approach involves real-time price adjustment based on dynamic factors such as demand patterns, seasonality, and external events. By leveraging artificial intelligence and predictive analytics, businesses can dynamically adapt pricing to maximize revenue during peak periods, capitalize on sudden increases in demand, and stay competitive during off-peak times. This flexibility ensures that pricing aligns with current market dynamics, allowing businesses to allocate resources and meet the fluctuating demands of travelers efficiently.

Dynamic pricing enhances revenue management and benefits consumers by enabling more competitive pricing and tailored offerings (Talón-Ballestero et al., 2022). It represents a strategic shift from static pricing models, providing businesses with the agility needed to navigate the dynamic landscape of the tourism industry. In conclusion, dynamic pricing strategies, driven by advanced technologies, are pivotal for businesses seeking to optimize revenue and maintain competitiveness in the ever-evolving landscape of Hospitality.

## AUGMENTED REALITY (AR) AND VIRTUAL REALITY (VR) IN MARKETING

The integration of Augmented Reality (AR) and Virtual Reality (VR) in marketing has ushered in a new era of immersive and engaging experiences within the Hospitality sector. As Thaduri (2021) highlighted, AR and VR technologies enable businesses to create interactive and visually compelling marketing campaigns. AR enhances the real-world environment by overlaying digital information, offering travelers interactive experiences like virtual city tours or on-site information about landmarks. On the other hand, VR immerses users in virtual environments, allowing them to explore accommodations, destinations, or experiences before making travel decisions.

These technologies not only captivate the attention of potential customers but also contribute to informed decision-making. For instance, virtual hotel tours provide a realistic preview of accommodations, influencing booking choices. AR-powered mobile apps offer on-the-go information, enhancing the exploration of destinations

(Mathioudakis et al., 2021). The adoption of AR and VR in marketing strategies signifies a transformative approach, bringing destinations and experiences closer to consumers in ways previously unimaginable.

### Immersive Marketing Experiences

Leveraging Augmented Reality (AR) and Virtual Reality (VR) in immersive marketing campaigns is a cutting-edge strategy that transforms customer engagement (Cordero Alvarez, 2022). AR seamlessly integrates Digital content into the real world, while VR creates fully immersive simulated environments. In the context of pre-travel experiences, these technologies redefine customer interactions with destinations and services. For instance, AR may enable customers to virtually visualize their accommodation or experience local attractions, enhancing anticipation. As highlighted by McLean & Barhorst (2022), VR can immerse customers in virtual travel scenarios, providing a taste of destinations before the actual journey. Examples include AR-enhanced travel brochures and VR-powered pre-travel experiences, contributing to heightened customer excitement and involvement in travel planning.

### Virtual Tours and Destination Marketing

Virtual Reality (VR) for virtual destination tours and marketing is revolutionizing the travel industry (Oncioiu & Priescu, 2022). VR lets customers virtually explore destinations, hotels, and attractions, offering a realistic preview of what to expect. This immersive experience profoundly influences customer decision-making and the overall travel experience. As discussed by X. Li et al. (2021), VR-powered virtual tours provide customers with a more comprehensive understanding of destinations, influencing their preferences and choices. The impact goes beyond mere visualization; it shapes perceptions, instills confidence, and contributes to a more informed and satisfying travel decision. The integration of VR in destination marketing is a powerful tool for engaging customers, enhancing their connection with potential travel experiences, and influencing their choices.

## CASE STUDIES

### Marriott's AI-Powered Customer Engagement

Marriott's implementation of AI for personalized marketing and guest services showcases a pioneering approach to enhancing customer engagement. By leveraging AI technologies, Marriott can analyze vast customer data to gain insights into individual preferences, behaviors, and booking patterns (Štilić et al., 2023). This enables the hotel chain to offer highly personalized marketing messages, tailor promotions, and anticipate guests' needs. The utilization of AI in guest services further enhances the overall experience by providing instant responses to inquiries, offering personalized recommendations, and ensuring a seamless and customized stay. While specific details may vary, studies such as those by Manser Payne et al. (2021)highlight the broad implementation of AI in the hospitality sector, emphasizing its dynamic capabilities in transforming customer engagement and service delivery.

### Airbnb's Dynamic Pricing Algorithm

Airbnb's dynamic pricing algorithm is a prime example of how AI is harnessed to optimize pricing strategies based on demand and supply dynamics. The platform utilizes sophisticated machine learning algorithms to analyze various factors, including location, time of year, local events, and user behavior, to adjust property prices dynamically. This ensures that prices align with market demand, maximizing revenue for hosts while offering competitive rates to users(Lähteenmäki, 2021). Airbnb's approach to dynamic pricing is a strategic use of AI in the sharing economy, balancing the satisfaction of both hosts and guests. While specific details of Airbnb's algorithm are proprietary, the broader concept aligns with research on dynamic pricing strategies in the hospitality industry, as Grewal et al. (2021) discussed, emphasizing AI's role in adapting pricing models for optimal profitability.

## FUTURE TRENDS AND CHALLENGES

Looking ahead, the landscape of AI-powered marketing in the Hospitality sector is poised for dynamic shifts, bringing forth both promising trends and substantial challenges.

### Emerging AI Technologies

The future of Hospitality marketing is on the brink of transformative advancements with the emergence of cutting-edge AI technologies. As Al-Surmi et al. (2022) highlight, the continuous evolution of artificial intelligence is expected to revolutionize customer engagement, operational efficiency, and strategic decision-making within the industry. Innovations in machine learning algorithms are anticipated to enable more sophisticated and accurate predictions, enhancing the personalization of customer experiences. Natural language processing enhancements will refine chatbots and virtual assistants, enabling more seamless and context-aware interactions.

Additionally, integrating blockchain technology may introduce unprecedented levels of transparency and security in data management, addressing concerns related to privacy and trust (Yaqoob et al., 2021). These emerging technologies hold the potential to redefine marketing strategies in the Hospitality sector. For instance, advanced machine learning algorithms can analyze vast datasets to offer more precise recommendations, virtual assistants may become more adept at understanding and responding to nuanced customer inquiries, and blockchain can instill greater confidence in the security of customer data. As the industry progresses, staying abreast of these emerging AI technologies will be essential for businesses to remain competitive and innovative in delivering unparalleled experiences to travelers.

## Overcoming Implementation Challenges

Integrating AI-powered marketing in the Hospitality sector is challenging, necessitating a strategic approach to overcome implementation hurdles. As elucidated by Cheng et al. (2021), a key challenge lies in the ethical considerations surrounding AI applications, including privacy, data security, and algorithmic bias. Implementing robust ethical frameworks and compliance measures becomes imperative to build and maintain customer trust, ensuring responsible and transparent use of AI technologies.

Furthermore, organizational readiness and the availability of a skilled workforce present challenges. Adapting to rapid technological advancements requires businesses to invest in employee training and development, as highlighted by Talukder (2023). Creating a culture that embraces AI technologies and fostering interdisciplinary collaboration between technologists and marketers are crucial steps in overcoming the human-centric challenges associated with AI implementation. Addressing these challenges requires a holistic approach that combines technological solutions, ethical considerations, and organizational adaptability. By acknowledging and actively working to overcome these challenges, businesses can unlock the full potential of AI in marketing, creating a symbiotic relationship between technology and human expertise.

*Figure 1. Implication of AI-powered marketing strategies in the hospitality sector* *(Author's Compilation)*

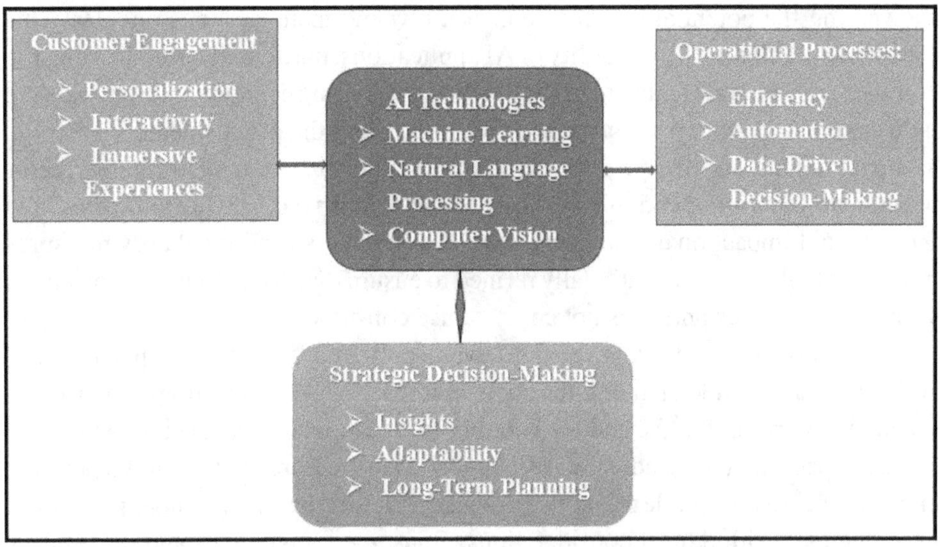


## CONCLUSION AND FUTURE RESEARCH

In conclusion, integrating AI-powered marketing strategies into the Hospitality sector marks a transformative juncture, reshaping the industry's landscape regarding customer engagement, operational efficiency, and strategic decision-making. The case studies of Marriott and Airbnb offer glimpses into the potential benefits of AI, demonstrating its capacity to enhance personalization, optimize services, and refine revenue strategies. As businesses in the sector navigate this paradigm shift, it is crucial to recognize and address the associated challenges.

Marriott's implementation of AI for customer engagement illustrates the potential for personalization in the hospitality sector. Using AI technologies like machine learning and natural language processing, Marriott can analyze vast datasets to understand individual preferences, booking behaviors, and guest expectations. This results in tailored marketing messages, personalized promotions, and anticipatory guest services. The real-time nature of AI allows Marriott to create a dynamic and responsive customer experience, fostering loyalty and satisfaction. This case study exemplifies the tangible benefits that AI can bring to customer-centric businesses within the industry.

Similarly, Airbnb's dynamic pricing algorithm showcases the strategic use of AI to optimize revenue. Using machine learning algorithms, Airbnb adjusts pricing based on demand, supply, and various contextual factors. This ensures hosts maximize their revenue during peak periods and provides users competitive and flexible pricing. The algorithmic approach allows Airbnb to adapt swiftly to market fluctuations, showcasing the potential for AI to enhance revenue management strategies. This case study highlights the versatility of AI applications, particularly in addressing the complex and dynamic nature of pricing within the sharing economy. However, as the industry embraces these transformative technologies, ethical considerations emerge as a paramount concern. AI's responsible and ethical use in the Hospitality sector necessitates careful attention to issues such as data privacy, algorithmic bias, and the potential impact on employment. Ethical frameworks and regulatory measures must be established and continually refined to ensure that AI implementation aligns with societal values and does not compromise consumer trust.

Future research endeavors should delve deeply into the ethical implications of AI in the sector. Understanding the societal impact of AI applications, uncovering potential algorithm biases, and formulating frameworks for responsible AI use are critical aspects that demand scholarly attention. This research strand aims to address current concerns and guide the industry toward a future where AI technologies coexist harmoniously with ethical considerations. Consumer perceptions and preferences regarding AI-driven experiences represent another crucial area for future investigation. Unraveling these nuances can provide invaluable insights into tailoring AI applications to meet and exceed consumer expectations, enhancing overall satisfaction. Effective human-AI collaboration models within organizational structures constitute another avenue for exploration. Understanding how employees can work synergistically with AI technologies, leveraging human intuition and machine precision strengths, is pivotal for fostering a workplace culture that embraces innovation while preserving the human touch. Adapting marketing and operational strategies to the evolving landscape of AI technologies remains a perpetual challenge. Future research should focus on identifying adaptive strategies that enable businesses to stay ahead of emerging AI technologies, ensuring that their marketing approaches align seamlessly with the capabilities and potentials offered by these innovations.

Lastly, the impact of regulatory frameworks on ensuring responsible AI practices within the hospitality sector is an area ripe for exploration. Assessing the effectiveness of existing regulations, identifying gaps, and proposing enhancements will contribute to the establishment of a robust regulatory environment that balances innovation with consumer protection. Therefore, integrating AI in the Hospitality sector represents both a promise and a challenge. While the case studies of Marriott and Airbnb showcase the transformative potential, the industry must navigate ethical considerations, understand consumer perceptions, foster effective human-AI collaboration, adapt strategies, and ensure a regulatory framework that promotes responsible AI practices. This multifaceted research agenda will guide the sector toward a future where AI enhances customer experiences while upholding ethical and societal standards.

## REFERENCES

Al-Surmi, A., Bashiri, M., & Koliousis, I. (2022). AI-based decision making: Combining strategies to improve operational performance. *International Journal of Production Research, 60*(14), 4464–4486. doi:10.1080/00207543.2021.1966540

Allioui, H., & Mourdi, Y. (2023). Unleashing the potential of AI: Investigating cutting-edge technologies that are transforming businesses. [IJCEDS]. *International Journal of Computer Engineering and Data Science, 3*(2), 1–12.

Barlette, Y., & Baillette, P. (2022). Big data analytics in turbulent contexts: Towards organizational change for enhanced agility. *Production Planning and Control, 33*(2–3), 105–122. doi:10.1080/09537287.2020.1810755

Bharadiya, J. P. (2023). The role of machine learning in transforming business intelligence. *International Journal of Computing and Artificial Intelligence, 4*(1), 16–24. doi:10.33545/27076571.2023.v4.i1a.60

Boute, R. N., Gijsbrechts, J., & Van Mieghem, J. A. (2022). Digital lean operations: Smart automation and artificial intelligence in financial services. *Innovative Technology at the Interface of Finance and Operations, I*, 175–188. doi:10.1007/978-3-030-75729-8_6

Buhalis, D., & Moldavska, I. (2022). Voice assistants in hospitality: Using artificial intelligence for customer service. *Journal of Hospitality and Tourism Technology, 13*(3), 386–403. doi:10.1108/JHTT-03-2021-0104

Bulchand-Gidumal, J., William Secin, E., O'Connor, P., & Buhalis, D. (2023). Artificial intelligence's impact on hospitality and tourism marketing: Exploring key themes and addressing challenges. *Current Issues in Tourism*, 1–18. doi:10.1080/13683500.2023.2229480

Buzzacchi, L., Milone, F. L., Paolucci, E., & Raguseo, E. (2023). How to react to a shock? Effects of Airbnb hosts' choices and market segmentation at the time of Covid-19. *Information & Management, 60*(7), 103857. doi:10.1016/j.im.2023.103857

Canhoto, A. I., Quinton, S., Pera, R., Molinillo, S., & Simkin, L. (2021). Digital strategy aligning in SMEs: A dynamic capabilities perspective. *The Journal of Strategic Information Systems, 30*(3), 101682. doi:10.1016/j.jsis.2021.101682

Chandra, S., Verma, S., Lim, W. M., Kumar, S., & Donthu, N. (2022). Personalization in personalized marketing: Trends and ways forward. *Psychology and Marketing*, *39*(8), 1529–1562. doi:10.1002/mar.21670

Cheng, L., Varshney, K. R., & Liu, H. (2021). Socially responsible ai algorithms: Issues, purposes, and challenges. *Journal of Artificial Intelligence Research*, *71*, 1137–1181. doi:10.1613/jair.1.12814

Chi, N. T. K. (2021). Innovation capability: The impact of e-CRM and COVID-19 risk perception. *Technology in Society*, *67*, 101725. doi:10.1016/j.techsoc.2021.101725

Chiny, M., Bencharef, O., Hadi, M. Y., & Chihab, Y. (2021). A client-centric evaluation system to evaluate guest's satisfaction on AirBNB using machine learning and NLP. *Applied Computational Intelligence and Soft Computing*, *2021*, 1–14. doi:10.1155/2021/6675790

Cichy, P., Salge, T. O., & Kohli, R. (2021). PRIVACY CONCERNS AND DATA SHARING IN THE INTERNET OF THINGS: MIXED METHODS EVIDENCE FROM CONNECTED CARS. *Management Information Systems Quarterly*, *45*(4), 1863–1892. doi:10.25300/MISQ/2021/14165

Code, I., & No, T. (2022). [AI]. *Artificial Intelligence*.

Cordero Alvarez, J. A. (2022). *An investigation into how marketers use Virtual Reality (VR) technology to enhance consumer interaction*. National College of Ireland.

Feng, C., Patel, P. C., & Fay, S. (2021). The value of the structural power of the chief information officer in enhancing forward-looking firm performance. *Journal of Management Information Systems*, *38*(3), 765–797. doi:10.1080/07421222.2021.1962599

Filieri, R., Lin, Z., Pino, G., Alguezaui, S., & Inversini, A. (2021). The role of visual cues in eWOM on consumers' behavioral intention and decisions. *Journal of Business Research*, *135*, 663–675. doi:10.1016/j.jbusres.2021.06.055

Grewal, D., Gauri, D. K., Roggeveen, A. L., & Sethuraman, R. (2021). Strategizing retailing in the new technology era. *Journal of Retailing*, *97*(1), 6–12. doi:10.1016/j.jretai.2021.02.004

Guerra-Montenegro, J., Sanchez-Medina, J., Lana, I., Sanchez-Rodriguez, D., Alonso-Gonzalez, I., & Del Ser, J. (2021). Computational intelligence in the hospitality industry: A systematic literature review and a prospect of challenges. *Applied Soft Computing*, *102*, 107082. doi:10.1016/j.asoc.2021.107082

Jiang, N., Liu, X., Liu, H., Lim, E. T. K., Tan, C.-W., & Gu, J. (2023). Beyond AI-powered context-aware services: The role of human–AI collaboration. *Industrial Management & Data Systems*, *123*(11), 2771–2802. doi:10.1108/IMDS-03-2022-0152

Kamal, M., & Himel, A. S. (2023). Redefining Modern Marketing: An Analysis of AI and NLP's Influence on Consumer Engagement, Strategy, and Beyond. *Eigenpub Review of Science and Technology*, *7*(1), 203–223.

Kumar, S., Talukder, M. B., Kabir, F., & Kaiser, F. (2024). Challenges and Sustainability of Green Finance in the Tourism Industry: Evidence From Bangladesh. In Sustainable Investments in Green Finance (pp. 97-111). IGI Global. doi:10.4018/979-8-3693-1388-6.ch006

Lähteenmäki, J. (2021). The evolution paths of neutral host businesses: Antecedents, strategies, and business models. *Telecommunications Policy*, *45*(10), 102201. doi:10.1016/j.telpol.2021.102201

Lee, M., Kwon, W., & Back, K.-J. (2021). Artificial intelligence for hospitality big data analytics: Developing a prediction model of restaurant review helpfulness for customer decision-making. *International Journal of Contemporary Hospitality Management*, *33*(6), 2117–2136. doi:10.1108/IJCHM-06-2020-0587

Li, H., Wu, Y., Cao, D., & Wang, Y. (2021). Organizational mindfulness towards digital transformation as a prerequisite of information processing capability to achieve market agility. *Journal of Business Research*, *122*, 700–712. doi:10.1016/j.jbusres.2019.10.036

Li, X., Gong, J., Gao, B., & Yuan, P. (2021). Impacts of COVID-19 on tourists' destination preferences: Evidence from China. *Annals of Tourism Research*, *90*, 103258. doi:10.1016/j.annals.2021.103258 PMID:34924648

Malik, D. (2023). Practical lessons from implementing a data-driven approach to passenger flow optimisation and airport capacity management. *Journal of Airport Management*, *17*(3), 218–235.

Manser Payne, E. H., Dahl, A. J., & Peltier, J. (2021). Digital servitization value co-creation framework for AI services: A research agenda for digital transformation in financial service ecosystems. *Journal of Research in Interactive Marketing*, *15*(2), 200–222. doi:10.1108/JRIM-12-2020-0252

Mathioudakis, G., Klironomos, I., Partarakis, N., Papadaki, E., Anifantis, N., Antona, M., & Stephanidis, C. (2021). Supporting Online and On-Site Digital Diverse Travels. *Heritage*, *4*(4), 4558–4577. doi:10.3390/heritage4040251

McLean, G., & Barhorst, J. B. (2022). Living the experience before you go... but did it meet expectations? The role of virtual reality during hotel bookings. *Journal of Travel Research, 61*(6), 1233–1251. doi:10.1177/00472875211028313

Mikołajczyk, K. (2022). Changes in the approach to employee development in organisations as a result of the COVID-19 pandemic. *European Journal of Training and Development, 46*(5/6), 544–562. doi:10.1108/EJTD-12-2020-0171

Niaz, M. (2022). Revolutionizing Inventory Planning: Harnessing Digital Supply Data through Digitization to Optimize Storage Efficiency Pre-and Post-Pandemic. *BULLET: Jurnal Multidisiplin Ilmu, 1*(03).

Oncioiu, I., & Priescu, I. (2022). The use of virtual reality in tourism destinations as a tool to develop tourist behavior perspective. *Sustainability (Basel), 14*(7), 4191. doi:10.3390/su14074191

Rapp, A., Curti, L., & Boldi, A. (2021). The human side of human-chatbot interaction: A systematic literature review of ten years of research on text-based chatbots. *International Journal of Human-Computer Studies, 151*, 102630. doi:10.1016/j.ijhcs.2021.102630

Riaz, H., Baig, U., Meidute-Kavaliauskiene, I., & Ahmed, H. (2021). Factors effecting omnichannel customer experience: Evidence from fashion retail. *Information (Basel), 13*(1), 12. doi:10.3390/info13010012

Rosário, A. T., & Dias, J. C. (2023). How has data-driven marketing evolved: Challenges and opportunities with emerging technologies. *International Journal of Information Management Data Insights, 3*(2), 100203. doi:10.1016/j.jjimei.2023.100203

Said, S. (2023). The Role of Artificial Intelligence (AI) and Data Analytics in Enhancing Guest Personalization in Hospitality. *Journal of Modern Hospitality, 2*(1), 1–13. doi:10.47941/jmh.1556

Sandeep, S. R., Ahamad, S., Saxena, D., Srivastava, K., Jaiswal, S., & Bora, A. (2022). To understand the relationship between Machine learning and Artificial intelligence in large and diversified business organisations. *Materials Today: Proceedings, 56*, 2082–2086. doi:10.1016/j.matpr.2021.11.409

Sann, R., Lai, P.-C., Liaw, S.-Y., & Chen, C.-T. (2022). Predicting online complaining behavior in the hospitality industry: Application of big data analytics to online reviews. *Sustainability (Basel), 14*(3), 1800. doi:10.3390/su14031800

Sayers, D., Sousa-Silva, R., Höhn, S., Ahmedi, L., Allkivi-Metsoja, K., Anastasiou, D., Beňuš, Š., Bowker, L., Bytyçi, E., & Catala, A. (2021). *The Dawn of the Human-Machine Era: A forecast of new and emerging language technologies.*

Şeker, F. (2023). Evolution of Machine Learning in Tourism: A Comprehensive Review of Seminal Research. *Journal of Artificial Intelligence and Data Science, 3*(2), 54–79.

Štilić, A., Nicić, M., & Puška, A. (2023). Check-in to the future: Exploring the impact of contemporary information technologies and artificial intelligence on the hotel industry. *Turističko Poslovanje, 31.*

Suo, L., & Huang, Y. (2023). Brand Authenticity and Consumers' Willingness to Recommend by Word-of-Mouth: The Mediating Effect of Brand Attachment. [Humanities and Social Sciences]. *Journal of Community Development Research, 16*(4), 73–90.

Talón-Ballestero, P., Nieto-García, M., & González-Serrano, L. (2022). The wheel of dynamic pricing: Towards open pricing and one to one pricing in hotel revenue management. *International Journal of Hospitality Management, 102*, 103184. doi:10.1016/j.ijhm.2022.103184

Talukder, M. B. (2020). An Appraisal of the Economic Outlook for the Tourism Industry, Specially Cox's Bazar in Bangladesh. *i-manager's Journal on Economics & Commerce, 2*(1), 23-35.

Talukder, M. B. (2020b). The Future of Culinary Tourism: An Emerging Dimension for the Tourism Industry of Bangladesh. I-Manager's. *Journal of Management, 15*(1), 27. doi:10.26634/jmgt.15.1.17181

Talukder, M. B. (2021). An assessment of the roles of the social network in the development of the Tourism Industry in Bangladesh. *International Journal of Business, Law, and Education*, 2(3), 85–93. doi:10.56442/ijble.v2i3.21

Talukder, M. B., & Hossain, M. M. (2021). Prospects of Future Tourism in Bangladesh: An Evaluative Study. I-Manager's. *Journal of Management, 15*(4), 1–8. doi:10.26634/jmgt.15.4.17495

Talukder, M. B., Kabir, F., Muhsina, K., & Das, I. R. (2023). Emerging Concepts of Artificial Intelligence in the Hotel Industry: A Conceptual Paper. *International Journal of Research Publication and Reviews, 4*(9), 1765–1769. doi:10.55248/gengpi.4.923.92451

Talukder, M. B., Kumar, S., Sood, K., & Grima, S. (2023). Information Technology, Food Service Quality and Restaurant Revisit Intention. *International Journal of Sustainable Development and Planning*, *18*(1), 295–303. doi:10.18280/ijsdp.180131

Thaduri, U. R. (2021). Virtual Reality & Artificial Intelligence in Real Estate Business: A Tool for Effective Marketing Campaigns. *Asian Journal of Applied Science and Engineering*, *10*(1), 56–65. doi:10.18034/ajase.v10i1.54

Verma, S., Sharma, R., Deb, S., & Maitra, D. (2021). Artificial intelligence in marketing: Systematic review and future research direction. *International Journal of Information Management Data Insights*, *1*(1), 100002. doi:10.1016/j.jjimei.2020.100002

Yaqoob, I., Salah, K., Jayaraman, R., & Al-Hammadi, Y. (2021). Blockchain for healthcare data management: Opportunities, challenges, and future recommendations. *Neural Computing & Applications*, 1–16.

# Compilation of References


(2020). Syakir Amir1, Nur'Hidayah Dura, Muhamad Asrah Yusof, Hitoshi Nakamura & Rahmat Abu Nong. (2020). Challenges of Smart Tourism in Malaysia Ecotourism Destinations. *Journal of the Malaysian Institute of Planners.*, *18*(4), 442–451.

Pine, B. J., & Gilmore, J. H. (1999). *The Experience Economy: Work is Theatre and Every Business a Stage*. Harvard Business School Press.

Abdul-Rahman, K. H., Shahidehpour, S. M., & Daneshdoost, M. (1995). AI APPROACH TO OPTIMAL VAR CONTROL WITH FUZZY REACTIVE LOADS. In 88 IEEE Transactions on Power Systems. IEEE.

Abdulwahid, A. H., Pattnaik, M., Palav, M. R., Babu, S. T., Manoharan, G., & Selvi, G. P. (2023, April). Library Management System Using Artificial Intelligence. In *2023 Eighth International Conference on Science Technology Engineering and Mathematics (ICONSTEM)* (pp. 1-7). IEEE.

Abumandil, M. S., Ekmeil, F. A., Younus, A. M., & Alkhawaja, M. I. (2022). Mobile Augmented Reality Elements and Social Media Usage on Smart Tourism in Penang: Malaysian. *ECS Transactions*, *107*(1), 10935–10943. doi:10.1149/10701.10935ecst

Abumandil, M. S., Halim, M. S., & Alshuaibi, A. S. (2020). Ibrahim, & Siam, M.I. (2020). Factors Affecting the Adoption of Smart Tourism App Study Among Tourism Stakeholders In Malaysia. *Journal of Critical Reviews*, *7*(02).

Abu-Taieh, E., AlHadid, I., Masa'deh, R., Alkhawaldeh, R. S., Khwaldeh, S., & Alrowwad, A. (2022). Factors Influencing YouTube as a Learning Tool and Its Influence on Academic Achievement in a Bilingual Environment Using Extended Information Adoption Model (IAM) with ML Prediction—Jordan Case Study. *Applied Sciences (Basel, Switzerland)*, *12*(12), 5856. doi:10.3390/app12125856

Adachi, R., Cramer, E. M., & Song, H. (2022). Using virtual reality for tourism marketing: A mediating role of self-presence. *The Social Science Journal*, *59*(4), 657–670. doi:10.1080/03623319.2020.1727245

Agrawal, A., Gans, J., & Goldfarb, A. (2019). *The economics of artificial intelligence : an agenda.*

Ahani, A., Nilashi, M., Ibrahim, O., Sanzogni, L., & Weaven, S. (2019). Market segmentation and travel choice prediction in Spa hotels through TripAdvisor's online reviews. *International Journal of Hospitality Management, 80*, 52–77. doi:10.1016/j.ijhm.2019.01.003

Ahaskar, A. (2020, July 10). Virtual tours over Zoom call keep tourists, guides happy amid COVID disruption. *Mint.* https://www.livemint.com/news/india/virtual-tours-over-zoom-call-keep-tourists-guides-happy-amid-covid-disruption-11594382679649.html

Al-Amri, R., Murugesan, R. K., Man, M., Abdulateef, A. F., Al-Sharafi, M. A., & Alkahtani, A. A. (2021). A review of machine learning and deep learning techniques for anomaly detection in iot data. In Applied Sciences (Switzerland). MDPI AG. doi:10.3390/app11125320

Alcañiz, M., Bigné, E., & Guixeres, J. (2019). Virtual Reality in Marketing: A Framework, Review, and Research Agenda. *Frontiers in Psychology, 10*, 1530. doi:10.3389/fpsyg.2019.01530 PMID:31333548

Allam, S. (2016). The Impact of Artificial Intelligence on Innovation - An Exploratory Analysis. *International Journal of Creative Research Thoughts, 4*(4), 810–814.

Allioui, H., & Mourdi, Y. (2023). Unleashing the potential of AI: Investigating cutting-edge technologies that are transforming businesses. [IJCEDS]. *International Journal of Computer Engineering and Data Science, 3*(2), 1–12.

Al-Safi, J. K. S., Bansal, A., Aarif, M., Almahairah, M. S. Z., Manoharan, G., & Alotoum, F. J. (2023). Assessment Based On IoT For Efficient Information Surveillance Regarding Harmful Strikes Upon Financial Collection. *2023 International Conference on Computer Communication and Informatics (ICCCI)*, Coimbatore, India. 10.1109/ICCCI56745.2023.10128500

Al-Surmi, A., Bashiri, M., & Koliousis, I. (2022). AI-based decision making: Combining strategies to improve operational performance. *International Journal of Production Research, 60*(14), 4464–4486. doi:10.1080/00207543.2021.1966540

Altexsoft. (2018). How the hospitality industry uses performance-enhancing artificial intelligence and data science. Altexsoft. https://www. altexsoft.com/blog/datascience/how-the-hospitality-industry-uses-performance-enhancing-artificial-intelligence-and-data-science/.

Analytics, F. (2023, March 17). 7 Ways smart technology is reshaping the hotel industry. *Flame Analytics.* https://flameanalytics.com/en/blog/7-ways-smart-technology-is-reshaping-the-hotel-industry/#:~:text=With%20smart%20EMS%2C%20hotel%20staff,a%20much%20more%20costly%20one

Ancarani, A., Di Mauro, C., & Mascali, F. (2019). Backshoring strategy and the adoption of Industry 4.0: Evidence from Europe. *Journal of World Business, 54*(4), 360–371. doi:10.1016/j.jwb.2019.04.003

Anurag. (2018). 4 Emerging trends of artificial intelligence in travel. *New Gen Apps.* www.newgenapps. com/blog/artificial-intelligence-in-travel-emerging-trends

Aslan, A., Altinoz, B., & Özsolak, B. (2021). The nexus between economic growth, tourism development, energy consumption, and CO 2 emissions in Mediterranean countries. *Environmental Science and Pollution Research International, 28*(3), 3243–3252. doi:10.1007/s11356-020-10667-6 PMID:32910404

Atembe, R. (2015, December). The Use of Smart Technology in Tourism: Evidence from Wearable Devices [Austria.]. *Journal of Tourism and Hospitality Management, 3*(11-12), 224–234.

Azadeh, A., Yazdanparast, R., Abdolhossein Zadeh, S., & Keramati, A. (2018). An intelligent algorithm for optimising emergency department job and patient satisfaction. *International Journal of Health Care Quality Assurance, 31*(5), 374–390. doi:10.1108/IJHCQA-06-2016-0086 PMID:29865961

Azis, N., Amin, M., Chan, S., & Aprilia, C. (2020). How smart tourism technologies affect tourist destination loyalty. *Journal of Hospitality and Tourism Technology, 11*(4), 603–625. doi:10.1108/JHTT-01-2020-0005

Azmi, A., & Ahmad, J. A. (2022, August). Developing Malaysia's Smart Community-Based Tourism Model. *Jurnal Intelek, 17*(2), 2022. doi:10.24191/ji.v17i2.18172

Babić Rosario, A., Sotgiu, F., De Valck, K., & Bijmolt, T. H. (2016). The effect of electronic word of mouth on sales: A meta-analytic review of platform, product, and metric factors. *JMR, Journal of Marketing Research, 53*(3), 297–318. doi:10.1509/jmr.14.0380

Bailenson, J. (2018). *Experience on Demand: What Virtual Reality Is, how it Works, and what it Can Do*. W. W. Norton & Company.

Baker, D. (2015). *Tourism and Terrorism: Terrorists Threats to Commercial Aviation Safety & Security*.

Bakici, T., Almirall, E., & Wareham, J. (2013). A smart city initiative: The case of Barcelona. *Journal of the Knowledge Economy, 4*(2), 135–148. doi:10.1007/s13132-012-0084-9

Balasubramanian, K., Kunasekaran, P., Konar, R., & Sakkthivel, A. M. (2022). Integration of Augmented Reality (AR) and Virtual Reality (VR) as Marketing Communications Channels in the Hospitality and Tourism Service Sector. In Marketing Communications and Brand Development in Emerging Markets Volume II: Insights for a Changing World (pp. 55-79). Cham: Springer International Publishing.

Barbosa, B., Saura, J. R., Zekan, S. B., & Ribeiro-Soriano, D. (2023). Defining content marketing and its influence on online user behavior: A data-driven prescriptive analytics method. *Annals of Operations Research*, 1–26. doi:10.1007/s10479-023-05261-1

Barlette, Y., & Baillette, P. (2022). Big data analytics in turbulent contexts: Towards organizational change for enhanced agility. *Production Planning and Control, 33*(2–3), 105–122. doi:10.1080/09537287.2020.1810755

Basha, M. J., Vijayakumar, S., Jayashankari, J., Alawadi, A. H., & Durdona, P. (2023). Advancements in Natural Language Processing for Text Understanding. *E3S Web of Conferences, 399*. doi:10.1051/e3sconf/202339904031

Bearse, C., & de Jong, E. J. (2008). Cultural and linguistic investment: Adolescents in a secondary two-way immersion program. *Equity & Excellence in Education, 41*(3), 325–340. doi:10.1080/10665680802174817

Beerli, A., & Martin, J. D. (2004). Factors influencing destination image. *Annals of Tourism Research, 31*(3), 657–681. doi:10.1016/j.annals.2004.01.010

Beh, L. S., & Lin, W. L. (2022). Impact of COVID-19 on ASEAN tourism industry. *Journal of Asian Public Policy, 15*(2), 300–320. doi:10.1080/17516234.2020.1871180

Belanche, D., Casalo, L. V., Flavin, C., & Schepers, J. (2019). Service robot implementation: A theoretical framework and research agenda. *Service Industries Journal.*

Beneke, J., de Sousa, S., Mbuyu, M., & Wickham, B. (2016). The effect of negative online customer reviews on brand equity and purchase intention of consumer electronics in South Africa. *International Review of Retail, Distribution and Consumer Research, 26*(2), 171–201. doi:10.1080/09593969.2015.1068828

Berezina, K., Ciftci, O., & Cobanoglu, C. (2019). *Robots, Artificial Intelligence, and Service Automation in Restaurants. In Robots, Artificial Intelligence, and Service Automation in Travel, Tourism, and Hospitality*. Emerald Publishing Limited.

Berger, H., Dittenbach, M., Merkl, D., Bogdanovych, A., Simoff, S., & Sierra, C. (2007). Opening new dimensions for e-tourism. *Virtual Reality (Waltham Cross), 11*(2-3), 75–87. doi:10.1007/s10055-006-0057-z

Beriša, H., & Zorić, O. (2019). *Safety Culture Of Touris M S Ector In The Function Of S Strengthening The Security Culture Of Citizens.*

Bharadiya, J. P. (2023). The role of machine learning in transforming business intelligence. *International Journal of Computing and Artificial Intelligence, 4*(1), 16–24. doi:10.33545/27076571.2023.v4.i1a.60

Bharwani, S., & Mathews, D. (2021). Post-pandemic pressures to pivot: Tech transformations in luxury hotels. *Worldwide Hospitality and Tourism Themes, 13*(5), 569–583. doi:10.1108/WHATT-05-2021-0072

Bhave, D. P., Teo, L. H., & Dalal, R. S. (2020). Privacy at work: A review and a research agenda for a contested terrain. *Journal of Management, 46*(1), 127–164. doi:10.1177/0149206319878254

Bigne, E., Ruiz, C., Cuenca, A., Perez, C., & Garcia, A. (2021). What drives the helpfulness of online reviews? A deep learning study of sentiment analysis, pictorial content, and reviewer expertise for mature destinations. *Journal of Destination Marketing & Management, 20*, 100570. doi:10.1016/j.jdmm.2021.100570

Bijeta, B., Sharma, V., Lourens, M., Kumar, A., & Hinge, P. (2024). Design and Empirical Analysis of a Artificial Intelligence-Based Human Resource Management Processing Systems for Detecting Personal Stress. 6th International Conference on Contemporary Computing and Informatics (IC3I), 2421-2426.

Biscotti, L. (2023). Restaurants Face Backlash As QR Code Fatigue and Tech Costs Increase. *Forbes*. https://www.forbes.com/sites/louisbiscotti/2023/07/10/restaurants-face-tech-backlash-as-qr-code-fatigue-technology-costs-and-complexity-increase/?sh=1bc01c5b2552

Bisoi, S., Mou Roy, D., & Samal, A. (2020). Impact of Artificial Intelligence in the Hospitality Industry. *International Journal of Advanced Science and Technology*, *29*(5), 4265–4276.

Bogicevic, V., Seo, S., Kandampully, J. A., Liu, S. Q., & Rudd, N. A. (2019). Virtual reality presence as a preamble of tourism experience: The role of mental imagery. *Tourism Management*, *74*(5), 55–64. doi:10.1016/j.tourman.2019.02.009

Boniface, P., & Fowler, P. (2002). *Heritage and tourism in the global village*. Routledge. doi:10.4324/9780203033685

Bourgeon-Renault, D., Urbain, C., Petr, C., Le Gall-Ely, M., & Gombault, A. (2006). An experiential approach to the consumption value of arts and culture: The case of museums and monuments. *International Journal of Arts Management*, 35–47. https://www.jstor.org/stable/41064896

Boute, R. N., Gijsbrechts, J., & Van Mieghem, J. A. (2022). Digital lean operations: Smart automation and artificial intelligence in financial services. *Innovative Technology at the Interface of Finance and Operations*, *I*, 175–188. doi:10.1007/978-3-030-75729-8_6

Bowen, J., & Morosan, C. (2018). Beware hospitality industry: The robots are coming. *Worldwide Hospitality and Tourism Themes*, *10*(6), 726–733. doi:10.1108/WHATT-07-2018-0045

Bowyer, K. W. (2004). Face recognition technology: Security versus privacy. *IEEE Technology and Society Magazine*, *23*(1), 9–19. doi:10.1109/MTAS.2004.1273467

Boyd, S. (2002). Cultural and heritage tourism in Canada: Opportunities, principles and challenges. *Tourism and Hospitality Research*, *3*(3), 211–233. doi:10.1177/146735840200300303

Brady, M., Fellenz, M. R., & Brookes, R. (2008). Researching the role of information and communications technology (ICT) in contemporary marketing practices. *Journal of Business and Industrial Marketing*, *23*(2), 108–114. doi:10.1108/08858620810850227

Brazil, C., Neri, S. B., Soriano, A. Y., Victorio, C. F., & Grimaldo, J. R. (2022). The Effect of Online Wet Markets Website Quality on the Purchase Intention of Consumers in Caloocan City. *Journal of Business and Management Studies*, *4*(2), 136–149. doi:10.32996/jbms.2022.4.2.11

Brem, A., Viardot, E., & Nylund, P. A. (2021). Implications of the coronavirus (COVID-19) outbreak for innovation: Which technologies will improve our lives? *Technological Forecasting and Social Change*, *163*, 120451. doi:10.1016/j.techfore.2020.120451 PMID:33191956

Brohm, D., Domurath, N., Glanz-Chanos, V., & Grunert, K. G. (2017). In L. W. S. Loijens (Ed.), *"Future trends of augmented reality," in Augmented Reality for Food Marketers and Consumers* (pp. 1681–1685). Wageningen Academic Publishers.

Brouder, P. (2020). Reset redux: Possible evolutionary pathways towards the transformation of tourism in a COVID-19 world. *Tourism Geographies*, *22*(3), 484–490. doi:10.1080/14616688.2020.1760928

Brown, J. (2020). The Tax Benefits of Hosting Business Events at Hotels and Resorts. *Forbes*. Https://Www.Forbes.Com/Sites/Jonathanbrown/2020/12/10/The-Tax-Benefits-Of-Hosting-Business-Events-At-Hotels-And-Resorts/?Sh=3e7ed6355741

Buckley, R. (2004). The effects of World Heritage listing on tourism to Australian national parks. *Journal of Sustainable Tourism*, *12*(1), 70–84. doi:10.1080/09669580408667225

Budarick, B. (2004). Rest and relaxation in Coffs Harbour. *Civil Engineers Australia*, *76*(8), 62. https://www.scopus.com/inward/record.uri?eid=2-s2.0-4344568624&partnerID=40&md5=9a3264e11a136260bd6cec8e2d91cb59

Budhwar, P., Malik, A., De Silva, M. T., & Thevisuthan, P. (2022). Artificial intelligence–challenges and opportunities for international HRM: A review and research agenda. *International Journal of Human Resource Management*, *33*(6), 1065–1097. doi:10.1080/09585192.2022.2035161

Buhalis, D. (2018). *Technological disruptions in Services: lessons from Tourism and Hospitality*. Manuscript Central. http://mc.manuscriptcentral.com/josm

Buhalis, D., & Amaranggana, A. (2014). Smart tourism destination, 553-564.

Buhalis, D., & Amaranggana, A. (2015). Smart tourism destinations enhancing tourism experience through personalization of services. In *Information and Communication Technologies in Tourism 2015* (pp. 377–389). Springer. doi:10.1007/978-3-319-14343-9_28

Buhalis, D., Harwood, T., Bogicevic, V., Viglia, G., Beldona, S., & Hofacker, C. (2019). Technological disruptions in services: Lessons from tourism and hospitality. *Journal of Service Management*, *30*(4), 484–506. doi:10.1108/JOSM-12-2018-0398

Buhalis, D., & Moldavska, I. (2022). Voice assistants in hospitality: Using artificial intelligence for customer service. *Journal of Hospitality and Tourism Technology*, *13*(3), 386–403. doi:10.1108/JHTT-03-2021-0104

Buhalis, D., O'Connor, P., & Leung, R. (2023). Smart hospitality: From smart cities and smart tourism towards agile business ecosystems in networked destinations. *International Journal of Contemporary Hospitality Management*, *35*(1), 369–393. doi:10.1108/IJCHM-04-2022-0497

Bulchand-Gidumal, J. (2020). Impact of Artificial Intelligence in Travel, Tourism, and Hospitality. In *Handbook of e-Tourism* (pp. 1–20). Springer International Publishing. doi:10.1007/978-3-030-05324-6_110-1

Bulchand-Gidumal, J., William Secin, E., O'Connor, P., & Buhalis, D. (2023). Artificial intelligence's impact on hospitality and tourism marketing: Exploring key themes and addressing challenges. *Current Issues in Tourism*, 1–18. doi:10.1080/13683500.2023.2229480

Burke, R. (2018). Virtual reality for marketing research. In L. Moutinho & M. Sokele (Eds.), Innovative Research Methodologies in Management (pp. 63–82). Palgrave Macmillan. doi:10.1007/978-3-319-64400-4_3

Burt, M., & Louw, C. (2019). Virtual reality enhanced roller coasters and the future of entertainment – audience expectations. *World Leisure Journal*, *61*(3), 183–199. doi:10.1080/16078055.2019.1639274

Buzzacchi, L., Milone, F. L., Paolucci, E., & Raguseo, E. (2023). How to react to a shock? Effects of Airbnb hosts' choices and market segmentation at the time of Covid-19. *Information & Management*, *60*(7), 103857. doi:10.1016/j.im.2023.103857

Calver, S. J., & Page, S. J. (2013). Enlightened hedonism: Exploring the relationship of service value, visitor knowledge and interest, to visitor enjoyment at heritage attractions. *Tourism Management*, *39*, 23–36. doi:10.1016/j.tourman.2013.03.008

Canhoto, A. I., Quinton, S., Pera, R., Molinillo, S., & Simkin, L. (2021). Digital strategy aligning in SMEs: A dynamic capabilities perspective. *The Journal of Strategic Information Systems*, *30*(3), 101682. doi:10.1016/j.jsis.2021.101682

Cao, D., Sun, Y., Goh, E., Wang, R., & Kuiavska, K. (2022). Adoption of smart voice assistants technology among Airbnb guests : A revised self-efficacy-based value adoption model (SVAM). *International Journal of Hospitality Management*, *101*, 1–20. doi:10.1016/j.ijhm.2021.103124

Cappelli, P., Tambe, P., & Yakubovich, V. (2018). Artificial Intelligence in Human Resources Management: Challenges and a Path Forward. SSRN *Electronic Journal*. doi:10.2139/ssrn.3263878

Car, T. & Stifanich, L. P. (2020). Mobile Technology: a Tool To Increase Hotel Sales and Revenue. *Economics Business and Organization Research*, 454–464.

Carter, R. (2020, November 13). *Hilton Hotels and How VR is Changing Hospitality*. XR TODAY. https://www.xrtoday.com/virtual-reality/hilton-hotels-and-how-vr-is-changing-hospitality/

Caton, K., & Santos, C. A. (2007). Heritage tourism on Route 66: Deconstructing nostalgia. *Journal of Travel Research*, *45*(4), 371–386. doi:10.1177/0047287507299572

Çeltek, E., & İlhan, İ. (2020). *Big Data*. Artificial Intelligence, and Their Implications in the Tourism Industry.

Chandler, J. A. (2004). Comparing visitor profiles at heritage tourism destinations in Eastern North Carolina. *Journal of Travel & Tourism Marketing*, *16*(1), 53–63. doi:10.1300/J073v16n01_06

Chandra, S., Verma, S., Lim, W. M., Kumar, S., & Donthu, N. (2022). Personalization in personalized marketing: Trends and ways forward. *Psychology and Marketing*, *39*(8), 1529–1562. doi:10.1002/mar.21670

Chathoth, P. K., Ungson, G. R., Harrington, R. J., & Chan, E. S. W. (2016). Co-creation and higher order customer engagement in hospitality and tourism services: A critical review. *International Journal of Contemporary Hospitality Management*, *28*(2), 222–245. doi:10.1108/IJCHM-10-2014-0526

Chaves, A. P., & Gerosa, M. A. (2019). *How should my chatbot interact? A survey on human-chatbot interaction design*. Taylor & Francis. doi:10.1080/10447318.2020.1841438

Chawla, S. (2019). 7 Successful applications of AI & machine learning in the travel industry. *Hacker Noon*. https://hackernoon.com/successful-implications-of-ai-machine-learning-in-travel-industry-3040f3e1d48c

Chen, C. (2020). The Influence of Smart Tourism on Tourist Experience Toward Travel Intention and Satisfaction: Evidence from China. *International Journal of Marketing Studies*, *12*(3), 65. doi:10.5539/ijms.v12n3p65

Chen, C. C., & Tseng, Y.-D. (2011). Quality evaluation of product reviews using an information quality framework. *Decision Support Systems*, *50*(4), 755–768. doi:10.1016/j.dss.2010.08.023

Chen, C. F., & Chen, F. S. (2010). Experience quality, perceived value, satisfaction and behavioral intentions for heritage tourists. *Tourism Management*, *31*(1), 29–35. doi:10.1016/j.tourman.2009.02.008

Chen, C.-C., & Chang, Y.-C. (2018). What drives purchase intention on Airbnb? Perspectives of consumer reviews, information quality, and media richness. *Telematics and Informatics*, *35*(5), 1512–1523. doi:10.1016/j.tele.2018.03.019

Cheng, L., Varshney, K. R., & Liu, H. (2021). Socially responsible ai algorithms: Issues, purposes, and challenges. *Journal of Artificial Intelligence Research*, *71*, 1137–1181. doi:10.1613/jair.1.12814

Chen, K.-H., Liu, H.-H., & Chang, F.-H. (2013). Essential customer service factors and the segmentation of older visitors within wellness tourism based on hot springs hotels. *International Journal of Hospitality Management*, *35*, 122–132. doi:10.1016/j.ijhm.2013.05.013

Chen, Y.-L., Chang, C.-L., & Sung, A.-Q. (2021). Predicting eWOM's Influence on Purchase Intention Based on Helpfulness, Credibility, Information Quality and Professionalism. *Sustainability (Basel)*, *13*(13), 7486. doi:10.3390/su13137486

Cheong, R. (1995). The virtual threat to travel and tourism. *Tourism Management*, *16*(6), 417–422. doi:10.1016/0261-5177(95)00049-T

Cheriyan, J. (2021). *Consumer Acceptance towards AI-enabled Chatbots; case of Travel and Tourism Industries*. Journal PPW. http://journalppw.com

Chesney, T., Chuah, S.-H., Dobele, A. R., & Hoffmann, R. (2017). Information richness and trust in v-commerce: Implications for services marketing. *Journal of Services Marketing*, *31*(3), 295–307. doi:10.1108/JSM-02-2015-0099

Chevalier, J. A., & Mayzlin, D. (2006). The effect of word of mouth on sales: Online book reviews. *JMR, Journal of Marketing Research*, *43*(3), 345–354. doi:10.1509/jmkr.43.3.345

Che, Y., Cao, Y., Wu, R., Liu, J., Chen, L., & Wu, J. (2022). Spatio-Temporal Pattern of World Heritage and Its Accessibility Assessment in China. *Sustainability (Basel)*, *14*(5), 3033. doi:10.3390/su14053033

Chicchi Giglioli, I. A., Pravettoni, G., Sutil Martín, D. L., Parra, E., & Raya, M. A. (2017). A novel integrating virtual reality approach for the assessment of the attachment behavioral system. *Frontiers in Psychology*, *8*, 959. doi:10.3389/fpsyg.2017.00959 PMID:28701967

Chigozie, O. (2020). Tourism and virtual reality (VR) in developing nations. *African Journal of Hospitality, Tourism and Leisure*. doi:10.1080/01629778.2018.1455719

Chi, N. T. K. (2021). Innovation capability: The impact of e-CRM and COVID-19 risk perception. *Technology in Society*, *67*, 101725. doi:10.1016/j.techsoc.2021.101725

Chiny, M., Bencharef, O., Hadi, M. Y., & Chihab, Y. (2021). A client-centric evaluation system to evaluate guest's satisfaction on AirBNB using machine learning and NLP. *Applied Computational Intelligence and Soft Computing*, *2021*, 1–14. doi:10.1155/2021/6675790

Choi, A. S., Ritchie, B. W., Papandrea, F., & Bennett, J. (2010). Economic valuation of cultural heritage sites: A choice modeling approach. *Tourism Management*, *31*(2), 213–220. doi:10.1016/j.tourman.2009.02.014

Chowdhury, S., Dey, P., Joel-Edgar, S., Bhattacharya, S., Rodriguez-Espindola, O., Abadie, A., & Truong, L. (2023). Unlocking the value of artificial intelligence in human resource management through AI capability framework. *Human Resource Management Review*, *33*(1), 100899. doi:10.1016/j.hrmr.2022.100899

Ciapponi, D. (n.d.). *Why empathy skills are crucial for hoteliers*. EHL Insights. https://hospitalityinsights.ehl.edu/empathy-skills-crucial-hoteliers

Cichy, P., Salge, T. O., & Kohli, R. (2021). PRIVACY CONCERNS AND DATA SHARING IN THE INTERNET OF THINGS: MIXED METHODS EVIDENCE FROM CONNECTED CARS. *Management Information Systems Quarterly*, *45*(4), 1863–1892. doi:10.25300/MISQ/2021/14165

Citak, J., Owoc, M. L., & Weichbroth, P. (2021). A Note on the Applications of Artificial Intelligence in the Hospitality Industry: Preliminary Results of a Survey. *Procedia Computer Science*, *192*, 4552–4559. doi:10.1016/j.procs.2021.09.233

Code, I., & No, T. (2022). [AI]. *Artificial Intelligence*.

Çolak, O. (2023). The Role of Generative Pre-trained Transformers (GPT) in Recreational Tourism: An Interview with ChatGPT. *Spor Bilimleri Araştırmaları Dergisi*, *8*(3), 733–748. doi:10.25307/jssr.1341967

Cole, R., Stevenson, M., & Aitken, J. (2019). Blockchain technology: Implications for operations and supply chain management. *Supply Chain Management, 24*(4), 469–483. doi:10.1108/SCM-09-2018-0309

Colque, J., Manoharan A., Thomson Fredrik, E., Kumar, N., & Torres-Cruz, F. (2024). A Deep Learning Approaches for Natural Language Processing and Sentiment Analysis in Social Media. *6th International Conference on Contemporary Computing and Informatics (IC3I),* (pp. 1746-1750). IEEE.

Conyette, M. (2015). *21 Century Travel using Websites, Mobile and Wearable Technology Devices*. Research Gate. https://www.researchgate.net/publication/328712383_21_Century_Travel_using_We bsites_Mobile_and_Wearable_Technology_Devices.

Cordero Alvarez, J. A. (2022). *An investigation into how marketers use Virtual Reality (VR) technology to enhance consumer interaction.* National College of Ireland.

Correia Loureiro, S. M. (2022). Chapter 38 VIRTUAL REALITY, AUGMENTED REALITY AND TOURISM EXPERIENCE. In The Routledge handbook of tourism experience management and marketing (Issue 351, pp. 439–452). Routledge.

Cowan, K., & Ketron, S. (2019). Prioritizing marketing research in virtual reality: Development of an immersion/fantasy typology. *European Journal of Marketing, 53*(8), 1585–1611. doi:10.1108/EJM-10-2017-0733

Crosby, P., & McKenzie, J. (2022). Survey evidence on the impact of COVID-19 on Australian musicians and implications for policy. *International Journal of Cultural Policy, 28*(2), 166–186. doi:10.1080/10286632.2021.1916004

Cubric, M. (2020). Drivers, barriers and social considerations for AI adoption in business and management: A tertiary study. *Technology in Society, 101257*, 101257. doi:10.1016/j.techsoc.2020.101257

Cuccia, T., & Cellini, R. (2007). Is cultural heritage really important for tourists? A contingent rating study. *Applied Economics, 39*(2), 261–271. doi:10.1080/00036840500427981

Dabre, R., Chu, C., & Kunchukuttan, A. (2020). A Survey of Multilingual Neural Machine Translation. *ACM Computing Surveys, 53*(5), 1–38. doi:10.1145/3406095

Daengbuppha, J., Hemmington, N., & Wilkes, K. (2006). Using grounded theory to model visitor experiences at heritage sites: Methodological and practical issues. *Qualitative Market Research, 9*(4), 367–388. doi:10.1108/13522750610689096

Das, S., Nayak, J., & Naik, B. (2022). Impact of COVID-19 on Indian Education System: Practice and Applications of Intelligent Technologies. *In Future of Work and Business in Covid-19 Era: Proceedings of IMC-2021* (pp. 265-283). Springer Nature Singapore. 10.1007/978-981-19-0357-1_23

Das, S., Nayak, J., & Subudhi, S. (2022, April). An Impact Study on Covid-19 with Sustainable Sports Tourism: Intelligent Solutions, Issues and Future Challenges. *In International Conference on Computational Intelligence in Pattern Recognition* (pp. 605-624). Singapore: Springer Nature Singapore. 10.1007/978-981-19-3089-8_57

Das, S., Nayak, J., & Naik, B. (2023). An impact study on Covid-19 and tourism sustainability: Intelligent solutions, issues and future challenges. *World Review of Science, Technology and Sustainable Development*, *19*(1-2), 92–119. doi:10.1504/WRSTSD.2023.127268

Daugherty, P. R., Wilson, H. J., & Chowdhury, R. (2018). Using artificial intelligence to promote diversity. *MIT Sloan Management Review Magazine*. https://sloanreview.mit.edu/article/using-artificial-intelligence-to-promote-diversity/

Davenport, T., Guha, A., Grewal, D., & Bressgott, T. (2020). How Artificial Intelligence Will Change the Future of Marketing. *Journal of the Academy of Marketing Science*, *48*(1), 24–42. doi:10.1007/s11747-019-00696-0

de Lurdes Calisto, M., & Sarkar, S. (2024). A systematic review of virtual reality in tourism and hospitality: The known and the paths to follow. *International Journal of Hospitality Management*, *116*, 103623. doi:10.1016/j.ijhm.2023.103623

Debata, B., Patnaik, P., & Mishra, A. (2020). COVID-19 pandemic! It's impact on people, economy, and environment. *Journal of Public Affairs*, *20*(4), e2372. doi:10.1002/pa.2372

Decker, A. (2023, March 15). *What is Branding? Understanding its Importance in 2023*. Hubspot. https://blog.hubspot.com/marketing/branding#:~:text=Your%20brand%20is%20arguably%20one,and%20brings%20your%20employees%20pride

Dentzel, Z. (2013). How the internet has changed everyday life. *Ch@ Nge, 19*, 235–252.

Desai, P. R., Desai, P. N., Ajmera, K. D., & Mehta, K. (2014). A Review Paper on Oculus Rift-A Virtual [IJETT]. *International Journal of Engineering Trends and Technology*, *13*(4), 175–179. doi:10.14445/22315381/IJETT-V13P237

Deshpande, M., Munje, P., Zilpelwar, T., Narnawre, V., Sharma, A. K., Thakre, B., & Purohit, N. (2022). *An AI Integrated Online Hotel Management System*. https://doi.org/ doi:10.37591/JoWET

Deviprasad, S., Madhumithaa, N., Vikas, I. W., Yadav, A., & Manoharan, G. (2023). The Machine Learning-Based Task Automation Framework for Human Resource Management in MNC Companies. *Engineering Proceedings*, *59*(1), 63.

Dey Sharmistha, S. D. (2022). *Analytical study on use of AI techniques in tourism sector for smarter customer experience management*.

Dhiraj, A., Kumar, S., Rani, D., Grima, S., & Sood, K. (2023). Blockchain Payment Services in the Hospitality Sector: The Mediating Role of Data Security on Utilisation Efficiency of the Customer. *Data*, *8*(8), 123. doi:10.3390/data8080123

Didascalou, E., & Lagos, D. (2009). Wellness tourism: Evaluating destination attributes for tourism planning in a competitive segment market. *Tourismos*, *4*(4), 113–126.

Dierking, L. D., & Falk, J. H. (1992). Redefining the museum experience: The interactive experience model. *Visitor Studies*, *4*(1), 173–176.

Divekar, R. R., Drozdal, J., Chabot, S., Zhou, Y., Su, H., Chen, Y., Zhu, H., Hendler, J. A., & Braasch, J. (2022). Foreign language acquisition via artificial intelligence and extended reality: Design and evaluation. *Computer Assisted Language Learning*, *35*(9), 2332–2360. doi:10.1080/09588221.2021.1879162

Doborjeh, Z., Hemmington, N., Doborjeh, M., & Kasabov, N. (2022). Artificial intelligence: A systematic review of methods and applications in hospitality and tourism. *International Journal of Contemporary Hospitality Management*, *34*(3), 1154–1176. doi:10.1108/IJCHM-06-2021-0767

Doğan, M. (2019). The Effects of Interactive Applications On Visitors' Experience: A Case of Gobeklitepe, Turkey. *Social Science Studies Journal. Vol*, *4*(27), 6125–6135. doi:10.26449/sssj.1084

Dogru, T., Line, N. D., Mody, M., Hanks, L., Abbott, J., Acikgoz, F., Assaf, A. G., Bakir, S., Berbekova, A., Bilgihan, A., Dalton, A. N., Erkmen, E., Geronasso, M., Gomez, D., Graves, S., Iskender, A., Ivanov, S., Kizildag, M., Lee, M., & Zhang, T. C. (2023). Generative Artificial Intelligence in the Hospitality and Tourism Industry: Developing a Framework for Future Research. *Journal of Hospitality & Tourism Research (Washington, D.C.)*, 10963480231188663. doi:10.1177/10963480231188663

Dou, X., Walden, J. A., Lee, S., & Lee, J. Y. (2012). Does source matter? Examining source effects in online product reviews. *Computers in Human Behavior*, *28*(5), 1555–1563. doi:10.1016/j.chb.2012.03.015

Drexler, N., & Lapré, V. B. (2019). For Better or For Worse: Shaping the Hospitality Industry Through Robotics and Artificial Intelligence. Research in Hospitality Management, 9(2), 117-120. Springer.

Du Cros, H., Bauer, T., Lo, C., & Rui, S. (2005). Cultural heritage assets in China as sustainable tourism products: Case studies of the Hutongs and the Huanghua section of the Great Wall. *Journal of Sustainable Tourism*, *13*(2), 171–194. doi:10.1080/09669580508668484

Du, H., Sun, W., Jiao, Y., Li, J., & Liu, L. (2022). Countermeasures for the Development of Data Integration of the Internet Ice and Snow Tourism Industry under the Background of Artificial Intelligence. *Applied Bionics and Biomechanics*, *2022*, 2022. doi:10.1155/2022/8496766 PMID:35528531

Duro, J. A., Perez-Laborda, A., Turrion-Prats, J., & Fernández-Fernández, M. (2021). Covid-19 and tourism vulnerability. *Tourism Management Perspectives*, *38*, 100819. doi:10.1016/j.tmp.2021.100819 PMID:34873568

Duy, N. T., Mondal, S. R., Van, N. T. T., Dzung, P. T., Minh, D. X. H., & Das, S. (2020). A study on the role of web 4.0 and 5.0 in the sustainable tourism ecosystem of Ho Chi Minh City, Vietnam. *Sustainability (Basel)*, *12*(17), 7140. doi:10.3390/su12177140

Edwards, M. R., Charlwood, A., Guenole, N., & Marler, J. (2022). HR analytics: An emerging field finding its place in the world alongside simmering ethical challenges. *Human Resource Management Journal*, 1748-8583.12435. doi:10.1111/1748-8583.12435

El-Moffock, N. (2023a). *Economic Studies Digital Transformation and AI in Tourism: Trends.* Challenges, and Successful Experiences.

El-Said, O., & Aziz, H. (2021). Virtual Tours a Means to an End: An Analysis of Virtual Tours' Role in Tourism Recovery Post COVID-19. *Journal of Travel Research*. doi:10.1177/0047287521997567

Ensemble, Q. (2020). Ways Social Media Has Transformed Tourism Marketing. *Hospitality Tourism.* https://hospitalitytech.com/5-ways-social-media-has-transformed[REMOVED HYPERLINK FIELD]tourism-marketing

Erenay, O., & Hashemipour, M. (2003). Virtual Reality in Engineering Education: A CIM Case Study. *The Turkish Online Journal of Educational Technology*, *2*(2), 51–56. http://www.tojet.net/articles/v2i2/228.pdf

Erkan, I., & Evans, C. (2016). The influence of eWOM in social media on consumers' purchase intentions: An extended approach to information adoption. *Computers in Human Behavior*, *61*, 47–55. doi:10.1016/j.chb.2016.03.003

Escobar, M. C. (2019). *IHG CEO discusses company's progress on loyalty, Concerto*. Hospitality Technology. https:// hospitalitytech.com/ihg-ceo-discusses-companys-progress-loyalty- concerto

Eskerod, P., Hollensen, S., Morales-Contreras, M. F., & Arteaga-Ortiz, J. (2019). Drivers for pursuing sustainability through IoT technology within high-end hotels-An exploratory study. *Sustainability (Basel)*, *11*(19), 5372. doi:10.3390/su11195372

Familmaleki, M., Aghighi, A., & Hamidi, K. (2015). Analyzing the Influence of Sales Promotion on Customer Purchasing Behavior. *International Journal of Economics and Management Sciences*, *4*(4). doi:10.4172/2162-6359.1000243

Fang, W. (2022). Cultural Tourism Industry Feature Extraction Based on Multiscale Feature Fusion Algorithm and Artificial Intelligence. *Mathematical Problems in Engineering*, *2022*, 1–8. doi:10.1155/2022/5946166

Feng, C., Patel, P. C., & Fay, S. (2021). The value of the structural power of the chief information officer in enhancing forward-looking firm performance. *Journal of Management Information Systems*, *38*(3), 765–797. doi:10.1080/07421222.2021.1962599

Filieri, R. (2015). What makes online reviews helpful? A diagnosticity-adoption framework to explain informational and normative influences in e-WOM. *Journal of Business Research*, *68*(6), 1261–1270. doi:10.1016/j.jbusres.2014.11.006

Filieri, R., D'Amico, E., Destefanis, A., Paolucci, E., & Raguseo, E. (2021a). Artificial intelligence (AI) for tourism: An European-based study on successful AI tourism start-ups. *International Journal of Contemporary Hospitality Management*, *33*(11), 4099–4125. doi:10.1108/IJCHM-02-2021-0220

Filieri, R., Lin, Z., Pino, G., Alguezaui, S., & Inversini, A. (2021). The role of visual cues in eWOM on consumers' behavioral intention and decisions. *Journal of Business Research*, *135*, 663–675. doi:10.1016/j.jbusres.2021.06.055

Filieri, R., McLeay, F., Tsui, B., & Lin, Z. (2018). Consumer perceptions of information helpfulness and determinants of purchase intention in online consumer reviews of services. *Information & Management*, *55*(8), 956–970. doi:10.1016/j.im.2018.04.010

Fino, E. R., Martín-Gutiérrez, J., López, D. C., Fernández, M. D., Hernández, V. M., & Penate, F. M. (2013). *An Augmented Tourist Guide of a World Heritage City*. Interacción. doi:10.1007/978-3-642-39476-8_58

Fisher, Greg and Beatson, A. T. (2002). The impact of culture on self-service technnology adoption in the hotel indistry. *International Journal of Hospitality and Tourism Administration*, *3*(3), 59–77. http://eprints.qut.edu.au/21114/1/c21114.pdf

Flowers, J., & Easterling, K. (2006). Growing South Carolina's tourism cluster. *Business and Economic Review*, *52*(3), 15–20.

Font, X., & Harris, C. (2004). Rethinking standards from green to sustainable. *Annals of Tourism Research*, *31*(4), 986–1007. doi:10.1016/j.annals.2004.04.001

Frey, B. S., & Briviba, A. (2021). A policy proposal to deal with excessive cultural tourism. *European Planning Studies*, *29*(4), 601–618. doi:10.1080/09654313.2021.1903841

Frintrop, S., Rome, E., & Tech, G. (2010). Computational Visual Attention Systems and their Cognitive Foundations. *ACM Transactions on Applied Perception*, *7*(1), 1–39. doi:10.1145/1658349.1658355

Fritz, F., & Susperregui, A. (2005). *Enhancing Cultural Tourism experiences with Augmented Reality Technologies*.

Fronzetti Colladon, A., Guardabascio, B., & Innarella, R. (2019). Using social network and semantic analysis to analyze online travel forums and forecast tourism demand. *Decision Support Systems*, *123*, 113075. Advance online publication. doi:10.1016/j.dss.2019.113075

Fyall, A., & Garrod, B. (1998). Heritage tourism: At what price? *Managing Leisure*, *3*(4), 213–228. doi:10.1080/136067198375996

Gaberamos, O., & Pasaribu, L. H. (2022). The Effect Of Information Quality, Customer Experience, Price, And Service Quality On Purchase Intention By Using Customer Perceived Value As Mediation Variables (Study On Gofood Applications On The Millenial Generation). *Jurnal Mantik*, *5*(4), 2470–2480.

Gajdošík, T. (2018). Smart Tourism: Concepts and Insights from Central Europe. *Czech Journal of Tourism*, *7*(1), 25–44. doi:10.1515/cjot-2018-0002

Gajdošík, T., & Orelová, A. (2020). Smart Technologies for Smart Tourism Development. In R. Silhavy (Ed.), *Artificial Intelligence and Bioinspired Computational Methods. CSOC 2020. Advances in Intelligent Systems and Computing* (Vol. 1225). Springer. doi:10.1007/978-3-030-51971-1_27

Galanos, V. (2023). Expectations And Expertise. *In Artificial Intelligence: Specialist Views And Historical Perspectives On Conceptualisation, Promise, And Funding.*

Gamwell, B. (2022). *California Consumer Protection Act (CCPA): Narrowing CCPA Exemptions Will Ensur emptions Will Ensure Greater Priv eater Privacy Protections otections.* GGU Law Review Blog.

García-Madurga, M., & Grilló-Méndez, A. (2023). Artificial Intelligence in the Tourism Industry: An Overview of Reviews. *Administrative Sciences*, *13*(8), 172. doi:10.3390/admsci13080172

Garg, A., & Kumar, J. (2021). Social media marketing influence on Boutique Hotel customers' purchase intention in Malaysia. *Tourism & Management Studies*, *17*(3), 51–62. doi:10.18089/tms.2021.170304

Gaur, L., Afaq, A., Singh, G., & Dwivedi, Y. K. (2021). Role of artificial intelligence and robotics to foster the touchless travel during a pandemic: A review and research agenda. *International Journal of Contemporary Hospitality Management*, *33*(11), 4079–4098. doi:10.1108/IJCHM-11-2020-1246

Geisler, R. (2018). *Artificial Intelligence in the Travel & Tourism industry Adoption and impact.* [Thesis, NOVA School of Business and Economics].

Gelter, H. (2017). Digital tourism -An analysis of digital trends in tourism and customer digital mobile behavior for the Visit Arctic Europe project. Report of Europe.

Ghandour, A., Kintonova, A., Demidchik, N., & Sverdlikova, E. (2021). Solving tourism management challenges by means of mobile augmented reality applications. [IJWLTT]. *International Journal of Web-Based Learning and Teaching Technologies*, *16*(6), 1–16. doi:10.4018/IJWLTT.293280

Ghose, A., & Ipeirotis, P. G. (2008). *Estimating the socio-economic impact of product reviews: Mining text and reviewer characteristics.*

Ghosh, A., Nundy, S., & Mallick, T. K. (2020). How India is dealing with COVID-19 pandemic. *Sensors International*, *1*, 100021. doi:10.1016/j.sintl.2020.100021 PMID:34766039

Gibson, A., & O'Rawe, M. (2018). Virtual reality as a travel promotional tool: Insights from a consumer travel fair. *Augmented reality and virtual reality: Empowering human, place and business*, 93-107.

Gilmore, A., Carson, D., & Ascenção, M. (2007). Sustainable tourism marketing at a World Heritage site. *Journal of Strategic Marketing*, *15*(2-3), 253–264. doi:10.1080/09652540701318930

Global Wellness Institute. (n.d.). *Home*. Global Wellness Institute. https://globalwellnessinstitute.org/

Goel, R., Singh, T., Baral, S. K., Sahdev, S. L., & Gupta, S. (2022). The Era of Artificial Intelligence Reforming Tourism Industry in Society 5.0. *2022 10th International Conference on Reliability, Infocom Technologies and Optimization (Trends and Future Directions) (ICRITO)*, (pp. 1-4). IEEE.

Goel, P., Kaushik, N., Sivathanu, B., Pillai, R., & Vikas, J. (2022). Consumers' Adoption of Artificial Intelligence and Robotics in Hospitality and Tourism Sector: Literature Review and Future Research Agenda. *Tourism Review*, *77*(4), 1–16. doi:10.1108/TR-03-2021-0138

Gombault, A., & Petr, C. (2007). *La réputation des musées et des monuments superstars* (No. halshs-00260154).

Gosjen, D. I., Haryadi, K. H., Nicholas, Gunawan, A. A. S., Djuwita, C. M., & Adiati, M. P. (2022). Nicholas, Gunawan, A. A. S., Djuwita, C. M., & Adiati, M. P. (2022). Implementation e-concierge in hotel. *Procedia Computer Science*, *216*, 485–498. doi:10.1016/j.procs.2022.12.161

Goulding, P., & Pomfret, G. (2022). Managing temporal variation at visitor attractions. In *Managing visitor attractions* (pp. 213–233). Routledge. doi:10.4324/9781003041948-15

Government of India. (2023). Digital Personal Data Protection Act 2023. *The Gazette of India, DI*. https://www.meity.gov.in/writereaddata/files/Digital Personal Data Protection Act 2023.pdf

Gretzel, U., Siagala, M., Xiang Z., & Koo, C. (2015). *Smart Tourism: Foundations and Developments*. Springer. https://link.springer.com/article/10.1007/s12525-015-0196-8

Gretzel, U. (2011). Intelligent systems in tourism: A social science perspective. *Annals of Tourism Research*, *38*(3), 757–779. doi:10.1016/j.annals.2011.04.014

Gretzel, U., Sigala, M., Xiang, Z., & Koo, C. (2015). Smart tourism: Foundations and developments. *Electronic Markets*, *25*(3), 179–188. doi:10.1007/s12525-015-0196-8

Gretzel, U., Zhong, L., & Koo, C. (2016). Application of smart tourism to cities. *International Journal of Tourism Cities*, *2*(2). doi:10.1108/IJTC-04-2016-0007

Grewal, D., Gauri, D. K., Roggeveen, A. L., & Sethuraman, R. (2021). Strategizing retailing in the new technology era. *Journal of Retailing*, *97*(1), 6–12. doi:10.1016/j.jretai.2021.02.004

Grewal, D., Roggeveen, A. L., & Nordfält, J. (2017). The future of retailing. *Journal of Retailing*, *93*(1), 1–6. doi:10.1016/j.jretai.2016.12.008

Guerra-Montenegro, J., Sanchez-Medina, J., Lana, I., Sanchez-Rodriguez, D., Alonso-Gonzalez, I., & Del Ser, J. (2021). Computational intelligence in the hospitality industry: A systematic literature review and a prospect of challenges. *Applied Soft Computing*, *102*, 107082. doi:10.1016/j.asoc.2021.107082

Gupta, S., Modgil, S., Lee, C. K., & Sivarajah, U. (2023a). The future is yesterday: Use of AI-driven facial recognition to enhance value in the travel and tourism industry. *Information Systems Frontiers*, *25*(3), 1179–1195. doi:10.1007/s10796-022-10271-8 PMID:35529102

Guttentag, D. A. (2010). Virtual reality: Applications and implications for tourism. *Tourism Management*, *31*(5), 637–651. doi:10.1016/j.tourman.2009.07.003

Hall, C. M., Gössling, S., Peeters, P., Hall, C. M., Ceron, J., & Dubois, G. (2012). Tourism and Water Use : Supply, Demand and Security – An International Review Tourism and water use : Supply, demand, and security. An international review. *Tourism Management*, *33*(1), 1–15. doi:10.1016/j.tourman.2011.03.015

Han, D., Weber, J., Bastiaansen, M., Mitas, O., & Lub, X. (2019). *Virtual and Augmented Reality Technologies to enhance the visitor experience in cultural tourism.*

Han, D.-I. D., Weber, J., Bastiaansen, M., Mitas, O., & Lub, X. (2019). Virtual and Augmented Reality Technologies to Enhance the Visitor Experience in Cultural Tourism. *Augmented Reality and Virtual Reality: The Power of AR and VR for Business*, 113–128. doi:10.1007/978-3-030-06246-0_9

Hao, F., & Chon, K. K. S. (2022). Contactless service in hospitality: Bridging customer equity, experience, delight, satisfaction, and trust. *International Journal of Contemporary Hospitality Management*, *34*(1), 113–134. doi:10.1108/IJCHM-05-2021-0559

Harrison, C., Eckman, B., Hamilton, R., Hartswick, P., Kalagnanam, J., Paraszczak, J., & Williams, P. (2010). Foundations for smarter cities. *IBM Journal of Research and Development*, *54*(4), 1–16. doi:10.1147/JRD.2010.2048257

Hartanti, F. T., Abawajy, J. H., Chowdhury, M., & Shalannanda, W. (2021). Citizens' Trust Measurement in Smart Government Services. *IEEE Access : Practical Innovations, Open Solutions*, *9*, 150663–150676. doi:10.1109/ACCESS.2021.3124206

Hasan, M. R., Abdunurova, A., Wang, W., Zheng, J., & Shams, S. R. (2021). Using deep learning to investigate digital behavior in culinary tourism. *Journal of Place Management and Development*, *14*(1), 43–65. https://www.statista.com/statistics/187122/movie-releases-in-north-america-since-2001/ https://www.worldometers.info/coronavirus/. doi:10.1108/JPMD-03-2020-0022

Hassan Editor, A. (2022). *Handbook of Technology Application in Tourism in Asia.*

Hertzman, E., Anderson, D., & Rowley, S. (2008). Edutainment heritage tourist attractions: A portrait of visitors' experiences at Storyeum. *Museum Management and Curatorship*, *23*(2), 155–175. doi:10.1080/09647770802012227

Hilton Worldwide Holdings Inc. (n.d.). Digital Transformation Strategies. *Global Data.* https://www.globaldata.com/store/report/hilton-worldwide-holdings-inc-enterprise-tech-analysis/)

Ho, L.-H., Lu, M.-H., Ho, H.-Y., & Peng, T.-F. (2011). A Study of Website Optimization Strategy and Implementation. In William, Z and Xiong, F (Ed.), COMPUTATIONAL MATERIALS SCIENCE, PTS 1-3. doi:10.4028/www.scientific.net/AMR.268-270.829

Hobson, J. S. P., & Williams, A. P. (1995). Virtual Reality: A new horizon for the tourism industry. *Journal of Vacation Marketing*, *1*(2), 125–135.

Hoffmann, T., & Vargas, P. L. P. de M. (2022). LGPD Et Al. – Report on the Law of Data Disclosure in Brazil. SSRN *Electronic Journal, April*. doi:10.2139/ssrn.4082390

Höjer, M., & Wangel, J. (2015). Smart Sustainable Cities: Definition and Challenges. In L. M. Hilty & B. Aebischer (Eds.), *ICT Innovations for Sustainability, Advances in Intelligent Systems and Computing* (pp. 333–349). Springer. doi:10.1007/978-3-319-09228-7_20

Hollander, J. (2023). *Marriott Data Breach FAQ: What Really Happened?* HotelTechReport. https://hoteltechreport.com/news/marriott-data-breach

Holmes, K., Jones, P., Lockwood, A., Miller, G., Scarles, C., Szivas, E., & Tribe, J. (2006). An eclectic agenda for Tourism and Hospitality Research. *Tourism and Hospitality Research*, *7*(1), 76–82. doi:10.1057/palgrave.thr.6050035

Hua, L. Y., Ramayah, T., Ping, T. A., & Cheah, J. (2017). Social Media as a Tool to Help Select Tourism Destinations: The Case of Malaysia. *Information Systems Management*, *34*, 265–279. doi:10.1080/10580530.2017.1330004

Huang, A. H., Chen, K., Yen, D. C., & Tran, T. P. (2015). A study of factors that contribute to online review helpfulness. *Computers in Human Behavior*, *48*, 17–27. doi:10.1016/j.chb.2015.01.010

Huang, A., Chao, Y., de la Mora Velasco, E., Bilgihan, A., & Wei, W. (2022). When artificial intelligence meets the hospitality and tourism industry: An assessment framework to inform theory and management. *Journal of Hospitality and Tourism Insights*, *5*(5), 1080–1100. doi:10.1108/JHTI-01-2021-0021

Huang, C. H., Tsaur, J. R., & Yang, C. H. (2012). Does world heritage list really induce more tourists? Evidence from Macau. *Tourism Management*, *33*(6), 1450–1457. doi:10.1016/j.tourman.2012.01.014 PMID:32287738

Hughes, H. (2013). *Arts, entertainment and tourism*. Taylor & Francis. doi:10.4324/9780080499468

Hughes, H. L., & Benn, D. (1995). *Entertainment: its role in the tourist experience*. Leisure Studies Association.

Huh, J., & Uysal, M. (2004). Satisfaction with cultural/heritage sites: Virginia historic triangle. *Journal of Quality Assurance in Hospitality & Tourism*, *4*(3-4), 177–194. doi:10.1300/J162v04n03_12

Hu, N., Liu, L., & Zhang, J. J. (2008). Do online reviews affect product sales? The role of reviewer characteristics and temporal effects. *Information Technology and Management*, *9*(3), 201–214. doi:10.1007/s10799-008-0041-2

Hunter, W. C., Chung, N., Gretzel, U., & Koo, C. (2015). Constructivist research in smart tourism. *APJIS*, *25*(1), 105–120. doi:10.14329/apjis.2015.25.1.105

Iansiti, M., & Lakhani, K. R. (2017). The truth about blockchain. *Harvard Business Review, 2017*(January-February).

Ismagilova, E., Slade, E., Rana, N. P., & Dwivedi, Y. K. (2020). The effect of characteristics of source credibility on consumer behavior: A meta-analysis. *Journal of Retailing and Consumer Services, 53*, 101736. doi:10.1016/j.jretconser.2019.01.005

Issa, H., Sun, T., & Vasarhelyi, M. A. (2016). Research ideas for artificial intelligence in auditing: The formalization of audit and workforce supplementation. *Journal of Emerging Technologies in Accounting, 13*(2), 1–20. doi:10.2308/jeta-10511

Itani, O. S., & Hollebeek, L. D. (2021). Light at the end of the tunnel: Visitors' virtual reality (versus in-person) attraction site tour-related behavioral intentions during and post-COVID-19. *Tourism Management, 84*, 104290. doi:10.1016/j.tourman.2021.104290 PMID:36530603

Ivanov, S., & Webster, C. (2017). Adoption of Robots, Aritificial Intelligence and Service Automation by Travel, Tourism and Hospitality Companies - A cost-benefit Analysis. *International Scientific Conference "Contemporary Tourism – Traditions and Innovations*. IEEE.

Ivanov, S., & Webster, C. (2017). Adoption of robots, artificial intelligence and service automation by travel, tourism and hospitality companies – a cost-benefit analysis. *International Scientific Conference Contemporary tourism – traditions and innovations*. Sofia University.

Ivanov, S., Webster, C., & Berezina, K. (2017). Adoption of Robots and Service Automation by Tourism and Hospitality Companies. *Revista Tur smo & Dese nv olvimento*, no. 27/28. https:// ssrn. com/abstract=2964308.

Ivanov, S. H., Webster, C., & Berezina, K. (2017). Adoption of robots and service automation by tourism and hospitality companies. *Revista Turismo & Desenvolvimento (Aveiro), 27*(28), 1501–1517.

Ivanov, S., & Webster, C. (2019). *Conceptual Framework of the Use of Robots, Artificial Intelligence and Service Automation in Travel, Tourism, and Hospitality Companies. Robots, Artificial Intelligence, and Service Automation in Travel, Tourism, and Hospitality*. Emerald Publishing Limited.

Jabeen, F., Al Zaidi, S., & Al Dhaheri, M. H. (2022). Automation and artificial intelligence in hospitality and tourism. *Tourism Review, 77*(4), 1043–1061. doi:10.1108/TR-09-2019-0360

Jabeen, F., Zaidi, S. A., & Dhaheri, M. H. (2021). Automation and artificial intelligence in hospitality and tourism. *Tourism Review*.

Jaipuria, S., Parida, R., & Ray, P. (2021). The impact of COVID-19 on tourism sector in India. *Tourism Recreation Research, 46*(2), 245–260. doi:10.1080/02508281.2020.1846971

Jalilvand, M. R., & Heidari, A. (2017). Comparing face-to-face and electronic word-of-mouth in destination image formation: The case of Iran. *Information Technology & People, 30*(4), 710–735. doi:10.1108/ITP-09-2016-0204

Jasrotia, A., & Gangotia, A. (2018). *Smart Cities to Smart Tourism Destinations: A Review Paper*. Research Gate. https://www.researchgate.net/publication/327536704_Smart_Cities_To_Smart_Touri sm_Destinations_A_Review_Paper_ISSN_2249-7307.

Jelski, C. (2022). Working during vacation: Hotels respond to bleisure's flipside. *Travel Weekly*. https://www.travelweekly.com/Travel-News/Hotel-News/The-flipside-of-bleisure-working-during-vacation

Jiang, F., Du, C., Fu, T., & Xiao, R. (2018). Research on the application intelligence in human resource management. The *4th Annual 2018 International Conference on Management Science and Engineering (MSE2018)*. Francis Academic Press. https://doi.org/ 10.25236/mse.2018.054

Jiang, G., Liu, F., Liu, W., Liu, S., Chen, Y., & Xu, D. (2021). Effects of information quality on information adoption on social media review platforms: Moderating role of perceived risk. *Data Science and Management*, *1*(1), 13–22. doi:10.1016/j.dsm.2021.02.004

Jiang, N., Liu, X., Liu, H., Lim, E. T. K., Tan, C.-W., & Gu, J. (2023). Beyond AI-powered context-aware services: The role of human–AI collaboration. *Industrial Management & Data Systems*, *123*(11), 2771–2802. doi:10.1108/IMDS-03-2022-0152

Jimura, T. (2011). The impact of world heritage site designation on local communities–A case study of Ogimachi, Shirakawa-mura, Japan. *Tourism Management*, *32*(2), 288–296. doi:10.1016/j.tourman.2010.02.005

Jung, T., Tom Dieck, M. C., Lee, H., & Chung, N. (2016). *Effects of Virtual Reality and Augmented Reality on Visitor Experiences in Museum*. 621–635. https://doi.org/ doi:10.1007/978-3-319-28231-2-45

Kabassi, K. (2010). Personalizing recommendations for tourists. In Telematics and Informatics, 27(1), 51–66. doi:10.1016/j.tele.2009.05.003

Kakoulli, M. S. P. and E. (2023). *IoT for Sustainable Hospitality: A Systematic Review of Opportunities and Challenges for the Hospitality Industry Revolution. 19th International Conference on Distributed Computing in Smart Systems and the Internet of Things (DCOSS-IoT)*, Pafos, Cyprus, 2023, 740–747. 10.1109/DCOSS-IoT58021.2023.00116

Kamal, M., & Himel, A. S. (2023). Redefining Modern Marketing: An Analysis of AI and NLP's Influence on Consumer Engagement, Strategy, and Beyond. *Eigenpub Review of Science and Technology*, *7*(1), 203–223.

Kang, J.-W., & Namkung, Y. (2019). The information quality and source credibility matter in customers' evaluation toward food O2O commerce. *International Journal of Hospitality Management*, *78*, 189–198. doi:10.1016/j.ijhm.2018.10.011

Kannan, P. K., & Li, H. A. (2017). Digital marketing: A framework, review and research agenda. *International Journal of Research in Marketing*, *34*(1), 22–45. doi:10.1016/j.ijresmar.2016.11.006

Kannan, P., & Bernoff, J. (2019). The future of customer service is AI-Human collaboration. *MIT Sloan Management Review*.

Kansakar, P., Munir, A., & Shabani, N. (2019). Technology in the Hospitality Industry: Prospects and Challenges. *IEEE Consumer Electronics Magazine*, *8*(3), 60–65. doi:10.1109/MCE.2019.2892245

Kapur, M. (2020, August 21). Indians holiday around the world during the pandemic—from inside their living rooms. *Quartz India*. https://qz.com/india/1893473/indians-take-online-holidays-on-tourhq-viator-amid-covid-19/

Kar, A. K., Choudhary, S. K., & Ilavarasan, P. V. (2023). How can we improve tourism service experiences: Insights from multi-stakeholders' interaction. *Decision (Washington, D.C.)*, *50*(1), 73–89. doi:10.1007/s40622-023-00338-z

Kariru, D. (2023). Contemporary Trends and Issues in The Hospitality and Tourism Industry. *International Journal of Research and Innovation in Social Science*, *VII*(IV), 970–986. doi:10.47772/IJRISS.2023.7481

Kaur, J. (2023, March 21). *RPA for Reservation in Travel and Hospitality Industry*. Xenonstack. https://www.xenonstack.com/insights/rpa-in-travel-hospitality

Kaur, B. (2021). A Study of Barriers to Environmentally Sustainable Practices in Hotel Businesses in Punjab, India: Preliminary Findings. *Academica Turistica*, *14*(1), 71–86. doi:10.26493/2335-4194.14.71-86

Kaur, K., & Kumar, P. (2022). Social media: A blessing or a curse? Voice of owners in the beauty and wellness industry. *The TQM Journal*, *34*(5), 1039–1056. doi:10.1108/TQM-03-2021-0074

Kaushik, N., Kaushik, J., Sharma, P., & Rani, S. (2010). Factors influencing choice of tourist destinations: A study of North India. *IUP Journal of Brand Management*, *7*(1/2), 116–132.

Kazak, A. N., Chetyrbok, P. V., & Oleinikov, N. N. (2020). Artificial intelligence in the tourism sphere. *IOP Conference Series. Earth and Environmental Science*, *421*(4), 042020. Advance online publication. doi:10.1088/1755-1315/421/4/042020

Kemp, S. (2023). *Digital 2023: Malaysia*. Data Portal. https://datareportal.com/reports/digital-2023-malaysia#:~:text=Malaysia's%20internet%20penetration%20rate%20stood,percent)%20 between%202022%20and%202023.

Kempiak, J., Hollywood, L., Bolan, P., & McMahon-Beattie, U. (2017). The heritage tourist: An understanding of the visitor experience at heritage attractions. *International Journal of Heritage Studies*, *23*(4), 375–392. doi:10.1080/13527258.2016.1277776

Kemska, A. S. (2021). Virtual tourism in Ukraine - Features and prospects. Polit. *Challenges of science Today*. http://fmv.nau.edu.ua/wp-content/uploads/2021/04/%D0%9F%D0%BE%D0%BB%D1%96%D1%82-2021.pdf#page=274

Kerstetter, D. L., Confer, J. J., & Graefe, A. R. (2001). An exploration of the specialization concept within the context of heritage tourism. *Journal of Travel Research*, *39*(3), 267–274. doi:10.1177/004728750103900304

Khalid, U., Okafor, L. E., & Burzynska, K. (2021). Does the size of the tourism sector influence the economic policy response to the COVID-19 pandemic? *Current Issues in Tourism, 24*(19), 2801–2820. doi:10.1080/13683500.2021.1874311

Khanna, A., Sah, A., Choudhury, T., & Maheshwari, P. (2020). Blockchain Technology for Hospitality Industry. *Lecture Notes in Business Information Processing, 402*(November), 99–112. doi:10.1007/978-3-030-63396-7_7

Kim, E. Y., & Kim, Y.-K. (2004). Predicting online purchase intentions for clothing products. *European Journal of Marketing.*

Kim, J., Hlee, S., & Joun, Y. (2016). Green practices of the hotel industry: Analysis through the windows of smart tourism system. *International Journal of Information Management, 36*(6), 1340–1349. doi:10.1016/j.ijinfomgt.2016.05.001

Kim, T., Kim, M. C., Moon, G., & Chang, K. (2014). Technology-based self-service and its impact on customer productivity. *Services Marketing Quarterly, 35*(3), 255–269. doi:10.1080/15332969.2014.916145

Kim, Y., Wang, Q., & Roh, T. (2021). Do information and service quality affect perceived privacy protection, satisfaction, and loyalty? Evidence from a Chinese O2O-based mobile shopping application. *Telematics and Informatics, 56*, 101483. doi:10.1016/j.tele.2020.101483

Knani, M. (2014). Ethics in the Hospitality Industry: Review and Research Agenda. *International Journal of Business and Management, 9*(3), 1. doi:10.5539/ijbm.v9n3p1

Knight, D. W., Xiong, L., Lan, W., & Gong, J. (2020). Impact of COVID-19: Research note on tourism and hospitality sectors in the epicenter of Wuhan and Hubei Province, China. *International Journal of Contemporary Hospitality Management, 32*(12), 3705–3719. doi:10.1108/IJCHM-04-2020-0278

Kober, S. E., & Neuper, C. (2013). Personality and presence in virtual reality: Does their relationship depend on the used presence measure? *International Journal of Human-Computer Interaction, 29*(1), 13–25. doi:10.1080/10447318.2012.668131

Kolar, T., & Zabkar, V. (2010). A consumer-based model of authenticity: An oxymoron or the foundation of cultural heritage marketing? *Tourism Management, 31*(5), 652–664. doi:10.1016/j.tourman.2009.07.010

Kong, H., Wang, K., Qiu, X., Cheung, C., & Bu, N. T. (2022). 30 years of artificial intelligence (AI) research relating to the hospitality and tourism industry. *International Journal of Contemporary Hospitality Management.*

Kontogianni, A., & Alepis, E. (2020). Smart tourism: State of the art and literature review for the last six years. *Array, 6*(September 2019), 100020. doi:10.1016/j.array.2020.100020

Koo, C., Xiang, Z., Gretzel, U., & Sigala, M. (2021). Artificial Intelligence (AI) and Robotics in Travel, Hospitality, and Leisure. *Electronic Markets, 31*(3), 473–476. doi:10.1007/s12525-021-00494-z PMID:35603226

Kottum Elmar, C. (2019). *Charting Artificial Intelligence in Reality and Fiction.*

Kovach, K. A., & Cathcart, C. E. Jr. (1999). Human resource information systems (HRIS): Providing business with rapid data access, information exchange and strategic advantage. *Public Personnel Management, 28*(2), 275–282. doi:10.1177/009102609902800208

Kumar, S., Kumar, V., & Attri, K. (2021). Impact of Artificial Intelligence and Service Robots in Tourism and Hospitality Sector: Current Use & Future Trends. *Administrative Development: A Journal of HIPA, 8*(SI-1), 59-83.

Kumar, S., Talukder, M. B., Kabir, F., & Kaiser, F. (2024). Challenges and Sustainability of Green Finance in the Tourism Industry: Evidence From Bangladesh. In Sustainable Investments in Green Finance (pp. 97-111). IGI Global. doi:10.4018/979-8-3693-1388-6.ch006

Kumar, J., Konar, R., & Balasubramanian, K. (2020). The impact of Social Media on Consumers' purchasing behaviour in Malaysian Restaurants. *Journal of Spatial and Organizational Dynamics, 8*(3), 197–216.

Kumar, J., Nazir, F., & Nisar, Q. (2023). Empowering wellness worldwide: A critical analysis of the Global Wellness Institute (GWI) journey 2014-2021. *Journal of Tourism & Development, 41*, 263–287. doi:10.34624/rtd.v41i0.29731

Kumar, S., Dhiraj, A., & Hassan, S. C. C. (2023). Metaverse and Cultural Marketing in Hospitality and Tourism. In *Cultural Marketing and Metaverse for Consumer Engagement* (pp. 224–233). IGI Global. doi:10.4018/978-1-6684-8312-1.ch016

Kumar, S., Dhiraj, A., & Rani, D. (2023). Challenges and Advantages of Location-Based Services in Tourism Industries. In *Enhancing Customer Engagement Through Location-Based Marketing* (pp. 66–76). IGI Global. doi:10.4018/978-1-6684-8177-6.ch006

Kumar, S., Dhiraj, A., Shah, M. A., & Rani, D. (2023). Application of Metaverse in the Hospitality Industry. In *Influencer Marketing Applications Within the Metaverse* (pp. 178–194). IGI Global. doi:10.4018/978-1-6684-8898-0.ch011

Kumar, S., Kumar, P., Ahmad, S. S., Jayasaradadevi, P., Rajeyyagari, S., Manoharan, G., & Radhakrishnan, V. (2024). A Novel Approach for IoT-Based Cloud Computing Technology and its Impact on Business Entrepreneurship. *International Journal of Intelligent Systems and Applications in Engineering, 12*(10s), 624–628.

Kunekar, P., Manoharan, G., Mekala, S., Bhuvana, M., Brat Gupta, D., & Bhatt, V. (2024). Natural Language Processing and Deep Learning Techniques to Improve Sentiment Analysis in Social Media Texts. *6th International Conference on Contemporary Computing and Informatics (IC3I),* (pp. 1751-1755). IEEE.

Kusdibyo, L. (2021). *Tourist loyalty to hot springs destination: the role of tourist motivation, destination image, and tourist satisfaction*. Leisure/Loisir. doi:10.1080/14927713.2021.1986420

Lähteenmäki, J. (2021). The evolution paths of neutral host businesses: Antecedents, strategies, and business models. *Telecommunications Policy, 45*(10), 102201. doi:10.1016/j.telpol.2021.102201

Laing, J., Wheeler, F., Reeves, K., & Frost, W. (2014). Assessing the experiential value of heritage assets: A case study of a Chinese heritage precinct, Bendigo, Australia. *Tourism Management*, *40*, 180–192. doi:10.1016/j.tourman.2013.06.004

Landgrebe, J., & Smith, B. (2022). *Why Machines will Never Rule the World; Artificial Intelligence without Fear.*

Larivière, B., Bowen, D., Andreassen, T. W., Kunz, W., Sirianni, N. J., Voss, C., Wünderlich, N. V., & De Keyser, A. (2017). "Service Encounter 2.0": An investigation into the roles of technology, employees and customers. *Journal of Business Research*, *79*, 238–246. doi:10.1016/j.jbusres.2017.03.008

Lau, A. (2020). New technologies used in COVID-19 for business survival: Insights from the Hotel Sector in China. *Information Technology & Tourism*, *22*(4), 497–504. doi:10.1007/s40558-020-00193-z

Laura, S. D., Verma, R., Ph, D., Clough, R., Gilman, G., Practices, E., & Llp, G. (2010). *How Travelers Use Online and Social Media Channels to Make Hotel-choice Decisions, 10*(11).

Laurent, P., Chollet, T., & Herzberg, E. (2015). *Intelligent automation entering the business world.* Deloitte. https://www2.deloitte.com/eg/en.html

Laurent, P., Chollet, T., & Herzberg, E. (2015). *Intelligent automation entering the business world.* Deloitte. www2.deloitte.com/content/dam/Deloitte/lu/Documents/operations/lu-intelligent-automation business-world.pdf.

LEE, S. K., & MIN, S. R. (2021). Effects of Information Quality of Online Travel Agencies on Trust and Continuous Usage Intention: An Application of the SOR Model. The Journal of Asian Finance. *Economics and Business*, *8*(4), 971–982.

Lee, J. H., Hancock, M. G., & Mei-Chih, H. (2014). Towards an effective framework for building smart cities: Lessons from Seoul and San Francisco. *Technological Forecasting and Social Change*, *89*, 80–99. doi:10.1016/j.techfore.2013.08.033

Lee, M., Kwon, W., & Back, K.-J. (2021). Artificial intelligence for hospitality big data analytics: Developing a prediction model of restaurant review helpfulness for customer decision-making. *International Journal of Contemporary Hospitality Management*, *33*(6), 2117–2136. doi:10.1108/IJCHM-06-2020-0587

Lehto, X. Y., Brown, S., Chen, Y., & Morrison, A. M. (2006). Yoga tourism as a niche within the wellness tourism market. *Tourism Recreation Research*, *31*(1), 25–35. doi:10.1080/02508281.2006.11081244

Leong, L. Y., Hew, T. S., Lee, V. H., & Ooi, K. B. (2015). An SEM–artificial-neural-network analysis of the relationships between SERVPERF, customer satisfaction and loyalty among low-cost and full-service airline. *Expert Systems with Applications*, *42*(19), 6620–6634. doi:10.1016/j.eswa.2015.04.043

Lewis, H., Schrier, T., & Xu, S. (2022). Dark tourism: Motivations and visit intentions of tourists. *International Hospitality Review*, *36*(1), 107–123. doi:10.1108/IHR-01-2021-0004

Liang, X., Hu, X., Islam, T., & Mubarik, M. S. (2021). Social support, source credibility, social influence, and solar photovoltaic panels purchase intention. *Environmental Science and Pollution Research International*, *28*(41), 57842–57859. doi:10.1007/s11356-021-14750-4 PMID:34097220

Li, H., Hu, M., & Li, G. (2020). Forecasting tourism demand with multisource big data. *Annals of Tourism Research*, *83*, 102912. doi:10.1016/j.annals.2020.102912

Li, H., Wu, Y., Cao, D., & Wang, Y. (2021). Organizational mindfulness towards digital transformation as a prerequisite of information processing capability to achieve market agility. *Journal of Business Research*, *122*, 700–712. doi:10.1016/j.jbusres.2019.10.036

Li, J. J., Bonn, M. A., & Ye, B. H. (2019). Hotel employee's artificial intelligence and robotics awareness and its impact on turnover intention: The moderating roles of perceived organizational support and competitive psychological climate. *Tourism Management*, *73*, 172–181. doi:10.1016/j.tourman.2019.02.006

Li, K., Zhou, C., Luo, X. R., Benitez, J., & Liao, Q. (2022). Impact of information timeliness and richness on public engagement on social media during COVID-19 pandemic: An empirical investigation based on NLP and machine learning. *Decision Support Systems*, *162*, 113752. doi:10.1016/j.dss.2022.113752 PMID:35185227

Limna, P. (2023). Artificial Intelligence (AI) in the hospitality industry: A review article. *International Journal of Computing Sciences Research*, *7*, 1306–1317. doi:10.25147/ijcsr.2017.001.1.103

Lin, L.-Y., & Chen, C.-S. (2006). The influence of the country-of-origin image, product knowledge and product involvement on consumer purchase decisions: An empirical study of insurance and catering services in Taiwan. *Journal of Consumer Marketing*, *23*(5), 248–265. doi:10.1108/07363760610681655

Lin, X., & Falk, M. T. (2022). Nordic stock market performance of the travel and leisure industry during the first wave of Covid-19 pandemic. *Tourism Economics*, *28*(5), 1240–1257. doi:10.1177/1354816621990937

Lisi, F. A., & Esposito, F. (2015). An AI application to integrated tourism planning. Lecture Notes in Computer Science (Including Subseries Lecture Notes in Artificial Intelligence and Lecture Notes in Bioinformatics), 9336 LNCS, 246–259. Springer. doi:10.1007/978-3-319-24309-2_19

Li, X., Gong, J., Gao, B., & Yuan, P. (2021). Impacts of COVID-19 on tourists' destination preferences: Evidence from China. *Annals of Tourism Research*, *90*, 103258. doi:10.1016/j.annals.2021.103258 PMID:34924648

Li, Y., & Peng, Y. (2021). Influencer marketing: Purchase intention and its antecedents. *Marketing Intelligence & Planning*, *39*(7), 960–978. doi:10.1108/MIP-04-2021-0104

Lommatzsch, A. (2018). A next generation Chatbot-Framework for the public administration. *International Conference on Innovations for Community Services*. Springer. 10.1007/978-3-319-93408-2_10

Lourens, M., Raman, R., Vanitha, P., Singh, R., Manoharan, G., & Tiwari, M. (2022). *Agile Technology and Artificial Intelligent Systems in Business Development.* 2022 5th International Conference on Contemporary Computing and Informatics (IC3I), Uttar Pradesh, India. 10.1109/IC3I56241.2022.10073410

Luhar, H. (2021). An Analytical Study on Economy Upliftment through Virtual Tourism with special reference to Vasai Virar City. *Palarch's Journal Of Archaeology Of Egypt/Egyptology 18*(7).

Lukanova, G., & Ilieva, G. (2019). Robots, artifiial intelligence, and service automation in hotels. In Robots, Artificial Intelligence and Service Automation in Travel, Tourism and Hospitality. Emerald. doi:10.1108/978-1-78756-687-320191009

Lu, L.-C., Chang, W.-P., & Chang, H.-H. (2014). Consumer attitudes toward blogger's sponsored recommendations and purchase intention: The effect of sponsorship type, product type, and brand awareness. *Computers in Human Behavior*, *34*, 258–266. doi:10.1016/j.chb.2014.02.007

Mahato, R. (2021). *Artificial Intelligence Language Learning And Communication: Exploring The Intersection Of Technology And Education*. Research Gate. https://www.researchgate.net/publication/371830162

Mah, P. M., Skalna, I., & Muzam, J. (2022). Natural Language Processing and Artificial Intelligence for Enterprise Management in the Era of Industry 4.0. *Applied Sciences (Basel, Switzerland)*, *12*(18), 9207. doi:10.3390/app12189207

Malik, A., Budhwar, P., Patel, C., & Srikanth, N. R. (2022). May the bots be with you! Delivering HR cost-effectiveness and individualised employee experiences in an MNE. *International Journal of Human Resource Management*, *33*(6), 1148–1178. doi:10.1080/09585192.2020.1859582

Malik, A., Budhwar, P., & Srikanth, N. R. (2020). Gig economy, 4IR and artificial intelligence: Rethinking strategic HRM. In *Human & technological resource management (HTRM): New insights into revolution 4.0* (pp. 75–88). Emerald Publishing Limited. doi:10.1108/978-1-83867-223-220201005

Malik, D. (2023). Practical lessons from implementing a data-driven approach to passenger flow optimisation and airport capacity management. *Journal of Airport Management*, *17*(3), 218–235.

Manoharan, G., & Narayanan, S. (2021). A research study to investigate the feasibility of digital marketing strategies in advertising. *PalArch's Journal of Archaeology of Egypt/Egyptology, 18*(09), 450-456.

Manoharan, G., Ashtikar, S., Nithya, P., & Maheshwari, V. (2023). Social media marketing influence on usage as a brand choice towards users in varied district. *BioGecko*, *12*(2), 2234-2242.

Manoharan, G., Durai, S., Ashtikar, S. P., & Kumari, N. (2024). Artificial Intelligence in Marketing Applications. In Artificial Intelligence for Business (pp. 40-70). Productivity Press.

Manoharan, G., Durai, S., Rajesh, G. A., Razak, A., Rao, C. B., & Ashtikar, S. P. (2023). A study of postgraduate students' perceptions of key components in ICCC to be used in artificial intelligence-based smart cities. In *Artificial Intelligence and Machine Learning in Smart City Planning* (pp. 117–133). Elsevier. doi:10.1016/B978-0-323-99503-0.00003-X

Manoharan, G., Durai, S., Rajesh, G. A., Razak, A., Rao, C. B., & Ashtikar, S. P. (2023). A study on the perceptions of officials on their duties and responsibilities at various levels of the organizational structure in order to accomplish artificial intelligence-based smart city implementation. In *Artificial Intelligence and Machine Learning in Smart City Planning* (pp. 1–10). Elsevier. doi:10.1016/B978-0-323-99503-0.00007-7

Manoharan, K. G., Nehru, J. A., & Balasubramanian, S. (2021). *Artificial Intelligence and IoT*. Springer. doi:10.1007/978-981-33-6400-4

Manoharan, T. R., Muralidharan, C., & Deshmukh, S. G. (2011). An integrated fuzzy multi-attribute decision-making model for employees' performance appraisal. *International Journal of Human Resource Management*, *22*(3), 722–745. doi:10.1080/09585192.2011.543763

Manser Payne, E. H., Dahl, A. J., & Peltier, J. (2021). Digital servitization value co-creation framework for AI services: A research agenda for digital transformation in financial service ecosystems. *Journal of Research in Interactive Marketing*, *15*(2), 200–222. doi:10.1108/JRIM-12-2020-0252

Margherita, A. (2022). Human resources analytics: A systematization of research topics and directions for future research. *Human Resource Management Review*, *32*(2), 100795. doi:10.1016/j.hrmr.2020.100795

Mariani, M., & Baggio, R. (2022). Big data and analytics in hospitality and tourism: A systematic literature review. *International Journal of Contemporary Hospitality Management*, *34*(1), 231–278. doi:10.1108/IJCHM-03-2021-0301

Marinakis, V., & Doukas, H. (2018). An advanced IoT-based system for intelligent energy management in buildings. *Sensors (Basel)*, *18*(2), 610. doi:10.3390/s18020610 PMID:29462957

Marketing Dive. (n.d.). *Marriott makes more room for chatbots to enhance guest experiences.* https://www.marketingdive.com/news/marriott-makes-more-room-for-chatbots-to-enhance-guest-experiences/510117/

Martínez-Molés, V., Jung, T. H., Pérez-Cabañero, C., & Cervera-Taulet, A. (2022). Gathering pre-purchase information for a cruise vacation with virtual reality: The effects of media technology and gender. *International Journal of Contemporary Hospitality Management*, *34*(1), 407–429. doi:10.1108/IJCHM-04-2021-0500

Mastercard. (2021). *Mastercard New Payments Index: Consumer Appetite for Digital Payments Takes Off*. Mastercard. https://www.mastercard.com/news/latin-america/en/newsroom/press-releases/pr-en/2021/may/mastercard-new-payments-index-consumer-appetite-for-digital-payments-takes-off/

Mathioudakis, G., Klironomos, I., Partarakis, N., Papadaki, E., Anifantis, N., Antona, M., & Stephanidis, C. (2021). Supporting Online and On-Site Digital Diverse Travels. *Heritage*, *4*(4), 4558–4577. doi:10.3390/heritage4040251

Mathur, S., Tewari, A., & Singh, A. (2021). Modeling the factors affecting online purchase intention: The mediating effect of consumer's attitude towards user-generated content. *Journal of Marketing Communications*, 1–20.

Mattan, M. (2023). *The Role of Artificial Intelligence in Augmented Reality and Virtual Reality.* Barnd XR. https://www.brandxr.io/the-role-of-ai-in-augmented-and-virtual-reality#:~:text=AI%20significantly%20enhances%20the%20user,the%20learner's%20progress%20and%20understandi-ng

Matute, J., Polo-Redondo, Y., & Utrillas, A. (2016). The influence of EWOM characteristics on online repurchase intention: Mediating roles of trust and perceived usefulness. *Online Information Review*, *40*(7), 1090–1110. doi:10.1108/OIR-11-2015-0373

Mccalla, G. (2000). The Fragmentation of Culture, Learning, Teaching and Technology: Implications for the Artificial Intelligence in Education Research Agenda in 2010. In International Journal of Artificial Intelligence in Education, 11.

Mccarty, K., & Orientale, P. (2010). Technology & Hospitality. *HOSTEUR*, *19*(1), 1–43.

McCormick, J. Doty, C.A. Sridharan, S. Curran, R. Evelson, B. Hopkins, B. Little, C. Leganza, G. Purcell, B. & Miller, E. (2016). *Predictions 2017: artificial intelligence will drive the insights revolution.* FORRESTER research for customer insights professionals.

McGovern, S. L., Pandey, V., Gill, S., Aldrich, T., Myers, C., Desai, C., & Balasubramanian, V. (2018). The new age: artificial intelligence for human resource opportunities and functions. Ey. com.

McKinsey & Company. (2020). The COVID-19 recovery will be digital: A plan for the first 90 days. McKinsey & Company.

McKinsey. (2019). *How Artificial Intelligence will transform Nordic businesses*. McKinsey. https://www.mckinsey.com/featured-insights/artificial-intelligence/how-artificial-intelligence-will-transform-nordic-businesses

McLean, G., & Barhorst, J. B. (2022). Living the experience before you go... but did it meet expectations? The role of virtual reality during hotel bookings. *Journal of Travel Research*, *61*(6), 1233–1251. doi:10.1177/00472875211028313

MCMC - Communications and Multimedia Malaysia. (2019). *National Fiberisation and Connectivity Plan (NFCP) 2019-2023.* MCMC.

MCMC - Communications and Multimedia Malaysia. (2022). *5G Drives Malaysia's Digitalisation.* MCMC. https://www.mcmc.gov.my/en/media/press-clippings/5g-drives-malaysia-s-digitalisation#:~:text=5G%20TECHNOLOGY%20was%20launched%20here,successor%20of%204G%20cellular%20networks

Md Khairi, N. D., Ismail, H. N., & Syed Jaafar, S. M. R. (2022). Knowledge of tourist spatial behaviour to improve Melaka world heritage site management. *International Journal of Tourism Cities*, *8*(1), 88–106. doi:10.1108/IJTC-01-2021-0018

Meenaakumari, M., Jayasuriya, P., Dhanraj, N., Sharma, S., Manoharan, G., & Tiwari, M. (2022, December). Loan Eligibility Prediction using Machine Learning based on Personal Information. In *2022 5th International Conference on Contemporary Computing and Informatics (IC3I)* (pp. 1383-1387). IEEE. 10.1109/IC3I56241.2022.10073318

Mensah, I., & Blankson, E. J. (2014). Commitment to Environmental Management in Hotels in Accra. *International Journal of Hospitality & Tourism Administration*, *15*(2), 150–171. doi:10.1080/15256480.2014.901064

Miah, S. J., Vu, H. Q., Gammack, J., & McGrath, M. (2017). A big data analytics method for tourist behaviour analysis. *Information & Management*, *54*(6), 771–785. doi:10.1016/j.im.2016.11.011

Mikołajczyk, K. (2022). Changes in the approach to employee development in organisations as a result of the COVID-19 pandemic. *European Journal of Training and Development*, *46*(5/6), 544–562. doi:10.1108/EJTD-12-2020-0171

Miller, C., Thomas, B. C., & Roeller, M. (2020). Innovation management processes and sustainable iterative circles: An applied integrative approach. *Journal of Work-Applied Management*, *12*(1), 69–90. doi:10.1108/JWAM-11-2019-0037

Milton, T. (2023). *Artificial Intelligence in Tourism-A review of Trends Opportunities and Challenges*. Chandigarh Philosophers. www.chandigarhphilosophers.com

Ministry of Housing and Local Government. (2018). *Smart City Framework Malaysia*. MHLG.

Mohamed Sofian, I. N., Padlee, S. F., & Hussin, N. Z. (2021). Tourists Satisfaction Towards Smart Tourism Services in Malaysia. *Proceeding for Global Tourism Conference (GTC) 2021*. IEEE. 10.46754/gtc.2021.11.008

Mohd Shith Putera, N. S., Saripan, H., Mohd Bajury, M. S., & Ya'cob, S. N. (2022). *Artificial Intelligence in the Tourism Industry: A privacy impasse*. Environment-Behaviour Proceedings Journal.

Muda, M., & Hamzah, M. I. (2021). Should I suggest this YouTube clip? The impact of UGC source credibility on eWOM and purchase intention. *Journal of Research in Interactive Marketing*, *15*(3), 441–459. doi:10.1108/JRIM-04-2020-0072

Mudambi, S. M., & Schuff, D. (2010). Research note: What makes a helpful online review? A study of customer reviews on Amazon. com. *MIS Quarterly*, 185–200.

Murphy, J., Hofacker, C., & Gretzel, U. (2017). Dawning of the age of robots in hospitality and tourism: Challenges for teaching and research. *European Journal of Tourism Research*, *15*, 104–111. doi:10.54055/ejtr.v15i.265

Nabella, S. D. (2021). Improve Consumer Purchasing Decisions Through Quality of Service, Promotion And Quality of Information At PT. Ng Tech Supplies. International Journal of Science. *Technology & Management*, *2*(3), 880–889.

Naeem, M., Rizvi, S. T. H., & Coronato, A. (2020). A Gentle Introduction to Reinforcement Learning and its Application in Different Fields. *IEEE Access : Practical Innovations, Open Solutions*, *8*, 209320–209344. doi:10.1109/ACCESS.2020.3038605

Nagaraj, S. (2019). AI enabled marketing: What is it all about? *International Journal of Research in Commerce, Economics and Management*, *8*(6), 501–518.

Nagaraj, S. (2020). Marketing analytics for customer engagement: A viewpoint [IJISSC]. *International Journal of Information Systems and Social Change*, *11*(2), 41–55. doi:10.4018/IJISSC.2020040104

Nagar, R., Singh, Y., Gobinath, R., & Manoharan, G. (2022). Aspects of medical tourism in India: A review. *AIP Conference Proceedings*, *2418*, 020030. doi:10.1063/5.0093282

National Restaurant Association. (2022). *High-tech hospitality*. NRA. https://restaurant.org/education-and-resources/resource-library/high-tech-hospitality/

Naumov, N. (2019). *The Impact of Robots, Artificial Intelligence, and Service Automation on Service Quality and Service Experience in Hospitality. Robots, Artificial Intelligence, and Service Automation in Travel, Tourism, and Hospitality*. Emerald Publishing Limited.

Nayak, J., Mishra, M., Naik, B., Swapnarekha, H., Cengiz, K., & Shanmuganathan, V. (2022). An impact study of COVID-19 on six different industries: Automobile, energy and power, agriculture, education, travel and tourism and consumer electronics. *Expert Systems: International Journal of Knowledge Engineering and Neural Networks*, *39*(3), e12677. doi:10.1111/exsy.12677 PMID:33821074

Nayyar, A., Mahapatra, B., Le, D., & Suseendran, G. (2018). Virtual Reality (VR) & Augmented Reality (AR) technologies for tourism and hospitality industry. *International journal of engineering & technology, 7*(2.21), 156-160.

Nayyar, A., Mahapatra, B., Le, D. N., & Suseendran, G. (2018). Virtual Reality (VR) & Augmented Reality (AR) technologies for tourism and hospitality industry. *International Journal of Engineering and Technology(UAE)*, *7*(2), 156–160. doi:10.14419/ijet.v7i2.21.11858

Nayyar, A., Mahapatra, B., Le, D., & Suseendran, G. (2018). Virtual Reality (VR) & Augmented Reality (AR) technologies for tourism and hospitality industry. [). www.sciencepubco.com/index.php/IJET]. *IACSIT International Journal of Engineering and Technology*, *7*(2).

Nero, S. (2009). Inhabiting the other's world: Language and cultural immersion for us-based teachers in the dominican republic. *Language, Culture and Curriculum*, *22*(3), 175–194. doi:10.1080/07908310903203066

Neslin, S. A., Grewal, D., Leghorn, R., Shankar, V., Teerling, M. L., Thomas, J. S., & Verhoef, P. C. (2006). Challenges and opportunities in multichannel customer management. *Journal of Service Research, 9*(2), 95–112. doi:10.1177/1094670506293559

Newsome, D. (2021). The collapse of tourism and its impact on wildlife tourism destinations. *Journal of Tourism Futures, 7*(3), 295–302. doi:10.1108/JTF-04-2020-0053

Nghiem-Phu, B. (2019). What determines the loyalty of airline passengers? Findings of a quantitative data-mining study. *MARKET-TRZISTE, 31*(1), 23–37. doi:10.22598/mt/2019.31.1.23

Nguyen, B., Pantano, E., Dennis, C., & Gerlach, S. (2016). *Internet Retailing and Future Perspectives*. Routledge.

Nhamo, G., Dube, K., Chikodzi, D., Nhamo, G., Dube, K., & Chikodzi, D. (2020). Implications of COVID-19 on gaming, leisure and entertainment industry. *Counting the cost of COVID-19 on the global tourism industry*, 273-295.

Niaz, M. (2022). Revolutionizing Inventory Planning: Harnessing Digital Supply Data through Digitization to Optimize Storage Efficiency Pre-and Post-Pandemic. *BULLET: Jurnal Multidisiplin Ilmu, 1*(03).

Nicastro, D. (2020). 7 ways artificial intelligence is reinventing Human Resources. *Digital workplace*. https://www.cmswire.com/digital-workplace/7-ways-artificial-intelligence-is-reinventing-human-resources/

Nwokorie, E. C., & Igbojekwe, P. (2019). Security challenges for the hotel industry. In Academica Turistica-Tourism and Innovation Journal.

Obeidy, W. K., Arshad, H., & Huang, J. (2018). TouristicAR: A Smart Glass Augmented Reality Application for UNESCO World Heritage Sites in Malaysia. *Journal of Telecommunication, Electronic and Computer Engineering, 10*, 101–108.

OECD. (2009). *The Impact of Culture on Tourism*. OECD Publishing.

OECD. O. (2014). OECD Tourism trends and policies 2014. OECD Publishing.

Oh, H., Fiore, A. M., & Jeoung, M. (2007). Measuring experience economy concepts: Tourism applications. *Journal of Travel Research, 46*(2), 119–132. doi:10.1177/0047287507304039

Okech, R. N. (2014). Promoting the spa tourism industry: Focus on coastal resorts in Kenya. *Athens Journal of Tourism, 1*(1), 67–77. doi:10.30958/ajt.1-1-4

Oncioiu, I., & Priescu, I. (2022). The use of virtual reality in tourism destinations as a tool to develop tourist behavior perspective. *Sustainability (Basel), 14*(7), 4191. doi:10.3390/su14074191

Oren, G., Poria, Y., & Reichel, A. (2022). The positive role of negative emotions in heritage-site visits: The case of Auschwitz Death Camp. *Journal of Heritage Tourism, 17*(2), 158–173. doi:10.1080/1743873X.2021.1937186

Osei, B. A., Ragavan, N. A., Kandappan, B., & Mensah, H. K. (2020). Hospitality revolution 4.0: A literature review on a unified typology of IR 4.0 technologies for the tourism and hospitality industry in the era of COVID-19. *Asia-Pacific Journal of Innovation in Hospitality and Tourism*, *9*(1), 25–45.

Ospina-Pinillos, L., Davenport, T. A., Ricci, C. S., Milton, A. C., Scott, E. M., & Hickie, I. B. (2018). Developing a Mental Health eClinic to Improve Access to and Quality of Mental Health Care for Young People: Using Participatory Design as Research Methodologies. *Journal of Medical Internet Research*, *20*(5), e188. doi:10.2196/jmir.9716 PMID:29807878

Ozdemir, D. Y., Singh, H., & Sarkar, S. (2021). *Credibility*. Novelty and Helpfulness in Online Reviews.

Özkul, E., & Kumlu, S. T.ÖZKUL. (2019). Augmented Reality Applications in Tourism. *International Journal of Contemporary Tourism Research*, *3*, 107–122. doi:10.30625/ijctr.625192

Palmer, C. (1999). Tourism and the symbols of identity. *Tourism Management*, *20*(3), 313–321. doi:10.1016/S0261-5177(98)00120-4

Pandey, U., Islam, M. T., & Hossain, M. I. (2023). Servicescape, E-WoM, and satisfaction on tourists' revisit intention to yoga tourist destination: Evidence from Patanjali Yogpeeth, India. *Revista Turismo & Desenvolvimento (Aveiro)*, *44*, 313–333.

Pan, Y., Froese, F., Liu, N., Hu, Y., & Ye, M. (2022). The adoption of artificial intelligence in employee recruitment: The influence of contextual factors. *International Journal of Human Resource Management*, *33*(6), 1125–1147. doi:10.1080/09585192.2021.1879206

Park, C. W., Sutherland, I., & Lee, S. K. (2021). Effects of online reviews, trust, and picture-superiority on intention to purchase restaurant services. *Journal of Hospitality and Tourism Management*, *47*, 228–236. doi:10.1016/j.jhtm.2021.03.007

Park, D.-H., & Lee, J. (2008). EWOM overload and its effect on consumer behavioral intention depending on consumer involvement. *Electronic Commerce Research and Applications*, *7*(4), 386–398. doi:10.1016/j.elerap.2007.11.004

Park, Y.-J. (2018). Predicting the helpfulness of online customer reviews across different product types. *Sustainability (Basel)*, *10*(6), 1735. doi:10.3390/su10061735

Penela, D., Estevao, J., & Gregory, A. (2019). Accounting and financial antecedents of corporate spin-offs in the lodging industry. *International Journal of Hospitality Management*, *83*, 151–158. doi:10.1016/j.ijhm.2019.05.007

Peranzo, P. (2019). *AI assistant: the future of travel industry with the increase of artificial intelligence*. Imaginovation. www.imaginovation.net/blog/the-future-of-travel-with-the-increase-of-ai/

Pereira, V., Hadjielias, E., Christofi, M., & Vrontis, D. (2023). A systematic literature review on the impact of artificial intelligence on workplace outcomes: A multi-process perspective. *Human Resource Management Review*, *33*(1), 100857. doi:10.1016/j.hrmr.2021.100857

Petr, C. (2002). Tourist apprehension of heritage: A semiotic approach to behaviour patterns. *International Journal of Arts Management*, 25–38. https://www.jstor.org/stable/41064753

Petr, C. (2009). Fame is not always a positive asset for heritage equity! Some clues from buying intentions of national tourists. *Journal of Travel & Tourism Marketing*, *26*(1), 1–18. doi:10.1080/10548400802656694

Petr, C. (2015). How heritage site tourists may become monument visitors. *Tourism Management*, *51*, 247–262. doi:10.1016/j.tourman.2015.05.018

Pillai, R., & Sivathanu, B. (2020). Adoption of AI-Based Chatbots for Hospitality and Tourism. *International Journal of Contemporary Hospitality Management*, *32*(10), 3199–3226. doi:10.1108/IJCHM-04-2020-0259

Pine, B. J., & Gilmore, J. H. (1998). Welcome to the experience economy. *Harvard Business Review*, *76*(4), 97–105. PMID:10181589

Ping, Y., Buoye, A., & Vakil, A. (2023). Enhanced review facilitation service for C2C support: Machine learning approaches. *Journal of Services Marketing*, *37*(5), 620–635. doi:10.1108/JSM-01-2022-0005

Polachowska, K. (2019). *12 challenges of AI adoption*. Neoteric. https://neoteric.eu/blog/12-challenges-of-ai-adoption/

Ponduri, S. B., Ahmad, S. S., Ravisankar, P., Thakur, D. J., Chawla, K., Chary, D. T., & Sharma, S. (2024). A Study on Recent Trends of Technology and its Impact on Business and Hotel Industry. *Migration Letters : An International Journal of Migration Studies*, *21*(S1), 801–806.

Popescul, D., Diana, L., & Alexandru, R. (2016). Data Security in Smart Cities: Challenges and Solutions. *Informações Econômicas*, *20*(1), 29–38. doi:10.12948/issn14531305/20.1.2016.03

Popesku, J., & Zlatanov, S. (2019). Current Applications of Artificial Intelligence In Tourism And Hospitality. *International Scientific Conference on Information Technology and Data Related Research*. Research Gate. https://www.researchgate.net/publication/333242550_Current_Applications_of_Artificial_Intelligence_in_Tourism_and_Hospitality

Poria, Y., Butler, R., & Airey, D. (2003). The core of heritage tourism. *Annals of Tourism Research*, *30*(1), 238–254. doi:10.1016/S0160-7383(02)00064-6

Poria, Y., Butler, R., & Airey, D. (2004). Links between tourists, heritage, and reasons for visiting heritage sites. *Journal of Travel Research*, *43*(1), 19–28. doi:10.1177/0047287504265508

Poria, Y., Reichel, A., & Biran, A. (2006). Heritage site perceptions and motivations to visit. *Journal of Travel Research*, *44*(3), 318–326. doi:10.1177/0047287505279004

Prahalad, C. K., & Ramaswamy, V. (2004). Co-creating unique value with customers. *Strategy and Leadership*, *32*(3), 4–9. doi:10.1108/10878570410699249

Prentice, C., Dominique Lopes, S., & Wang, X. (2020). The impact of artificial intelligence and employee service qualityon customer satisfaction and loyalty. *Journal of Hospitality Marketing & Management*, *29*(7), 739–756. doi:10.1080/19368623.2020.1722304

Punia, S., & Shankar, S. (2022). Predictive analytics for demand forecasting: A deep learning-based decision support system. *Knowledge-Based Systems*, *258*, 109956. doi:10.1016/j.knosys.2022.109956

Qamar, Y., & Samad, T. A. (2022). Human resource analytics: A review and bibliometric analysis. *Personnel Review*, *51*(1), 251–283. doi:10.1108/PR-04-2020-0247

Quinn, B. (2006). Problematising 'festival tourism': Arts festivals and sustainable development in Ireland. *Journal of Sustainable Tourism*, *14*(3), 288–306. doi:10.1080/09669580608669060

Rahman, S. A., Dura, N., Yusof, M. A., Nakamura, H., & Nong, R. A. (2020). Challenges of Smart Tourism in Malaysia Eco-Tourism Destinations. *Planning Malaysia Journal*, *18*(4), 442–451. doi:10.21837/pm.v18i14.844

Ramadanty, M. L., & Kartikasari, D. (2021). *Purchase Intention of E-Payment: The Substitute or Complementary Role of Brand*. Sales Promotions, and Information Quality.

Ramsey, D., & Everitt, J. (2008). If you dig it, they will come!: Archaeology heritage sites and tourism development in Belize, Central America. *Tourism Management*, *29*(5), 909–916. doi:10.1016/j.tourman.2007.11.002

Ranasinghe, R., Karunarathne, A. C. I. D., & Herath, J. (2021). After corona (COVID-19) impacts on global poverty and recovery of tourism based service economies: An appraisal. *International Journal of Tourism and Hospitality*, *1*(1), 52–64.

Ransbotham, S., Khodabandeh, S., Kiron, D., Candelon, F., Chu, M., & LaFountain, B. (2020). *Expanding AI's impact with organizational learning*. MIT Sloan Management Review and Boston Consulting Group.

Ransbotham, S., Kiron, D., & Reeves, M. (2017). Research Report: Reshaping business with artificial intelligence. *MIT Sloan Management Review*, 1–17.

Rapp, A., Curti, L., & Boldi, A. (2021). The human side of human-chatbot interaction: A systematic literature review of ten years of research on text-based chatbots. *International Journal of Human-Computer Studies*, *151*, 102630. doi:10.1016/j.ijhcs.2021.102630

Ratten, V. Álvarez-García, J., & Río Rama, M. de la C. del. (2019). Entrepreneurship, Innovation and Inequality : Exploring Territorial Dynamics and Development. Routledge.

Razak, A., Nayak, M. P., Manoharan, G., Durai, S., Rajesh, G. A., Rao, C. B., & Ashtikar, S. P. (2023). Reigniting the power of artificial intelligence in education sector for the educators and students competence. In *Artificial Intelligence and Machine Learning in Smart City Planning* (pp. 103–116). Elsevier. doi:10.1016/B978-0-323-99503-0.00009-0

Reddy, R. (2006). Robotics and intelligent systems in support of society. *IEEE Intelligent Systems*, *21*(3), 24–31. doi:10.1109/MIS.2006.57

Revfine. (n. d.). *How to use Artificial Intelligence in the Hospitality Industry*. Revfine. https://www.revfine.com/artificial-intelligence-hospitality-industry/

Riaz, H., Baig, U., Meidute-Kavaliauskiene, I., & Ahmed, H. (2021). Factors effecting omnichannel customer experience: Evidence from fashion retail. *Information (Basel)*, *13*(1), 12. doi:10.3390/info13010012

Richards, G. (2001). The experience industry and the creation of attractions. In *Cultural attractions and European tourism* (pp. 55–69). Cabi Publishing. doi:10.1079/9780851994406.0055

Richards, G. (2012). An overview of food and tourism trends and policies. In *Food and the tourism experience: The OECD-Korea workshop* (pp. 13–46). The OECD Tourism Studies. doi:10.1787/9789264171923-3-en

Richards, G., & Wilson, J. (2006). Developing creativity in tourist experiences: A solution to the serial reproduction of culture? *Tourism Management*, *27*(6), 1209–1223. doi:10.1016/j.tourman.2005.06.002

Riswanto, A. L., & Kim, H.-S. (2023). An Investigation of The Key Attributes of Korean Wellness Tourism Customers Based on Online Reviews. *Sustainability (Basel)*, *15*(8), 6702. doi:10.3390/su15086702

Rodríguez, B., Molina, J., Pérez, F., & Caballero, R. (2012). Interactive design of personalised tourism routes. *Tourism Management*, *33*(4), 926–940. doi:10.1016/j.tourman.2011.09.014

Rogers, E. M. (2010). *Diffusion of innovations*. Simon and Schuster.

Rosário, A. T., & Dias, J. C. (2022). Sustainability and the Digital Transition: A Literature Review. *Sustainability (Basel)*, *14*(7), 4072. doi:10.3390/su14074072

Rosário, A. T., & Dias, J. C. (2023). How has data-driven marketing evolved: Challenges and opportunities with emerging technologies. *International Journal of Information Management Data Insights*, *3*(2), 100203. doi:10.1016/j.jjimei.2023.100203

Ruel, H., & Njoku, E. (2021). AI Redefining the Hospitality Industry. Journal of Tourism Futures, 7, 53-66. doi:10.1108/JTF-03-2020-0032

Rula, A. (2022). How smart is e-tourism? A systematic review of smart tourism recommendation system applying data management. *Computer Science Review*, *39*, 2021.

Rusdiana, A., Suroso, A., & Suwandari, L. (2020). The Effect of e-WOM Source Credibility on Purchase Intentions with Consumer Involvement as a Moderating Variable. *ICORE*, *5*(1).

Russell, S., & Norvig, P. (2016). *Artificial Intelligence: A Modern Approach*. Pearson.

Ryan, C., & Higgins, O. (2006). Experiencing cultural tourism: Visitors at the Maori arts and crafts institute, New Zealand. *Journal of Travel Research*, *44*(3), 308–317. doi:10.1177/0047287505279002

Saariluoma, P., & Karvonen, A. (2023). Theory languages in designing artificial intelligence. *AI & Society*. doi:10.1007/s00146-023-01716-y

Sahoo, M., & Mishra, S. (2023). A Bibliometric Analysis of Artificial Intelligence and Human Resource Management. In *International Conference on ICT for Sustainable Development,* (pp. 33-40). Singapore: Springer Nature Singapore. 10.1007/978-981-99-5652-4_4

Said, S. (2023). The Role of Artificial Intelligence (AI) and Data Analytics in Enhancing Guest Personalization in Hospitality. *Journal of Modern Hospitality*, *2*(1), 1–13. doi:10.47941/jmh.1556

Saleem, A., & Ellahi, A. (2017). Influence of electronic word of mouth on purchase intention of fashion products in social networking websites. [PJCSS]. *Pakistan Journal of Commerce and Social Sciences*, *11*(2), 597–622.

Salvatore, C., Biffignandi, S., & Bianchi, A. (2021). Social media and Twitter data quality for new social indicators. *Social Indicators Research*, *156*(2), 601–630. doi:10.1007/s11205-020-02296-w

Sandeep, S. R., Ahamad, S., Saxena, D., Srivastava, K., Jaiswal, S., & Bora, A. (2022). To understand the relationship between Machine learning and Artificial intelligence in large and diversified business organisations. *Materials Today: Proceedings*, *56*, 2082–2086. doi:10.1016/j.matpr.2021.11.409

Sann, R., Lai, P.-C., Liaw, S.-Y., & Chen, C.-T. (2022). Predicting online complaining behavior in the hospitality industry: Application of big data analytics to online reviews. *Sustainability (Basel)*, *14*(3), 1800. doi:10.3390/su14031800

Sarker, I. H. (2021). Deep Learning: A Comprehensive Overview on Techniques, Taxonomy, Applications and Research Directions. In SN Computer Science, 2(6). Springer. doi:10.1007/s42979-021-00815-1

Sarmah, B., Kamboj, S., & Kandampully, J. (2018). Social media and co-creative service innovation: An empirical study. *Online Information Review*, *42*(7), 1146–1179. doi:10.1108/OIR-03-2017-0079

Satpathy, A., Samal, A., Gupta, S., Kumar, S., Sharma, S., Manoharan, G., Karthikeyan, M., & Sharma, S. (2024). To Study the Sustainable Development Practices in Business and Food Industry. *Migration Letters : An International Journal of Migration Studies*, *21*(S1), 743–747. doi:10.59670/ml.v21iS1.6400

Sayers, D., Sousa-Silva, R., Höhn, S., Ahmedi, L., Allkivi-Metsoja, K., Anastasiou, D., Beňuš, Š., Bowker, L., Bytyçi, E., & Catala, A. (2021). *The Dawn of the Human-Machine Era: A forecast of new and emerging language technologies.*

Schoorman, F. D. (1988). Escalation Bias in Performance Appraisals: An Unintended Consequence of Supervisor Participation in Hiring Decisions. *The Journal of Applied Psychology*, *73*(1), 58–62. doi:10.1037/0021-9010.73.1.58

Şeker, F. (2023). Evolution of Machine Learning in Tourism: A Comprehensive Review of Seminal Research. *Journal of Artificial Intelligence and Data Science*, *3*(2), 54–79.

Sekhon, G., & Ahuja, S. (2023). Review Machine Learning Models for Managing Hotel Cancellations in the Tourism Industry. *2023 3rd International Conference on Intelligent Technologies, CONIT 2023*. IEEE. 10.1109/CONIT59222.2023.10205827

Sen Chiang, H., & Huang, T. C. (2015). User-adapted travel planning system for personalized schedule recommendation. *Information Fusion*, *21*(1), 3–17. doi:10.1016/j.inffus.2013.05.011

Seyidov, J., & Adomaitiene, R. (2016). Factors influencing local tourists' decision-making on choosing a destination: A case of Azerbaijan. *Ekonomika (Nis)*, *95*(3), 112–127. doi:10.15388/Ekon.2016.3.10332

Shabani, N., & Munir, A. (2020). A Review of Cyber Security Issues in Hospitality Industry. *Advances in Intelligent Systems and Computing*, *1230 AISC*(July), 482–493. doi:10.1007/978-3-030-52243-8_35

ShabaniN. (2017). *A study of cyber security in hospitality industry- threats and countermeasures: case study in Reno, Nevada* (Issue April). University of South Florida Sarasota. http://arxiv.org/abs/1705.02749

Shameem, A., Ramachandran, K. K., Sharma, A., Singh, R., Selvaraj, F. J., & Manoharan, G. *The Rising Importance of AI in Boosting the Efficiency of Online Advertising in Developing Countries*. 2023 3rd International Conference on Advance Computing and Innovative Technologies in Engineering (ICACITE), Greater Noida, India. 10.1109/ICACITE57410.2023.10182754

Shank, D. B., Graves, C., Gott, A., Gamez, P., & Rodriguez, S. (2019). Feeling our way to machine minds: People's emotions when perceiving mind in artificial intelligence. *Computers in Human Behavior*, *98*, 256–266. doi:10.1016/j.chb.2019.04.001

Sharif, M. A. (2016). Electronic word of mouth: Investigating the influence of electronic message source credibility, message appeal and brand equity on consumer purchase intention. *City University Research Journal*, *6*(1).

Sharma, S. P., Singh, L., & Tiwari, R. (2023). Prediction of Customer Review's Helpfulness Based on Feature Engineering Driven Deep Learning Model. [IJSI]. *International Journal of Software Innovation*, *11*(1), 1–16.

Shin, H. H., & Jeong, M. (2022). Does a virtual trip evoke travelers' nostalgia and derive intentions to visit the destination, a similar destination, and share?: Nostalgia-motivated tourism. *Journal of Travel & Tourism Marketing*, *39*(1), 1–17. doi:10.1080/10548408.2022.2044972

Shin, H.-R., & Choi, J.-G. (2021). The Moderating Effect of 'Generation'on the Relations between Source Credibility of Social Media Contents, Hotel Brand Image, and Purchase Intention. *Sustainability (Basel), 13*(16), 9471. doi:10.3390/su13169471

Shore, S. (2010). Cultural and heritage tourism-international. *Travel & Tourism Analyst*, 8.

Sigala, M. (2020). Tourism and COVID-19: Impacts and implications for advancing and resetting industry and research. *Journal of Business Research, 117*(June), 312–321. doi:10.1016/j.jbusres.2020.06.015 PMID:32546875

Sihombing, L. H., Lestari, P., & Dante, J. (2022). The effects of COVID-19 pandemic towards conventional theaters and online streaming services in Indonesia. *International Journal of Communication and Society, 4*(1), 153–162. doi:10.31763/ijcs.v4i1.337

Singer, R. (2016). *Robots and Artificial Intelligence in The Hotel Industry*. ITB Berlin.

Singh, A. (2023). *How Remote Work is Reshaping the Future of Tourism*. LinkedIn. https://www.linkedin.com/pulse/how-remote-work-reshaping-future-tourism-aastha-singh/

Singh, A. L., Jamal, S., & Ahmad, W. S. (2021). Impact assessment of lockdown amid COVID-19 pandemic on tourism industry of Kashmir Valley, India. *Research in Globalization, 3*, 100053. doi:10.1016/j.resglo.2021.100053

Singh, N. (2023). AI in Inventory Management: Applications, Challenges, and Opportunities. *International Journal for Research in Applied Science and Engineering Technology, 11*(11), 2049–2053. doi:10.22214/ijraset.2023.57010

Siriwardhana, Y., De Alwis, C., Gür, G., Ylianttila, M., & Liyanage, M. (2020). The fight against the COVID-19 pandemic with 5G technologies. *IEEE Engineering Management Review, 48*(3), 72–84. doi:10.1109/EMR.2020.3017451

Sithambaram, R. A., & Tajudeen, F. P. (2023). Impact of artificial intelligence in human resource management: A qualitative study in the Malaysian context. *Asia Pacific Journal of Human Resources, 61*(4), 821–844. doi:10.1111/1744-7941.12356

Skard, S., Knudsen, E. S., Sjåstad, H., & Thorbjørnsen, H. (2021). How virtual reality influences travel intentions: The role of mental imagery and happiness forecasting. *Tourism Management, 87*, 104360. doi:10.1016/j.tourman.2021.104360

Škare, M., Soriano, D. R., & Porada-Rochoń, M. (2021). Impact of COVID-19 on the travel and tourism industry. *Technological Forecasting and Social Change, 163*, 120469. doi:10.1016/j.techfore.2020.120469 PMID:35721368

Slater, M., & Sanchez-Vives, M. V. (2016). Enhancing Our Lives with Immersive Virtual Reality. *Frontiers in Robotics and AI, 3*, 1–47. doi:10.3389/frobt.2016.00074

Sobhani, S. R., Armaghan, N., Haghir, S., & Garmaroodi, A. A. (2022). The Impact of Interactive technology by using Artificial Intelligence on the Formation of Social Interactions: A Study in Tourism Industry 4.0. *2022 IEEE 28th International Conference on Engineering, Technology and Innovation (ICE/ITMC) & 31st International Association For Management of Technology (IAMOT) Joint Conference*, (pp. 1-7). IEEE.

Solakis, K., Katsoni, V., Mahmoud, A.B., & Grigoriou, N. (2022). Factors affecting value co-creation through artificial intelligence in tourism: a general literature review. *Journal of Tourism Futures*.

Spita, M., Peitzika, E., & Chatzi, S. (2020). Social media adoption among small and medium-sized Greek hotels: A survey about its antecedents and its impact on performance outcomes. *International Journal of Decision Sciences. Risk Management*, *9*(1/2), 23. doi:10.1504/IJDSRM.2020.110144

Stamboulis, Y., & Skayannis, P. (2003). Innovation strategies and technology for experience-based tourism. *Tourism Management*, *24*(1), 35–43. doi:10.1016/S0261-5177(02)00047-X

Starkov, M. (2019). Hospitality Digital Technology: Challenges, Priorities, and Buzzwords. *Next Guest*. https://www.nextguest.com/blog/hospitality-digitaltech/HARE

Statista. (2023). *Mobile payments in the United States - statistics & facts*. Statista. https://www.statista.com/topics/982/mobile-payments/#topicOverview

Stephen, C., & Barth, D. S. B. (2017). *Hospitality Law: Managing Legal Issues in the Hospitality Industry*. John Wiley & Sons, Ltd. https://books.google.co.in/books?hl=en&lr=&id=Z5VFEAAAQBAJ&oi=fnd&pg=PR13&dq=Data+Protection+and+Privacy+in+the+Hospitality+Industry&ots=RH_flR0pZ3&sig=layJuMY7zsqwPsCcrBj3VC-zGvc#v=onepage&q=Data Protection and Privacy in the Hospitality Industry&f=false

Stewart, S. L. K., Wright, C., & Atherton, C. (2019). Deception Detection and Truth Detection Are Dependent on Different Cognitive and Emotional Traits: An Investigation of Emotional Intelligence, Theory of Mind, and Attention. *Personality and Social Psychology Bulletin*, *45*(5), 794–807. doi:10.1177/0146167218796795 PMID:30264653

Štilić, A., Nicić, M., & Puška, A. (2023). Check-in to the future: Exploring the impact of contemporary information technologies and artificial intelligence on the hotel industry. *Turističko Poslovanje, 31*.

Subawa, N. S., Widhiasthini, N. W., Astawa, I. P., Dwiatmadja, C., & Permatasari, N. P. I. (2021). The practices of virtual reality marketing in the tourism sector, a case study of Bali, Indonesia. *Current Issues in Tourism*, *24*(23), 3284–3295. https://www.revfine.com/virtual-reality-hospitality-industry/. doi:10.1080/13683500.2020.1870940

Sudheer, S., Reddy, M. S. K., & Manideep, A. S. (2019). The Influence of Source Credibility, Endorser Credibility and Message Appeal on Consumers' Purchase Intention: An Empirical Analysis. *International Journal of Recent Technology and Engineering*, *8*(1), 2845–2850.

Sun, S., Li, Y., Guo, J.-E., & Wang, S. (2021). *Tourism Demand Forecasting: An Ensemble Deep Learning Approach.*

Sundar, S. S. (2008). *The MAIN model: A heuristic approach to understanding technology effects on credibility.* MacArthur Foundation Digital Media and Learning Initiative Cambridge.

Suo, L., & Huang, Y. (2023). Brand Authenticity and Consumers' Willingness to Recommend by Word-of-Mouth: The Mediating Effect of Brand Attachment. [Humanities and Social Sciences]. *Journal of Community Development Research, 16*(4), 73–90.

Susanto, E. H., Novianti, S., Rafdinal, W., Prawira, M. F., & Septyandi, C. B. (2020). Visiting Tourism Destination: Is It Influenced by Smart Tourism Technology? *Journal of Indonesian Tourism and Development Studies, 8*(3), 145–155. doi:10.21776/ub.jitode.2020.008.03.04

Suseno, Y., Chang, C., Hudik, M., & Fang, E. S. (2022). Beliefs, anxiety and change readiness for artificial intelligence adoption among human resource managers: The moderating role of high-performance work systems. *International Journal of Human Resource Management, 33*(6), 1209–1236. doi:10.1080/09585192.2021.1931408

Suttikun, C., Chang, H. J., & Bicksler, H. (2018). A qualitative exploration of day spa therapists' work motivations and job satisfaction. *Journal of Hospitality and Tourism Management, 34*, 1–10. doi:10.1016/j.jhtm.2017.10.013

Su, Y. W., & Lin, H. L. (2014). Analysis of international tourist arrivals worldwide: The role of world heritage sites. *Tourism Management, 40*, 46–58. doi:10.1016/j.tourman.2013.04.005

Swan, M. (2015). *Blockchain: Blueprint for a new economy.* O'Reilly Media, Inc. https://books.google.co.in/books?hl=en&lr=&id=RHJmBgAAQBAJ&oi=fnd&pg=PR3&dq=Blockchain:+Blueprint+for

Syakir, A., Nur'hidayah, D., Asrah, Y. M., Hitoshi, N., & Abu, N. R. (2020). Challenges of Smart Tourism In Malaysia Ecotourism Destinations. *Journal of the Malaysian Institute of Planners VOLUME, 18*(4), 442–451.

Szromek, A. R., & Polok, G. (2022). A Business Model for Spa Tourism Enterprises: Transformation in a Period of Sustainable Change and Humanitarian Crisis. *Journal of Open Innovation, 8*(2), 72. doi:10.3390/joitmc8020072

Talón-Ballestero, P., Nieto-García, M., & González-Serrano, L. (2022). The wheel of dynamic pricing: Towards open pricing and one to one pricing in hotel revenue management. *International Journal of Hospitality Management, 102*, 103184. doi:10.1016/j.ijhm.2022.103184

Talukder, M. B. (2020). An Appraisal of the Economic Outlook for the Tourism Industry, Specially Cox's Bazar in Bangladesh. *i-manager's Journal on Economics & Commerce, 2*(1), 23-35.

Talukder, M. B. (2020b). The Future of Culinary Tourism: An Emerging Dimension for the Tourism Industry of Bangladesh. I-Manager's. *Journal of Management, 15*(1), 27. doi:10.26634/jmgt.15.1.17181

Talukder, M. B. (2021). An assessment of the roles of the social network in the development of the Tourism Industry in Bangladesh. *International Journal of Business, Law, and Education, 2*(3), 85–93. doi:10.56442/ijble.v2i3.21

Talukder, M. B., & Hossain, M. M. (2021). Prospects of Future Tourism in Bangladesh: An Evaluative Study. I-Manager's. *Journal of Management, 15*(4), 1–8. doi:10.26634/jmgt.15.4.17495

Talukder, M. B., Kabir, F., Muhsina, K., & Das, I. R. (2023). Emerging Concepts of Artificial Intelligence in the Hotel Industry: A Conceptual Paper. *International Journal of Research Publication and Reviews, 4*(9), 1765–1769. doi:10.55248/gengpi.4.923.92451

Talukder, M. B., Kumar, S., Sood, K., & Grima, S. (2023). Information Technology, Food Service Quality and Restaurant Revisit Intention. *International Journal of Sustainable Development and Planning, 18*(1), 295–303. doi:10.18280/ijsdp.180131

Tambe, P., Cappelli, P., & Yakubovich, V. (2019). Artificial Intelligence in Human Resources Management: Challenges and a Path Forward. *California Management Review, 61*(4), 15–42. doi:10.1177/0008125619867910

Tan, D. R. (1999). Personal Privacy in the Information Age: Comparison of Internet Data Protection Regulations in the United Stats and European Union. *Loyola of Los Angeles International and Comparative Law Journal, 21*(4), 661–684. http://heinonlinebackup.com/hol-cgi-bin/get_pdf.cgi?handle=hein.journals/loyint21&section=28

Tarute, A., Nikou, S., & Gatautis, R. (2017). Mobile application driven consumer engagement. *Telematics and Informatics, 34*(4), 145–156. doi:10.1016/j.tele.2017.01.006

Tasatanattakool, P., & Techapanupreeda, C. (2018). Blockchain: Challenges and applications. *International Conference on Information Networking, 24*(4), 473–475. 10.1109/ICOIN.2018.8343163

Taye, M. M. (2023). Understanding of Machine Learning with Deep Learning: Architectures, Workflow, Applications and Future Directions. In Computers, 12(5). MDPI. doi:10.3390/computers12050091

Teo, W.-P., Muthalib, M., Yamin, S., Hendy, A. M., Bramstedt, K., Kotsopoulos, E., Perrey, S., & Ayaz, H. (2016). Does a combination of virtual reality, neuromodulation and neuroimaging provide a comprehensive platform for neurorehabilitation? – a narrative review of the literature. *Frontiers in Human Neuroscience, 10*, 284. doi:10.3389/fnhum.2016.00284 PMID:27445739

Terry, L. (2018). *Why Wearable Technology Is Hotel Management's Next Big Thing*. Samsung. https://insights.samsung.com/2018/10/19/why-wearable[REMOVED HYPERLINK FIELD]technology-is-hotel-managements-next-big-thing

Thaduri, U. R. (2021). Virtual Reality & Artificial Intelligence in Real Estate Business: A Tool for Effective Marketing Campaigns. *Asian Journal of Applied Science and Engineering, 10*(1), 56–65. doi:10.18034/ajase.v10i1.54

Thavamani, S., Mahesh, D., Sinthuja, U., & Manoharan, G. (2022, May). Crucial attacks in internet of things via artificial intelligence techniques: The security survey. In AIP Conference Proceedings (Vol. 2418, No. 1). AIP Publishing.

The Star. (2022). 5G Drives Malaysia's Digitalization. *The Star.* https://www.thestar.com.my/news/nation/2022/01/26/5g-drives-malaysias-digitalisation

Theam, T. S., Veloo, P., Hussain, N. H., & Luu, Y. K. (2021). *Travellers' Satisfaction on the Applications of Artificial Intelligence in Malaysia's Tourism and Hospitality Industry.* Asia Proceedings of Social Sciences.

Timothy, D. J. (1997). Tourism and the personal heritage experience. *Annals of Tourism Research, 24*(3), 751–754. doi:10.1016/S0160-7383(97)00006-6

Timothy, D. J. (2011). *Cultural heritage and tourism: An introduction* (Vol. 4). Channel View Publications. doi:10.21832/9781845411787

Timothy, D. J., & Boyd, S. W. (2003). *Heritage tourism.* Pearson Education.

Ting, S.-H., Ng, Y.-J., & Neelam, M. (2021). *Aspects of Artificial Intelligence.* Research Gate. https://www.researchgate.net/publication/358119068

Topsakal, Y., Bahar, M. & Yüzbaşioğlu, N. (2020). Review of Smart Tourism Literature by Bibliometric And Visualization Analysis. *Journal of Tourism Intelligence and Smartness, 3*(1).

Trihas, N., & Konstantarou, A. (2016). Spa-goers' characteristics, motivations, preferences and perceptions: Evidence from Elounda, Crete. Almatourism-Journal of Tourism. *Culture and Territorial Development, 7*(14), 106–127.

Tripathi, M. A., Tripathi, R., Effendy, F., Manoharan, G., John Paul, M., & Aarif, M. (2023). An In-Depth Analysis of the Role That ML and Big Data Play in Driving Digital Marketing's Paradigm Shift. *2023 International Conference on Computer Communication and Informatics (ICCCI)*, Coimbatore, India. 10.1109/ICCCI56745.2023.10128357

Tsang, S. (2022, April 27). What's Employee Branding and How to Build It. *Fond.* https://www.fond.co/blog/whats-employee-branding-and-how-to-build-it/#:~:text=Employee%20branding%20is%20an%20internal,being%20part%20of%20your%20organization

Tung, V. W., Cheong, T. M., & To, S. J. (2019). Tourism Management in The Era of Smart Mobility: A Perspective Article. *Tourism Review, 75*(1), 283–285. doi:10.1108/TR-05-2019-0180

Tuo, Y., Ning, L., & Zhu, A. (2021). How Artificial Intelligence Will Change the Future of Tourism Industry: The Practice in China. In W. Wörndl, C. Koo, & J. L. Stienmetz (Eds.), *Information and Communication Technologies in Tourism.* Springer. doi:10.1007/978-3-030-65785-7_7

Tussyadiah, I. P., Wang, D., & Jia, C. (2017). Virtual Reality and Attitudes Toward Tourism Destinations. In R. Schegg & B. Stangl (Eds.), *Information and Communication Technologies in Tourism 2017.* Springer. doi:10.1007/978-3-319-51168-9_17

Tussyadiah, I. P., Wang, D., Jung, T. H., & Tom Dieck, M. C. (2018). Virtual reality, presence, and attitude change: Empirical evidence from tourism. *Tourism Management*, *66*, 140–154. doi:10.1016/j.tourman.2017.12.003

Tussyadiah, I., & Miller, G. (2019). Perceived impacts of artificial intelligence and responses to positive behaviour change intervention. In *Information and communication technologies in tourism 2019* (pp. 359–370). Springer. doi:10.1007/978-3-030-05940-8_28

Uglis, J., Jęczmyk, A., Zawadka, J., Wojcieszak-Zbierska, M. M., & Pszczoła, M. (2022). Impact of the COVID-19 pandemic on tourist plans: A case study from Poland. *Current Issues in Tourism*, *25*(3), 405–420. doi:10.1080/13683500.2021.1960803

Ukpabi, D. C., Aslam, B., & Karjaluoto, H. (2019). Chatbot adoption in tourism services: A conceptual exploration. In Robots, Artificial Intelligence and Service Automation in Travel, Tourism and Hospitality (pp. 105–121). Emerald Group Publishing Ltd. doi:10.1108/978-1-78756-687-320191006

Umair, M., Cheema, M. A., Cheema, O., Li, H., & Lu, H. (2021). Impact of COVID-19 on IoT adoption in healthcare, smart homes, smart buildings, smart cities, transportation and industrial IoT. *Sensors (Basel)*, *21*(11), 3838. doi:10.3390/s21113838 PMID:34206120

Um, S., Chon, K., & Ro, Y. H. (2006). Antecedents of revisit intention. *Annals of Tourism Research*, *33*(4), 1141–1158. doi:10.1016/j.annals.2006.06.003

UNWTO. (2010). *World Tourism Barometer January 2010*. UNWTO.

UNWTO. (2020). *International tourism growth continues to outpace the global economy*. UN. https://www.unwto.org/ international-tourism-growth-continues-to-outpace-the-economy

Upadhyay, A. K., & Khandelwal, K. (2018). Applying artificial intelligence: Implications for recruitment. *Strategic HR Review*, *17*(5), 255–258. doi:10.1108/SHR-07-2018-0051

Vafeiadis, M. (2021). Message interactivity and source credibility in online dental practice reviews: Responding to reviews triggers positive consumer reactions regardless of review valence. *Health Communication*, 1–11. PMID:34080513

Vajirakachorn, T., & Chongwatpol, J. (2017). Application of business intelligence in the tourism industry: A case study of a local food festival in Thailand. *Tourism Management Perspectives*, *23*, 75–86. doi:10.1016/j.tmp.2017.05.003

Valva, P. (2014). Shared Living and Sustainability: Emerging Trends in the Tourism Industry. *Almatourism-Journal Of Tourism Culture And Territorial Development*, *5*(3, SI), 1–18.

van Nuenen, T., & Scarles, C. (2021). Advancements in technology and digital media in tourism. *Tourist Studies*, *21*(1), 119–132. doi:10.1177/1468797621990410

Vanolo, A. (2013). Smartmentality: The smart city as disciplinary strategy. *Urban Studies (Edinburgh, Scotland)*, *51*(5), 883–898. doi:10.1177/0042098013494427

Varkaris, E., & Neuhofer, B. (2017). The influence of social media on the consumers' hotel decision journey. *Journal of Hospitality and Tourism Technology*, *8*(1), 101–118. doi:10.1108/JHTT-09-2016-0058

Vasavada, M., & Padhiyar, Y. Y. (2016). "Smart Tourism"; Growth for Tomorrow. *Journal for Research*, *1*(12), 55–61.

Vashi, S., Ram, J., Modi, J., Verma, S., & Prakash, C. (2017). Internet of Things (IoT): A vision, architectural elements, and security issues. *Proceedings of the International Conference on IoT in Social, Mobile, Analytics and Cloud, I-SMAC 2017, December*, (pp. 492–496). IEEE. 10.1109/I-SMAC.2017.8058399

Vaughan, N., Gabrys, B., & Dubey, V. N. (2016). An Overview of Self-Adaptive Technologies Within Virtual Reality Training. In *Computer Science Review*. https://www.oculus.com

Verhoef, P. C., Kannan, P. K., & Inman, J. J. (2015). From multi-channel retailing to omni-channel retailing: Introduction to the special issue on multi-channel retailing. *Journal of Retailing*, *91*(2), 174–181. doi:10.1016/j.jretai.2015.02.005

Verma, S., Sharma, R., Deb, S., & Maitra, D. (2021). Artificial intelligence in marketing: Systematic review and future research direction. *International Journal of Information Management Data Insights*, *1*(1), 100002. doi:10.1016/j.jjimei.2020.100002

Viglia, G., Furlan, R., & Ladron-de-Guevara, A. (2014). Please, talk about it! when hotel popularity boosts preferences. *International Journal of Hospitality Management*, *42*, 155–164. doi:10.1016/j.ijhm.2014.07.001

VISA. (2022). *No TitleContactless payments witnessed a 6x growth in the last 3 years: Visa and Worldline India Whitepaper*. VISA. Https://Www.Visa.Co.In/About-Visa/Newsroom/Press-Releases/Contactless-Payments-Witnessed-A-6x-Growth-In-The-Last-3-Years-Visa-And-Worldline-India-Whitepaper.Html

Vishwakarma, P., Mukherjee, S., & Datta, B. (2020). Travelers' intention to adopt virtual reality: A consumer value perspective. *Journal of Destination Marketing & Management*, *17*, 100456. doi:10.1016/j.jdmm.2020.100456

Walten, L., & Wiedmann, K.-P. (2022). How product information and source credibility affect consumer attitudes and intentions towards innovative food products. *Journal of Marketing Communications*, 1–17.

Wang, G., Dong, T., Chu, Y., Shi, D., Ding, J., & Chen, C. (2021). The Integrated Development Evaluation of Tourism Industry from the Perspective of Global Tourism Based on Artificial Intelligence Model. *2021 3rd International Conference on Artificial Intelligence and Advanced Manufacture*.

Wang, X., Li, X. R., Zhen, F., & Zhang, J. H. (2016). How smart is your tourist attraction?: Measuring tourist preferences of smart tourism attractions via a FCEM-AHP and IPA approach. *Tourism Management*, *54*, 309–320. doi:10.1016/j.tourman.2015.12.003

Wen, J., Kozak, M., Yang, S., & Liu, F. (2021). COVID-19: Potential effects on Chinese citizens' lifestyle and travel. *Tourism Review, 76*(1), 74–87. doi:10.1108/TR-03-2020-0110

Williams, P., & Hobson, J. P. (1995). Virtual reality and tourism: Fact or fantasy? *Tourism Management, 16*(6), 423–427. doi:10.1016/0261-5177(95)00050-X

Wilson, H. J., Daugherty, P., & Bianzino, N. (2017). The jobs that artificial intelligence will create. *MIT Sloan Management Review, 58*(4), 14. http://mitsmr.com/2odREFJ

Wisskirchen, G., Biacabe, B., Bormann, U., Muntz, A., Niehaus, A., Soler, G., & Brauchitsch, B. (2017). *Artificial Intelligence and Robotics and Their Impact on the Workplace*. IBA Global Employment Institute.

Wong, K. Y. (2021). Virtual Reality Marketing in Hospitality and Tourism. *University of South Florida M3 Center Publishing, 18*(9781732127586), 6.

Wortham, R. (2018). *Using Other Minds: Transparency as a Fundamental Design Consideration for Artificial Intelligent Systems*. Taylor & Francis.

Wright, P. M., & Snell, S. A. (1991). Toward an Integrative View of Strategic Human Resource Management. *Human Resource Management Review, 1*(3), 203–225. doi:10.1016/1053-4822(91)90015-5

Wu, W., Lee, C. C., Xing, W., & Ho, S. J. (2021). The impact of the COVID-19 outbreak on Chinese-listed tourism stocks. *Financial Innovation, 7*(1), 1–18. doi:10.1186/s40854-021-00240-6 PMID:35024277

Xiang, Z., Du, Q., Ma, Y., & Fan, W. (2017). A comparative analysis of major online review platforms: Implications for social media analytics in hospitality and tourism. *Tourism Management, 58*(February), 51–65. doi:10.1016/j.tourman.2016.10.001

Xiang, Z., & Fesenmaier, D. R. (2017). Big Data Analytics, Tourism Design and Smart Tourism. In Z. Xiang & D. Fesenmaier (Eds.), *Analytics in Smart Tourism Design. Tourism on the Verge*. Springer., doi:10.1007/978-3-319-44263-1_17

Xie, D., Xiao, F., & Pedrycz, W. (2022). Information quality for intuitionistic fuzzy values with its application in decision making. *Engineering Applications of Artificial Intelligence, 109*, 104568. doi:10.1016/j.engappai.2021.104568

Xue, M., Cao, X., Feng, X., Gu, B., & Zhang, Y. (2022). Is college education less necessary with AI? Evidence from firm-level labor structure changes. *Journal of Management Information Systems, 39*(3), 865–905. doi:10.1080/07421222.2022.2096542

Xu, F., Nash, N., & Whitmarsh, L. (2020). Big data or small data? A methodological review of sustainable tourism. *Journal of Sustainable Tourism, 28*(2), 147–166. doi:10.1080/09669582.2019.1631318

Yang, C. H., Lin, H. L., & Han, C. C. (2010). Analysis of international tourist arrivals in China: The role of World Heritage Sites. *Tourism Management*, *31*(6), 827–837. doi:10.1016/j.tourman.2009.08.008 PMID:32287732

Yang, S.-B., Hlee, S., Lee, J., & Koo, C. (2017). An empirical examination of online restaurant reviews on Yelp. com: A dual coding theory perspective. *International Journal of Contemporary Hospitality Management*, *29*(2), 817–839. doi:10.1108/IJCHM-11-2015-0643

Yang, T., Lai, I., Fan, Z. B., & Mo, Q. M. (2021). The impact of a 360° virtual tour on the reduction of psychological stress caused by COVID-19. *Technology in Society*, *64*, 101514. doi:10.1016/j.techsoc.2020.101514 PMID:33424061

Yaqoob, I., Salah, K., Jayaraman, R., & Al-Hammadi, Y. (2021). Blockchain for healthcare data management: Opportunities, challenges, and future recommendations. *Neural Computing & Applications*, 1–16.

Ye, B. H., Ye, H., & Law, R. (2020). Systematic Review of Smart Tourism Research. *Sustainability (Basel)*, *12*(8), 3401. doi:10.3390/su12083401

Yoon, S., Erdem, M., Schuckert, M., & Lee, P. C. (2021). Revisiting the impact of VR applications on hotel bookings. *Journal of Hospitality and Tourism Technology*, *12*(3), 489–511. doi:10.1108/JHTT-04-2019-0057

You, Y., Vadakkepatt, G. G., & Joshi, A. M. (2015). A meta-analysis of electronic word-of-mouth elasticity. *Journal of Marketing*, *79*(2), 19–39. doi:10.1509/jm.14.0169

Yung, R., & Khoo-Lattimore, C. (2019). New realities: A systematic literature review on virtual reality and augmented reality in tourism research. *Current Issues in Tourism*, *22*(17), 2056–2081. doi:10.1080/13683500.2017.1417359

Yung, R., Khoo-Lattimore, C., & Ellen Potter, L. (2021). Virtual reality and tourism marketing: Conceptualizing a framework on presence, emotion, and intention. *Current Issues in Tourism*, *24*(11), 1505–1525. doi:10.1080/13683500.2020.1820454

Zarzuela, M. M., Pernas, F. J. D., Calzón, S. M., Ortega, D. G., & Rodríguez, M. A. (2013). Educational Tourism through a Virtual Reality Platform. *Procedia Computer Science*, *25*, 382–388. doi:10.1016/j.procs.2013.11.047

Zeithaml, V. A. (1988). Consumer perceptions of price, quality, and value: A means-end model and synthesis of evidence. *Journal of Marketing*, *52*(3), 2–22. doi:10.1177/002224298805200302

Zeng, H. (2020). Adaptability of artificial intelligence in human resources management in this era. *International Journal of Sciences*, *7*(1), 271–276.

Zhang, B., Ritchie, B., Mair, J., & Driml, S. (2019). Is the airline trustworthy? The impact of source credibility on voluntary carbon offsetting. *Journal of Travel Research*, *58*(5), 715–731. doi:10.1177/0047287518775781

Zhang, H., Lu, Y., Gupta, S., & Zhao, L. (2014). What motivates customers to participate in social commerce? the impact of technological environments and virtual customer experiences. *Information & Management*, *51*(8), 1017–1030. doi:10.1016/j.im.2014.07.005

Zhang, K., Chen, Y., & Li, C. (2019). Discovering the tourists' behaviors and perceptions in a tourism destination by analyzing photos' visual content with a computer deep learning model: The case of Beijing. *Tourism Management*, *75*, 595–608. doi:10.1016/j.tourman.2019.07.002

Zhang, S. N., Li, Y. Q., Ruan, W. Q., & Liu, C. H. (2022). Would you enjoy virtual travel? The characteristics and causes of virtual tourists' sentiment under the influence of the COVID-19 pandemic. *Tourism Management*, *88*, 104429. doi:10.1016/j.tourman.2021.104429

Zhang, T., Li, B., Milman, A., & Hua, N. (2022). Assessing technology adoption practices in Chinese theme parks: Text mining and sentiment analysis. *Journal of Hospitality and Tourism Technology*, *13*(1), 195–213. doi:10.1108/JHTT-05-2020-0126

Zhang, Y., Sotiriadis, M. D., & Shen, S. (2022). Investigating the Impact of Smart Tourism Technologies on Tourists' Experiences. *Sustainability (Basel)*, *2022*(14), 3048. doi:10.3390/su14053048

Zhou, W. (2019). The impact of AI on the hospitality industry. *Towards Data Science*. https://towardsdatascience.com/the-impact-of -ai-on-the hospitality-industry-8ba7adb66be

Zhou, J., Cao, Z., Dong, X., & Vasilakos, A. V. (2017). Security and Privacy for Cloud-Based IoT: Challenges. *IEEE Communications Magazine*, *55*(1), 26–33. doi:10.1109/MCOM.2017.1600363CM

Zhou, X., & Chen, Z. (2023). Destination attraction clustering: Segmenting tourist movement patterns with geotagged information. *Tourism Geographies*, *25*(2-3), 797–819. doi:10.1080/14616688.2021.2006769

Zlatanov, S., & Popesku, J. (2019). *Current Applications of Artificial Intelligence in Tourism and Hospitality*. 84–90. doi:10.15308/Sinteza-2019-84-90

Zohar, A. (2015). Bitcoin: Under the hood. *Communications of the ACM*, *58*(9), 104–113. doi:10.1145/2701411

# About the Contributors

**Sanjeev Kumar** is an accomplished expert in Food and Beverage. He currently holds the positions of Professor at the Lovely Professional University, Punjab, India. With over a decade of experience in the field, food Service Industry, his research focuses on Alcoholic beverages, Event management and Sustainable Management Practices, Metaverse and Artificial Intelligence. He has published more than 35 research papers, articles and chapters in Scopus Indexed, UGC Approved and peer reviewed Journals and books. Dr. Sanjeev Kumar participated and acted as resource person in various National and International conferences, seminars, research workshops and industry talks and his work has been widely cited.

**Mohammad Badruddoza Talukder** is an Associate Professor and head of the Department of Tourism and Hospitality Management, Daffodil Institute of Information Technology (at the National University), Dhaka, Bangladesh. He completed his Ph.D. in Hotel Management at the School of Hotel Management and Tourism, Lovely Professional University, India. He holds a bachelor's and a master's degree in Hotel Management from India. He has been teaching various courses in the Department of Tourism and Hospitality at various universities in Bangladesh since 2009. His research areas include tourism management, hotel management, hospitality management, food and beverage management, and accommodation management, where he has published research papers in well-known journals in Bangladesh and abroad. Dr. Talukder is one of the executive members of the Tourism Educators Association of Bangladesh. He has led training and counseling for various hospitality organizations in Bangladesh. As an administrator, Dr. Talukder served as a debate advisor at the University coordinator for courses and exams in the Department of Tourism and Hotel Management. He has experience as a manager in various business-class hotels in Bangladesh. He is one of the certified trainers for the food and beverage service department of the SIEP project from Bangladesh. He became an honorary facilitator at Bangladesh Tourism Board's Bangabandhu International Tourism and Hospitality Training Institute.

**Ana Pego** holds a Ph.D. in Geography and Territorial Planning (Universidade Nova de Lisboa, Portugal), an MBA (Open University, Portugal) and a BSC in Economics (Universidade de Évora, Portugal). She is an integrated researcher at CICS Nova- Research Center in Social Sciences; in her research, she focuses on the circular economy, offshore energy, smart cities and tourism. She is a coordinator of five European projects as Erasmus and Horizon Europe. She is an author of several articles about offshore energy clusters, tourism, and the circular economy. She also collaborates with Open University in Macroeconomics and Business Management classes.

***

**Sunitha Purushottam Ashtikar** is pursuing her Ph.D. program under, School of Business, SR University, Warangal, Telangana, India

**Rohit Bansal** is working as Associate Professor in Department of Management Studies in Vaish College of Engineering, Rohtak. He is a perseverant, passionate academician cum seasoned professional. He obtained Ph.D. in Management from Maharshi Dayanand University, Rohtak. With a rich experience of 15 years, he has achieved growth through robust and proactive academic initiatives. He has authored & edited 25 books with renowned national & international publishers including IGI Global USA, Scrivener-Wiley Publishing, De Gruyter, Weser Books, Scholar's Press, Germany etc. In addition to, Dr. Rohit has published 150 research papers and chapters in journals of repute including Scopus indexed as well as edited books. He has also presented papers in 50 conferences and seminars. His area of interest includes marketing management, organizational behaviour, services marketing, customer engagement, digital marketing, human resource management and organizational development. He is on Editorial Advisory Board as a member in 125 national and international peer reviewed journals. He has acted as session chair in many international conferences.

**Prof. Dina Darwish**, Vice dean, faculty of computer science and information technology, Ahram Canadian university, Egypt. She obtained her Ph.D from Cairo university at 2009, engineering faculty. She is professor since 2020, also her special domain is artificial intelligence and she has many publications in the following topics, including: Artificial intelligence, wireless ad hoc networks, Internet of things, Big data analytics, Blockchain applications, Cloud computing applications, Web technologies, intelligent systems and others.

**Iva Rani Das** is a dynamic individual, currently pursuing her MPhil in the Marketing Department of Dhaka University. Alongside her academic pursuits, she holds key positions as an Assistant Director at the Daffodil Institute of Technology and serves as Guest Faculty in the Business Faculty at the Asian Institute of Business and Technology. Her scholarly achievements extend beyond the classroom, with publications in esteemed national and international journals. Iva's dedication to education and research makes her a driving force in the fields of business and marketing.

**Saumendra Das** presently working as an Associate Professor at the School of Management Studies, GIET University, Gunupur, Odisha. He has more than 20 years of teaching, research, and industry experience. He has published more than 52 articles in national and international journals, conference proceedings, and book chapters. He also authored one book on advertising effectiveness. Dr Das has participated and presented many papers in seminars, conferences, and workshops in India and abroad. He has organized many FDPs and workshops in his career. He is an academician, author, and editor. He has also published two patents also. He is an active member of various professional bodies such as ICA, ISTE and RFI. In the year 2023, he has been awarded as the best teacher by Research Foundation India.

**Parul Gupta**, currently an Assistant Professor (Selection Grade) at Welcomgroup Graduate School of Hotel Administration, Manipal Academy of Higher Education, holds a B.Sc. in Hospitality & Hotel Administration from IHM Lucknow, an MBA (HRM) from Banasthali Vidyapith, and a PhD from Bundelkhand University. With over 10 years of industry and academic experience, she commenced her career at Leela Kempinski Hotel & Residences, Gurgaon. Dr. Gupta has also served as faculty at various institutions, presenting research papers in international conferences and contributing to journals and books. She has also qualified UGC JRF-NET in HRM/Industrial Relations, and she has undergone training programs at esteemed institutions and participated in various workshops

**Tariqul Islam**, a Ph.D. candidate in Hospitality and Tourism at Taylor's University, Malaysia. He holds a Master of Science (by research) in Tourism from Universiti Putra Malaysia, Malaysia. He graduated with distinction in Airlines, Tourism, and Hospitality from Lovely Professional University, India. Tariqul has published several research articles in ABDC- listed and Scopus-indexed journals and presented the findings of his research at various national and international conferences. His area of research includes consumer behaviour and technology adoption.

**Baljit Kaur** is an outstanding authority in Hospitality Management, boasts a tremendous educational journey and a wealthy tapestry of the hotel industry spanning over 25 years. Earning a Ph.D. In Hospitality Management, an MBA specializing in Hospitality, and a Master's in Tourism, Dr. Baljit Kaur possesses a sturdy educational basis that supports her understanding. Dr. Baljit Kaur's professional voyage encompasses pivotal roles in esteemed hotels including Le Meridien and Holiday Inn, wherein she performed a crucial part in raising excellence. Beyond the company realm, Dr. Baljit Kaur has committed a huge element of her career to academia. Holding positions as the Head of Departments in diverse renowned universities and establishments, she remained instrumental in shaping the destiny of aspiring hospitality professionals. A luminary in studies, Dr. Baljit Kaur has contributed drastically to the instructional norm with several research papers posted in esteemed journals. Additionally, her insights have been preserved in book publications, solidifying her status in the concerned area.

**Jeetesh Kumar** is Senior Lecturer at the School of Hospitality, Tourism and Events; Associate Director for Information Management & Documentation at Centre for Research and Innovation in Tourism (CRiT), and also Hub Leader - "Responsible Tourism for Inclusive Economic Growth" hub under Sustainable Tourism Impact Lab at Taylor's University, Malaysia. His doctorate is from Taylor's University in Hospitality and Tourism, with research on Economic Impacts of Business Events in Malaysia. His research areas include Economic Impacts, Economic Modelling, MICE, Medical Tourism, Behavioural Studies.

**Dwipanita Mishra** is currently pursuing her PhD at GIET University. Her research interest is in tourism study and management research. She is an active researcher and a true academician. She attended many conferences and published papers in many journals.

**Smriti Mishra** is an Architect and Urban Planner and is currently working as an Associate Professor as Head in the Department of Architecture and Planning, Birla Institute of Technology, Mesra, Ranchi, India. She has research interests in the field of urban and regional planning, tourism heritage management, perception studies, riverfront development, reclamation strategies for abandoned mines, vernacular architecture, urban environmental management, energy conservation and heat mitigation, vulnerability of peri-urban areas and has numerous publications in her records.

**N. V. J. Rao** is a versatile personality and thought leader with more than 25 years of administrative experience across various areas in addition to the existing profile.

He has done an MBA and PhD in Management. He served the GIET University, Gunupur, Odisha from its inception in 1997. He has a strong moral character and integrity in handling university policies and his leadership ability is imperative for effective supervision. From the beginning, his main motive is to help the students both with academic and non-academic problems and counsel them in shaping to be worthy in the present market conditions which helps both the students as well as the university.

**Aditi Nag** is an Architect and Urban Planner, pursuing a Ph.D. in the Department of Architecture and Planning, Birla Institute of Technology, Mesra, Ranchi, India. She has done research in the field of urban and rural planning and has a few publications in her record. She is the 1st to have been awarded the DST Inspire Fellowship in the field of Architecture and Planning by the Ministry of Science and Technology, Govt. of India.

**Biswabhusan Pradhan** is a research scholar in the Department of Tourism and Travel Management, Central University of Jammu, India, His research area focuses on smart tourism, Heritage tourism, Hotel and Restaurant, Rural tourism. His publications have been published in Emerald, IGI global and various UGC care journals.

**Sanjeev Kumar Saxena** holds a Ph.D. in Human Resources, MBA, M.Com (Gold Medalist), B.Sc in H&HA, and a 3-year Diploma in Hotel Management. He has further enhanced his expertise through various certificate courses from prestigious institutions such as IIM Bangalore, IIT Kanpur, and IIT Kharagpur. Currently serving as an Associate Professor at Assam University, Silchar, Dr. Saxena has had a great career for 32 years. He worked in the industry for 21 years and taught in academia for 11 years. His professional journey commenced in 1992 at The Taj Group of Hotels, where he began as a Management Trainee. After an impactful tenure of over 5 years with The Taj Group, Dr. Saxena transitioned to the Institute of Hotel Management, Jodhpur, serving as a lecturer for more than 9 years. In 2007, he joined Jaypee Hotels & Resorts as a Learning & Development Manager for 5+ years before taking on the role of Principal at IHM Silvassa. Subsequently, he rejoined Jaypee Hotels & Resorts in 2013, holding the position of Additional General Manager (HRD) for 8 years. In academia, Dr. Saxena has built an impressive portfolio, with 25 research papers and 6 authored books covering topics such as Human Resource Management, Front Office & F&B Service. Additionally, he has supervised two Ph.D. scholars and one MPhil scholar. His specialized knowledge spans the fields of Human Resource, Strategic Management, Marketing, and Hospitality.

**Partho Pratim Seal** is an Associate Professor with Welcomgroup Graduate School of Hotel Administration, Manipal Academy of Higher Education and has more than two decades of experience in academics and hospitality industry. An avid wordsmith who believes that writing is the most influential and resourceful medium to disseminate information has authored four books Computers in Hotels: Concepts and Application, Food & Beverage Management, How to Succeed in Hotel Management Job Interviews, and Food Anthropology in India. His research interests are in Hospitality, Education, Anthropology and Gastronomy

**Milan Sharma** is a research scholar in the School of Hotel Management and Tourism at Lovely Professional University, Punjab, India and Working as Assistant Professor in SGT University, Gurugram, India. His research area focuses on Innovative High-tech Services, AI,VR, Hotel Performance, Restaurant, Marketing, Consumer Behaviours. His work published in IEEE conferences (Scopus Indexed), conferences, peer-reviewed journal.

**Amrik Singh** is working as Professor in the School of Hotel Management and Tourism at Lovely Professional University, Punjab, India. He obtained his Ph.D. degree in Hotel Management from Kurukshetra University, Kurukshetra. He started his academic career at Lovely Professional University, Punjab, India in the year 2007. He has published more than 40 research papers in UGC and peer-reviewed and Scopus/Web of Science) journals. He has published 12 patents and 01 patent has been granted in the inter-disciplinary domain. Dr. Amrik Singh participated and acted as a resource person in various national and international conferences, seminars, research workshops, and industry talks. His area of research interest is accommodation management, ergonomics, green practices, human resource management in hospitality, waste management, AR VR in hospitality, etc. He is currently guiding 8Ph.D. scholars and 2 Ph.D. scholars have been awarded Ph.D.

**Anthony Tee Mooi Kwong** is a scholar in the field of sustainable tourism development and currently serving as Assistant Professor in Universiti Tunku Abdul Rahman. Holding a Ph.D. in the subject, he has dedicated his career to advancing knowledge and practices in tourism planning and development. As an active researcher, he has contributed significantly to the discourse on sustainable tourism. In addition to research, he also served as a consultant in tourism planning and development.

# Index

## A



## B



## C



## D

## P



## R



## S



## T



## V

# W

www.ingramcontent.com/pod-product-compliance
Lightning Source LLC
LaVergne TN
LVHW080340011026
849161LV00009B/2133
* 9 7 9 8 3 6 9 3 1 9 7 8 9 *